MESSIAH IN HIS SANCTUARY

The Author

Messiah in His Sanctuary

A SERIES OF BIBLE STUDIES ON THE 'SANCTUARY AND
ITS SERVICES, IN BOTH TYPE AND ANTITYPE,
WITH PARTICULAR APPLICATION TO THE
CHURCH FOLLOWING THE ADVENT
MOVEMENT OF THE YEARS
1834-1844

By F. C. GILBERT

Author of "Practical Lessons From the Experience
of Israel;" "From Judaism to Christianity;"
"Divine Predictions," and other works.

TEACH Services, Inc.
New York

2010 11 12 13 14 · 5 4 3 2 1

Published by

TEACH Services, Inc.
www.TEACHServices.com

Introduction

THERE is no literary production in all history comparable to the Sacred Scripture. Translated into almost a thousand languages, in part or as a whole, it is still in greater demand than any other literature. The themes recorded in the Bible deal with the past, with the present, and with the future. They clarify creation, redemption, the restoration of this world, and the future of the human race. The Bible foretells the tomorrow of the nations, ages, and generations. It deals with events taking place in heaven, and it also describes existing conditions on earth.

In this Holy Book the Creator has revealed His plans in regard to the reward of the righteous and the final disposition of evildoers. The divine Lord is not responsible for unhallowed practices. Sin was not included in God's program for this earth. This world was made to be inhabited by righteous, not by wicked, men. Satan, the originator of lawlessness, is an innovator. He has no right to inject into this earth disobedience to God's commands. If misery and death were to be perpetuated eternally, there might be ground for believing that God is responsible for the existence of evil. But the Most High has assured us in His word that the root and branches of sin shall be consumed into smoke and into ashes. Evil shall not rise the second time.

Through the ages, as noted in sacred history, the Lord has repeatedly revealed by seer and by messenger, in type and in object lesson, the means He will use through the mighty power of the divine Saviour to bring to an end this reign of wrong and death. These types and object lessons are found in the services and ceremonies of the ancient sanctuary. The fullness of light of this heavenly teaching has been committed to the present generation.

Nearly twenty-five centuries ago, through the prophet Daniel, the angel Gabriel foretold the time when Christ would transfer His ministry from the holy place to the most holy place of the heavenly sanctuary, preparatory to the time when the divine intercession for man's salvation would be finished. To this prophet, by this same heavenly messenger, was revealed the sequence of events leading to the time when sin and sinners shall cease.

The subject of the heavenly sanctuary and its ministry, illustrated by the tabernacle in the wilderness, and later by the temple in Jerusalem, with the priesthood, sacrifices, and other ritual services, was to diffuse bright beams of heavenly light upon all nations, kindreds, tongues, and peoples at the close of the longest prophetic period mentioned in the Bible, namely, the two thousand three hundred days of Daniel 8:14. In "the time of the end," when this twenty-three-century prophecy would meet its fulfillment, the sealed book of Daniel would be unlocked, and the wise would understand.

The first mention of the sanctuary is found in the second book of the Bible; the last time the temple ministry is spoken of is in the closing book of the Scriptures. Between these two books of the Sacred Volume is revealed one of the most fascinating and inspiring themes that can occupy the human mind. The sanctuary and its cleansing may properly engage the heartiest interest of the one who desires to understand the purposes of the Creator in the salvation of the righteous and the final disposition of evil.

The sanctuary and its ministry are considered and explained in this series of Bible studies. Each study contains a series of questions. At the close of each question, Bible texts are cited and notes or quotations presented which deal with the question. Every Bible lesson, with its explanations, is complete in itself. In this way the reader has before him all necessary information on each study. The four final studies are devoted to a consideration of the atonement.

The author commits these studies to the reader with the hope and prayer that they may render helpful service to those who accept God's message for these last days. May these lessons afford confirmation and stabilization of God's precious truth to those who have accepted the faith once delivered to the saints.

Quotations From the Spirit of Prophecy Upon the Subject of the Sanctuary

"THERE are many precious truths contained in the word of God, but it is '*present truth*' that the flock needs now. I have seen the danger of the messengers' running off from the important points of present truth, to dwell upon subjects that are not calculated to unite the flock and sanctify the soul. Satan will here take every possible advantage to injure the cause.

"But such subjects as the sanctuary, in connection with the twenty-three hundred days, the commandments of God and the faith of Jesus, are perfectly calculated to explain the past advent movement, and show what our present position is, establish the faith of the doubting, and give certainty to the glorious future. These, I have frequently seen, were the principal subjects on which the messengers should dwell."—"*Early Writings,*" p. 63.

"In His word, God has revealed saving truths. As a people we should be earnest students of prophecy; we should not rest until we become intelligent in regard to the subject of the sanctuary, which is brought out in the visions of Daniel and John. This subject sheds great light on our present position and work, and gives us unmistakable proof that God has led us in our past experience. It explains our disappointment in 1844, showing us that the sanctuary to be cleansed was not the earth, as we had supposed, but that Christ then entered into the most holy apartment of the heavenly sanctuary, and is there performing the closing work of His priestly office, in fulfillment of the words of the angel to the prophet Daniel, 'Unto two thousand and three hundred days; then shall the sanctuary be cleansed.' Dan. 8:14.

"Our faith in reference to the messages of the first, second, and third angels was correct. The great waymarks we have passed are immovable. Although the hosts of hell may try to tear them from their foundation, and triumph in the thought that they have succeeded, yet they do not succeed. These pillars of truth stand firm as the eternal hills, unmoved by all the efforts of men combined with those of Satan and his host. We can learn much, and should be constantly searching the Scriptures to see if these things are so. God's people are now to have their eyes fixed on the heavenly sanctuary, where the final ministration of our great High Priest in the work of the judgment is going forward,—where He is interceding for His people."—"*Life Sketches,*" p. 278, 1915 edition.

"We are to be established in the faith, in the light of the truth given us in our early experience. At that time one error after another pressed in upon us; ministers and doctors brought in new doctrines. We would search the Scriptures with much prayer, and the Holy Spirit would bring the truth to our minds. Sometimes whole nights would be devoted to searching the Scriptures, and earnestly asking God for guidance. Companies of devoted men and women assembled for this purpose. The power of God would come upon me, and I was enabled clearly to define what is truth and what is error.

"As the points of our faith were thus established, our feet were placed upon a solid foundation. We accepted the truth point by point, under the demonstration of the Holy Spirit. I would be taken off in vision, and explanations would be given me. I was given illustrations of heavenly things, and of the sanctuary, so that we were placed where light was shining on us in clear, distinct rays.

"I know that the sanctuary question stands in righteousness and truth, just as we have held it for so many years. It is the enemy that leads minds off on sidetracks. He is pleased when those who know the truth become engrossed in collecting scriptures to pile around erroneous theories, which have no foundation in truth.

"The scriptures thus used are misapplied; they were not given to substantiate error, but to strengthen truth."—*"Gospel Workers,"* pp. 302, 303.

Contents

I. Origin and Definition of the Sanctuary - - - - - 11
II. God's Design in Giving the Sanctuary to the Israelites - - 14
III. Why Moses Was Summoned to an Interview With God - 20
IV. Moses Communicates to the People the Sacred Trust Committed to Him - - - - - - - - - - - 24
V. God Outlines the Plans for All Parts of the Sanctuary - 29
VI. Moses Commanded to Make Garments for the Priests, Also the Anointing Oil and the Incense - - - - - - 34
VII. The Sanctuary Built, Inspected, Accepted, and Approved of Heaven - - - - - - - - - - 37
VIII. Dedication of the Sanctuary, Consecration and Inauguration of the Priesthood - - - - - - - - - - 41
IX. The Ministry in the Sanctuary—The Work of the Priests - 47
X. The Ministry in the Sanctuary—The Daily Offerings - - 52
XI. The Ministry in the Sanctuary by the Priests—The Day of Atonement - - - - - - - - - - - 60
XII. The Ministry in the Sanctuary—The Day of Atonement (Concluded) - - - - - - - - - - - 67
XIII. Beginning and Ending of Earthly Sacrifices and Priesthood - 75
XIV. When Did God Design the Sacrificial System to Cease? Why? 84
XV. God's Outstanding Purpose in the Gift of the Scriptures - 93
XVI. Old Testament Prophecies and Symbols Illuminated by the New Testament - - - - - - - - - - , 98
XVII. Christ the Central Theme of the Prophetic Scriptures - - 105
XVIII. Christ Described in the Scriptures by Three Outstanding Terms 112
XIX. God's Call to the Church to Prepare for Christ's Second Advent 119
XX. The Angel Gabriel Visits the Prophet Daniel - - - - 124
XXI. Daniel Studied the Scriptures to Understand the 2300 Days - 127
XXII. The Seventy Weeks Explained to Daniel by the Angel Gabriel 131
XXIII. The Seventy-Week Prophecy Fulfilled, and the Rest of the 2300 Days Explained - - - - - -. - - - - 140
XXIV. How God Through the Ages Gave Light on the Sanctuary - 147
XXV. Christ the Fulfillment of the Law and of the Types - - - 152
XXVI. Christ the Spotless Lamb of God - - - - - 159
XXVII. Christ's Death, Burial, Resurrection, and Ascension - - - 162
XXVIII. The Anointing of the Heavenly Sanctuary - - - - · 167
XXIX. Christ Enters Upon His Work as High Priest - - - 170
XXX. The Great Advent Movement of the Years 1834-44 - - 174
XXXI. Christ Entered the Most Holy Place in the Heavenly Sanctuary in 1844 - - - - - - - - - - - 180
XXXII. Christ's Ministry in the Most Holy Place in the Heavenly Temple 184
XXXIII. A Special Message to a Particular People - - - - 189
XXXIV. The Investigative Judgment; The Close of Human Probation 196

XXXV. Cleansing of the Heavenly Sanctuary; The Church of Christ Prepared for Her Lord - - - - - - - 203
XXXVI. Our Lord Returns for His People; Reunion of God's Family 207
XXXVII. A Study of the Atonement—Part 1. The Principle of Substitution Introduced - - - - - - - - - 212
XXXVIII. A Study of the Atonement—Part 2. The Son of God Becomes the Second Adam and Lives the Life of Man - - - 216
XXXIX. A Study of the Atonement—Part 3. Christ's Death and Resurrection Make Possible Man's Reconciliation to His Maker 220
XL. A Study of the Atonement—Part 4. What Christ's Intercession Means to the Atonement - - - - - - - 223

Illustrations

The Author - - - - - - - - - - Frontispiece
Eating the Passover - - - - - - - - - - 16
Moses Returning From Mt. Sinai With the Law of God - - - - 22
Interior View of the Sanctuary, Showing Articles of Furniture and Ministry of the Priest - - - - - - - - - - - 26
Bird's-Eye View Showing the Artist's Conception of the Ancient Typical Sanctuary and the Camp of Israel - - - - - - - 30
Anointing of the Priest - - - - - - - - - 42
Over the Head of the Innocent Lamb the Penitent Sinner Confessed His Sin 54
The High Priest With His Censer - - - - - - - 60
The Sacred Ark Containing the Law of God - - - - - - 64
The Scapegoat on the Day of Atonement - - - - - - 70
Abraham Upon Mt. Moriah Preparing to Offer His Son Isaac - - - 78
The Children of Israel Crossing the Jordan River Into the Promised Land 87
Jacob's Ladder Reaching From Earth to Heaven - - - - - 103
Ancient Manuscript Scrolls Illustrating the Manner in Which the Sacred Scriptures Were Prepared - - - - - - - - 110
The Time Is Fulfilled - - - - - - - - - 137
Diagram of Seventy Weeks and Twenty-three Hundred Days - - - 143
Hebrew Alphabet - - - - - - - - - - 155
Diagram Illustrating the Sanctuary of Israel, and Showing the Arrangement of the Furniture - - - - - - - - - - 186
Israel Worshiping the Sun, With Their Backs to the Law of God, Enshrined in His Temple - - - - - - - - - - 187

Origin and Definition of the Sanctuary

1. WHERE in the Bible do we first meet the term "sanctuary"? Ex. 15:17.

To no peoples prior to the deluge, nor following the antediluvian era until we reach the times of the seed of Abraham, was there given a knowledge of this most interesting and profound Bible theme. There is no account of the sanctuary and its ministry anywhere recorded during the first twenty-five centuries of human history. We first learn from the writings of Moses, recorded in the book of Exodus, the purpose of erecting the tabernacle, which service meant so much for fifteen centuries to the literal seed of Abraham.

On page 209 of "Daniel and the Revelation," the author, Uriah Smith, says: "The word 'sanctuary' occurs in the Old and New Testaments one hundred and forty-four times, and from the definitions of lexicographers, and its use in the Bible, we learn that it is used to signify a holy or sacred place, a dwelling place for the Most High. If, therefore, the earth is the sanctuary, it must answer to this definition; but what single characteristic pertaining to this earth is found which will satisfy the definition? It is neither a holy nor a sacred place, nor is it a dwelling place for the Most High. . . .

"Is the land of Canaan the sanctuary? So far as we may be governed by the definition of the word, it can present no better claim than the earth to that distinction. If we inquire where in the Bible it is called the sanctuary, a few texts are brought forward which seem to be supposed by some to furnish the requisite testimony. The first of these is Exodus 15:17."

2. With what similar words is the term "sanctuary" associated? Holy, holiness, sanctify, sanctification.

The Hebrew word in Exodus 25:8 for sanctuary is מִקְרָשׁ (*miqdash*). The Hebrew root for *miqdash* is קְרָשׁ (*qadesh*), which means to set apart, to be separated for a holy or sacred purpose.

God is holy. Lev. 11:44, 45; 19:2; 1 Peter 1:16. Everything associated with God's service is of a holy character. Separation from uncleanness or defilement is necessary to the worshiper of God, if he is to understand the pure and lofty ideals of divine service. Since the sanctuary was to be a dwelling place for God, it must be a holy institution. The Hebrew noun קְרָשׁ (*qodesh*), indicates holiness, sanctification, sacredness.

There is another Hebrew word used in the Old Testament that is translated "holy." This word is חָסִיד (*chasid*). This word *chasid* on several occasions is applied to the Saviour. In Psalms 16:10 we read: "Thou wilt not leave My soul in hell; neither wilt Thou suffer Thine Holy One [*chasid*] to see corruption." "Thou spakest in vision to Thy Holy One [*chasid*], and saidst, I have laid help upon One that is mighty." Ps. 89:19. In its primary use the word *chasid* means kindness, zeal, love, mercy.

3. What institution did God first make holy? Gen. 2:3.

The Sabbath of the Lord was made before the existence of sin. God set apart the seventh day as His holy day. The Creator, at the close of His six days of labor, in which He made heaven and earth, pronounced His works very good. The seventh day was consecrated by the Lord as the memorial of His created works.

Only God could make the Sabbath, for only the Creator had the ability to make the world. Man had no part in creation, for Adam was not formed till toward the close of the sixth day. Our Lord said the Sabbath was made *for* man, not *by* man.

This seventh day at creation was set apart for man, in which man was to worship his Creator. Therefore, this seventh day is called God's holy day. The Lord Himself originated the word "holiness" when He set apart for a holy and sacred purpose the seventh day. The word "sanctify" in Genesis 2:3 is *qadesh*.

4. For what purpose was the sanctuary to be erected? Ex. 25:8.

A holy God was to dwell with a holy people. The Hebrew word שכן (*shaken*), "dwell," means to neighbor. To this day among the Jewish people a *shaken* (neighbor) is a desirable person to have in the community.

There are several words in the Old Testament translated "dwell." The word *shaken* (dwell) means, literally, to tabernacle, to become a permanent dweller, a settler in a community. The word *shaken* expresses the idea of permanency, continuity. (See Ex. 29:45, 46.)

This Hebrew word *shaken* also implies rest. Num. 10:12. This word is closely related to the word שכינה (*Shekinah*), the resting place of God. God wanted Israel to learn that He desired permanently to settle among them; then they would have rest.

God dwelt in the sanctuary among the children of Israel. He desires to dwell in the human heart by His Spirit. The apostle Paul conveys this idea when he refers to Exodus 29:45. (See 2 Cor. 6:16.)

5. To what people did God entrust the sanctuary and its services? Ex. 25:1-9.

6. Why did God choose this people? Ex. 19:3-6; Amos 3:2; Deut. 10:15.

The Scriptures repeatedly declare that God is no respecter of persons. (See 2 Sam. 14:14; 2 Chron. 19:7; Acts 10:34.) There is no partiality with the Creator. In choosing the Israelites to be the depositaries of His truth, He was carrying out a promise He had made to His faithful servants, the patriarchs. (See Rom. 15:8.)

7. What two institutions did God charge the Israelites to guard sacredly? Lev. 19:30; 26:2.

Leviticus 19:30 and 26:2 are identical in the Hebrew Scriptures. These statements to His people were to remind the Israelites of the close relationship which existed between the Sabbath of the Lord and God's dwelling place. Jehovah sought to impress His people with the sacredness of His work and of His institutions.

8. Of what were the Israelites repeatedly reminded? Deut. 7:6-8.

9. Why did God commit to the Israelites His statutes and judgments? Deut. 4:5-9.

10. Were the Israelites to mingle with the heathen nations in their social life? Ex. 33:16; Num. 23:9.

The Lord did not plan for His people to be ascetics or hermits. The Israelites were to be a light to the nations about them. This light was to shine forth through godly living, through sacredly observing the Sabbath of Jehovah, and through proper conduct of His sacred institutions. By strictly observing

God's commands, Israel was to reveal the glory of God to the heathen round about.

For centuries, the Israelites disregarded the divine instructions to be a separated people. They united with the heathen among whom they lived, adopted their customs, followed their ways and manners, and, in fact, did worse than the heathen. (See 2 Chron. 33:9.) God was obliged to send His people into captivity in Babylon.

Following the delivery of Israel from the Babylonian exile, the leaders urged the people to keep themselves free from heathen manners. But prior to the advent of the Messiah, this purpose of God for Israel not to follow the customs of the heathen was perverted by the Pharisees. The Pharisees were an exclusive people. They feared to come into contact even with certain classes of Jews whom they regarded as defiled. Their separateness was external, ceremonial.

"External ceremonies and a theoretical knowledge of truth constituted Pharisaical righteousness. . . . While they were punctilious in ritual observances, their lives were immoral and debased. . . .

"The greatest deception of the human mind in Christ's day was, that a mere assent to the truth constitutes righteousness. . . . The Pharisees claimed to be children of Abraham, . . . yet these advantages did not preserve them from selfishness, malignity, greed for gain, and the basest hypocrisy. . . . The ceremonies required in the service of God are not meaningless rites, like those of the hypocritical Pharisees."—*"The Desire of Ages,"* pp. 309, 310.

The Lord intended Israel to keep themselves from following in the ways of the heathen. Israel was to be an outstanding people. It is interesting to note that the Hebrew word rendered "separated," in Exodus 33:16, is more frequently translated "wonderful."

God intended that His people should be regarded by the surrounding nations as a wonderful people. If Israel would closely and carefully follow the statutes and instructions of the Most High, the people about them would regard them as an outstanding race. God's people would not adopt heathen customs and manners if they bore in mind that God's presence was constantly with them.

11. With what assurance did God encourage His people? Ex. 33: 13-15.

12. That the Israelites might understand they were especially chosen of the Lord from other nations, with what were they sprinkled? Ex. 24:6-8; Heb. 9:19-22.

13. How were the priests set apart to indicate their sacred work? Ex. 28:3, 41; 40:13.

God's Design in Giving the Sanctuary Service to the Israelites

1. WHAT prediction did God make to Abraham in regard to his posterity? Gen. 15:13-16.

Following the deluge, the Lord chose the patriarch Abraham, through whose seed He would teach the plan of salvation by type and symbol.

"After the dispersion from Babel, idolatry again became well-nigh universal, and the Lord finally left the hardened transgressors to follow their evil ways, while He chose Abraham, of the line of Shem, and made him the keeper of His law for future generations. . . . Faithful among the faithless, uncorrupted by the prevailing apostasy, he [Abraham] steadfastly adhered to the worship of the one true God. . . . [God] communicated His will to Abraham, and gave him a distinct knowledge of the requirements of His law, and of the salvation that would be accomplished through Christ.

"There was given to Abraham the promise, especially dear to the people of that age, of a numerous posterity and of national greatness: 'I will make of thee a great nation, and I will bless thee, and make thy name great; and thou shalt be a blessing.' And to this was added the assurance, precious above every other to the inheritor of faith, that of his line the Redeemer of the world should come: 'In thee shall all families of the earth be blessed.'"—*"Patriarchs and Prophets,"* p. 125.

"The Lord condescended to enter into a covenant with His servant, employing such forms as were customary among men for the ratification of a solemn engagement. By divine direction, Abraham sacrificed a heifer, a she-goat, and a ram, each three years old, dividing the bodies and laying the pieces a little distance apart. To these he added a turtle dove and a young pigeon, which, however, were not divided. This being done, he reverently passed between the parts of the sacrifice, making a solemn vow to God of perpetual obedience. Watchful and steadfast, he remained beside the carcasses till the going down of the sun, to guard them from being defiled or devoured by birds of prey. About sunset he sank into a deep sleep; and, 'lo, a horror of great darkness fell upon him.' And the voice of God was heard, bidding him not to expect immediate possession of the Promised Land, and pointing forward to the sufferings of his posterity before their establishment in Canaan. The plan of redemption was here opened to him, in the death of Christ, the great sacrifice, and His coming in glory."—*Id.*, p. 137.

The Israelites were to experience the suffering, agony, and torture of physical slavery, a type of sin, in order that when they were delivered from their bondage in Egypt, they might better appreciate the blessings and freedom from sin in the symbolic service, by which they would be instructed through the ministry of the sanctuary.

2. What would follow this period of bondage? Was this prophecy accurately fulfilled? Ex. 12:40, 41.

"That day completed the history revealed to Abraham in prophetic vision centuries before: 'Thy seed shall be a stranger in a land that is not theirs, and shall serve them; and they shall afflict them four hundred years; and also that nation, whom they shall serve, will I judge; and afterward shall they come out with great substance.' The four hundred years had been fulfilled. 'And it came to pass the selfsame day, that the Lord did bring the children of Israel out of the land of Egypt by their armies.' "—*Id.*, pp. 281, 282.

"But like the stars in the vast circuit of their appointed path, God's purposes know no haste and no delay. Through the symbols of the great darkness and the smoking furnace, God had revealed to Abraham the bondage of Israel in Egypt, and had declared that the time of their sojourning should be four hundred years. . . . Against that word, all the power of Pharaoh's proud empire battled in vain. On 'the selfsame day' appointed in the divine promise, 'it came to pass that all the hosts of the Lord went out from the land of Egypt.' "—*The Desire of Ages,*" pp. 31, 32.

3. Was Abraham assured that his posterity would enjoy an inheritance? Gen. 13:14-17; 15:18-21.

When Joseph sent for his father Jacob to come and spend his last days in Egypt, where he could nourish and care for his aged parent, the patriarch seemed fearful to enter that land, but the assurance came to Jacob, "Fear not to go down into Egypt; for I will there make of thee a great nation." Gen. 46:3.

In regard to this fear of Jacob's, we have the following observation made by the Spirit of prophecy concerning the possession of Canaan by the descendants of the patriarchs:

"The promise had been given to Abraham of a posterity numberless as the stars; but as yet the chosen people had increased but slowly. And the land of Canaan now offered no field for the development of such a nation as had been foretold. It was in the possession of powerful heathen tribes, that were not to be dispossessed until 'the fourth generation.' If the descendants of Israel were here to become a numerous people, they must either drive out the inhabitants of the land or disperse themselves among them. The former, according to the divine arrangement, they could not do; and should they mingle with the Canaanites, they would be in danger of being seduced into idolatry. Egypt, however, offered the conditions necessary to the fulfillment of the divine purpose."—*"Patriarchs and Prophets,"* p. 232.

"The posterity of Canaan descended to the most degrading forms of heathenism. Though the prophetic curse had doomed them to slavery, the doom was withheld for centuries. God bore with their impiety and corruption until they passed the limits of divine forbearance."—*Id.*, p. 118.

4. When did God begin to fulfill this promise? Ex. 3:6-10; Deut. 6:21-23.

The forty years' wandering in the wilderness was an emergency situation. It was no part of God's program that the Israelites should wander in the desert for twoscore years. God had planned to place the seed of Abraham in the land of Canaan as soon as they would make the journey following the exodus. The reason the Lord led them by way of the wilderness is given as follows:

"It came to pass, when Pharaoh had let the people go, that God led them not through the way of the land of the Philistines, although that was near; for God said, Lest peradventure the people repent when they see war, and they return to Egypt: but God led the people about, through the way of the wilderness of the Red Sea." Ex. 13:17, 18.

But we are told in Scripture that "there are eleven days' journey from Horeb by the way of Mount Seir unto Kadesh-barnea." Deut. 1:2. Kadesh-barnea was the border of the Promised Land. Verses 19-21. The people failed to heed the counsel of God to enter the land when they were commanded to. The Lord confirmed the desire of the people,—that they should wander in the wilderness until that whole generation passed off the stage of

EATING THE PASSOVER

When the Lord was about to deliver Israel from Egypt, He commanded that a lamb
should be slain, that its blood should be sprinkled upon the doorpost, and that the
flesh should be eaten in haste, the family being prepared for instant flight.

action. Num. 14:1, 2, 28-35. The Israelites remained in that desert for forty
years. When Moses presented to Israel the statutes and judgments which he
received from the Lord, he emphasized repeatedly that these instructions, with
the laws regarding sacrifices and offerings, were to be followed when they were
come into the land of Canaan. Ex. 23:23, 27-33; Deut. 12:1-11; 16:1-8, etc.

5. At the time of Israel's deliverance from Egypt, what sacred service did God introduce among them? Ex. 12:14-20.

"The observance of the Passover began with the birth of the Hebrew nation.
On the last night of their bondage in Egypt, when there appeared no token of
deliverance, God commanded them to prepare for an immediate release. He
had warned Pharaoh of the final judgment on the Egyptians, and He directed
the Hebrews to gather their families within their own dwellings. Having
sprinkled the doorposts with the blood of the slain lamb, they were to eat the
lamb, roasted, with unleavened bread and bitter herbs."—*The Desire of Ages,*
page 76.

6. What was the center of the Passover service? Ex. 12:1-6, 8-12.

"The Lord had commanded that the Passover should be yearly kept. 'It
shall come to pass,' He said, 'when your children shall say unto you, What
mean ye by this service? that ye shall say, It is the sacrifice of the Lord's
Passover, who passed over the houses of the children of Israel when He smote
the Egyptians.' . . .

"The Passover was followed by the seven days' feast of unleavened bread.
On the second day of the feast, the first fruits of the year's harvest, a sheaf
of barley, was presented before the Lord. All the ceremonies of the feast were

types of the work of Christ. The deliverance of Israel from Egypt was an object lesson of redemption, which the Passover was intended to keep in memory."—*Id.*, p. 77.

7. Which homes were assured of freedom from death? Ex. 12: 7, 13.

"It was not enough that the paschal lamb be slain; its blood must be sprinkled upon the doorposts; so the merits of Christ's blood must be applied to the soul. We must believe, not only that He died for the world, but that He died for us individually. We must appropriate to ourselves the virtue of the atoning sacrifice."—*"Patriarchs and Prophets,"* p. 277.

"The Israelites obeyed the directions that God had given. Swiftly and secretly they made their preparations for departure. Their families were gathered, the paschal lamb slain, the flesh roasted with fire, the unleavened bread and bitter herbs prepared. The father and priest of the household sprinkled the blood upon the doorpost, and joined his family within the dwelling. In haste and silence the paschal lamb was eaten. In awe the people prayed and watched, the heart of the eldest born, from the strong man down to the little child, throbbing with indefinable dread. Fathers and mothers clasped in their arms their loved first-born, as they thought of the fearful stroke that was to fall that night. But no dwelling of Israel was visited by the death-dealing angel. The sign of blood—the sign of a Saviour's protection—was on their doors, and the destroyer entered not."—*Id.*, p. 279.

8. Of what was the blood of the paschal lamb typical? 1 Peter 1:2; 1 Cor. 5:7.

"By the paschal service, God was seeking to call His people away from their worldly cares, and to remind them of His wonderful work in their deliverance from Egypt. In this work He desired them to see a promise of deliverance from sin. As the blood of the slain lamb sheltered the homes of Israel, so the blood of Christ was to save their souls; but they could be saved through Christ only as by faith they should make His life their own. There was virtue in the symbolic service, only as it directed the worshipers to Christ as their personal Saviour. God desired that they should be led to prayerful study and meditation in regard to Christ's mission."—*"The Desire of Ages,"* page 82.

9. What strict prohibition did God make in regard to the eating of sacrifices? Lev. 17:10, 12-14.

From the earliest times, man was prohibited from eating blood. When permission was given for man to eat flesh, the command was imperative that blood be not eaten. "Flesh with the life thereof, which is the blood thereof, shall ye not eat." Gen. 9:4.

Repeatedly Israel was forbidden the eating of blood. "Ye shall not eat anything with the blood." Lev. 19:26. "Only be sure that thou eat not the blood: for the blood is the life; and thou mayest not eat the life with the flesh." Deut. 12:23.

The eating of blood was so great a sin that the record states: "Whatsoever soul it be that eateth any manner of blood, even that soul shall be cut off from his people." Lev. 7:27.

Because the people were hungry in the days of King Saul, some "flew upon the spoil, and took sheep, and oxen, and calves, and slew them on the ground: and the people did eat them with the blood. Then they told Saul, saying, Behold, the people sin against the Lord, in that they eat with the blood. And he said, Ye have transgressed." 1 Sam. 14:32, 33.

To this day the orthodox Jew refuses to eat any flesh with the blood. All

2

orthodox Jewish communities have their own men who are set apart to slaughter the animal in accordance with the Jewish law, and the blood is carefully drained from the animal. The Jewish housewife performs all necessary rabbinical requirements in the preparation of the meat, that no blood shall be found in the animal when it is ready for food.

The instruction to refrain from the eating of blood is carried over into the New Testament. The first general council convened by the apostles in Jerusalem commanded all the Christian churches to abstain from eating blood. Acts 15:20. This command was reinforced by the Holy Ghost. Verse 28.

The precious blood of the Son of God, which was spilled in Gethsemane and shed on Calvary, made atonement for the soul of man. The blood of God's Son cleanseth from all sin. God desired that man should recognize the purpose of the blood.

10. Why was such a statute enacted? Lev. 17:11.

11. What does the apostle Paul declare is necessary for the remission of sins? Heb. 9:22.

"A solemn statement was made to ancient Israel that the man who should remain unclean and refuse to purify himself, should be cut off from among the congregation. This has a special meaning for us. If it was necessary in ancient times for the unclean to be purified by the blood of sprinkling, how essential for those living in the perils of the last days, and exposed to the temptations of Satan, to have the blood of Christ applied to their hearts daily. 'For if the blood of bulls and of goats . . . sanctifieth to the purifying of the flesh, how much more shall the blood of Christ, who through the eternal Spirit offered Himself without spot to God, purge your conscience from dead works to serve the living God?' "—"Testimonies for the Church," Vol. IV, p. 123.

The sin of the sons of Eli, the high priest, was so great that the Lord said of the house of Eli: "I have told him that I will judge his house forever for the iniquity which he knoweth; because his sons made themselves vile, and he restrained them not. And therefore I have sworn unto the house of Eli, that the iniquity of Eli's house shall not be purged with sacrifice nor offering forever." 1 Sam. 3:13, 14.

When sin entered the world, God immediately introduced the plan of salvation. Gen. 3:15. In the Garden of Eden God offered Christ, His Son, as man's substitute. He then gave to Adam a sacrificial system by which it was possible for man to show his confidence in God's provision. The principle of substitution was understood by Adam and Eve, and they taught their sons to bring offerings to the Lord. (See Gen. 4:3, margin.)

"Cain and Abel, the sons of Adam, differed widely in character. . . . These brothers were tested, as Adam had been tested before them. . . . They were acquainted with the provision made for the salvation of man, and understood the system of offerings which God had ordained. They knew that in these offerings they were to express faith in the Saviour whom the offerings typified. . . . Without the shedding of blood, there could be no remission of sin; and they were to show their faith in the blood of Christ as the promised atonement, by offering the firstlings of the flock in sacrifice."—"Patriarchs and Prophets," p. 71.

12. What was Israel's response to God's requests? Ex. 19:4-8.

From the beginning of their national life, the Lord demanded of Israel implicit obedience to His commands. After they had crossed the Red Sea and seen the great victory the Lord had wrought for them by destroying the hosts of Egypt in the waters, the Lord made them the following promise:

"If thou wilt diligently hearken to the voice of the Lord thy God, and wilt do that which is right in His sight, and wilt give ear to His commandments, and keep all His statutes, I will put none of these diseases upon thee, which I have brought upon the Egyptians: for I am the Lord that healeth thee." Ex. 15:26.

Nearly nine centuries later the people were reminded of this experience through the prophet Jeremiah. Jer. 7:22-24.

13. As a witness to this promise of obedience on the part of the people, what act did Moses perform? Ex. 24:6-8.

14. What was the outstanding reason for the building of the sanctuary, and later for the building of the temple? 2 Chron. 2:6; 7:12.

From a multiplicity of scriptures, it would appear that the outstanding object in erecting the sanctuary among the Israelites was to provide for the sacrificial offerings and the symbolic gospel ministry. (See Deut. 12:5-12.) But when Jesus came, rabbinical traditions and Pharisaical rites had obscured the significance of these sacrifices.

"Numerous ceremonies were enjoined upon the people without the proper instruction as to their import. The worshipers offered their sacrifices without understanding that they were typical of the only perfect Sacrifice. And among them, unrecognized and unhonored, stood the One symbolized by all their service. He had given directions in regard to the offerings. He understood their symbolical value, and He saw that they were now perverted and misunderstood."— *"The Desire of Ages,"* p. 157.

LESSON III

Why Moses Was Summoned to an Interview With God

1. FOLLOWING the giving of the law on Mt. Sinai, what invitation did the Lord extend to Moses? Ex. 24:1, 12, 15.

The second greatest event in the annals of human history is the giving of the ten commandments on Mt. Sinai in the hearing of the Israelites. The Scripture says:

"Ask now of the days that are past, which were before thee, since the day that God created man upon the earth, and ask from the one side of heaven unto the other, whether there hath been any such thing as this great thing is, or hath been heard like it? Did ever people hear the voice of God speaking out of the midst of the fire, as thou hast heard, and live?" Deut. 4:32, 33.

The proclamation of God's holy law on Mt. Sinai was a glorious and awesome occasion. There were present at this solemn meeting on Mt. Sinai tens of thousands of holy angels, for the record says:

"The Lord came from Sinai, and rose up from Seir unto them; He shined forth from Mount Paran, and He came with ten thousands of saints: from His right hand went a fiery law for them." Deut. 33:2.

The law and the gospel are intimately connected. They are closely associated. If the divine law had never been transgressed, there would have been no need of the gospel. Since the basis of God's government and authority is the immutable law, when this divine code was violated, a remedy for sin was essential. The saving grace of God is His only remedy.

Before the children of Israel could appreciate the gospel, they must know and understand the meaning, the grandeur, the majesty, and the purpose of God's universal law. Having heard the divine precepts from the mouth of the Lord, having already promised to obey whatever God required of them, when the Israelites sinned, and found themselves under condemnation of death because of their failure in their own strength to keep this immutable heavenly law, they were in a position to value the divine remedy for sin and transgression. Through the ministry and services of the sanctuary, Israel would understand God's remedy for sin.

"In the ministration of the tabernacle, and of the temple that afterward took its place, the people were taught each day the great truths relative to Christ's death and ministration."—"*Patriarchs and Prophets*," p. 358.

2. How long did this interview last? Ex. 24:18.

3. Was this the only lengthy interview Moses had with God? Ex. 34:1-4, 28; Deut. 10:1-5.

The two interviews which Moses had with God on the mount greatly affected the physical person of the prophet. Of this experience the Scripture says:

"It came to pass, when Moses came down from Mt. Sinai with the two tables of testimony in Moses' hand, when he came down from the mount, that Moses wist not that the skin of his face shone while He talked with him. And when Aaron and all the children of Israel saw Moses, behold, the skin of his face shone; and they were afraid to come nigh him. And Moses called unto them; and Aaron and all the rulers of the congregation returned unto him: and Moses talked with them. And afterward all the children of Israel came nigh: and he gave them in commandment all that the Lord had spoken with him in Mt. Sinai. And till Moses had done speaking with them, he put a veil on his face. But when Moses went in before the Lord to speak with Him, he took the veil off, until he came out. And he came out, and spake unto the children of Israel that which he was commanded. And the children of Israel saw the face of Moses, that the skin of Moses' face shone: and Moses put the veil upon his face again, until he went in to speak with Him." Ex. 34:29-35.

Israel's prophet was unconscious of the glory which rested upon him. Moses' close and constant communion with God resulted in a manifestation of the glory of God in the prophet's countenance. Likewise, in a spiritual sense, it is man's privilege to make manifest the outshining of God's glory as a result of close communion with Christ.

4. Was Moses sustained with physical food during the weeks he spent with God on the mount? Ex. 34:28; Deut. 9:9.

According to the Scriptures already noted under question 3, it would appear that Moses was in the mount with God on at least two occasions. Each time the prophet was on Sinai forty days and forty nights. The entire time, therefore, that Moses was secreted with the Lord was eighty days and eighty nights. This was almost twelve weeks. Yet the Scriptures tell us that during these days, weeks, and months, the prophet neither ate bread nor drank water. What a precious experience may come to the servant of God who craves the personal presence of God and His close communion. It was our Saviour who said, "Blessed are they which do hunger and thirst after righteousness: for they shall be filled." Matt. 5:6.

The heavenly manna which falls from heaven, and the water of life which flows from the throne of God, give lasting and refreshing satisfaction to the soul.

5. What instruction did Moses receive while he was on Mt. Sinai? Ex. 25:8, 9, 40; 26:30; 27:8; Num. 8:4.

The experience Moses enjoyed during the days and weeks He was with God was most unusual and outstanding. He did not read, he did not study, nor did he eat. By day and by night the prophet was intensively observing what was before him. To Moses was being revealed the sanctuary in heaven. His mind and thought were concentrated on what was being shown to him. Repeatedly the admonition was given: Look! See! Watch! Make all things according to the pattern.

God impressed upon the mind of Moses the scenes which were being revealed to the prophet. Moses was commanded to make such careful and strict observations that every detail of the sanctuary he was to erect would be in perfect accord with what was revealed to him. The sanctuary with its services and its furnishing, was given to Moses by revelation. Let the reader please note that the sanctuary and its ministration originated with God. It did not come to Israel through any man's study, or by investigation, or by research. It came to Moses from the Lord directly by revelation. It was for this purpose that God summoned Moses to the mount. Even Moses' associates were left behind. Only the prophet of God was to see the pattern of the sacred tabernacle and its services, a symbol of the ministry of the blessed Messiah.

"The solemn service of sacrifice and worship at the sanctuary, and the utterances of the prophets, were a revelation of God."—"*Patriarchs and Prophets*," p. 592.

"The earthly sanctuary was built by Moses according to the pattern shown him in the mount."—*Id.*, p. 356.

MOSES RETURNING FROM MT. SINAI WITH THE LAW OF GOD

The salvation of man and the restoration of the world is God's plan, and not man's. Man is unable to save himself. Inspiration has recorded the following: "None of them can by any means redeem his brother, nor give to God a ransom for him: (for the redemption of their soul is precious, and it ceaseth forever)." Ps. 49:7, 8.

The following parable, spoken by the wise woman of Tekoah when she appeared before David to appeal for the return of Absalom, well illustrates God's arrangement for the restoration of man: "We must needs die, and are as water spilt on the ground, which cannot be gathered up again; neither doth God respect any person: yet doth He devise means, that His banished be not expelled from Him." 2 Sam. 14:14.

6. What was revealed to Moses during these days and weeks he was shut in with the Lord? Exodus 25 to 30.

7. What two men did God appoint to be associated with Moses in carrying out the instruction given to the prophet? Ex. 31:1-11.

8. How much of the information which Moses imparted to these two assistants did he receive by revelation? Heb. 8:5; Ex. 36:1-3.

It cannot be emphasized too strongly that the gospel in type, given through Moses in the services of the sanctuary, was divinely communicated. In his writings the apostle Paul says repeatedly that the gospel is made known by revelation. The reader should not gather from what has just been stated that it is unnecessary to investigate the Sacred Scriptures. The contrary of this is true. Paul admonishes us to study to show ourselves approved of God. 2 Tim. 2:15. Peter tells us to be ready always to give an answer to every person who asks us a reason for the hope. 1 Peter 3:15. Yet the true understanding of the gospel, given to man through the Holy Scriptures, must come by revelation. Gal. 1:11, 12; Eph. 3:3-8; Rom. 16:25, 26.

Sin is blinding. Sin has darkened the mind. Unaided by the Holy Spirit, man cannot comprehend things divine. Says the apostle Paul: "If our gospel be hid, it is hid to them that are lost: in whom the god of this world hath blinded the minds of them which believe not, lest the light of the glorious gospel of Christ, who is the image of God, should shine unto them." 2 Cor. 4:3, 4.

"Having the understanding darkened, being alienated from the life of God through the ignorance that is in them, because of the blindness of their heart." Eph. 4:18.

The Scriptures tell us: "The prophecy came not in old time by the will of man: but holy men of God spake as they were moved by the Holy Ghost." 2 Peter 1:21.

LESSON IV

Moses Communicates to the People the Sacred Trust Committed to Him

1. WHEN Moses was charged by God to erect the sanctuary, what divine command was he to convey to the Israelites? Ex. 25:1-7; 35:4-9.

Since the gospel is God's free gift to man, it is essential that man show a measure of appreciation of this divine benefit by cooperating with heaven. In the construction of the sanctuary, the Lord desired the Israelites to show a willing spirit toward His plan which He was to put into effect by the symbolic service of the sanctuary. God opened the way for the people to offer these gifts, if the desire to do this were in their hearts. The Lord moved upon the Egyptians to contribute gold, silver, and other precious metals to Israel before their departure from the land of their slavery. God promised Moses that He would give the Israelites favor with the Egyptians; the former should not leave Egypt empty-handed. Ex. 3:21, 22.

What the Egyptians gave to Israel, the latter had really earned when they built those treasure cities for Pharaoh. "Before leaving Egypt, the people, by the direction of Moses, claimed a recompense for their unpaid labor; and the Egyptians were too eager to be freed from their presence to refuse them. The bondmen went forth laden with the spoil of their oppressors."—"Patriarchs and Prophets," p. 281. It was this favor of God which enabled the descendants of Jacob to make the offering toward the building of the sanctuary.

2. What response did Moses receive from the people to this heavenly request? Ex. 35:21-29.

Three times in the Scriptures of the Old Testament and the New we have record of God's people being called upon for gifts with which to carry forward God's cause. In addition to the call for gifts to build the sanctuary in the wilderness, was the call made in the days of David to erect the temple which was later constructed by King Solomon.

There was also the call for assistance, in the days of the apostles, for means to save the needy poor in Jerusalem, who would face famine. This took place in the days of Claudius Caesar. Acts 11:28-30; Rom. 15:26; 1 Cor. 16:1-3. Aside from these appeals, we find no record of general calls for means with which to carry on God's work, except those ordained arrangements of tithes and offerings, which had been known to the Israelites since the days of Abraham and Jacob, and which were included in the instruction given to Moses in the wilderness.

If God's people would respond to Heaven's plans, inaugurated for the carrying forward of the work of God, there would be an abundance of gifts to supply all the needs of every part of the work of God.

"If one and all would accept it [the tithing system], each would be made a vigilant and faithful treasurer for God; and there would be no want of means with which to carry forward the great work of sounding the last message of warning to the world. The treasury will be full if all adopt this system, and the contributors will not be left the poorer."—"Testimonies for the Church," Vol. III, p. 389.

3. What reaction to this call and response was reported by Bezaleel and Aholiab? Ex. 36:5-7.

Every part of the sanctuary ministry was directly ordered of God. The Lord chose two outstanding men whom he associated with Moses, and to these He gave wisdom and skill, in order that they might erect the sacred building in full harmony with God's plan. To these men, Bezaleel and Aholiab, was committed the task of making all the furnishings for the holy sanctuary. Moses called upon the congregation to furnish the means and the material with which to do this work. The response was so unanimous and the provisions brought by the people so abundant that Bezaleel and Aholiab appealed to Moses to restrain the people from bringing more, for they already had sufficient to do all that was required for the erection of the sanctuary, and for the furnishing of it. (See Ex. 36:1-4.)

"While the building of the sanctuary was in progress, the people, old and young,—men, women, and children,—continued to bring their offerings, until those in charge of the work found that they had enough, and even more than could be used. And Moses caused to be proclaimed throughout the camp, 'Let neither man nor woman make any more work for the offering of the sanctuary. So the people were restrained from bringing.'"—*"Patriarchs and Prophets,"* p. 344.

4. What description of the ark is given in the Scriptures? Ex. 25:10-15.

5. How does the Bible describe the mercy seat? Ex. 25:17-21.

On each side of the mercy seat was a cherub. The plural for cherub is cherubim or cherubs. The Hebrew plural is formed by the Hebrew letter מ (mem). (See the word "mem" heading verse 97 in Psalms 119; see also Esther 9:26, where the letter mem, which harmonizes with the English M, is added to the singular. The word in the singular is פור (*pur*), whereas in the plural it is פורים (*purim*).

6. What did the Lord say should be placed in the ark? Ex. 25:16; Heb. 9:3, 4.

Moses was commanded to put the testimony in the ark. The testimony is the ten commandments. (See Ex. 31:18; 34:28.) In addition to the ten commandments, originally there were also deposited in the ark the pot of manna and Aaron's rod that budded. Heb. 9:3, 4. In regard to the manna we find the following:

"Moses said unto Aaron, Take a pot, and put an omer full of manna therein, and lay it up before the Lord, to be kept for your generations. As the Lord commanded Moses, so Aaron laid it up before the testimony, to be kept." Ex. 16:33, 34. According to our measure, an omer is seven and one-half pints, almost four quarts.

The word "before," in the foregoing scriptures, is the Hebrew word לפני (*liphene*). Of this word *liphene*, Gesenius, in his Hebrew and English Lexicon (ed. 1871), says: "In the presence of any one, in his sight, under his eyes, he being present and beholding, before any one."

From this understanding of the word *liphene*, it would appear that the pot of manna was placed beside the testimony, the law of God, in the ark; that is, Moses told Aaron to place this pot of manna inside the ark with the decalogue. The prophet said that the Lord commanded him to so instruct his brother.

The reason for placing the pot of manna in the ark is thus stated: "This is the thing which the Lord commandeth, Fill an omer of it to be kept for your generations; that they may see the bread wherewith I have fed you in the wilderness, when I brought you forth from the land of Egypt." Ex. 16:32.

INTERIOR VIEW OF THE SANCTUARY, SHOWING ARTICLES OF FURNITURE AND MINISTRY OF THE PRIEST

This manna was a miracle bread. It was not a food resulting from the raising of any grain, but it was rained down from heaven. Of the manna, the psalmist writes as follows: "And had rained down manna upon them to eat, and had given them of the corn of heaven. Man did eat angels' food: He sent them meat to the full." Ps. 78:24, 25.

"For forty years they were daily reminded by this miraculous provision, of God's unfailing care and tender love. . . . They were daily taught that, having God's promise, they were as secure from want as if surrounded by fields of waving grain on the fertile plains of Canaan."—"*Patriarchs and Prophets*," p. 297.

"In the wilderness, when all means of sustenance failed, God sent His people manna from heaven; and a sufficient and constant supply was given. This provision was to teach them that while they trusted in God, and walked in His ways, He would not forsake them."—"*The Desire of Ages*," p. 121.

But why was this pot of manna placed in the ark? Only the high priest was permitted to see the ark, and he could see it only when he ministered before the ark on the Day of Atonement in the most holy place of the sanctuary. No person was allowed to open the sacred chest, on pain of death. 1 Sam. 6:19. It is true that the ark was carried upon the shoulders of the Levites, when Israel journeyed from place to place. Num. 7:9. At such a time the ark was covered with the veil of the sanctuary which separated the holy place from the most holy place. Num. 4:5. The people could not know what was in the ark, only as they were told by the high priest.

The Israelites were ever to be reminded that the food their fathers ate in the wilderness was provided by the Lord Himself in a miraculous manner, for where their ancestors lived during the forty years' wilderness wandering, there was no opportunity of raising food. The Scripture says of that experience:

"Who led thee through that great and terrible wilderness, wherein were fiery serpents, and scorpions, and drouth, where there was no water; who brought thee forth water out of the rock of flint; who fed thee in the wilderness with manna, which thy fathers knew not." Deut. 8:15, 16.

The Scriptures tell us that whatsoever was written aforetime was written for our learning, particularly for those who should live at the time of the end of the world. (See Rom. 15:4; 1 Cor. 10:11.) In the days of King Solomon, the record says, "there was nothing in the ark save the two tables of stone, which Moses put there at Horeb, when the Lord made a covenant with the children of Israel." 1 Kings 8:9. What then became of the pot of manna and Aaron's rod that budded?

In "Early Writings," page 32, we read: "In the holiest I saw an ark; on the top and sides of it was purest gold. . . . In the ark was the golden pot of manna, Aaron's rod that budded." The servant of the Lord saw these objects in the most holy place in the heavenly sanctuary at the time the Lord gave her the first vision of the sanctuary. Read pages 32 and 33 of "Early Writings." The pot of manna and Aaron's rod were taken up from earth to heaven. But our heavenly High Priest is at present ministering in the most holy place of the heavenly sanctuary. The pot of manna in the ark in heaven is placed along-side the law of God. The people of God who are faithful to God's commandments in these last days may rest assured that the Saviour will feed them, even though it be necessary to work a miracle in their behalf, as the Lord cared for Israel in the wilderness when they were unable to secure their usual food. The Lord Jesus still cares for His people.

The word "manna" is derived from the two Hebrew words מן הוא (*man hu*), meaning, "What is it?" or, "What is this?" (See Ex. 16:15, margin.) When the Israelites awoke in the morning and saw the ground covered with this white substance, in their language they cried out, "*Man hu*"—"What is this?" The translators of the Bible anglicized these two Hebrew words into the one word, manna. A description of the manna is found in Exodus 16:31.

Aaron's rod budded through a miracle of the Lord. The children of Israel murmured repeatedly against God. The Lord decided to make a test among the Israelites, that they might know whom God had chosen to be leaders of the people. Each tribe was commanded to select a rod and give it to Moses. The latter was charged to place these rods before the testimony. The rod which blossomed would determine which tribe of the twelve had been chosen for leadership, and to whom belonged the priesthood. The Lord said that then the murmurings of the people should cease. The multitude, especially the leaders, murmured against God because of the food they were having, and against Moses and Aaron because of the priesthood. Their murmurings were many. So the Lord said:

"The man's rod, whom I shall choose, shall blossom: and I will make to cease from Me the murmurings of the children of Israel, whereby they murmur against you." Num. 17:5.

The day after Moses had placed the rods in the ark, he brought them forth, "and, behold, the rod of Aaron for the house of Levi was budded, and brought forth buds, and bloomed blossoms, and yielded almonds." "And the Lord said unto Moses, Bring Aaron's rod again before the testimony, to be kept for a token against the rebels; and thou shalt quite take away their murmurings from Me, that they die not." Verses 8, 10.

Regarding this experience with the rods of the tribes, we read the following: "By divine direction each tribe prepared a rod, and wrote upon it the name of the tribe. The name of Aaron was upon that of Levi. The rods were laid up in the tabernacle, 'before the testimony.' The blossoming of any rod was to be a token that the Lord had chosen that tribe for the priesthood. . . . 'The rod of Aaron for the house of Levi was budded.'. . . It was shown to the people, and afterward laid up in the tabernacle as a witness to succeeding generations. This miracle effectually settled the question of the priesthood."—"Patriarchs and Prophets," p. 403. This rod is at the present time in heaven.

7. Where did God manifest His presence? Ex. 25:22.

The mercy seat was placed on top of the ark. On the mercy seat, between the cherubim, the Lord would meet with His people, and from the mercy seat God would communicate His instruction to the people through His servant, the prophet. To this day the Jewish people regard this place between the cherubim as the place where the Shekinah rested.

8. What was one of the articles of furniture placed in the holy place of the sanctuary? Ex. 25:31-40.

9. What other article of furniture was placed in the holy place? Ex. 30:1-10.

10. What description is given of still another article of furniture in the sanctuary. Ex. 25:23-30.

LESSON V

God Outlines the Plans for All Parts of the Sanctuary

1. By what name did God call that part of the sanctuary which housed the ark, the golden altar of incense, the table of showbread, and the golden candlestick? Ex. 26:1; 36:8; Heb. 9:2-4.

The tabernacle of the sanctuary was called by different names. It was sometimes known as the מִשְׁכָּן (mishkan), "tabernacle." Ex. 26:1. At other times, as for example in 1 Kings 1:39, it was called in the Hebrew אֹהֶל (ohel), "tent." Again, as in Exodus 29:44, it was called אֹהֶל מוֹעֵד (ohel moed), "tabernacle of assembly." Still again it was called מִשְׁכַּן הָעֵדוּת (mishkan ha-eduth), "tabernacle of testimony." Ex. 38:21. Hebrew writers claimed that the reason the tabernacle was given different names was that the tabernacle was the place of the assembly of the people, and that Jehovah made this the meeting place with His people. Since the law of God was placed in the inner part of the tabernacle, and the decalogue was God's witness of Himself, of His character, of His immutability, the tabernacle of testimony was a fitting name to be given to the sanctuary.

2. How was this tabernacle constructed? Ex. 26:1-29.

"The tabernacle was so constructed that it could be taken apart and borne with the Israelites in all their journeyings. . . . Yet it was a magnificent structure. The wood employed for the building and its furniture was that of the acacia tree, which was less subject to decay than any other to be obtained at Sinai. The walls consisted of upright boards, set in silver sockets, and held firm by pillars and connecting bars; and all were overlaid with gold, giving to the building the appearance of solid gold. The roof was formed of four sets of curtains, the innermost of 'fine-twined linen, and blue, and purple, and scarlet, with cherubim of cunning work;' the other three respectively were of goats' hair, rams' skins dyed red, and sealskins, so arranged as to afford complete protection."—"Patriarchs and Prophets," p. 347.

3. How did the Lord emphasize the importance of accuracy in building the tabernacle? Ex. 26:30.

It is interesting to note how frequently the Lord stressed the thought that Moses must make the tabernacle and all connected therewith according to the pattern shown him in the mount. There must be no deviation from the plan of God. Everything must be built according to the heavenly design. No part of the sanctuary was left for man to originate.

"Chosen men were especially endowed by God with skill and wisdom for the construction of the sacred building. God Himself gave to Moses the plan of that structure, with particular directions as to its size and form, the materials to be employed, and every article of furniture which it was to contain."—Id., p. 343.

4. Into how many parts did God divide the tabernacle? Ex. 26:33.

5. How was this division in the tabernacle effected? Verses 31-33.

29

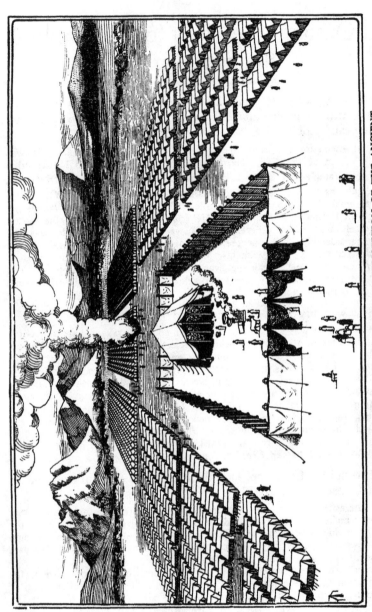

BIRD'S-EYE VIEW SHOWING THE ARTIST'S CONCEPTION OF THE ANCIENT
TYPICAL SANCTUARY AND THE CAMP OF ISRAEL

30

The veil (Hebrew, פרכת (*paroketh*), hanging, curtain, covering) was used for at least three purposes in connection with the sanctuary service. Its primary use was to form a door of separation between the holy and the most holy place. When the curtain was suspended, it formed a dividing line in the tabernacle. That portion of the tabernacle back of the veil toward the west was designated the most holy place. In the most holy place were the ark, the cherubim, and the mercy seat. In the ark were the ten commandments. No person, except the high priest, was permitted to enter the most holy place at any time, on punishment of death; and he was allowed to serve in that most holy apartment only once a year, on the Day of Atonement. (See Lev. 16:2.)

The veil was used also to cover the ark of the testimony when the sanctuary was moved from place to place. Num. 4:5.

Upon the veil the priest sprinkled the blood of the offerings brought to the sanctuary by the sinner for the remission of his sins. Lev. 4:6.

6. What were the dimensions of the tabernacle? Ex. 26:15-29; 36:20-34.

It is believed that the tabernacle was oblong in form, thirty cubits long, ten cubits wide, and ten cubits high. The Hebrew word for "cubit" is אמה (*ammah*). In regard to the length of the *ammah*, or cubit, Gesenius, in his Hebrew Lexicon (ed. 1871), says: "The common cubit of the Hebrews (2 Chron. 3:3) was reckoned at six palms, or eighteen inches; though some, without good reason, make it only four palms, or twelve inches."

The Popular and Critical Encyclopedia makes the following observation on the cubit:

"The length of the cubit has varied in different nations, and at different times. Derived as the measure is from a part of the human body, and as the human stature has been of very dissimilar length, the cubit must of necessity have been various. That the cubit, *ammah*, among the Hebrews was derived as a measure from the human body, is clear from Deuteronomy 3:11, 'after the cubit of a man.' But it is difficult to determine whether this cubit was understood as extending to the wrist or the end of the third finger. As the latter, however, seems most natural, since men, when ignorant of anatomy, and seeking in their own frame standards of measure, were likely to take both the entire foot and the entire forearm, the probability is that the longer was the original cubit, namely, the length from the elbow to the extremity of the longest finger.

"The Egyptian cubit, which it is likely the Hebrews would adopt, consisting of six handbreadths, is found on the ruins of Memphis. . . . The rabbins also . . . assign six handbreadths to the Mosaic cubit. By comparing Josephus (Antiq. 3:6, 5) with Exodus 25:10, it will, moreover, be found that the weight of his authority is in the same scale. According to him, a cubit is equal to two spans. Now, a span is equal to three handbreadths; . . . a cubit therefore is equal to six handbreadths. The handbreadth is found as a measure in 1 Kings 7:26. . . . Still no absolute and invariable standard presents itself. If the question, What is a hand or finger breadth? be asked, the answer can be only an approximation to fact."—Vol. II, p. 479.

Of the dimension of the tabernacle we find the following in the Spirit of prophecy:

"It [the tabernacle] was therefore small, being not more than fifty-five feet in length, and eighteen in breadth and height."—*"Patriarchs and Prophets,"* p. 347.

The Jews still reckon the *ammah*, cubit, at eighteen inches.

7. How were the furnishings in the sanctuary arranged? Ex. 26:34; 25:21; 26:35; 30:1-10.

The tabernacle which housed the solid gold and the gold-covered furnishings, as the table of showbread, the seven-branched candlestick, the solid-gold altar of incense, the ark which contained the decalogue, the pot of manna, Aaron's rod that budded, the cherubim, and the mercy seat, was lined and draped with the most beautiful and ornamental curtains. There were ten curtains covering the whole of the tabernacle. Five curtains were placed on each side, each curtain measuring forty feet long by six feet wide. These curtains were joined by loops and taches.

In the holy place of the sanctuary were the golden altar of incense, the table of showbread, and the golden candlestick. The golden altar of incense was placed in front of the veil. Ex. 40:26. The table of showbread was on the north side of the tabernacle. Opposite the table, on the south side of the tabernacle, was the branched candlestick. This geographical location was by order from the Lord. Ex. 26:35; 40:22, 24. The ark and mercy seat, with the law, were therefore placed in the west end of the structure, and the worshiper's entrance to the sanctuary was at the east, with the face of the worshiper always toward the west.

In the most holy place dwelt the Shekinah, the glory of God. The Scriptures repeatedly say that the Lord dwells between the cherubim. (See Ps. 80:1; 99:1; Isa. 37:15, 16.) The Lord also met the priests and people at the *door* of the sanctuary, as may be seen from the following:

"This shall be a continual burnt offering throughout your generations at the door of the tabernacle of the congregation before the Lord: where I will meet you, to speak there unto thee. And there I will meet with the children of Israel, and the tabernacle shall be sanctified by My glory. And I will sanctify the tabernacle of the congregation, and the altar: I will sanctify also both Aaron and his sons, to minister to Me in the priest's office." Ex. 29:42-44.

We find that the Lord came to the door of the tabernacle of the congregation when He spoke to Moses, Aaron, and Miriam, at the time the two latter murmured against their brother. Num. 12:1, 2, 4, 5.

Exodus 29:42 teaches that the Lord met with His people and with the priests at the time the sacrifices were offered each day. The Lord promised He would meet His people day by day when their prayers ascended to heaven at the time of the offering of the sacrifices. (See verse 43.) God was present with His people in the holy places.

8. With what was the tabernacle enclosed? Ex. 27:9-17; 38:9-20; 40:8.

"The sacred tent was enclosed in an open space called the court, which was surrounded by hangings, or screens, of fine linen, suspended from pillars of brass. The entrance to this enclosure was at the eastern end. It was closed by curtains of costly material and beautiful workmanship, though inferior to those of the sanctuary. The hangings of the court being only about half as high as the walls of the tabernacle, the building could be plainly seen by the people without."—"*Patriarchs and Prophets,*" p. 347.

9. What were the dimensions of the court? Ex. 27:18.

If the *ammah* (cubit) be taken as eighteen inches, the length of the court would be one hundred fifty feet, and the width seventy-five feet. The gate or entrance to the court was thirty feet. The hangings of the court were seven and one-half feet high.

10. What was placed in the court near its entrance? Ex. 27:1-8; 38:1-7; 40:6.

The altar of burnt offering was seven and one-half feet square, and four and one-half feet high. It was covered or filled in with brass. The Hebrew word נחשת (*nechosheth*), translated "brass," is also translated "copper." Gesenius says the following on this word *nechosheth*: "Anything made of brass or copper, . . . money, brass or copper coin, . . . a chain, fetter, of brass or copper. Lam. 3:7."—*Hebrew Lexicon, ed. 1871.*

Following the rebellion of Korah, Dathan, and Abiram, when the earth opened her mouth and swallowed them up, and the two hundred fifty sympathizers with them, Moses was commanded to take the censers of those rebels, and make covers of them for the altar of burnt offering. (See Num. 16:36-40.)

11. What other article of furniture was placed in the court, and where? Ex. 30:18-21; 38:8; 40:7.

Jewish writers claim that the laver consisted of two parts, a basin and a stand. The Hebrew word for foot in verse 18 is כֵּן (*ken*). This word is rendered in other parts of the Old Testament, "base," "stand," "pedestal." (See 1 Kings 7:27, 37.)

The text of Exodus 38:8 is not very clear; but the following comment on the laver assists in clarifying the text:

"Between the altar and the door of the tabernacle was the laver, which was also of brass, made from the mirrors that had been the freewill offering of the women of Israel."—*"Patriarchs and Prophets,"* p. 347.

Fourteen years after "Patriarchs and Prophets" was published, the Jewish Encyclopedia, prepared by more than four hundred of the most scholarly rabbis and educators, was published by Funk and Wagnalls, New York. This encyclopedia says the following of the laver:

"It was made of brass from the mirrors given by the women [Ex. 38:8], . . . and stood between the door of the tabernacle and the altar of burnt offering." —Vol. VII, pp. 630-632, edition 1904.

"At the laver the priests were to wash their hands and their feet whenever they went into the sacred apartments, or approached the altar to offer a burnt offering."—*"Patriarchs and Prophets,"* pp. 347, 348.

LESSON VI

Moses Commanded to Make Garments for the Priests, Also the Anointing Oil and the Incense

1. IF Israel would be obedient to the Lord, what kind of people did He promise to make them? Ex. 19:5, 6.

2. What special claim did God make upon the Israelites? Ex. 22: 29, last clause; Ex. 13:1, 2.

3. What was the basis for such a demand? Ex. 13:14, 15.

"The first-born of both man and beast were to be the Lord's to be bought back only by a ransom, in acknowledgment that when the first-born of Egypt perished, that of Israel, though graciously preserved, had been justly exposed to the same doom but for the atoning sacrifice. 'All the first-born are Mine,' the Lord declared; 'for on the day that I smote all the first-born in the land of Egypt, I hallowed unto Me all the first-born in Israel, both man and beast: Mine they shall be.' After the institution of the tabernacle service, the Lord chose unto Himself the tribe of Levi for the work of the sanctuary, instead of the first-born of the people."—"*Patriarchs and Prophets*," pp. 274-277.

4. After Moses and Aaron had taken the census of the Israelites, what command came to Moses? Num. 3:5-10.

"By divine direction the tribe of Levi was set apart for the service of the sanctuary. In the earliest times every man was the priest of his own household. In the days of Abraham, the priesthood was regarded as the birthright of the eldest son. Now, instead of the first-born of all Israel, the Lord accepted the tribe of Levi for the work of the sanctuary. By this signal honor He manifested His approval of their fidelity, both in adhering to His service and in executing His judgments when Israel apostatized in the worship of the golden calf."—*Id.*, p. 350.

5. What reason did the Lord give for this arrangement of transfer? Num. 3:11-13.

"'Instead of the first-born of all the children of Israel, have I taken them unto Me.' All the people were, however, still required, in acknowledgment of God's mercy, to pay a redemption price for the first-born son."—*Id.*, p. 277.

This custom of redeeming the first-born son is still in vogue among the Jewish people. In certain countries where Jewish orthodoxy is rigidly followed, the oldest son has to attend the synagogue on the anniversary of his birth, and contribute a sum of money to acknowledge his debt of gratitude for the redemption of the first-born in the days of Israel's deliverance when the Egyptian first-born were slain. This service is known ,as *Pid-yan A-ben*, the redemption of the son.

It is well, also, to recognize that God Himself introduces the principle of substitution. Occasionally in the Scriptures we have object lessons which impress the reader with the divine recognition of substitution.

34

6. What formal service was inaugurated to separate the Levites? Num. 8:5-22.

We frequently meet in the Sacred Record with dedication services, consecrations, and services of separation. These rites were made impressive. The Lord wished the people to understand that those whom He had chosen for a special purpose, whatever that purpose might be, must recognize its sacredness and importance.

7. What special work was given to the Levites? Num. 3:5, 6, 9, 10; 8:9; 18:1, 2.

8. To prepare Aaron and his sons for the priesthood, what was Moses commanded to make for them? Ex. 28:1, 2.

A most interesting chapter of Scripture is that which describes the particular garments necessary for the high priest and the associate priests to wear when conducting the sacred service in the sanctuary of the Lord.

"Everything connected with the apparel and deportment of the priests was to be such as to impress the beholder with a sense of the holiness of God, the sacredness of His worship, and the purity required of those who came into His presence."—*Id.*, p. 351.

In regard to the length of the priest's robe, we read: "The robe of the common priest was of white linen, and woven in one piece. It extended nearly to the feet, and was confined about the waist by a white linen girdle, embroidered in blue, purple, and red."—*Id.*, p. 350.

Of the dress of the high priest, the Spirit of prophecy says: "The garments of the high priest were of costly material and beautiful workmanship, befitting his exalted station. In addition to the linen dress of the common priest, he wore a robe of blue, also woven in one piece."—*Id.*, pp. 350, 351.

The purpose of God in directing the high priest to wear such apparel was to "impress the beholder with the holiness of God, the sacredness of His worship, and the purity required of those who came into His presence." The Lord never lowers His standard of piety and purity. His worship ever has been and always will be sacred. He expects His people, when they come into His presence, to be clothed in an acceptable manner. Our High Priest's dress is thus described by the apostle John, to whom a revelation of Jesus Christ was given on the Isle of Patmos: "In the midst of the seven candlesticks one like unto the Son of man, clothed with a garment down to the foot, and girt about the paps with a golden girdle." Rev. 1:13.

In the first vision given the servant of the Lord in these last days, we find a description of the dress of the saints as they stand on the sea of glass when they are translated to heaven:

"Some crowns appeared heavy with stars, while others had but few. All were perfectly satisfied with their crowns. And they were all clothed with a glorious white mantle from their shoulders to their feet."—*"Early Writings,"* pp. 16, 17.

9. What was included in this special command? Ex. 28:4, 36-38; 39:27-29.

10. How were these articles to be made? Ex. 28:6-43.

11. Why did the Lord command Moses to choose various spices? Ex. 30:22-25.

The prescription given to Moses for the preparation of the oil of consecration for the anointing of the sanctuary and for the consecration of Aaron and his sons to the priesthood, originated with God. The Lord calls this oil "a holy anointing oil." The sanctuary ministry could not commence, nor could the ministry of the priesthood become effective until both the sanctuary and the priests were set apart by this holy anointing oil. Nor could this prescription be used by the laity for their personal use. The priests could avail themselves of this oil only at the time when they were consecrated to the work of ministry. To use this oil contrary to the command of God meant instant death. God was extremely particular that the anointing oil should be used for one and only one purpose,—the anointing of the sanctuary and the inauguration of the priests. There could be no ministry of the priesthood until there had been a dedication and a consecration of the sanctuary and of the priests.

12. For what purpose was this oil made? Ex. 30:26-30; 28:41; 29:7-9.

13. Was this holy anointing oil to be used by the people in general? Ex. 30:31-33.

14. What other compound was Moses instructed to make for the services of the sanctuary? Ex. 30:34-36.

15. Could the rank and file of the Israelites make a similar prescription for their own personal use? Ex. 30:37, 38.

Sacred perfume was to be used in connection with the sanctuary service. God is a lover of the beautiful and the fragrant; but fragrance and beauty with the Lord are associated with character building. God inaugurated the use of sweet odors, for they are pleasant and agreeable to Him; but these were not designed for use as a personal attraction. To duplicate those perfumes for personal use meant instant death. These fragrant odors were for daily use in the sanctuary service. The Spirit of prophecy offers the following comment on their use:

"Just before the veil separating the holy place from the most holy and the immediate presence of God, stood the golden altar of incense. Upon this altar the priest was to burn incense every morning and evening. . . . Day and night the holy incense diffused its fragrance throughout the sacred apartments, and without, far around the tabernacle."—*"Patriarchs and Prophets,"* p. 348.

"In the offering of incense the priest was brought more directly into the presence of God than in any other act of the daily ministration. As the inner veil of the sanctuary did not extend to the top of the building, the glory of God, which was manifested above the mercy seat, was partially visible from the first apartment. When the priest offered incense before the Lord, he looked toward the ark; and as the cloud of incense arose, the divine glory descended upon the mercy seat and filled the most holy place. . . .

"The ·incense, ascending with the prayers of Israel, represents the merits and intercession of Christ, His perfect righteousness, which through faith is imputed to His people, and which can alone make the worship of sinful beings acceptable to God."—*Id.,* p. 353.

The Sanctuary Built, Inspected, Accepted, and Approved of Heaven

1. WHAT is said of the work of the two men who were especially selected to cooperate with Moses in the building of the sanctuary? Ex. 36:1.

It is easy to conclude, as we read the Scriptures, that Aholiab and Bezaleel accepted the charge from Moses, at the mouth of the Lord, with earnestness and zeal. They "wrought," the text says. And how faithfully they did their work! Moses used his influence to encourage the people to recognize that the Lord had especially chosen these two men to lead out in this particular task, and the multitude were encouraged to give full cooperation; for it is written: "Moses said unto the children of Israel, See, the Lord hath called by name Bezaleel the son of Uri, the son of Hur, of the tribe of Judah; and He hath filled him with the spirit of God, in wisdom, in understanding, and in knowledge, and in all manner of workmanship; and to devise curious works, to work in gold, and in silver, and in brass, and in the cutting of stones, to set them, and in carving of wood, to make any manner of cunning work. And He hath put in his heart that he may teach, both he, and Aholiab, the son of Ahisamach, of the tribe of Dan. Them hath He filled with wisdom of heart, to work all manner of work." Ex. 35:30-35.

From the very beginning of this work, God was in the movement, and He stayed with it until the work was completed. From the greatest in the assembly to the last man, all recognized that the erection of the sanctuary was by the express command of the Lord.

"The murmurings of the Israelites and the visitations of God's judgments because of their sins, are recorded as a warning to after generations. And their devotion, their zeal and liberality, are an example worthy of imitation. All who love the worship of God, and prize the blessing of His sacred presence, will manifest the same spirit of sacrifice in preparing a house where He may meet with them. They will desire to bring to the Lord an offering of the very best that they possess."—*Patriarchs and Prophets,*" p. 344.

2. Were only these two men engaged in doing the work of the sanctuary? Ex. 36:2-4; 35:21, 25, 26.

3. How long a time did it take to build the sanctuary?

While we do not find in the Scriptures a detailed record of just how long it required Aholiab, Bezaleel, and their coworkers to make the furnishings of the sanctuary, including the court, the Spirit of prophecy makes the following observation on this point: "A period of about half a year was occupied in the building of the tabernacle."—*Id.,* p. 349.

4. What does the Scripture say of the workmanship of these men when they had finished building the sanctuary? Ex. 39:32.

Aholiab and Bezaleel continued the work committed to their charge until the task was completed. How honored they must have felt to be entrusted with so sacred a work! They were not working at a job; they were given a task to perform for God. All features of the Lord's work are sacred, and they should ever be so regarded. Says the servant of the Lord: "God's work is to become increasingly sacred to His people. In every way we are to magnify the exalted character of the truth."—*"Testimonies for the Church,"* Vol. IX, p. 264.

5. What did Aholiab and Bezaleel do with the furnishings when the work was completed? Ex. 39:33-42.

6. When Moses examined all the work, what did he find? Verse 43.

When Moses inspected the finished work, it must have afforded him great satisfaction to know that every detail had been carried out in accordance with the instructions given him of God. Aholiab and Bezaleel doubtless were happy that their labors were approved of Moses. To receive divine approbation for carrying forward God's work is a source of encouragement and gratification. The blessing of the Lord was conferred upon Aholiab and Bezaleel, and upon all who participated in the sacred work. God's people may look forward with fond anticipation to the hour when they will hear the words of the Master that they have pleased God.

7. After the furniture for the sanctuary was inspected, what command came to Moses? Ex. 40:1, 2.

God was so particular in regard to the construction and erection of the sanctuary that He prescribed when and how the structure should be placed in order. Moses waited for God to command him when to take the next step. We find that when the prophet was ordered to set up the tabernacle, the command to put the furnishings in the sanctuary in definite and specific places, was given the third time. The Lord insists on order and harmony in His work.

"God is a God of order. Everything connected with heaven is in perfect order; subjection and thorough discipline mark the movements of the angelic host. Success can only attend order and harmonious action. God requires order and system in His work now no less than in the days of Israel. All who are working for Him are to labor intelligently, not in a careless, haphazard manner. He would have His work done with faith and exactness, that He may place the seal of His approval upon it."—*"Patriarchs and Prophets,"* p. 376.

8. Did Moses make this command effective? Ex. 40:16, 17.

Moses had learned the value of implicit obedience to the Lord's commands. According to the record, the prophet did not deviate from the exact instruction given to him. Moses taught Israel this same principle:

"Ye shall not add unto the word which I command you, neither shall ye diminish ought from it, that ye may keep the commandments of the Lord your God which I command you." Deut. 4:2. Moses was a faithful exponent of his own teaching. Only once did he depart from following the precise command of God, but this caused his exclusion from the Promised Land.

9. How was Moses guided in placing the articles of furniture in the sanctuary? Ex. 40:19, 21, 23, 25, 27, 29, last clause in each verse.

No less than seven times it is stated in this fortieth chapter of Exodus, following verse 17, that this man of God did "as the Lord commanded" him. He placed each piece of furniture in the exact spot commanded him. He was constantly conscious of the admonition given to him in the mount, "See . . . that thou make, all things according to the pattern." Heb. 8:5. Moses was following heaven's blueprint in placing the furnishings of the sanctuary. This man of God had a sense of God's holiness as well as of God's requirements. He placed the table in the holy place on the north, the candlestick on the south, and the ark on the west. Scripture writers approve of the faithfulness of Moses in all things that the Lord commanded him. God so appreciated this fine quality in this meek man that Aaron and Miriam were told that God would talk to Moses with unveiled face. (See Num. 12:7.) God could depend on Moses.

The apostle Paul states that Moses' faithfulness was an object lesson for later times. Says the apostle: "Moses verily was faithful in all his house, as a servant, for a testimony of those things which were to be spoken after." Heb. 3:5.

10. What does the record say of the task after Moses had reared up the court? Ex. 40:33.

11. How did God show His approval of the work done? Verse 34.

Covering the sanctuary with the cloud, and filling the tabernacle with the glory of God, was the ancient divine method of approval. This manifestation of divine sanction was present at the time when King Solomon's temple was accepted and approved by Heaven. (See 1 Kings 8:10.) It was the same as saying: "Well done, thou good and faithful servant." Matt. 25:21.

"With eager interest the multitudes of Israel crowded around to look upon the sacred structure. While they were contemplating the scene with reverent satisfaction, the pillar of cloud floated over the sanctuary, and descending, enveloped it. 'And the glory of the Lord filled the tabernacle.' There was a revealing of the divine majesty, and for a time even Moses could not enter. With deep emotion the people beheld the token that the work of their hands was accepted. There were no loud demonstrations of rejoicing. A solemn awe rested upon all. But the gladness of their hearts welled up in tears of joy, and they murmured low, earnest words of gratitude that God had condescended to abide with them."— *"Patriarchs and Prophets,"* pp. 349, 350.

12. How were the movements of the Israelites guided? Ex. 40:36-38.

What a beautiful demonstration of divine leadership and guidance the Israelites constantly enjoyed! They must have known by experience that Moses was in direct and close communication with heaven, and that their leader received all his orders from God. In addition to this divine leadership by the hand of Moses, the Lord gave that people an ever-abiding token that He was directly guiding them, as they constantly beheld the pillar of cloud by day and the pillar of fire by night. There was no avenue open to them to doubt the personal presence of God among them. The visible sign of God's leadership could be seen by all the people at all times, by day and by night. What a fortunate people the Israelites were to have God so nigh to them! Deut. 4:7. How could they have murmured against Him when there was such a constant manifestation of His presence among them!

13. How long a time did the people remain in one place in their journeyings? Num. 9:15-17.

14. What signal did the Lord give the Israelites when they were to move to another location? Verses 18-23.

15. Who were in the forefront, leading the hosts of the Lord? Num. 10:33-36.

The Lord offered the Israelites in their desert wanderings unfailing evidence of His love and care. The ark, borne by the priests who went before them, was the symbol of God's personal presence and leadership. In the ark was the law of God, the pledge of a covenant-keeping God. Beside that law in the ark was the pot of manna, the assurance that the Lord would work miracles for them to sustain their life when they needed food, if they would only obey Him. Aaron's rod, with its buds, blossoms, and almonds, should have reminded them that God is able to furnish a table for them in the wilderness. Num. 17:7-11; Ps. 23:4, 5; 78:18, 19. The rod of God in Moses' hand was an ever-present testimony that God could give them all the pure drinking water they needed. Ex. 17:5, 6. Yet the word of the Lord declares of that people: "They tempted the Lord, saying, Is the Lord among us, or not?" Ex. 17:7.

"The history of the wilderness life of Israel was chronicled for the benefit of the Israel of God to the close of time. The record of God's dealings with the wanderers of the desert in all their marchings to and fro, in their exposure to hunger, thirst, and weariness, and in the striking manifestations of His power for their relief, is fraught with warning and instruction for His people in all ages. . . . God would have His people in these days review with a humble heart and teachable spirit the trials through which ancient Israel passed, that they may be instructed in their preparation for the heavenly Canaan."—*"Patriarchs and Prophets,"* p. 293.

Dedication of the Sanctuary; Consecration and Inauguration of the Priesthood

1. WHAT exercises were necessary before the sanctuary service and that of the priesthood could begin? Ex. 29:44; 40:9; Lev. 8:10, 11; Num. 7:1; Ex. 29:7-9; 28:41.

In preparing the sanctuary and the priests for the holy work in the tabernacle, God designed to attach sacredness and reverence to the services which should be conducted. The Lord was to meet with His people. The priests were to conduct the solemn service and worship of the living God. For all future time, priests and laity must view in a reverential manner the ministry carried forward in these holy apartments.

No secular or common exercises could be conducted in these sacred shrines; all the worship to be performed by the priests for the people was dedicated to the salvation of man. Day by day man was to commune with God through the ministry of the priest; the people must understand the necessity of reverence and holiness in connection with this work. A holy preparatory service was therefore necessary to be conducted in the presence of the entire congregation of Israel. The sanctuary must be dedicated to the sacred worship of a pure and holy God; the priests must be set apart for their holy office.

"The people were to be impressed that everything connected with the service of God must be regarded with the greatest reverence."—*"Patriarchs and Prophets,"* p. 303.

"Jehovah, the eternal, self-existent, uncreated One, Himself the source and sustainer of all, is alone entitled to supreme reverence and worship."—*Id.,* p. 305.

"Humility and reverence should characterize the deportment of all who come into the presence of God. . . . There are those who conduct themselves in His house as they would not presume to do in the audience chamber of an earthly ruler. These should remember that they are in His sight whom seraphim adore, before whom angels veil their faces. God is greatly to be reverenced; all who truly realize His presence will bow in humility before Him."—*Id.,* p. 252.

When the Captain of the Lord's hosts appeared to Joshua, Israel's leader was commanded to remove his shoes, for the place whereon he stood was holy ground. Joshua 5:15.

2. What provision had been made for such a ceremony? Ex. 30:25-30.

From early times, holy oil has been used for anointing purposes in God's service. When the Lord appeared to Jacob at the time the patriarch fled from his brother Esau, and revealed to him the divine presence, Jacob "took the stone that he had put for his pillows, and set it up for a pillar, and poured oil upon the top of it." Gen. 28:18.

When later the angel of the Lord visited Jacob, and told him to return to his father's home, the heavenly messenger said to him: "I am the God of Bethel, where thou anointedst the pillar." Gen. 31:13.

When the prophet Samuel was commanded to set apart Saul the Benjamite to be king over Israel, he "took a vial of oil, and poured it upon his head, and

ANOINTING OF THE PRIEST

kissed him, and said, Is it not because the Lord hath anointed thee to be captain over His inheritance?" 1 Sam. 10:1.

Later, in telling Samuel to choose a king from the sons of Jesse, the Lord said to the prophet: "Fill thine horn with oil, and go, I will send thee to Jesse the Bethlehemite." 1 Sam. 16:1.

When Samuel was told that David was the Lord's choice in place of Saul, the son of Kish, he "took the horn of oil, and anointed him in the midst of his brethren: and the Spirit of the Lord came upon David from that day forward." Verse 13.

The Lord recognized the significance of the use of oil for setting people apart to His work and service. There are several Hebrew words in the Old Testament translated "anoint." The word מָשַׁח (mqshach) has the preponderance over all others. This Hebrew word mashach is the root from which we derive the word "Messiah."

3. By whose authority was this ceremony commanded? Lev. 8:5; Ex. 29:1.

Moses impressed the people with the idea that what he was about to undertake he was doing at the command of God, and not of his own volition. So often were Moses and Aaron accused of leading the people without divine authority, that the prophet of Israel assured the congregation that he was commanded of God to conduct this dedicatory service.

The Lord gave the Israelites sufficient evidence that God Himself was their leader; nevertheless, the people repeatedly accused Moses of usurping his authority. Never a day or an hour passed but that the people saw the pillar of cloud or the pillar of fire. This illuminated body was designed to be a constant reminder to them that they were under divine leadership.

"The standard of their invisible Leader was ever with them. By day the cloud directed their journeyings, or spread as a canopy above the host. It served as a protection from the burning heat, and by its coolness and moisture afforded grateful refreshment in the parched, thirsty desert. By night it became a pillar of fire, illuminating their encampment, and constantly assuring them of the divine presence."—"Patriarchs and Prophets," p. 282.

4. How many of the people were to attend this important ceremony? Lev. 8:1, 3, 4.

According to the census of the Israelites, taken by Moses and Aaron and recorded in Numbers 1, there were 603,550 males above the age of twenty-one years. Verse 46. What an experience it must have been to those tens of thousands, yes, hundreds of thousands, of men besides the women and children, to witness this solemn and significant service of the inauguration of the sanctuary and the dedication and consecration of the priests! Without doubt this service marked a new era in the experience of the Israelites. The Lord was introducing in an organized manner, by types and symbols, the great plan of salvation in behalf of the seed of Abraham, and through them, the light and knowledge of God's redemption for a lost world. Without doubt this great gathering was an object lesson of another and still greater inauguration, dedication, and consecration to be witnessed by a much greater audience in the royal courts above, when the heavenly priesthood was undertaken by man's divinely appointed Priest, who ministers in the sanctuary which the Lord appointed.

Dedicatory exercises for the worship of God were without doubt first introduced when the sanctuary in the wilderness was set apart for the service of God. What an influence that dedicatory service has exerted in the world!

5. How did Moses prepare Aaron and his sons for their anointing? Lev. 8:2, 6-9; Ex. 29:1, 4-9.

Moses was commanded to take Aaron and his sons and prepare them to be clothed with the special garments. First, these men called to the holy office of priesthood were to wash in the laver. "They were to leave their shoes in the court before entering the sanctuary, and also to wash both their hands and their feet before ministering in the tabernacle or at the altar of burnt offering. Thus was constantly taught the lesson that all defilement must be put away from those who would approach into the presence of God."—*Patriarchs and Prophets,"* p. 350.

When the priests were through with this cleansing preparation, Moses robed Aaron and his sons with the garments made for them. This clothing is described as follows:

"The garments of the high priest were of costly material and beautiful workmanship, befitting his exalted station. In addition to the linen dress of the common priest, he wore a robe of blue, also woven in one piece. Around the skirt it was ornamented with golden bells, and pomegranates of blue, purple, and scarlet. Outside of this was the ephod, a shorter garment of gold, blue, purple, scarlet, and white. It was confined by a girdle of the same colors, beautifully wrought. The ephod was sleeveless, and on its gold-embroidered shoulder pieces were set two onyx stones, bearing the names of the twelve tribes of Israel.

"Over the ephod was the breastplate, the most sacred of the priestly vestments. This was of the same material as the ephod. It was in the form of a square, measuring a span, and was suspended from the shoulders by a cord of blue from golden rings. The border was formed of a variety of precious stones, the same that form the twelve foundations of the city of God. Within the border were twelve stones set in gold, arranged in rows of four, and, like those in the shoulder pieces, engraved with the names of the tribes. The Lord's direction was, 'Aaron shall bear the names of the children of Israel in the breastplate of judgment upon his heart, when he goeth in unto the holy place, for a memorial before the Lord continually.' So Christ, the great high priest, pleading His blood before the Father in the sinner's behalf, bears upon His heart the name of every repentant, believing soul. Says the psalmist, 'I am poor and needy, yet the Lord thinketh upon me.'

"At the right and left of the breastplate were two large stones of great brilliancy. These were known as the Urim and Thummim. By them the will of God was made known through the high priest. . . .

"The miter of the high priest consisted of the white linen turban, having attached to it by a lace of blue, a gold plate bearing the inscription, 'Holiness to Jehovah.' Everything connected with the apparel and deportment of the priests was to be such as to impress the beholder with a sense of the holiness of God, the sacredness of His worship, and the purity required of those who came into His presence."—*Id.,* pp. 350, 351.

"The robe of the common priest was of white linen, and woven in one piece. It extended nearly to the feet, and was confined about the waist by a white linen girdle embroidered in blue, purple, and red. A linen turban, or miter, completed his outer costume. . . . The priests were not to enter the sanctuary with shoes upon their feet. Particles of dust cleaving to them would desecrate the holy place."—*Id.,* p. 350.

6. After Aaron and his sons were prepared for their consecration, what did Moses do? Ex. 30:26-29; Lev. 8:10, 11.

When the priests were clothed, Moses went into the sanctuary to anoint it. This was the command:

"Thou shalt anoint the tabernacle . . . and the ark of the testimony, and the table and all his vessels, and the candlestick and his vessels, and the altar of incense, and the altar of burnt offering with all his vessels, and the laver and his foot. And thou shalt sanctify them, that they may be most holy: whatsoever toucheth them shall be holy." Ex. 30:26-29.

"Moses took the anointing oil, and anointed the tabernacle, . . . and sanctified them. And he sprinkled thereof upon the altar seven times, and anointed the altar and all his vessels, both the laver and his foot, to sanctify them." Lev. 8:10, 11.

It was necessary that the holy places should first be set apart by the anointing oil before the priests were dedicated to their task. The priests could not enter upon their labors until the sanctuary had been anointed with this sacred oil.

7. What ministry did Moses then perform for Aaron and for his sons? Ex. 30:30; 29:7; Lev. 8:12; 21:10; Ex. 40:13-15.

8. How thoroughly were the high priest and the other priests anointed? Ps. 133:1, 2; Lev. 8:30, 24.

Upon Aaron and his sons Moses poured the oil of consecration. By this method they were set apart and inaugurated unto the sacred service of God. Never could they have entered upon their priestly ministry until this act of consecration had been performed.

This anointing was done thoroughly. From the crown of the priest's head to the bottom of his garments the oil ran down. The tips of the priests' ears, their great toes, representing the organs of the body, all were included in the setting of these men apart to their service. God expects of His servants complete consecration.

9. By what names was this service called? Ex. 28:41; Num. 18:8; Ex. 29:9, 29.

Various terms were used to indicate this service of setting apart the priests to their holy task. It was called anointing, consecrating, sanctifying. These chosen men were specially set apart to this ministry. They were not to engage in any other form of occupation. They were to be separated from all the people to this specific mission.

→ In consecrating and sanctifying the priests to this work, God did not intend or plan to make the priests an exclusive or superior class of people. God chose them for this special worship to represent the saving ministry of the gospel, through the typical services in the sanctuary. The priests were to mingle and associate with the people. They were to represent God to the people. Of one feature of their work we read as follows:

"Thou shalt come unto the priests the Levites, and unto the judge that shall be in those days, and inquire; and they shall show thee the sentence of judgment: and thou shalt do according to the sentence, which they of that place which the Lord shall choose shall show thee; and thou shalt observe to do according to all that they inform thee: according to the sentence of the law which they shall teach thee, and according to the judgment which they shall tell thee, thou shalt do: thou shalt not decline from the sentence which they shall show thee, to the right hand, nor to the left. And the man that will do presumptuously, and will not hearken unto the priest that standeth to minister there before the Lord thy God, or unto the judge, even that man shall die: and thou shalt put away the evil from Israel." Deut. 17:9-12.

When Canaan was divided among the tribes, the Levites received no inheritance in the land. The Lord provided for them, since they were dedicated to do His special work. God said He was their part and their inheritance among the people. Num. 18:20.

10. How long a time was devoted to this service of dedication and consecration? Lev. 8:33; Ex. 29:30, 35.

These exercises of inauguration and dedication lasted seven days. Those who were set apart were to give their entire time to this solemn and holy service. Nothing was permitted to interfere with these solemn rites. So sacred were these services that the priests were commanded to remain in the same place during the entire time of their consecration. To deviate in the least from the strict command of God meant death. These consecration services were performed in connection with the sanctuary which was built according to the pattern shown Moses in the mount. The sanctuary and true tabernacle, after which the earthly was built, was not on earth.

11. Where were the priests to remain during these days of consecration? Lev. 8 :33.

During these days of consecration no one was permitted to enter the most holy place. Moses entered the inner apartment to anoint the most holy, as he was instructed of the Lord; but the services themselves were conducted at the door of the sanctuary, at the entrance into the holy place. Of this "door of the tabernacle of the congregation," the Lord said: "There I will meet with the children of Israel, and the tabernacle shall be sanctified by My glory." Ex. 29 :43. It is well to remember this fact.

12. How was all the time of the priests occupied during this period of consecration? Lev. 8 :34, 35.

No person who was associated with the sanctuary ministry was permitted to perform any labor during these days of consecration. Day and night they were to abide at the same place while the consecration was continuing. They were exhorted to keep the charge of the Lord, that they die not. Moses was so commanded.

LESSON IX

The Ministry in the Sanctuary

The Work of the Priests

1. WHY did the Lord say He chose Aaron and his sons? Ex. 28: 1-4, 41; 29:44; Num. 3:2, 3.

It is true that Aaron showed a weakness at the time of the idolatry of the children of Israel at Sinai, when the people demanded that he make them a golden calf. Of his experience at this time we read:

"He to whom God had committed the government of the people in the absence of Moses, was found sanctioning their rebellion. 'The Lord was very angry with Aaron to have destroyed him.' But in answer to the earnest intercession of Moses, his life was spared; and in penitence and humiliation for his great sin, he was restored to the favor of God."—*"Patriarchs and Prophets,"* p. 323.

"The Lord had conferred upon the family of Aaron the office of the priesthood, and had honored him with the sacred consecration of high priest. He had sustained him in the holy office by the terrible manifestations of divine judgment in the destruction of Korah and his company. It was through Aaron's intercession that the plague was stayed."—*Id.,* pp. 425, 426.

2. Of what did the priest's office consist? Num. 18:1, 5, 7; Ex. 27:21; 30:7-10; Lev. 24:3, 4.

The entire responsibility for the sanctuary and its ministry rested upon the high priest and the associate priests. The priests were to supervise the erecting and the taking down of the sanctuary.

"When the camp setteth forward, Aaron shall come, and his sons, and they shall take down the covering veil, and cover the ark of testimony with it: and shall put thereon the covering of badgers' skins." Num. 4:5, 6.

"When Aaron and his sons have made an end of covering the sanctuary, and all the vessels of the sanctuary, as the camp is to set forward; after that, the sons of Kohath shall come to bear it. . . . And to the office of Eleazar the son of Aaron the priest pertaineth the oil for the light, and the sweet incense, and the daily meat offering, and the anointing oil, and the oversight of all the tabernacle, and of all that therein is, in the sanctuary, and in the vessels thereof." Verses 15, 16.

The priests were to take care of the lights in the golden candlestick. They were to see that the oil was constantly replenished and the lamps carefully trimmed, so that the lights would burn continually.

Each day the priests were to burn incense at the time the lamps were trimmed. There was a constant fire upon the altar. The use of strange fire incurred the penalty of death.

All the offerings were to be in charge of the priests, and a number of these offerings were given to the priest and his family as gifts from the people. (See Num. 18:8-20.) The priest was to represent the Lord, and the gifts given to the priest by the people were given as to the Lord.

"Aaron bore the names of Israel upon his breast. He communicated to the people the will of God. He entered the most holy place on the Day of Atonement, 'not without blood,' as a mediator for all Israel. He came forth from that work to bless the congregation, as Christ will come forth to bless His waiting people when His work of atonement in their behalf shall be ended. It was the exalted character of that sacred office as representative of our great High Priest, that made Aaron's sin at Kadesh of so great magnitude."—*"Patriarchs and Prophets,"* p. 426.

3. Could any besides the priests conduct priestly work? Num. 3:
10-38.

None but Aaron and his sons were permitted to conduct the work of the sanctuary. For any other person to attempt to do this' work meant death to him.

"The priesthood, however, was restricted to the family of Aaron. Aaron and
his sons alone were permitted to minister before the Lord; the rest of the tribe
were entrusted with the charge of the tabernacle and its furniture, and 'they were
to attend upon the priests in their ministration, but they were not to sacrifice, to
burn incense, or to see the holy things till they were covered."—Id., p. 350.

4. Were there others besides Aaron's family who desired the priesthood, or who attempted to usurp its authority? With what results?
Num. 16:8-10, 23-25, 39, 40; 2 Chron. 26:16-21.

The rebellion of Korah, Dathan, and Abiram against Moses and Aaron was
in reality an attempt to overthrow the government and authority of God. While
the rebels claimed they were desirous only to improve upon the organization
inaugurated by Moses and Aaron, they were attempting to destroy the system of
God's plan, and to substitute another priesthood.

"Moses said unto Korah, Hear, I pray you, ye sons of Levi: Seemeth it but
a small thing unto you, that the God of Israel hath separated you from the congregation of Israel, to bring you near to Himself to do the service of the tabernacle of the Lord, and to stand before the congregation to minister unto them?
And He hath brought thee near to Him, and all thy brethren the sons of Levi with
thee: and seek ye the priesthood also? For which cause both thou and all thy
company are gathered together against the Lord: and what is Aaron, that ye
murmur against him?" Num. 16:8-11.

"Korah, the leading spirit in this movement, was a Levite, of the family of
Kohath, and a cousin of Moses; he was a man of ability and influence. . . . He
had become dissatisfied with his position, and aspired to the dignity of the priesthood. The bestowal upon Aaron and his house of the priestly office . . . had given
rise to jealousy and dissatisfaction, and for some time Korah had been secretly
opposing the authority of Moses and Aaron, though he had not ventured upon
any open act of rebellion. He finally conceived the bold design of overthrowing
both the civil and the religious authority."—Id., p. 395.

Moses was not desirous of being the leader of the Israelites, neither was
Aaron insisting on having the priesthood; this arrangement of leadership was
ordered by the Lord. To give public demonstration that these men were the choice
of God—that Aaron had received the priesthood by divine authority—the Lord
introduced a remarkable test, as will be seen by the following experience:

"Moses said, Hereby ye shall know that the Lord hath sent me to do all these
works; for I have not done them of mine own mind. If these men die the common
death of all men, or if they be visited after the visitation of all men; then the Lord
hath not sent me. But if the Lord make a new thing, and the earth open her
mouth, and swallow them up, with all that appertain unto them, and they go down
quick into the pit; then ye shall understand that these men have provoked the
Lord.

"And it came to pass, as he had made an end of speaking all these words, that
the ground clave asunder that was under them: and the earth opened her mouth,
and swallowed them up, and their houses, and all the men that appertained unto
Korah, and all their goods. They, and all that appertained to them, went down
alive into the pit, and the earth closed upon them: and they perished from among
the congregation." Num. 16:28-33.

To give added proof of the choice of Aaron and his male successors to the
priesthood, the following command was given to Moses:

"Speak unto Eleazar the son of Aaron the priest, that he take up the censers
out of the burning, and scatter thou the fire yonder; for they are hallowed. The

censers of these sinners against their own souls, let them make them broad plates for a covering of the altar: for they offered them before the Lord, therefore they are hallowed: and they shall be a sign unto the children of Israel.

"And Eleazar the priest took the brazen censers, wherewith they that were burnt had offered; and they were made broad plates for a covering of the altar: to be a memorial unto the children of Israel, that no stranger, which is not of the seed of Aaron, come near to offer incense before the Lord; that he be not as Korah, and as his company: as the Lord said to him by the hand of Moses." Num. 16:37-40.

Yet another miracle was performed as further evidence that Aaron and his posterity were chosen for the priesthood. It is written:

"Speak unto the children of Israel, and take of every one of them a rod according to the house of their fathers, . . . twelve rods: write thou every man's name upon his rod. And thou shalt write Aaron's name upon the rod of Levi: for one rod shall be for the head of the house of their fathers. And thou shalt lay them up in the tabernacle of the congregation before the testimony, where I will meet with you. And it shall come to pass, that the man's rod, whom I shall choose, shall blossom: and I will make to cease from Me the murmurings of the children of Israel, whereby they murmur against you." Num. 17:2-5.

"And it came to pass, that on the morrow Moses went into the tabernacle of witness; and, behold, the rod of Aaron for the house of Levi was budded, and brought forth buds, and bloomed blossoms, and yielded almonds." Verse 8.

"And the Lord said unto Moses, Bring Aaron's rod again before the testimony, to be kept for a token against the rebels; and thou shalt quite take away their murmurings from Me, that they die not." Verse 10.

In spite of the record of these outstanding experiences through which the people passed to assure them and their descendants that the priesthood belonged to none save Aaron and his posterity, Uzziah, king of Judah, "transgressed against the Lord his God, and went into the temple of the Lord to burn incense upon the altar of incense." 2 Chron. 26:16.

Azariah the high priest and fourscore other priests followed the king into the temple of God, and appealed to the king to refrain from such a sinful act, for they said to him: "It appertaineth not unto thee, Uzziah, to burn incense unto the Lord, but to the priests the sons of Aaron, that are consecrated to burn incense: go out of the sanctuary; for thou hast trespassed; neither shall it be for thine honor from the Lord God." Verse 18.

Uzziah grew angry at the priests, and had the censer in his hand to offer the incense. But while his wrath was hot against the priests, "the leprosy even rose up in his forehead before the priests in the house of the Lord, from beside the incense altar. . . . And they thrust him out from thence; yea, himself hasted also to go out, because the Lord had smitten him." Verses 19, 20.

To the day of his death, Uzziah never recovered from his leprosy. He carried the marks of his disobedience all the rest of his days. How important it is to follow strictly the commands of the Lord!

"Neither his [Uzziah's] exalted position nor his long life of service could be pleaded as an excuse for the presumptuous sin by which he marred the closing years of his reign, and brought upon himself the judgment of Heaven."—"Prophets and Kings," p. 304.

5. How soon after the dedication of the sanctuary, and the consecration of the priests, did the ministry in the tabernacle begin? Lev. 9:1.

"After the dedication of the tabernacle, the priests were consecrated to their sacred office. These services occupied seven days, each marked by special ceremonies. On the eighth day they entered upon their ministration. Assisted by his sons, Aaron offered the sacrifices that God required, and he lifted up his hands and blessed the people. All had been done as God commanded, and He accepted the sacrifice, and revealed His glory in a remarkable manner; fire came from the

Lord, and consumed the offering upon the altar. The people looked upon this wonderful manifestation of divine power, with awe and intense interest. They saw in it a token of God's glory and favor, and they raised a universal shout of praise and adoration, and fell on their faces as if ,in the immediate presence of Jehovah."—*"Patriarchs and Prophets,"* p. 359.

The priests could not enter upon their labors until they had been anointed and consecrated. This manifestation of the glory of the Lord was Heaven's approval that the consecration service and the anointing of the priests were according to the will of God. The priests immediately entered upon their sacred duties.

6. What regular sacrifices were to be offered? Ex. 29:38-42; Num. 28:3-10.

The ministry of the sanctuary was ordained by the Lord. These ministrations were wholly of a sacred nature. The Lord recognized that it was necessary for the priests to carry forward on the Sabbath day, even as on other days, the ministry for salvation from sin. The priests were to perform double service on God's holy rest day.

When the Pharisees accused the disciples of violating the Sabbath at the time they plucked the ears of corn on that day, the Messiah vindicated their course by saying: "Have ye not read in the law, how that on the Sabbath days the priests in the temple profane the Sabbath, and are blameless?" Matt. 12:5.

We should differentiate between man working for himself and for his own interests on the Sabbath, and laboring in the service of God. Man is admonished to refrain from his own labors on God's holy Sabbath, but he is commanded to do the Lord's work in the Lord's way on this sacred day. Isa. 58:13.

"Now that the disciples are attacked, He [Jesus] cites His accusers to examples from the Old Testament, acts performed on the Sabbath by those who were in the service of God. . . .

"The priests in the temple performed greater labor on the Sabbath than upon other days. The same labor in secular business would be sinful; but the work of the priests was in the service of God. They were performing those rites that pointed to the redeeming power of Christ, and their labor was in harmony with the object of the Sabbath. But now Christ Himself had come. The disciples, in doing the work of Christ, were engaged in God's service, and that which was necessary for the accomplishment of this work, it was right to do on the Sabbath day.

"Christ would teach His disciples and His enemies that the service of God is first of all. The object of God's work in this world is the redemption of man; therefore that which is necessary to be done on the Sabbath in the accomplishment of this work, is in accord with the Sabbath law. Jesus then crowned His argument by declaring Himself the 'Lord of the Sabbath,'—One above all question and above all law. This infinite Judge acquits the disciples of blame, appealing to the very statutes they are accused of violating.

"Jesus did not let the matter pass with administering a rebuke to His enemies. He declared that in their blindness they had mistaken the object of the Sabbath. He said, 'If ye had known what this meaneth, I will have mercy, and not sacrifice, ye would not have condemned the guiltless.' Their many heartless rites could not supply the lack of that truthful integrity and tender love which will ever characterize the true worshiper of God.

"Again Christ reiterated the truth that the sacrifices were in themselves of no value. They were a means, and not an end. Their object was to direct men to the Saviour, and thus to bring them into harmony with God. It is the service of love that God values. When this is lacking, the mere round of ceremony is an offense to Him. So with the Sabbath. It was designed to bring men into communion with God; but when the mind was absorbed with wearisome rites, the object of the Sabbath was thwarted. Its mere outward observance was a mockery."—*The Desire of Ages,"* pp. 284-286.

7. What name was given to these daily offerings? Ex. 29:42; Num. 28:6.

The Hebrew word in Exodus 29:42 for "continual" is תָּמִיד (tamid). This same Hebrew word is translated variously in the Old Testament. In Exodus 27:20, tamid is translated "always." In Exodus 29:38 the same word is translated "continually." In Numbers 9:16, tamid is rendered "alway." In Psalms 25:15, this word tamid is translated "ever." The thought expressed by the word tamid is that the service must be conducted right along, all the time. It was a continual service. The word tamid has nothing in common with such words as יוֹם לְיוֹם (yom le yom), "day unto day," as found in Psalms 19:2.

8. Were these daily offerings the only sacrifices demanded by the Lord? Leviticus, chapters 1 to 9, 16, 17, 23, and 24; Num. 19:1-10; and chapters 28 and 29.

In addition to the daily offerings, the Lord required many other sacrifices to be devoted and consecrated to His service. There were the monthly offerings; these offerings were given at the beginning of each month. In the annual services. they had the sacrifice slain at the time of the Passover, at the Feast of Pentecost, and at the Feast of Tabernacles. Each day during the eight days of this last festival a number of sacrifices were to be offered.

On the first day of the seventh month, offerings were to be sacrificed to the Lord, besides the special sacrifices on the Day of Atonement. (See Num. 28:11-15, 16-25, 26-31; 29:1-6, 7-11, 12-38; Lev. 23:4-8, 9-22, 23-25, 26-32, 33-37, 39-42.) In addition to these already mentioned, there were special offerings for the poor and needy; the Levites also had to be remembered. Says the Scripture:

"These are the feasts of the Lord, which ye shall proclaim to be holy convocations, to offer an offering made by fire unto the Lord, a burnt offering, and a meat offering, a sacrifice, and drink offerings, everything upon his day: beside the Sabbaths of the Lord, and beside your gifts, and beside all your vows, and beside all your freewill offerings, which ye give unto the Lord." Lev. 23:37, 38.

The Lord did not command Israel to erect county homes or poor farms for those who should become impoverished by their liberality. The following comment by the Spirit of prophecy is interesting:

"The contributions required of the Hebrews for religious and charitable purposes amounted to fully one fourth of their income. So heavy a tax upon the resources of the people might be expected to reduce them to poverty; but, on the contrary, the faithful observance of these regulations was one of the conditions of their prosperity. On condition of their obedience, God made them this promise: 'I will rebuke the devourer for your sakes, and he shall not destroy the fruits of your ground; neither shall your vine cast her fruit before the time in the field. . . . And all nations shall call you blessed; for ye shall be a delightsome land, saith the Lord of hosts.'"—"Patriarchs and Prophets," p. 527.

9. Into how many general classes were the offerings divided? Leviticus, chapters 1-5.

There were five general classes into which the offerings were divided: The trespass offering (Leviticus 5), the sin offering (chapter 4), the burnt offering (chapter 1), the peace offerings (chapter 3), and the meat offering (chapter 2).

The meat offering was not the sacrificing of an animal. The word "meat" in the Old Testament does not always imply or mean "flesh." The first time we encounter the word "meat" is in Genesis 1:29. The Lord was giving to Adam and Eve their bill of fare. The first parents were commanded to eat of the products which grew above the ground. These were to be their "meat." The word rendered "meat" in Genesis 1:29 is אָכְלָה (oklah), meaning "food" or "diet."

LESSON X

The Ministry in the Sanctuary

The Daily Offerings

1. INTO how many classes was the camp of Israel divided? Lev. 4:3, 13, 22, 27.

With God there is no respect of persons. Acts 10:34. The Lord shows no partiality. He loves all peoples. To carry forward His work in the earth, He has it systematized. The Lord conducts His work in an organized manner. The apostle says that all things should "be done decently and in order." 1 Cor. 14:40.

The camp of Israel was classified into four divisions. There was the priest, who was the leader of the people. Then came the ruler, who was associated with the leader to assist in carrying forward the organization. Moses was advised by his father-in-law to associate with him a body of men to aid him in conducting the work in the wilderness. So we read of this class of associates:

"Moreover thou shalt provide out of all the people able men, such as fear God, men of truth, hating covetousness; and place such over them, to be rulers of thousands, and rulers of hundreds, rulers of fifties, and rulers of tens." Ex. 18:21. God approved of this plan of organization, as may be seen by reading verse 25 of this chapter in Exodus.

The priests and the rulers were the responsible men, upon whom rested heavy obligations. When men of this type departed from the ways of the Lord, they were summarily dealt with. (See Lev. 10:1, 2; Num. 16:1-3, 28-33.) God expects that the leaders of His work shall be men of piety—devout, God-fearing men. God carries forward His work in an organized and harmonious way.

Of course there was the large class of laymen to be considered, and offerings were made for the whole congregation.

2. If an individual in any of these classes committed a sin, what was he commanded to do? Lev. 4:2, 3, 13, 14, 22, 23, 27, 28.

3. What was the nature of the offering the sinner must bring? Lev. 4:3, 23, 28.

The kind of offering the sinner brought for his sin depended upon the individual who committed the wrong, and the nature of the wrong done. However, every offering brought for sacrifice by any class of persons must be without spot and without blemish. Whether the wrongdoer was poor or wealthy, his offering must be without spot and without blemish.

"God expressly directed that every offering presented for the service of the sanctuary should be 'without blemish.' The priests were to examine all animals brought as a sacrifice, and were to reject every one in which a defect was discovered. Only an offering 'without blemish' could be a symbol of His perfect purity who was to offer Himself as 'a lamb without blemish and without spot.'

"The apostle Paul points to these sacrifices as an illustration of what the followers of Christ are to become. He says: 'I beseech you therefore, brethren, by the mercies of God, that ye present your bodies a living sacrifice, holy, acceptable unto God, which is your reasonable service.' We are to give ourselves to the service of God, and we should seek to make the offering as nearly perfect as possible. God will not be pleased with anything less than the best we can offer. Those who love Him with all the heart, will desire to give Him the best service of the life, and they will be constantly seeking to bring every power of their being into harmony with the laws that will promote their ability to do His will."—*"Patriarchs and Prophets,"* pp. 352, 353.

4. Where was this offering to be presented? Lev. 4:4, 14.

The offering must be brought by the sinner to the door of the tabernacle of the congregation. Of the daily offering which was offered for the congregation by the priest, it is written:

"This shall be a continual burnt offering throughout your generations at the door of the tabernacle of the congregation before the Lord: where I will meet you, to speak there unto thee. And there I will meet with the children of Israel, and the tabernacle shall be sanctified by My glory, and I will sanctify the tabernacle of the congregation, and the altar: I will sanctify also both Aaron and his sons, to minister to Me in the priest's office." Ex. 29:42-44.

The ministry of the priest in the sanctuary was in the first apartment throughout the entire year, with the exception of one day. These daily services conducted by the high priest and his associates were in the holy, and not in the most holy place. The Lord declared He would sanctify the tabernacle with His glory; He would also sanctify the priests and their work in the tabernacle of the congregation.

5. After the offering was presented at the door of the tabernacle, what was the guilty person to do? Lev. 4:4, 15, 24, 29.

"The most important part of the daily ministration was the service performed in behalf of individuals. The repentant sinner brought his offering to the door of the tabernacle, and placing his hand upon the victim's head, confessed his sins, thus in figure transferring them from himself to the innocent sacrifice. By his own hand the animal was then slain."—*"Patriarchs and Prophets,"* p. 354.

When the sinner brought his offering to the door of the sanctuary and confessed his sin upon the head of the spotless offering, he was conscious of having accomplished two things in connection with the remission of his guilt:

First, he recognized that this blameless offering was his substitute. Therefore, the principle of substitution was known and accepted among the Israelites. Centuries prior to this time, the Lord had illustrated the principle of substitution. When Abraham was journeying with his son to offer the lad as a sacrifice to God, Isaac asked his father: "Behold the fire and the wood: but where is the lamb for a burnt offering? And Abraham said, My son, God will provide Himself a lamb for a burnt offering." Gen. 22:7, 8.

When God accepted Abraham's willing spirit, and restrained the patriarch from offering up Isaac, "Abraham lifted up his eyes, and looked, and behold behind him a ram caught in a thicket by his horns: and Abraham went and took the ram, and offered him up for a burnt offering in the stead of his son." Verse 13.

Having accepted this substitute, the sinner confessed his sins upon the head of the offering, and by this act the guilt of the transgressor was transferred to this spotless offering. The blameless animal, in the figure, became responsible for the guilt committed by the sinner. The spotless offering took the place of the transgressor.

Second, when the individual who brought this substitute took its life, he recognized that the just died for the unjust. He understood that the spotless offering became responsible for his evil act, and forfeited its life for the wrong he had done. Provision had been made whereby the sin of this wrongdoer might be expiated by another, so that the penalty for the guilt was paid, and yet the sinner could be pardoned for his sin and be set free.

How that beautiful prophecy of the Messiah written by the prophet Isaiah stands out in bold relief, in the light of what has just been written:

"Surely He hath borne our griefs, and carried our sorrows: yet we did esteem Him stricken, smitten of God, and afflicted. But He was wounded for our transgressions, He was bruised for our iniquities: the chastisement of our peace was upon Him; and with His stripes we are healed.

"All we like sheep have gone astray; we have turned every one to his own way; and the Lord hath laid on Him the iniquity of us all. He was oppressed, and

OVER THE HEAD OF THE INNOCENT LAMB THE PENITENT SINNER CONFESSED HIS SIN

He was afflicted, yet He opened not His mouth: He is brought as a lamb to the slaughter, and as a sheep before her shearers is dumb, so He openeth not His mouth. He was taken from prison and from judgment: and who shall declare His generation? for He was cut off out of the land of the living: for the transgression of my people was He stricken." Isa. 53:4-8.

6. When the offering was slain, what was the priest commanded to do? Lev. 4:5-7, 16, 17, 25, 30.

"The blood was carried by the priest into the holy place and sprinkled before the veil, behind which was the ark containing the law that the sinner had transgressed. By this ceremony the sin was, through the blood, transferred in figure to the sanctuary."—*Patriarchs and Prophets*," p. 354.

In view of the scriptures quoted, answering questions 4 and 5, these two acts—the sinner confessing his sin upon the head of the spotless offering, then with his own hand taking its life—were all that were demanded of the sinner to remedy the wrong he had done. The Lord in His mercy had made such a wonderful and beautiful provision for man's recovery and restoration from the terrible ruin which had overtaken him by sin, that all man had to do to be brought again into God's favor, was to accept a spotless substitute, acknowledge his guilt, confess his wrong, and then take the life of the blameless offering.

To this day the orthodox Jew recognizes and acknowledges the need of a substitutionary atonement by the course he pursues just before the beginning of the Day of Atonement. In the Jewish Prayer Book is found an article entitled, "Method of Atonements."

"It is the custom on the day before the atonement to make כפרה (*kapharoth*), "atonements." A rooster is taken for the male, and a hen for the female, of the family. The head of the family makes the atonement first for himself, as it was the custom of the high priest to make atonement first for himself, then for his family, then for the house of Israel.

"He takes the rooster in his hand and says the following verses: 'The children of men that sit in darkness and in the shadow of death, being bound in affliction and iron; He brought them out of darkness and the shadow of death, and brake their bands in sunder. Fools, because of their transgressions, and because of their iniquities are afflicted. . . . O that men would praise the Lord for His goodness and for His wonderful works to the children of men.'

" 'If there be for him an angel, an intercessor, one among a thousand, to show unto man His uprightness, then He is gracious unto him, and saith, Deliver him from going down into the pit; I have found a ransom.'

"He then moves the atonement around his head, while saying: 'This is my substitute; this is my offering; this is my atonement; this rooster goeth before me to death, and I be made free, and will walk in long life, in happiness, and in peace.' "

However, had not the priest taken the blood of the sinless offering into the holy place of the sanctuary, and sprinkled it, pardon for the wrong done would not have been given. It is the blood that makes atonement for the soul. It was the blood of the spotless offering which was accepted in place of the guilty sinner.

Israel was not permitted to eat blood. The Lord gave detailed commands forbidding them the eating of blood. Here is the record:

"Whatsoever man there be of the house of Israel, or of the strangers that sojourn among you, that eateth any manner of blood; I will even set My face against that soul that eateth blood, and will cut him off from among his people. For the life of the flesh is in the blood: and I have given it to you upon the altar to make an atonement for your souls: for it is the blood that maketh an atonement for the soul. Therefore I said unto the children of Israel, No soul of you shall eat blood, neither shall any stranger that sojourneth among you eat blood.

"And whatsoever man there be of the children of Israel, or of the strangers that sojourn among you, which hunteth and catcheth any beast or fowl that may be eaten; he shall even pour out of the blood thereof, and cover it with dust. For it is the life of all flesh; the blood of it is for the life thereof: therefore I said unto the children of Israel, Ye shall eat the blood of no manner of flesh: for the life of all flesh is the blood thereof: whosoever eateth it shall be cut off." Lev. 17:10-14.

The eating of blood is likewise prohibited in New Testament times, as may be seen from the following action taken at the first "general conference" held at Jerusalem: "That we write unto them, that they abstain from pollutions of idols, . . . and from blood." Acts 15 :20.

Fortunate for the sinner it was, that provision was made for the priest to take of the blood of the slain offering and sprinkle it in the sanctuary. For without the shedding of blood there can be no remission of sin.

But the blood must be taken into the sanctuary by the priest. It must be sprinkled before the veil. The words "before the veil" are in the Hebrew את פני פרכת (eth-pene paroketh), "the face of the veil." For the meaning of the Hebrew word פני (pene), "face," see Lesson 4, question 6. The Hebrew word לפני (liphene), from the Hebrew root pene, translated "before," means "face" or "presence." (See Ex. 33 :14, 15, 20, 23.) The words "presence," "before," "face," in these texts just mentioned, are all translated from the same Hebrew word pene.

The blood was sprinkled on the face of the veil. The veil became in this sense a preserver of records. That is, the blood sprinkled on this veil preserved the record of the sins of those who had confessed, who had brought their offering, and who had been forgiven of their wrongs. The veil was a typical record book, having preserved on the face of it the acknowledgment of guilt. Sin had been confessed and forgiven. "By this ceremony [sprinkling of the blood on the veil] the sin was, through the blood, transferred in figure to the sanctuary."—"Patriarchs and Prophets," p. 354. It should be remembered that the sins transferred to the sanctuary were not the sins of unrepentant sinners; they were the sins of those whose sins had been confessed and pardoned. The guilty person who harmonized with the requirements of God, went home free and accepted, and his sin was, in type, lodged in the sanctuary until the Day of Atonement. His sin was not held against him. He was a free man in the Lord.

7. What command was given to the priest in regard to the blood of the offering when it was not sprinkled on or before the veil? Lev. 6: 24-26, 30.

When the offering brought by the ruler or the common people was slain, the blood was not sprinkled on the veil in the holy place. The blood was caught in a basin, and the priest, with his finger, put some of the blood upon the horns of the altar of burnt offering. The rest of the blood was poured out at the foot of the altar. The flesh of the offering must be eaten by the priest in the holy place. In this way the confessed and forgiven sin of the wrongdoer was brought into the holy place of the sanctuary.

"In some cases the blood was not taken into the holy place; but the flesh was then to be eaten by the priest, as Moses directed the sons of Aaron, saying, 'God hath given it you to bear the iniquity of the congregation.' Lev. 10 :17. Both ceremonies alike symbolized the transfer of the sin from the penitent to the sanctuary.

"Such was the work that went on day by day throughout the year. The sins of Israel being thus transferred to the sanctuary, the holy places were defiled, and a special work became necessary for the removal of the sins."—"Patriarchs and Prophets," pp. 354, 355.

And Moses at the command of God emphasized the importance of this latter method of carrying the pardoned sin into the sanctuary, as will be seen by the following instruction:

"No sin offering, whereof any of the blood is brought into the tabernacle of the congregation to reconcile withal in the holy place, shall be eaten." Lev. 6:30.

"Moses diligently sought the goat of the sin offering, and, behold, it was burnt : and he was angry with Eleazar and Ithamar, the sons of Aaron, . . .

saying, Wherefore have ye not eaten the sin offering in the holy place, seeing it is most holy, and God hath given it you to bear the iniquity of the congregation, to make atonement for them before the Lord? Behold, the blood of it was not brought in within the holy place: ye should indeed have eaten it in the holy place, as I commanded." Lev. 10:16-18.

The reason for this twofold instruction is plain.· It was important that the blood be taken into the holy place, but to take the blood of one offering in twice would mar the typical service.

8. What blessing came to the sinner through this service? Lev. 4: 35, last clause.

When the priest had completed the service of sprinkling the blood upon the veil, or of eating the flesh of the offering in the holy place, the sin of the sinner who had brought the sacrifice was atoned for; for it is written: "The priest shall make an atonement for his sin that he hath committed, and it shall be forgiven him." Lev. 4:35, last clause.

9. What was this work of the priest called? Lev. 4:20, 26, 31; Num. 15:28.

The priest had made an atonement for the penitent man. The sinner had confessed his sin, and turned from it. He was reconciled to his God. His sin was forgiven. The man was in figure cleansed. He had the assurance that he was accepted by the Lord. He was no more under condemnation for the wrong he had committed. This atonement, however, did not imply that it would be impossible for the man, after this transaction had been completed, to repeat the wrong or become guilty of another sin. If the man again sinned, it was necessary for him to come again to the sanctuary with his sacrifice for repeated forgiveness. The provision for pardon by this method of bringing an offering to the sanctuary was ample and full; but the sinner was not, by this one act of atonement for his sin, ensured against further wrongdoing while he lived. He might fall again, and he must make repeated sacrifice for his sin.

The time must come, however, when the atonement for wrong would be completed, finished, when the wrongs of men would be blotted out, when there would be no further remembrance of sin preserved. Provision was made in the sanctuary service for just such an experience, as will be noted in later lessons.

10. What did the apostle Paul call this service of the priest for the people? Heb. 9:6.

The offering of these sacrifices for the sins of the people, with the ministry associated therewith, was called "the service of God." This form of service was the method of worship for that people, which God Himself introduced, and which continued for many centuries. It was to that people the gospel. The apostle Paul says of the Israelites: "Unto us was the gospel preached, as well as unto them." Heb. 4:2.

And the gospel which they enjoyed was the gospel of Christ; for it is written: "Moreover, brethren, I would not that ye should be ignorant, how that all our fathers were under the cloud, and all passed through the sea; and were all baptized unto Moses in the cloud and in the sea; and did all eat the same spiritual meat; and did all drink the same spiritual drink: for they drank of that spiritual Rock that followed them: and that Rock was Christ." 1 Cor. 10:1-4.

It was the privilege of that people, too, to enjoy the presence of the Holy Spirit; for it is written:

"I will mention the loving-kindness of the Lord, and the praises of the Lord, according to all that the Lord hath bestowed on us, and the great goodness toward the house of Israel, which He hath bestowed on them according to His mercies, and according to the multitude of His loving-kindnesses. For He said, Surely they are My people, children that will not lie: so He was their Saviour. In all their affliction He was afflicted, and the angel of His presence saved them: in His love and in His pity He redeemed them; and He bare them, and carried them all the days of old. But they rebelled, and vexed His Holy Spirit: . . . then He remembered the days of old, Moses, and His people, saying, Where is He that brought them up out of the sea with the shepherd of His flock? where is He that put His Holy Spirit within him?" Isa. 63:7-11.

The word "Saviour," in verse 8 of the foregoing quotation, is מוֹשִׁיעַ (moshia). The Greek word "Jesus" is translated from "Joshua," which comes from the same Hebrew root, יָשַׁע (Yasha), "Saviour."

11. How often does the apostle say this ministry for the people was conducted? Heb. 9:6.

12. Where does the apostle say this service of God took place? Heb. 9:6.

The service conducted in the first apartment of the tabernacle, in the holy place, is expressed by the apostle as continuing "always." That is to say, this ministry was performed all the time, every day. As we already have observed, the Sabbath also was occupied by the priests in this form of worship.

The reader will note that the sacrifices and offerings to be brought on the various holidays, new moons, and feast and fast days, must include the daily offering. This offering must never be forgotten. (See Num. 28:1-4, 9, 11-15, 17-23, etc.)

13. Does the apostle mention a further service in connection with this "service of God"? Heb. 9:7.

In connection with the offerings on special occasions, which included the daily offering, there were also to be offered peace offerings and meat offerings. The services in the first apartment of the sanctuary were indeed a constant ministry.

14. How often was the high priest to enter the second apartment? Heb. 9:7.

However, the yearly round of ministry of the sanctuary was not completed by the offerings in the holy place day by day. There was another service provided which was to be conducted in the second apartment, in the most holy place; but this latter service, says the apostle, was performed "once every year." A special work was to take place at this once-every-year ministry.

According to Scriptural reckoning of time, there were 360 days in the Bible year. This will be recognized by reading Genesis 7:11; 8:4, and comparing the two foregoing scriptures with Genesis 7:24; 8:3. The flood began on the seventeenth day of the second month in the six hundredth year of Noah's life, and the waters reached their height on the seventeenth day of the seventh month of the same year. From the time the waters began to descend from heaven until they reached their highest level, a period of five months intervened. The Scripture also declares that the waters of the deluge reached their height at the end of one hundred and fifty days. This makes the five months equal to one hundred and fifty days. Therefore at the time of the deluge, a millennium and a half from creation, thirty days equaled a Bible month.

In Revelation 12 it is recorded that the woman (the church) fled into the wilderness, where she was protected for a time, and times, and half a time, from the face of the serpent. The serpent (verse 9) is the devil. Satan persecuted the church for a time, times, and half a time. Daniel 4 declares that unless King Nebuchadnezzar would change his habits of life, he would lose his reason, and his kingdom would be taken from him for seven times. By comparing Daniel 4:16 with Daniel 11:13, margin, we learn that a time in prophecy represents a year. Since the church fled into the wilderness for three and a half prophetic times, she sought protection from her persecutors for three and a half prophetic years.

According to Exodus 12:1, 2; 16:1; 19:1; Jeremiah 39:2; 28:1; Haggai 1:1; Leviticus 23:26, 27; 1 Kings 12:32; Zechariah 7:1; Ezekiel 24:1; Deuteronomy 1:3; and Esther 9:1, compared with Numbers 28:14; 1 Kings 4:7; and 1 Chronicles 27:1-15, the Bible teaches that there are twelve months in the year.

In Revelation 13:5 it is said that the power used by Satan to persecute the woman (the church) had control over the church for forty and two months. There being twelve months to the Bible year, forty and two months equal three and a half years. This latter period harmonizes with the three and a half times (years) the church was in the wilderness.

In Revelation 12:6 the Scripture states that the woman (church) fled into the wilderness for twelve hundred and sixty days. By dividing the 1260 days by the forty and two months, we have thirty days to the month. So from the book of Genesis to the book of Revelation, the Bible reckons the period of thirty days to the month. Since there are twelve months to the year, the Scripture days of a year, therefore, are three hundred and sixty. The Jewish people have so arranged their calendar that the twelfth month (see Esther 9:1) is periodically repeated. This repetition of אדר (*Adar*), the twelfth month, is called ואדר (*We-Adar*), *Adar* over again. By this calendar arrangement the solar and lunar months are harmonized.

15. How often were the priests commanded to offer the incense in the holy place of the sanctuary? Ex. 30:7-9; Luke 1:8, 9.

The ministry of the priests in the first apartment of the sanctuary was conducted uninterruptedly for three hundred and fifty-nine days each year.

16. What would happen to a person who offered incense with fire not commanded by the Lord? Ex. 30:9; Lev. 10:1, 2.

Nadab and Abihu immediately lost their lives for their disobedience, when they used strange fire to offer incense before the Lord instead of using the fire which God had provided.

"At the hour of worship, as the prayers and praise of the people were ascending to God, two of the sons of Aaron took each his censer, and burned fragrant incense thereon, to rise as a sweet odor before the Lord. But they transgressed His command by the use of 'strange fire.' For burning the incense they took common instead of the sacred fire which God Himself had kindled, and which He had commanded to be used for this purpose. . . .

"Next to Moses and Aaron, Nadab and Abihu had stood highest in Israel. They had been especially honored by the Lord. . . . But their transgression was not therefore to be excused or lightly regarded. All this rendered their sin more grievous. . . .

"God designed to teach the people that they must approach Him with reverence and awe, and in His own appointed manner. He cannot accept partial obedience. It was not enough that in this solemn season of worship *nearly* everything was done as He had directed. God has pronounced a curse upon those who depart from His commandments, and put no difference between common and holy things. . . . Let no one deceive himself with the belief that a part of God's commandments are nonessential, or that He will accept a substitute for that which He has required."—*"Patriarchs and Prophets,"* pp. 359, 360.

The Ministry in the Sanctuary by the Priests

The Day of Atonement

1. IN addition to the regular offerings of the sanctuary, what special service was commanded of the Lord? Ex. 30:10; Lev. 16:34; Heb. 9:7, 25.

Provision was made for the sins of the people during the year. That forgiveness of wrong was ample, and that pardon was freely and fully granted. But the Lord arranged that "once every year" a special and important service should be conducted which completed the annual round of services in the sanctuary. This particular service included the offering of sacrifices, the purification or cleansing of the sanctuary itself, with the vessels used during the ministry by the priests.

"The sins of Israel being thus transferred to the sanctuary, the holy places were defiled, and a special work became necessary for the removal of the sins. God commanded that an atonement be made for each of the sacred apartments, as for the altar, to 'cleanse it, and hallow it from the uncleanness of the children of Israel.'

"Once a year, on the great Day of Atonement, the priest entered the most holy place, for the cleansing of the sanctuary. The work there performed, completed the yearly round of ministration."—*Patriarchs and Prophets,* p. 355.

2. At what time during the year was this special service to be performed? Lev. 16:29, 30.

THE HIGH PRIEST WITH HIS CENSER

It should be observed that the ministry performed upon this day was a thorough and extensive work. That the people must be cleansed from all their sins was the command of the Lord.

To prepare the camp of Israel for this significant and important event, ten days prior to this special occasion a solemn service was conducted, when the trumpet was blown and a warning sounded. This preceding service, observed on the first day of the seventh month, was a holy convocation. It was to be regarded as a sabbath. The people were prohibited from performing secular labor on this first day of the seventh month. An offering must be presented to the Lord. Lev. 23:23-25.

Till the present day the orthodox Jew in all parts of the world calls the ten days prior to the Day of Atonement, from the first day of the seventh month to the tenth day of this same month, "the ten days of repentance." These are preparatory days to the solemn Day of Atonement.

During many centuries of the Christian Era, the Jewish people have had this day, called in the Bible "The Blowing of Trumpets," grossly perverted. The day is not now called by this name; it is called ראש השנה (*Rosh Hashanah*), the Jewish New Year. To justify their course in calling this period *Rosh Hashanah*, New Year, there is a treatise in the *Mishna*, one of the Jewish commentaries, entitled *Rosh Hashanah*, in which the Talmudists say:

"There are four periods of commencement of years, viz, on the first of Nisan. Esther 3:7. This is the New Year to compute the kings and the festivals. The first of Elul, the sixth Jewish month (Neh. 6:15), is a New Year for the tithe of cattle. . . . The first of Tishri, the seventh Jewish month, is a New Year for the ordinary civil year, for the computation of the seventh years, and of the jubilees. Leviticus 25:1-6, also for the planting of the trees and herbs."—*Treatise VII, chap. I.*

The Talmud teaches that *Rosh Hashanah* is an important period. In the prayers for the New Year's we find the following written:

"On the New Year's day it is written, and on the Day of Atonement it is sealed, who shall pass away from the world, and who shall be created into the world; who shall live, and who shall die; who shall live the length of his days, and who shall have his days shortened."

Instead of the people's observing this one day as a sacred day, the first day of the seventh month, the rabbis have added a day. The pious Jew observes the first two days of the seventh month instead of one day. Both these days must be observed as a sabbath, and the people are not permitted to do any secular labor. Here is the Talmudical law enforcing this added day:

"These are the six days on which the Scripture has forbidden the doing of work. The first and the seventh day of Passover; the first and last day of the Feast of Tabernacles; the day of the Feast of Pentecost; and the first day of the seventh month. All these are called holy days."—*"Hilchoth Youm Tov"* (*Laws of the Holidays*).

"But to us who observe two days, what is unlawful on the first day is also unlawful on the second day; and he who disregards the latter, is to be excommunicated."—*"Orach Chayim"* (*The Ways of Life*).

"Though the second holy day *is of the words of the scribes only*, everything which is considered unlawful on the first, is not permitted on the second. And every one who profanes the second holy day, even though it be the New Year's [this New Year's is the first day of the seventh month, called in the Bible "the Blowing of Trumpets"], whether it be a matter relating to the Sabbath, or to work, or by going beyond the limit of the Sabbath, he is to be excommunicated, or to be beaten with the flogging of rebellion, provided he be not a Talmudist."—*"Hilchoth Youm Tov."*

What the Talmud means in regard to excommunication may be inferred from the following rabbinical laws:

"How is an excommunicated person to conduct himself, and how are others to conduct themselves toward him? It is unlawful for an excommunicated person, as for a mourner, to trim his beard or hair, or to wash himself all the days of his excommunication; neither is he to be associated in pronouncing the benediction; neither is he to be reckoned as one of ten, wherever ten persons are required. [According to rabbinical law, in order to conduct the worship of God in the synagogue, it is necessary to have ten males present who are above the age of thirteen years.] Neither may any one sit within four ells of him."

"But if he die in his excommunication, the tribunal send and lay a stone on his coffin to signify that they stone him, because he is separated from the congregation. And it is unnecessary to say that he is not mourned for, and that his funeral is not to be attended."

"Whosoever remains thirty days in his excommunication without seeking to be absolved, he is to be excommunicated the second time. If he abide thirty days more without seeking absolution, he is then to be anathematized."—*"Hilchoth Talmud Torah"* (*Laws of Teaching the Law*).

After the man has been anathematized, he is to be dealt with in the following manner:

"He is not to teach others nor to be taught; he may learn by himself that he may not forget the learning. He is not to be hired, nor to hire. Men have no dealings with him, nor any business, except a little, that he may get a livelihood."—*"Hilchoth Talmud Torah."*

A few of the laws of the "flogging of rebellion" for not sacredly observing a second holy day when the Scriptures say Israel should keep holy only one day for the "Blowing of Trumpets," follow:

"An Israelite who tells a Gentile to do a certain work for him on the Sabbath, although he has transgressed, and is to be flogged with the flogging of rebellion, yet he may lawfully make use of that work when the Sabbath is over, if he wait as long as it would take to accomplish the work."—*"Hilchoth Shabbath"* (*Laws of the Sabbath*).

"If a Gentile slaughters, even though he does it in the presence of an Israelite, with a proper knife, his slaughtering is carrion; and he that eats it is to be flogged according to the written law, for it is said, 'And one call thee, and thou eat of his sacrifice.' "—*"Hilchoth Shechita"* (*Laws of Slaughtering Animals*).

"If an Israelite does not know the five things which invalidate the act of slaughtering, as we have explained, and slaughters by himself, it is unlawful to eat of his slaughtering, both for himself and others; for this case is much the same as doubtful carrion. He that eats of it the quantity equal to an olive, is to be flogged with the flogging of rebellion."—*Ibid.*

"He is to be beaten until his soul goes out, without any consideration of his strength, and without dividing the flogging into three. And in like manner, whoever transgresses the words of the wise men, he is to be beaten without number, and without consideration. Why is this called, 'The flogging of rebellion'? Because he has rebelled against the words of the law, and against the words of the scribes."—*"Baal Aruch."*

To this day in Palestine the Jews who do not follow the teachings of the Talmud strictly, observe only one day instead of two days as holy time.

3. What name was given to this tenth day of the seventh month? Lev. 23:26, 27.

This special day is called in Scripture the "Day of Atonement." The Jewish people the world around also call it יום כפור (*Yom Kippur*), which means "Day of Atonement." Upon this day all wrongs are righted among that people. It is considered by the children of Abraham as the most sacred and solemn day of the year. The Jewish Encyclopedia, Volume II, page 288, published by Funk and Wagnalls Company, New York, makes the following comment in regard to this day:

"The serious character impressed upon the day from the time of its institution has been preserved to the present day. No matter how much else has fallen into desuetude, so strong is its hold upon the Jewish conscience that no Jew, unless he have cut himself entirely loose from the synagogue, will fail to observe the Day of Atonement by resting from his daily pursuits and attending service in the synagogue. With a few exceptions, the service even of the Reformed synagogue is continuous through the day."

4. How was the service conducted on this particular day? Lev. 16:5.

The services on the Day of Atonement centered in the most holy place of the sanctuary. From the people were to be received two' kids of the goats for a sin offering, and a ram for a burnt offering. The reason why the goats were taken from the congregation on this day was because the entire people of God were especially interested in the ministry of this important day.

The atonement on this day included "all the people of the congregation," "whether it be one of your own country, or a stranger that sojourneth among you." Lev. 16:33, 29.

5. What was the high priest to do with these goats? Lev. 16:7, 8.

When the congregation gave to the high priest these two goats, he brought them to the door of the tabernacle of the congregation. The priest then cast lots upon these animals, one lot for the Lord, the other lot for the scapegoat. The Hebrew expression for the casting of the two lots is as follows:

"One lot to Jehovah," גורל אחד ליהוה (*goral echad la-Yehovah*), "and one lot to Azazel," וגורל אחד לעזאזל (*we-goral echad la-Azazel*). The word "Azazel" is a proper noun, intended to represent Satan. While the text has rendered the Hebrew word "Azazel," "scapegoat," from time immemorial the Hebrew people have regarded the word "Azazel" as synonymous with the evil spirit, Satan. (See Lev. 16:8, margin.)

6. Following the casting of the lot, what was to be done with the animals? Lev. 16:9, 10.

Following the casting of the lot, when the decision was reached as to which of the goats was for the Lord and which for Azazel, the Lord's lot was to be offered for a sin offering. The other lot, the goat dedicated to Azazel, the scapegoat, must be presented alive before the Lord, and eventually this goat was sent away into the wilderness alive; it was not killed on this same day.

On the word "Azazel" the Jewish Encyclopedia makes the following remarks:

"*Azazel.*—The name of a supernatural being mentioned in connection with the ritual of the Day of Atonement. After Satan, for whom he was in some degree a preparation, Azazel enjoys the distinction of being the most extrahuman character in sacred literature. . . .

"Far from involving the recognition of Azazel as a deity, the sending of the goat was . . . a symbolic expression of the idea that the people's sins and their evil consequences were to be sent back to the spirit of desolation and ruin, the source of all impurity.

"The very fact that the two goats were presented before Jehovah before the one was sacrificed and the other sent into the wilderness, was proof that Azazel was not ranked with Jehovah, but regarded simply as the personification of wickedness in contrast with the righteous government of Jehovah. . . .

"Nay, more; as a demon of the desert, it seems to have been closely interwoven with the mountainous region of Jerusalem. . . .

"This is confirmed by the Book of Enoch, which brings Azazel into connection with the Biblical story of the fall of the angels. . . . Azazel is represented in the Book of Enoch as the leader of the rebellious giants in the time preceding the flood; he taught men the art of warfare, of making swords, knives, . . . and also revealed to the people the secrets of witchcraft and corrupted their manners, leading them into wickedness and impurity; until at last he was, at the Lord's command, bound hand and foot by the archangel Raphael* and chained to the

---

* There is only one archangel, or chief angel, and His name is not Raphael, but Michael. In Jude 9 we read that He contended with the devil over the body of Moses. In 1 Thessalonians 4:16 we are told that it is "the Lord Himself" who has the voice of the Archangel, and in Daniel 10:23 the angel Gabriel mentions "Michael your Prince." Michael it was who in the beginning fought with Satan and his angels. Rev. 12:7. Christ Himself will come as King of kings and Lord of lords. Rev. 19:16. Michael is Christ.

rough and jagged rocks, . . . where he is to abide in utter darkness until the great day of judgment, when he will be cast into the fire to be consumed forever."—Vol. II, pp. 365, 366.

The consensus of opinion among Hebrew writers and scholars from time immemorial is that Azazel represents the evil one, Satan.

7. What was the priest to do with the Lord's goat? Lev. 16:15, 16.

The priest was commanded to take the Lord's goat, and kill it for a sin offering for the people. The blood of this sin offering must be taken into the

THE SACRED ARK CONTAINING THE LAW OF GOD

most holy place of the sanctuary. The Scripture says that the blood of this offering must be brought "within the veil." Verse 15. In connection with taking the blood of the sin offering within the veil, the priest must "do with that blood as he did with the blood of the bullock." Verse 15.

What the priest did with the blood of the bullock which he offered for himself and his family, was to "sprinkle it with his finger upon the mercy seat eastward; and before the mercy seat shall he sprinkle of the blood with his finger seven times." Verse 14.

"On the Day of Atonement the high priest, having taken an offering for the congregation, went into the most holy place with the blood, and sprinkled it upon the mercy seat, above the tables of the law. Thus the claims of the law, which demanded the life of the sinner, were satisfied."—*"Patriarchs and Prophets,"* p. 356.

The apostle Paul emphasizes the taking of the blood into the most holy place on the Day of Atonement: "Into the second went the high priest alone once every year, not without blood, which he offered for himself, and for the errors of the people." Heb. 9:7. "Nor yet that he should offer Himself often, as the high priest entereth into the holy place every year with the blood of others." Verse 25.

8. Was the priest permitted to sprinkle the blood of an offering within the veil at any other time? Lev. 16:2.

Even though the high priest was commanded to enter into the most holy place "once every year," "not without blood," should he have attempted to enter into this most sacred shrine at any other time of the year, he would have met instant death. For the Scripture states:

"The Lord said unto Moses, Speak unto Aaron thy brother, that he come not at all times into the holy place within the veil before the mercy seat, which is upon the ark; that he die not." Lev. 16:2.

The utmost sacredness was associated with all the parts of the service of the sanctuary, but a special sanctity was commanded in connection with the entrance and ministry into the holy of holies. Under no circumstances was the priest permitted to approach the inner apartment of the sanctuary after the dedication exercises were completed and the structure was consecrated to the Lord's service, except on the tenth day of the seventh Bible month, the Day of Atonement.

9. For what purpose was this service instituted? Lev. 16:16.

The service of the Day of Atonement was instituted to provide for the closing up of the ministry of the sanctuary for the year. On this day everything connected with the sanctuary was to be made clean. It was in reality a cleaning-up day. The reason given for the service on this day is: "Because of the uncleanness of the children of Israel, and because of their transgressions in all their sins; and so shall he do for the tabernacle of the congregation, that remaineth among them in the midst of their uncleanness." Lev. 16:16.

During the year the sins of the people had been carried into the holy place of the tabernacle. The blood representing the sins forgiven was sprinkled against the veil before the most holy place. Blood of certain of the offerings was placed upon the horns of the altar. The sprinkling and the application of the blood in the sanctuary and upon the instruments in the holy place made defilement. This work in the tabernacle was carried on day by day. There was no cessation. The time came when there must be a thorough cleaning up of what had been taking place through the year. Then, too, there were Israelites who were neglectful during the year, who had not lived up to their privileges. These were to be given a final opportunity.

Every provision was made by the Lord for every soul—for the stranger and the sojourner—and for every occasion; for this cleansing from sin, conducted in the sanctuary, was figurative. While forgiveness and pardon were effective through the blood of the spotless sacrifices offered, there was a larger, a broader, and a more comprehensive work to be accomplished through the mediation of the great High Priest who would minister in the sanctuary and the tabernacle which the Lord pitched and not man. But we must not anticipate.

10. How many were permitted to minister in the sanctuary on this special day during the time the high priest was in the most holy place? Lev. 16:17.

During the time the high priest was officiating in the most holy place, no ministry was conducted in any other part of the sanctuary. The work conducted in the most holy place on the Day of Atonement, when the high priest was ministering in the inner apartment, was the exclusive work performed during this time, for the Scripture says: "There shall be no man in the tabernacle of the

5

congregation when he goeth in to make an atonement in the holy place, until he come out, and have made an atonement for himself, and for his household, and for all the congregation of Israel." Lev. 16:17.

Be it observed that the atonement was being made in the most holy place by the high priest. During the other days of the year, when sacrifices were offered, there was a portion of the ministry conducted by the associate priests. But at this particular time, during the period of the high priest's service in the most holy place, no ministry of any character was permitted in any other part of the sanctuary. Only the high priest officiated, from the time he began the work in the most sacred place.

Then, too, it should be remembered that the ministry of the priest in the most holy place was not alone for a single individual in Israel, nor for the priest himself, neither for the priest's family, but this "atonement" was "for himself, and for his household, and for all the congregation of Israel."

11. How comprehensive was the work to be accomplished on this Day of Atonement? Lev. 16:30, 33; 23:28.

From what has already been said of the work at this annual service, the high priest's mission on this day was a comprehensive one. The results of this day likewise were far-reaching for all the people.

First, the efforts of this day included the home-born Israelites and the stranger or sojourner who was among that people. Lev. 16:29.

Second, this day's services involved the atonement "to cleanse you, that ye may be clean from *all* your sins before the Lord." Lev. 16:30. That is to say, the ministry of this day was to involve a thorough cleansing of the people of all their sins, and a complete cleansing of all in the camp of Israel. When this day's ministry terminated, the people and the camp of Israel were wholly cleansed. If any of the people were not thus cleansed, they were cut off from Israel. The Day of Atonement was the outstanding cleaning-up day in God's symbolic plan of salvation for Israel.

Third, the services of this day meant "an atonement for the holy sanctuary, . . . an atonement for the tabernacle of the congregation, and for the altar, and . . . an atonement for the priests, and for all the people of the congregation." Lev. 16:33.

A most solemn and sacred obligation rested upon the high priest in his efforts to cleanse the camp of Israel on this most sacred of all days.

LESSON XII

The Ministry in the Sanctuary

The Day of Atonement (Concluded)

1. WHAT special commands were given to Israel, to be observed on the Day of Atonement? Lev. 16:29, 30; 23:27, 32; Num. 29:7.

While the high priest was seeking the Lord in behalf of the people on this sacred and solemn day, and while this holy man of God was making the final atonement for all the congregation, an important charge was given to the Israelites:

First, The people were commanded to afflict their souls.

Second, they were to do no work on this day. They were to abstain from all secular labor. They were to observe the day as a holy day, a sabbath day. This day was regarded as more sacred than a regular Sabbath. The Hebrew expression שבת שבתון (shabbath shabbathon), translated in our version, "It shall be unto you a sabbath of rest," really means "a sabbath of sabbaths." Writing on this point in the Jewish Encyclopedia, the author of an article on the "Atonement" says the following:

"All the various elements effecting atonement are in a marked degree combined in the Day of Atonement. . . . It is called 'shabbat shabbaton,' the holiest of rest days."—Vol. II, p. 280. (See Lev. 23:32.)

Third, the stranger and the sojourner must afflict the soul exactly as did the Israelite. Not a person in the camp of Israel was exempted from this command.

Fourth, it was to be a holy convocation. The people were to gather together for the worship of God, and to seek the Lord most heartily.

Fifth, the soul that did not afflict itself on this day was cut off from among the people.

Sixth, the person who violated any of the requirements in regard to this day was destroyed from among the people. The most solemn obligation rested upon the congregation to guard most jealously the commands of God in respect to this holy day.

"Every man was to afflict his soul while the work of atonement was going forward. All business was laid aside, and the whole congregation of Israel spent the day in solemn humiliation before God, with prayer, fasting, and deep searching of heart."—"Patriarchs and Prophets," p. 355.

The people were charged to seek the Lord with all their heart. An illustration of the manner in which the people, in olden times, sought God with all the heart, is found in the experience of the prophet Daniel. (See Dan. 9:3; compare with Jer. 29:13, 14.)

2. What disastrous results would overtake any among the people who did not follow the counsel of God in regard to this day? Lev. 23:29, 30.

The Day of Atonement meant life or death to the Israelite. Large numbers of people still feel the same way in regard to this most sacred day. The child of Abraham seeks thoroughly to investigate his life on this day, that no sin shall be recorded against him when the day terminates.

"On the Day of Atonement the pious Jew becomes forgetful of the flesh and its wants, and, banishing hatred, ill feeling, and all ignoble thoughts, seeks to be

67

occupied exclusively with things spiritual."—*The Jewish Encyclopedia*, Vol. II, p. 288.

No sacrifices, as in the days of the sanctuary and the days of the temple, are available. For this loss the Jew is sad and sorrowful. He greatly mourns the lack of an atonement. In his devotions during this day he offers the following prayer:

"Because of the abundance of our sins, we have no burnt offering, nor sin offering, no staves for the holy ark, no peace nor any meat offering, nor lot, nor heavenly fire, . . . *no sanctuary nor any sprinkling of the blood*, no trespass offering nor any sacrificing, no purifying with ashes, no red heifer, no Jerusalem nor any Lebanon, no laver nor any bread of the presence, no altar nor evening sacrifice, . . . no veil nor any atonement; . . . and all this because of the abundance of our sins, and the sins of our forefathers. We are diminished, and have not these things; and since that time, we have been destitute of these things."— *"Prayers for the Day of Atonement."*

The Jew spends the entire day in the synagogue. The pious believer eats no food nor drinks any water for at least twenty-four hours. He humiliates himself while in the synagogue by removing his shoes. He will not allow himself to be interrupted in his devotions to hold converse with his neighbor. Now that he has no mediator or substitute, he must permit no part of the day to pass without afflicting his soul, lest he be cut off at the close of the day. He must enter into no form of business deals, he must not even think of business enterprises, lest he be included among those who have performed work on that day, and be destroyed from among his people.

3. How much sacredness was attached to the strict observance of this Day of Atonement? Lev. 16:31; 23:27, 28, 31, 32.

The services of the orthodox Jew on the Day of Atonement are now divided into five parts. In the evening of the day, every member of the family repairs to the synagogue for worship. And they enter as they would enter on Sabbath evening; for this is a sabbath of sabbaths. This is the rendering of the Hebrew text in Leviticus 16:31—*shabbath shabbathon*, sabbath of sabbaths. Unusual sacredness is attached to this day.

At this evening service all vows, promises, oaths, and other forms of agreements and contracts which may not have been fulfilled, must be absolved. They must be atoned for; they must be pardoned. It is a solemn and holy convocation. The penitent weeps because of his having been remiss. He puts forth earnest and expressive intensity, for he craves and longs for forgiveness.

The services during the day are divided into four parts. The forenoon is devoted to thanks for life, and to special forms of expression used on Sabbath. At the additional service the law and the prophets are read, especially those portions which deal with fasting and affliction of the soul.

The time and work of judgment is read at the afternoon worship, and the worshiper then becomes absorbed in greater earnestness and devotion. There is no other opportunity for straightening matters out, except what is left on this day. The worshiper's repentance must be thorough and complete. In the Talmudic work, *"Hilchoth T-Choo-vah"* (*Laws of Repentance*), it is written:

"At this time when there is no temple in existence, when there is no altar, there is *no atonement, only repentance*. Repentance atones for all transgressions. Even a very wicked man, who, all the days of his life, has committed great wickedness, and repents at the last, not the least of all his evil deeds will ever be mentioned to him; for it is said: 'As for the wickedness of the wicked, he shall not fall thereby, in the day that he turneth from his wickedness.' The Day of Atonement itself also atones for them that repent, for it is said: 'For on that day he shall make an atonement for you.'"

At three o'clock of this day the final exercises begin. Solemn and sacred are the hours and moments until the setting of the sun of that day. In addition to the work of judgment pending during this day, the penitent soul is reminded that he must be sealed before the day closes. During these later hours of the day he prays:

"Our Father, our King, *seal* our name in the book of life; our Father, our King, *seal* our name in the book of remembrance; our Father, our King, *seal* our name in the book of success and prosperity."—*"Prayers for the Day of Atonement."*

The closing moments of the Day of Atonement are recognized by the literal seed of Abraham as the most momentous. To him this day is his final opportunity. As long as the high priest on the Day of Atonement was in the sanctuary, the person who conformed to the will of God on this day, irrespective of his past record, found mercy and pardon. His past was overlooked. It was the "one more chance" to amend his life. It was man's final hope of probation.

"Thus, the first ten days of Tishri [the seventh Bible month] grew to be the Penitential Days of the year, intended to bring about a perfect change of heart, and to make Israel like newborn creatures, . . . the culmination being reached on the Day of Atonement, when religion's greatest gift, God's condoning mercy, was to be offered to man. . . . The Day of Atonement was thenceforth made the annual day of divine forgiveness of sin, when Satan, the accuser, failed to find blame in the people of Israel, who on that day appeared pure from sin like the angels."—*The Jewish Encyclopedia,* Vol. II, p. 281.

At the close of the services of this day every man and woman meets friend and neighbor. They clasp each other by the hand, and they offer one another the glad expression, "Hope you have received a good seal."

4. As the high priest completed his work in the most holy place on this day, what was he commanded to do on his way out of the sanctuary? Lev. 16:18, 19.

The Day of Atonement meant everything to the high priest as well as to the people. This representative of God and man was placed in a singular position during the hours of this sacred day. As far as the people for whom he was officiating were concerned, he was mediating in their behalf for the last time, if there was any sin left in them. He must be clean. His family likewise must be separated from all uncleanness. According to Jewish writers, "so great . . . was the dread that some mishap might befall the high priest while officiating in the holy of holies, that at the conclusion of the service he was escorted home and congratulated by his friends, whom in turn the priest was wont to entertain in the evening at a feast."—*The Jewish Encyclopedia,* Vol. II, pp. 284-286.

In behalf of the sanctuary and the congregation, four definite acts were accomplished by the high priest on this sacred day:

First, the priest must make an *atonement for the sanctuary* (Lev. 16:33) ; that is, the sanctuary on this day must be cleansed. At the conclusion of his ministry in the holy of holies, "he shall go out unto the altar that is before the Lord, and make an atonement for it; and shall take of the blood of the bullock, and of the blood of the goat, and put it upon the horns of the altar round about. And he shall sprinkle of the blood upon it with his finger seven times, and cleanse it, and hallow it from the uncleanness of the children of Israel." Lev. 16:18, 19. By this act the priest cleansed the sanctuary. Then he removed from the sanctuary the sins which had gathered during the year, and carried them forth from the tabernacle of the congregation.

"In the type, this great work of atonement, or blotting out of sins, was represented by the services of the Day of Atonement,—the cleansing of the earthly sanctuary, which was accomplished by the removal, by virtue of the blood of the sin offering, of the sins by which it had been polluted."—*"Patriarchs and Prophets,"* p. 358.

THE SCAPEGOAT ON THE DAY OF ATONEMENT

Second, this Day of Atonement was a work of judgment. The man who fulfilled the requirements of God for this day was judged worthy of continued existence. All his sins were confessed and pardoned. There was no guilt attached to his record. He had rectified every wrong. He had put away every known sin. His case was decided. To this day the Jewish people call the Day of Atonement the הדין יום (yom haddin), "the day of judgment." The Scripture says; "On that day shall the priest make an atonement for you, to cleanse you, that ye may be clean *from all your sins* before the Lord." Lev. 16:30.

Third, this Day of Atonement was the time when *sins were blotted out.* When the high priest left the holy of holies to go out of the tabernacle, he took with him the record of the sins which had been confessed and forgiven on that day and during the year.

"Important truths concerning the atonement were taught the people by this yearly service. In the sin offerings presented during the year, a substitute had been accepted in the sinner's stead; but the blood of the victim had not made full atonement for the sin. It had only provided a means by which the sin was transferred to the sanctuary. By the offering of blood, the sinner acknowledged the authority of the law, confessed the guilt of his transgression, and expressed his faith in Him who was to take away the sin of the world; but he was not entirely released from the condemnation of the law.

"On the Day of Atonement the high priest, having taken an offering for the congregation, went into the most holy place with the blood, and sprinkled it upon the mercy seat above the tables of the law. Thus the claims of the law, which demanded the life of the sinner, were satisfied. Then in his character of mediator the priest took the sins upon himself, and leaving the sanctuary, he bore with him the burden of Israel's guilt. . . . And as the goat bearing these sins was sent away, they were with him regarded as forever separated from the people."—*"Patriarchs and Prophets,"* pp. 355, 356.

Fourth, this day was a *day of sealing.* This thought has been discussed in the Notes of this study under question 3. The Jewish Encyclopedia makes this observation on the sealing in connection with the Day of Atonement:

"Down to the first century, . . . the idea of the divine judgment was mainly eschatological in character, as deciding the destiny of the soul after death rather than of men on earth. But . . . the idea developed also in Jewish circles that on the first of Tishri [the seventh Bible month] the sacred New Year's Day, . . . man's doings were judged and his destiny was decided; and that on the tenth of Tishri [the Day of Atonement] the decree of heaven was sealed."—*Vol.* II, p. 281.

The belief in the sealing work on this most holy day has been prevalent and accepted among the seed of Abraham for many centuries. This idea is found in their literature through the ages.

With these four things definitely accomplished at the close of the Day of Atonement, not only were the people and the sanctuary cleansed, but the camp of Israel also was cleansed, for unless the congregation were cleansed, they would be cut off. The command was that those who failed to carry out Heaven's instruction for this day were to be cut off from among the people—destroyed from among the congregation. (See Lev. 23:29, 30.)

5. When the priest had ended his work of reconciliation in the sanctuary, what did he next proceed to do? Lev. 16:20.

The priest now calls for the live goat. Till this time there has been no need of Azazel in connection with the day's services. Not since the lot was cast has Azazel been considered. The work of atonement now is ended for the people and for the sanctuary. There has been no need of or demand for Azazel until the atonement is completed.

"When he hath made an end of reconciling the holy place, and the tabernacle of the congregation, and the altar, he shall bring the live goat." Lev. 16:20.

The command is specific, that the other offering was not necessary until the ministry of reconciliation was ended. Azazel was not essential for reconciliation for the congregation, or for the tabernacle ministry.

6. What singular ceremony did the priest then perform with this live goat, Azazel? Lev. 16:21.

Upon the head of Azazel must be placed the hands of the high priest. We learn from many scriptures (see Lev. 1:4; 3:2, 8, 13; 4:4, 15, etc.) that sin was confessed upon the head of an animal, when it was offered for sacrifice, by the laying on of the hands of the individual who brought the offering. Following the act of confession, the animal was sacrificed. Its blood was brought into the sanctuary when forgiveness was made possible. When the blood was sprinkled, the penitent was pardoned.

When the high priest laid his hands on Azazel, he confessed over the goat the sins of the children of Israel. All the transgressions of the entire people were placed upon its head. The live goat became responsible for the sins of the congregation. The sins which were placed on the goat were not unconfessed sins. What were placed on the head of Azazel were the sins of the people which had been confessed and pardoned. The priest's confession upon Azazel represented the guilt, which had been freely and fully forgiven, of those who during the year had acknowledged their wrongs, for which atonement already had been made. These were not the sins of sinners. They needed not to be atoned for by the death of Azazel; for Azazel's life was not taken. The live goat was not killed on that day, nor was the live goat sacrificed at any time for the sins which were confessed upon him. This live goat did not become a substitute for the congregation of Israel. Its blood was not needed for the people's reconciliation.

The opinion of a large class is that Azazel, the scapegoat, represents one phase of the ministry of Christ. But the type, the Scriptures, the plan of redemption, and the antitypical ministry of the Lord Jesus, man's High Priest, will not admit of such a suggestion. Let us consider a few facts in connection with the use and purpose of Azazel:

1. On the Day of Atonement the lot is cast, and Azazel is chosen. The choice is made at the direction and by the authority of the Lord. Lev. 16:7, 8.

2. Azazel has no part in the sanctuary ministry on the Day of Atonement.

3. The life of Azazel is not taken, nor is his blood needed for sacrificial purposes.

4. Azazel is caused no suffering during this holy day because of the sins of others.

5. The live goat has no part during the affliction of the congregation.

6. Since Azazel's blood has not been shed, he cannot be used for remission of sin, and without the shedding of blood there is no remission of sin.

7. Therefore Azazel makes no propitiation for sin.

8. Azazel is not used as man's substitute, as is the Lord's goat, the sin offering.

9. Azazel is given no consideration in the exercises of the Day of Atonement till the services are completed in the holy of holies.

10. After the ceremonies are officially at an end, Azazel is brought alive to the door of the tabernacle of the congregation.

11. Atonement has already been made for the sins which are placed upon the head of Azazel by the high priest. These sins have been brought out of the sanctuary.

12. Azazel does not die that day.

The Lord's lot, the sin offering, accomplished all that was essential and necessary to make amends for the broken law in the holy of holies, and for the sins of the people. This goat was offered as a חטאת (chattath), "sin offering." The sin offerings, noted in the fourth chapter of the book of Leviticus, were all offered to bear the sins of the people. The penitent sinner recognized in this sin offering his substitute, and he was pardoned of his sin when the blood of the animal was sprinkled in the holy place. Atonement was made for the sinner through the sacrifice, the sin offering. The *chattath,* "sin offering," was ample to meet the needs of the sinner. Therefore the *chattath* provided for both the sanctuary and the people on the Day of Atonement, and when offered by the priests, met every need for the ministry on this day.

The virtue of the sin offering, the Lord's goat, on the Day of Atonement was in the shedding of its blood. But as we have already observed, there was no blood of Azazel shed on that day. There was nothing in the use of Azazel which partook of the ministry of Christ, the Lamb of God which taketh away the sin of the world.

That Azazel, the scapegoat, does represent Satan, the devil, is clear, evident, forceful. The sins which are placed upon Azazel at the close of the ministry of the Day of Atonement are the sins of the righteous, and not of sinners. These sins which he bears have already been atoned for. Why should Satan bear the sins which have already been atoned for?

Man by nature is sinful. His nature does not desire regeneration. Christ, the Son of God, became man's substitute. Our Lord took the place of man. He volunteered to become man's Deliverer and Redeemer. Jesus bore man's sins. Through Christ it is possible for man again to be reconciled to God. In Christ, God and man are once more united; heaven and earth are again joined.

When the Spirit of God appeals to the sinner to return to the Father's home and the Father's heart, Satan immediately opposes this divine influence upon the sinner's heart. The enemy of righteousness puts forth every effort to hold the captive in his grasp. The soul that longs for freedom from the cruel, satanic bondage, appeals to the almighty Saviour to free him from the clutches of this relentless foe. The Son of God hears the cry of the burdened heart, and releases the sinner from his bondage of sin. Christ makes a man free.

The devil, seeing that his prey has been snatched from him, begins a warfare against the Lord Jesus in the person of the individual who has been delivered. Satan manifests fierce wrath to bring back, if possible, the captive whom the Son of God has made free. The snares, pitfalls, and traps of the enemy are many and varied; for Satan is artful, deceitful, and cruel. Through Satan's devices and cunning craftinesses he sometimes succeeds in causing the plucked captive to come again under his bondage. Once more this burdened soul cries to the Saviour for help and deliverance. Again Jesus rescues him, pardons him gladly and freely, and encourages him with heavenly assurance that He will hold him fast if the sinner will yield himself into the hand of the Deliverer. The battle wages between Christ and Satan in the man who has accepted the Lord as his Saviour and his Substitute. If Satan did not harass, bother, and trail the man delivered by the power of Christ, the captive would serve his Lord and Master devotedly. His enemy hounds him as a roaring lion seeks to terrify and slay its prey. By every means does Satan seek to destroy, if possible, the one who has been snatched from his grasp.

If through the power of Christ the ransomed one is in the end a conqueror, and has proved by a victorious life that he is prepared to live with the pure and the holy through the ceaseless ages of eternity, why would not Satan, the originator and perpetuator of sin, be responsible for the sins, the trespasses, and the transgressions he caused this child of God to commit when this redeemed one was endeavoring to serve his Saviour who gave him such deliverance? This is what took place at the close of the Day of Atonement in the typical service in the sanctuary.

"Aaron shall lay both his hands upon the head of the live goat, and confess over him all the iniquities of the children of Israel, and all their transgressions in all their sins, putting them upon the head of the goat, and shall send him away by the hand of a fit man into the wilderness." Lev. 16:21.

The sins confessed upon the live goat, Azazel, were not the sins of the wicked men of Israel, the ungodly of the congregation. They were the iniquities of the people who had been forgiven.

It was but right and just that Azazel should bear the sins of the forgiven and pardoned, when these justified ones fully harmonized with the requirements of the God of Israel on the Day of Atonement.

"As in the final atonement the sins of the truly penitent are to be blotted from the records of heaven, no more to be remembered or come into mind, so in the type they were borne away into the wilderness, forever separated from the congregation."—*"Patriarchs and Prophets,"* p. 358.

7. When the proper man took Azazel into the wilderness, what was the condition of the people and of the camp? Lev. 16:30, 33; 23:28.

By a fit man is Azazel taken into the wilderness, bearing the iniquities of the camp of Israel upon him. He does not return into the camp. He remains in this uninhabited land. His life is not taken by the man chosen to lead him out of the camp. He is forever barred from returning to the congregation.

"The goat that fell to Jehovah was slain as a sin offering for the people. But the goat of Azazel . . . was made the subject of a more striking ceremony. The high priest laid his hands upon its head and confessed over it the sins of the people. Then the victim was handed over to a man standing ready for the purpose, and, laden as it was with these . . . sins, it was 'led forth to an isolated region,' and then let go in the wilderness."

"Hence it was the practice in Jerusalem, according to Yoma [a Talmudic treatise], 7:4, to take the scapegoat to a cliff and push him over it out of sight. In this way the complete separation was effected."—*The Jewish Encyclopedia,* Vol. II, pp. 365, 367.

The people were free from their sins. The atonement now was completed. The tabernacle was cleansed. There was no more sin in the camp. The atonement was made for the sanctuary, and for all the congregation of Israel, before the Lord God. Lev. 23:28.

"Once a year, on the great Day of Atonement, the priest entered the most holy place for the cleansing of the sanctuary. The work there performed, completed the yearly round of ministration."—*"Patriarchs and Prophets,"* p. 355.

Beginning and Ending of Earthly Sacrifices and Priesthood

1. DID the sacrificial system begin with the Israelites in the wilderness? Gen. 8:20, 21; 14:18.

The impression prevails in some quarters that the Israelites were the first people who offered sacrifices. Such a view is not correct. It is a popular belief with some that the system of sacrifices in existence among the literal seed of Abraham afforded them a means of salvation through good works, and that they therefore knew nothing of God's true way of saving men,—by the gift and grace of the Lord Jesus.

The idea of offering sacrifices was in vogue in the earliest times. We read in Scripture that after the deluge, "Noah builded an altar unto the Lord; and took of every clean beast, and of every clean fowl, and offered burnt offerings on the altar. And the Lord smelled a sweet savor." Gen. 8:20, 21.

From Adam to the flood covered a period of more than sixteen hundred years. During this time, from the days of Adam, there lived three men who spanned this entire period till the deluge. These three persons were Adam, Methuselah, and Noah. The record says that Adam was 130 years old at the time of the birth of Seth. (See Gen. 5:3.) At the age of 105 years Seth begat Enos. Verse 6. When Enos was ninety years old, he became the father of Cainan. Verse 9. Mahalaleel was born when Cainan was seventy years old. Verse 12. Jared was born when Mahalaleel was sixty-five years old. Verse 15. When Jared was 162 years old, Enoch was born. Verse 18. When Enoch was sixty-five years of age, Methuselah was born. Verse 21. From the creation of Adam till the birth of Methuselah, was 687 years. We are told that Adam lived to be 930 years old. Verse 5. Methuselah lived contemporary with Adam 243 years; that is, when Methuselah was 243 years old, the first man died. Adam could have imparted most valuable information during the two hundred forty and more years he and Methuselah lived contemporaneously.

When Methuselah was 187 years old, Lamech was born. Verse 25. At the age of 182 Lamech begat Noah. Verse 28. When Noah was born, Methuselah was 369 years old. The Scripture says that Methuselah died at the age of 969 years. Verse 27. And the word of God declares that at the time of the flood, Noah was in his 600th year. Gen. 7:11. Methuselah and Noah lived as contemporaries for six centuries. The former died the year of the flood. Therefore Adam, Methuselah, and Noah span the era from creation to the deluge.

The history of more than fifteen hundred years is crowded into less than seven chapters of the Bible. The first chapter of Genesis deals with creation. The second chapter summarizes the events found in chapter one, with additions. The third chapter tells the story of the fall. So we have less than three chapters in which are given the history of creation and the rise and fall of the human race.

Details of the lives of the antediluvians are not recorded in these early chapters of sacred history. Many things that are not mentioned occurred during these centuries. When we read that the patriarch Noah offered up sacrifices to the Lord, and the Lord accepted these offerings as a sweet-smelling savor, we must conclude that sacrifices were offered in Noah's day.

2. When was the sacrificial system introduced, and by whom? Gen. 4:3-5.

From the reading of the fourth chapter of Genesis we learn that the system of sacrifices was in vogue and well established in the days of Cain and Abel. In the margin of verse three of this chapter, in place of the words of the text, "in process of time," the reading is "at the end of days." The rendering of the Hebrew text for the phrase "in process of time" is מִקֵּץ יָמִים (miqqets yamim), "the end of days." By reading Genesis 1:5, 8, 13, 19, 23, 31, and 2:2, 3, we learn that the world was made in six days, and that on the seventh day God rested from His labors, and blessed and sanctified this seventh day as His holy rest day. The cycle of seven days was thus established. The last of these days is the seventh. Inasmuch as the Scripture says וַיְהִי מִקֵּץ יָמִים (wa-yehi miqqets yamim), "And it came to pass at the end of the days," it is clear that the two sons of Adam each brought an offering unto the Lord at the close of the week, on the seventh day, or the Sabbath of the Lord.

We know that when the sacrificial system was introduced among the Israelites, the Lord required the priests to offer twice as many offerings on the Sabbath as on other days, for it is written: "On the Sabbath day two lambs of the first year without spot, and two tenth deals of flour for a meat offering. . . . This is the burnt offering of every Sabbath, beside the continual burnt offering, and his drink offering." Num. 28:9, 10. However, on the other days of the week, the Lord required but one offering in the morning and one in the evening. (See verses 1-6.)

The sacrificial system must have been introduced at a very early period of the world's history. Yes, Adam and Eve were acquainted with the system of sacrificial offerings in their day. In view of this fact, note the following:

"The sacrificial offerings were ordained by God to be to man a perpetual reminder and a penitential acknowledgment of his sin, and a confession of his faith in the promised Redeemer. . . . To Adam, the offering of the first sacrifice was a most painful ceremony. His hand must be raised to take life, which only God could give. It was the first time he had ever witnessed death. . . . As he slew the innocent victim, he trembled at the thought that his sin must shed the blood of the spotless Lamb of God."—*Patriarchs and Prophets,*" p. 68.

"Cain and Abel, the sons of Adam, differed widely in character. . . . These brothers were tested, as Adam had been tested before them. . . . They were acquainted with the provision made for the salvation of man, and understood the system of offerings which God had ordained. They knew that in these offerings they were to express faith in the Saviour whom the offerings typified. . . . Without the shedding of blood, there could be no remission of sin; and they were to show their faith in the blood of Christ as the promised atonement, by offering the firstlings of the flock in sacrifice."—*Id.,* p. 71.

3. How early in sacred history have we record of a priesthood? Gen. 14:18; 41:45; Ex. 2:16.

We have no written record as to how early in the history of the world priesthood was introduced. The Scriptures speak of Melchizedek, king of Salem, who was priest of the Most High God. Of his ancestry, pedigree, or genealogy, we have no record. This man Melchizedek is mentioned in the Old and New Testaments a number of times, but in no place have we any reference to his ancestry. The record says he was priest of the Most High God. He was influential, he held a high position; for to him Abraham gave tithes. He is the first character in Holy Writ called a priest.

We find also in this same book of Genesis that in the city of On, in Egypt, there was a man by the name of Potipherah who also was a priest. Joseph was married to this man's daughter. Gen. 41:45.

Where Moses spent forty years of his life as a shepherd, we find a man who was priest of Midian. In Genesis 41:45, as in this sixteenth verse of Exodus 2, the margin gives the word "prince" instead of "priest." But the original word for priest in all three places, including Genesis 14:18, is the same. The Hebrew word is כֹּהֵן (*kohen*), "priest," not נָשִׂיא (*nasi*), "prince." *Kohen*, priest, is the title given to Aaron the priest.

"In the earliest times every man was priest of his own household. In the days of Abraham, the priesthood was regarded as the birthright of the eldest son."—*"Patriarchs and Prophets,"* p. 350.

It has ever been Satan's purpose to counterfeit the work of God. We find a system of idolatrous worship and heathen priests in existence in Abraham's day.

"After the dispersion from Babel, idolatry again became well-nigh universal. . . . Abraham had grown up in the midst of superstition and heathenism. Even his father's household, by whom the knowledge of God had been preserved, were yielding to the seductive influences surrounding them, and they 'served other gods' than Jehovah. Joshua 24:2. . . . Idolatry invited him on every side, but in vain. Faithful among the faithless, uncorrupted by the prevailing apostasy, he steadfastly adhered to the worship of the one true God."—*"Patriarchs and Prophets,"* p. 125.

"By the laws of Egypt, all who occupied the throne of the Pharaohs must become members of the priestly caste; and Moses, as the heir apparent, was to be initiated into the mysteries of the national religion. This duty was committed to the priests. But while he was an ardent and untiring student, he could not be induced to participate in the worship of the gods. . . . He reasoned with priests and worshipers, showing the folly of their superstitious veneration of senseless objects."—*Id.,* p. 245.

"God entered into covenant with Abraham, and took to Himself a people to become the depositaries of His law. To seduce and destroy this people, Satan began at once to lay his snares. The children of Jacob were tempted to contract marriages with the heathen and to worship their idols. . . . It was to quench this light that Satan worked through the envy of Joseph's brothers to cause him to be sold as a slave in a heathen land.

"God overruled events, however, so that the knowledge of Himself should be given to the people of Egypt. Both in the house of Potiphar and in the prison, Joseph received an education and training that, with the fear of God, prepared him for his high position as prime minister of the nation. . . .

"The Israelites . . . such as were true to God exerted a widespread influence. The idolatrous priests were filled with alarm as they saw the new religion finding favor. Inspired by Satan with his own enmity toward the God of heaven, they set themselves to quench the light. To the priests was committed the education of the heir to the throne, and it was this spirit of determined opposition to God and zeal for idolatry that molded the character of the future monarch, and led to cruelty and oppression toward the Hebrews."—*Id.,* pp. 332, 333.

4. Was God worshiped by sacrifices prior to the sanctuary experience in the wilderness? Gen. 22:2, 7, 9, 10; 31:54.

In the days of Abraham the offering of sacrifices had become well established. Those who feared God recognized the necessity of a Saviour, and the sacrificing of animals had come to be regarded as a means of worshiping the true God.

"Abraham, 'the friend of God,' set us a worthy example. His life was a life of prayer. Wherever he pitched his tent, close beside it was set up his altar, calling all within his encampment to the morning and the evening sacrifice. When his tent was removed, the altar remained. In following years, there were those among the roving Canaanites who received instruction from Abraham; and whenever one of these came to that altar, he knew who had been there before him; and when he had pitched his tent, he repaired the altar, and there worshiped the living God."—*Id.,* p. 128.

"In early times the father was the ruler and priest of his own family. . . .

ABRAHAM UPON MT. MORIAH PREPARING TO OFFER HIS SON ISAAC

This patriarchal system of government Abraham endeavored to perpetuate, as it tended to preserve the knowledge of God. . . . The greatest care was exercised to shut out every form of false religion, and to impress the mind with the majesty and glory of the living God as the true object of worship."—*Id.*, p. 141.

Without doubt it was customary for Abraham and his son Isaac often to offer sacrifice unto the Lord. From the conversation between the father and son en route to sacrifice on Mt. Moriah, it is evident the young man was familiar with the arrangements necessary to sacrifice the offerings to the Lord. Said Isaac to his father:

"Behold the fire and the wood: but where is the lamb for a burnt offering?" Gen. 22:7.

To ensure lasting peace between Jacob and Laban, the former offered sacrifice upon the mount, and there they parted in friendship and harmony. For centuries before the sacrificial system was introduced among the Israelites in the wilderness, the saints of God had been familiar with the arrangement of sacrificial offerings to the true God. These offerings were intended to teach the plan of human redemption through the promised Messiah.

"Through type and promise, God 'preached before the gospel unto Abraham.' And the patriarch's faith was fixed upon the Redeemer to come. . . . The ram offered in the place of Isaac represented the Son of God, who was to be sacrificed in our stead. . . . It was to impress Abraham's mind with the reality of the gospel, as well as to test his faith, that God commanded him to slay his son."

"It had been difficult even for the angels to grasp the mystery of redemption,— to comprehend that the Commander of heaven, the Son of God, must die for guilty man. When the command was given to Abraham to offer up his son, the interest of all heavenly beings was enlisted. With intense earnestness they watched each step in the fulfillment of this command. When to Isaac's question, 'Where is the lamb for a burnt offering?' Abraham made answer, 'God will provide Himself a lamb;' and when the father's hand was stayed as he was about to slay his son, and the ram which God had provided was offered in the place of Isaac,—then light was shed upon the mystery of redemption, and even the angels understood more clearly the wonderful provision that God had made for man's salvation."—*"Patriarchs and Prophets,"* pp. 154, 155.

5. To whom did the heathen offer their sacrifices? Num. 25:1, 2; 1 Cor. 10:20.

"The sacrifices, pointing forward to the death of Christ, were designed to preserve in the hearts of the people faith in the Redeemer to come; hence it was of the greatest importance that the Lord's directions concerning them should be strictly heeded."—*Id.*, p. 576.

"Satan was seeking to bring contempt upon the sacrificial offerings that prefigured the death of Christ; and as the minds of the people were darkened by idolatry, he led them to counterfeit these offerings, and sacrifice their own children upon the altars of their gods."—*Id.*, pp. 120-123.

The heathen offered their sacrifices to the devil. In connection with their idolatrous worship, they perverted the service and the sacrifice of the true God, and became devotees of the evil one. "The heathen systems of sacrifice were a perversion of the system that God had appointed."—*"The Desire of Ages,"* p. 28.

6. Did the Lord introduce the sacrificial system immediately upon Israel's deliverance from Egypt? Ex. 12:3, 5, 6, 10; Jer. 7:21, 22.

Although the Passover was first observed by the Israelites prior to their departure from Egypt, the sacrificial system of the Levitical priesthood was not introduced immediately. There were other lessons necessary for them to learn and to understand. The Scripture says:

"Thus saith the Lord of hosts, the God of Israel: Put your burnt offerings unto your sacrifices, and eat flesh. For I spake not unto your fathers, nor commanded them in the day that I brought them out of the land of Egypt, concerning burnt offerings or sacrifices." Jer. 7:21, 22.

It was necessary for that people to have some token of their deliverance before they were freed from slavery.

"The deliverance of Israel from Egypt was an object lesson of redemption, which the Passover was intended to keep in memory. The slain lamb, the unleavened bread, the sheaf of first fruits, represented the Saviour."—*"The Desire of Ages,"* p. 77.

7. How did the Lord exhort His people, following their exodus from Egypt? Ex. 15:26; Isa. 1:19, 20; Jer. 7:23, 24.

The most important lesson that Israel first had to learn was prompt obedience to all of God's commands. It was this lack of obedience to God's requirements that caused the fall of Adam and Eve. It was necessary for the seed of Abraham to recognize that their primary obligation was strictly to conform their lives to the commands of God. God made that people unusual promises on their leaving Egypt, if they would diligently hearken unto His commandments. They were assured health, freedom from sickness, and every other blessing if they heeded the instructions of God.

To strengthen their faith in His unerring promises, God so preserved them that when they marched out of Egypt, there was not a weak person among all their tribes. Ps. 105:37. Not one feeble Israelite was found among the millions who came forth from the land of their exile. They had an abundance of evidence that God would fulfill His faithful word if they would only be willing and obedient. While in Egypt these people were under the lash. The Israelites were bondmen to the Egyptians. They were ruled by taskmasters. They were cruelly abused and ill-treated. God dealt with them tenderly and kindly. He led them gently. He was desirous, for their own good, that they should do exactly as He told them. Deut. 6:24. This was the first lesson Israel was to learn as God gave birth to this nation. "The observance of the Passover began with the birth of the Hebrew nation."—*"The Desire of Ages,"* p. 76.

8. Did Israel's stay in Egypt affect their religious ideas and devotions? Lev. 18:1-4; 20:22, 23; Jer. 7:25, 26.

The most vile forms of heathenism and idolatry were practiced by the Egyptian people. Every diabolical, sinful, and unclean ceremony which Satan could invent was practiced by the people of the Pharaohs. God repeatedly admonished the Israelites not to indulge in any of the abominable rites which they saw carried on in their slavery. The Egyptian abominations were similar to those of the Canaanitish people, and of the latter the Lord said that the land spewed out the inhabitants thereof.

"Through long intercourse with idolaters, the people of Israel had mingled many heathen customs with their worship." "The sacrificial system, committed to Adam, was also perverted by his descendants. Superstition, idolatry, cruelty, and licentiousness corrupted the simple and significant service that God had appointed."—*"Patriarchs and Prophets,"* p. 364.

"It was because the Israelites were so disposed to connect themselves with the heathen and imitate their idolatry that God had permitted them to go down into Egypt, where the influence of Joseph was widely felt, and where circumstances were favorable for them to remain a distinct people. Here also the gross idolatry of the Egyptians and their cruelty and oppression during the latter part of the Hebrew sojourn, should have inspired in them an abhorrence of idolatry, and should have led them to flee for refuge to the God of their fathers. This very providence Satan made a means to serve his purpose, darkening the minds of the Israelites, and leading them to imitate the practices of their heathen masters."—*Id.,* p. 333.

9. Why did God give Israel the ten commandments on Mt. Sinai? Ex. 20:18-20.

One reason the Lord gives for bringing Israel from Egypt was that they might keep His law. Ps. 105:43-45. During their sojourn among the heathen Egyptians, the people of Abraham had in a large degree lost the knowledge of God and a sense of the awfulness of sin. Evil and transgression did not appear so shocking to them. Before they as a nation could be accepted as the people of God's choice, they must have a sense of God's holiness, of His purity, of His majesty, and of the sinfulness of sin.

After the Lord had personally delivered the ten commandments on Mt. Sinai, the people appealed to Moses to talk with them and not let God talk to them, lest they die. "Moses said unto the people, Fear not: for God is come to prove you, and that His fear may be before your faces, that ye sin not." Ex. 20:20.

To understand the serious nature of sin, the people had to be impressed with the importance and obligation of God's sacred law.

"God accompanied the proclamation of His law with exhibitions of His power and glory, that His people might never forget the scene, and that they might be impressed with profound veneration for the Author of the law, the Creator of heaven and earth. He would also show to all men the sacredness, the importance, and the permanence of His law.

"The people of Israel were overwhelmed with terror. The awful power of God's utterances seemed more than their trembling hearts could bear. For as God's great rule of right was presented before them, they realized as never before, the offensive character of sin, and their own guilt in the sight of a holy God. They shrank away from the mountain in fear and awe. . . .

"The minds of the people, blinded and debased by slavery and heathenism, were not prepared to appreciate fully the far-reaching principles of God's ten precepts."—"*Patriarchs and Prophets,*" pp. 309, 310.

10. When was Moses called into the mount to meet with God to receive the revelation of the sanctuary and its ministry? Ex. 24:12-18; 25:1-9.

It was not until the Lord had given the Israelites the ten commandments that Moses was called into the mount to receive the revelation on the sanctuary. The sanctuary ritual was first given to the people through Moses. It was through Moses that the first ray of light on this subject of the sanctuary was communicated.

"Arrangements were now to be made for the full establishment of the chosen nation under Jehovah as their King. Moses had received the command, 'Come up unto the Lord.' "—*Id.,* p. 312.

"During his stay in the mount, Moses received directions for the building of a sanctuary in which the divine presence would be specially manifested."—*Id.,* p. 313.

"Henceforth the people were to be honored with the abiding presence of their King. . . . As the symbol of God's authority, and the embodiment of His will, there was delivered to Moses a copy of the decalogue engraved by the finger of God Himself upon two tables of stone, to be sacredly enshrined in the sanctuary, which, when made, was to be the visible center of the nation's worship.

"From a race of slaves the Israelites had been exalted above all peoples, to be the peculiar treasure of the King of kings. God had separated them from the world, that He might commit to them a sacred trust. He had made them the depositaries of His law, and He purposed, through them, to preserve among men the knowledge of Himself. Thus the light of heaven was to shine out to a world enshrouded in darkness, and a voice was to be heard appealing to all peoples to turn from their idolatry to serve the living God. If the Israelites would be true to their trust, they would become a power in the world. God would be their defense, and He would exalt them above all other nations. His light and truth would be revealed through them, and they would stand forth under His wise and holy rule as an example of the superiority of His worship over every form of idolatry."—*Id.*, p. 314.

11. How much was included in the revelation given to Moses while closeted with the Lord on Mt. Sinai? Num. 18:1-7; Ex. 28:1-3.

While Moses was in the mount with God, the entire system of sacrificial services and the ministry of the priesthood, with its significance, was revealed to the prophet of God.

"God had chosen Israel. He had called them to preserve among men the knowledge of His law, and of the symbols and prophecies that pointed to the Saviour. He desired them to be as wells of salvation to the world. What Abraham was in the land of his sojourn, what Joseph was in Egypt, and Daniel in the courts of Babylon, the Hebrew people were to be among the nations. They were to reveal God to men."—*"The Desire of Ages,"* p. 27.

"As they departed from God, the Jews in a great degree lost sight of the teaching of the ritual service. That service had been instituted by Christ Himself. In every part it was a symbol of Him; and it had been full of vitality and spiritual beauty."—*Id.*, p. 29.

"The Saviour typified in the rites and ceremonies of the Jewish law is the very same that is revealed in the gospel."—*"Patriarchs and Prophets,"* p. 373.

12. Was the system of sacrifices and offerings entrusted to any nation besides the Israelites? Deut. 4:32-35, 5-9; Rom. 3:1-3; 1 Cor. 10:18; Heb. 7:11.

To no nation but the children of Abraham did the Lord entrust the system of sacrifices and offerings. He had a purpose in so doing. Israel was instructed that if they observed the judgments and the commandments given them, they would be the wisest people upon earth. No other nation had God so nigh to them as had Israel. To them were committed the oracles of God. This was not done because this people was of greater value in God's sight than other peoples.

"God called Israel, and blessed and exalted them, not that by obedience to His law they alone might receive His favor, and become the exclusive recipients of His blessings, but in order to reveal Himself through them to all the inhabitants of the earth. It was for the accomplishment of this very purpose that He commanded them to keep themselves distinct from the idolatrous nations around them."—*"Patriarchs and Prophets,"* p. 369.

13. When did the system of the earthly priesthood and the offering of sacrifices terminate? Dan. 9:26, 27; Heb. 8:6, 7, 13; Matt. 21:43, 44; Luke 21:20-24.

God declared that sacrifices and offerings would come to an end when these types had accomplished their mission, when this symbolism had served its purpose. But the people to whom these types were entrusted lost the significance of these figures.

"The Jews lost the spiritual life from their ceremonies, and clung to the dead forms. They trusted to the sacrifices and ordinances themselves, instead of resting upon Him to whom they pointed. In order to supply the place of that which they had lost, the priests and rabbis multiplied requirements of their own; and the more rigid they grew, the less of the love of God was manifested. They measured their holiness by the multitude of their ceremonies, while their hearts were filled with pride and hypocrisy."—*"The Desire of Ages,"* p. 29.

In describing the action of the priest as he enrolled the name of the child Jesus among the records of the "first-born," the Spirit of prophecy says:

"He did not think that this Babe was He whose glory Moses had asked to see. But One greater than Moses lay in the priest's arms; and when he enrolled the child's name, he was enrolling the name of One who was the foundation of the whole Jewish economy. That name was to be its death warrant; for the system of sacrifices and offerings was waxing old; the type had almost reached its antitype, the shadow its substance."—*Id.*, p. 52.

The people rejected their own King. When their Lord had been set aside, the system He had given them to represent Him became valueless. They said they had no king but Caesar. In that renunciation they rejected the typical and symbolical ministry which pointed to the Messiah. At the death of our Lord, as He uttered the words, "It is finished," the veil of the temple was rent in twain from top to bottom. This miraculous rending, when no visible hand dared to remove that sacred partition, was Heaven's response to their statement: "We will not have this man to reign over us." It was also an indication that the typical service was at an end, that type had met antitype, that henceforth the Levitical order was to give place to the ministry of the Messiah, our great High Priest, who, after the order of Melchizedek, ministers in the true sanctuary in heaven.

Their sanctuary, their priesthood, their offerings, their nationalism, their prestige, their hold upon God,—all were gone. The typical service, the symbolical ritualism pointing to Messiah, was gone, and it was gone forever. The Messiah, the Lamb of God, the Holy One of Israel, had at last come. Earthly priesthood with divine significance had forever ceased.

LESSON XIV

When Did God Design the Sacrificial System to Cease? Why?

1. WAS it God's intention to confine the sacrificial system to the Israelites in the wilderness? Deut. 29:14, 15; 12:4-14.

It is claimed by some that the sacrificial system given to the Israelites was intended only for the time the people were to remain in the wilderness. To entertain such an idea is unfortunate. It must be remembered that the wilderness experience of the Israelites was an emergency situation. It was not in God's original program for the Israelites to spend any length of time in that desert land.

When the Lord appeared to Moses in the burning bush, He said: "I have surely seen the affliction of My people which are in Egypt, and have heard their cry by reason of their taskmasters; for I know their sorrows; and I am come down to deliver them out of the hand of the Egyptians, and to bring them up out of that land unto a good land and a large, unto a land flowing with milk and honey." Ex. 3:7, 8.

As that people left Egypt, the Lord guarded them from coming in contact with the warring Philistines. So we read: "When Pharaoh had let the people go, ... God led them not through the way of the land of the Philistines, although that was near; for God said, Lest peradventure the people repent when they see war, and they return to Egypt: but God led the people about, through the way of the wilderness." Ex. 13:17, 18.

When the Israelites left Egypt, they "took their dough before it was leavened, their kneading troughs being bound up in their clothes upon their shoulders." Ex. 12:34. We have no record of just how much food they carried with them. We read, however: "The Lord gave the people favor in the sight of the Egyptians, so that they lent unto them [Hebrew, וישאלום (*wayyashilum*), "and they solicited them"] such things as they required. And they spoiled the Egyptians." Verse 36.

Since the Lord said He would deliver the people from Egypt and bring them into a land flowing with milk and honey, the food they had with them would have been sufficient till they reached the Land of Promise. Within a few days after their departure from Egypt they began murmuring against Moses and Aaron. (See Ex. 14:10, 11.) Evidently they had enough food to last them till they reached the camp in the wilderness of Sin. Ex. 16:1-3. Thence onward the congregation continued their murmuring against God and against His servants. In another month they arrived in the wilderness of Sinai. Ex. 19:1. From Sinai the journey to Kadesh-barnea could be covered in eleven days. (See Deut. 1:2; Ex. 3:12; 18:5; 19:1, 2.) Kadesh-barnea was on the border of the Promised Land. Deut. 1:19-21.

When they reached this dividing line of their inheritance, Moses encouraged them to advance and take possession of the country. They refused to follow the counsel of their leader. They demanded that a delegation be sent to investigate the country. When the spies returned with their report, the people refused to enter the Land of Promise. They insisted that they preferred a grave in the wilderness to the enjoyment of the land of plenty. What could the Lord do with the people? He would not allow them to return to Egypt. However, they would not advance. The only thing the Lord could do was to give them the desire of their heart. Num. 14:28-30; Ps. 78:29; 106:15. In the wilderness they were to remain till all that generation died. Num. 14:32-35.

The Lord would not allow these millions of people to starve in that desert. Nothing could grow in the wilderness. Deut. 8:15, 16. Therefore the Lord performed continuous and uninterrupted miracles for the Israelites until that entire generation passed away, as may be seen by reading Numbers 26:1-3, 63-65.

He fed them with manna from heaven. The shoes on their feet and the clothes on their bodies did not wear out during the entire forty years' wanderings. Deut. 8:4; 29:5. This wilderness experience was no part of God's original program for the Israelites.

The Lord repeatedly said that the children of that generation would inherit the land promised to their fathers. Deut. 1:39. The instruction for the observance of the services and feasts included those who were not yet born. Deut. 29:14, 15. Repeatedly the command was given that the laws and the ordinances given to the people in the wilderness must be executed faithfully when the future generations inherited the goodly land. Deut. 6:1-3.

2. What special holy convocations were given to Israel in connection with the offering of sacrifices? Ex. 23:14-19; 34:22-25.

A series of feasts, holy days, and fasts were committed to the Israelites. The special feasts commanded them were the Passover, the Pentecost, or the Feast of Weeks, and the Feast of Tabernacles. In addition to these festivals they were to remember the "Blowing of the Trumpets" and the Day of Atonement.

The people were assured that during the time of these holy convocations "neither shall any man desire thy land, when thou shalt go up to appear before the Lord thy God thrice in the year." Ex. 34:24.

Special significance was attached to these holy occasions. The Passover was to be a perpetual reminder to that nation of the great wonders wrought for them when the Lord miraculously delivered them from the land of Egypt. The Passover also was to encourage them to look forward to the time when a Deliverer should come and release them from a still greater bondage than was the slavery of the land of Ham.

"The Passover was ordained as a commemoration of the deliverance of Israel from Egyptian bondage. God had directed that, year by year, as the children should ask the meaning of this ordinance, the history should be repeated. Thus the wonderful deliverance was to be kept fresh in the minds of all."—*"The Desire of Ages,"* p. 652.

The Feast of Weeks was observed fifty days after the Passover. This feast was called Pentecost. (See Acts 2:1.) The feast was also called the Feast of Harvest. Ex. 23:16.

Why this feast was called the Feast of Harvest may be gathered from the following:

"The Passover was followed by the seven days' Feast of Unleavened Bread. ... On the second day of the feast, the first fruits of the year's harvest were presented before God. ...

"Fifty days from the offering of first fruits, came the Pentecost. ... As an expression of gratitude for the grain prepared as food, two loaves baked with leaven were presented before God."—*"Patriarchs and Prophets,"* pp. 539, 540.

This putting in of the sickle on the second day of the feast was called among the Jewish people עֹמֶר (*omer*). From the first day of omer to the last day of omer was seven full weeks. The day following the last day of omer was Pentecost. The orthodox Jewish people to this day count the omer. The entire period, counting from the second day of the Passover, is called "counting the omer."

Pentecost, the Feast of Harvest, represented a beautiful symbolic truth:

"Christ arose from the dead as the first fruits of those that slept. He was the antitype of the wave sheaf, and His resurrection took place on the very day when the wave sheaf was to be presented before the Lord. For more than a thousand years this symbolic ceremony had been performed. From the harvest fields the first heads of ripened grain were gathered, and when the people went up to Jerusalem to the Passover, the sheaf of first fruits was waved as a thank offering before the Lord. Not until this was presented, could the sickle be put to the grain, and it be gathered into sheaves. The sheaf dedicated to God represented the harvest. So Christ the first fruits represented the great spiritual harvest to be gathered for the kingdom of God. His resurrection is the type and pledge of the resurrection of all the righteous dead."—"*The Desire of Ages,*" pp. 785, 786.

What an encouragement it was to the Saviour as well as to the disciples, on that memorable day of Pentecost, to see as a result of the outpouring of the Holy Spirit, three thousand souls gathered into the garner of the Lord. This, too, was an ingathering of souls from the seed sowing of our Lord during His three and one-half years of ministry among men.

There is a long-cherished belief among the Jewish people that it was on the day of Pentecost that the Lord gave His law to Israel on Mt. Sinai.

The Feast of Tabernacles was celebrated following the observance of the Day of Atonement. "This feast acknowledged God's bounty in the products of the orchard, the olive grove, and the vineyard. It was the crowning festal gathering of the year. The land had yielded its increase, the harvests had been gathered into the granaries, . . . and now the people came with their tributes of thanksgiving to God, who had thus richly blessed them."—"*Patriarchs and Prophets,*" p. 540.

"Jesus was in the court of the temple specially connected with the services of the Feast of Tabernacles. In the center of this court rose two lofty standards, supporting lamp stands of great size. After the evening sacrifice, all the lamps were kindled, shedding their light over Jerusalem. This ceremony was in commemoration of the pillar of light that guided Israel in the desert, and was also regarded as pointing to the coming of the Messiah. At evening when the lamps were lighted, the court was a scene of great rejoicing. Gray-haired men, the priests of the temple and the rulers of the people, united in the festive dances to the sound of instrumental music and the chants of the Levites.

"In the illumination of Jerusalem, the people expressed their hope of the Messiah's coming to shed His light upon Israel. But to Jesus the scene had a wider meaning. As the radiant lamps of the temple lighted up all about them, so Christ, the source of spiritual light, illumines the darkness of the world. . . . That great light which His own hand had set in the heavens was a truer representation of the glory of His mission."—"*The Desire of Ages,*" p. 463.

3. In what place did God specify that these feasts should be observed? Deut. 16:5-16; 6:1, 2.

That the wilderness was not intended to be a permanent location for the Israelites, is evident from the instruction given to that people in regard to the offering of the sacrifices in connection with these holy gatherings:

"Thou mayest not sacrifice the Passover within any of thy gates, which the Lord thy God giveth thee: but at the place which the Lord thy God shall choose to place His name in, there thou shalt sacrifice." Deut. 16:5, 6.

God had in mind a specific location where these holy seasons were to be observed, and where the offerings were to be sacrificed unto Him. For it is written: "When ye go over Jordan, and dwell in the land which the Lord your God giveth you to inherit, . . . then there shall be a place which the Lord your God shall choose to cause His name to dwell there; thither shall ye bring all that I command you; your burnt offerings, and your sacrifices, your tithes, and the heave offering of your hand, and all your choice vows which ye vow unto the Lord." Deut. 12:10, 11. (See also verse 21.)

This place of God's choice was Jerusalem, for we read in regard to the Holy City: Unto his son will I give one tribe, that David My servant may have a light alway before Me in Jerusalem, the city which I have chosen Me to put My name there." 1 Kings 11:36.

For well-nigh fifteen centuries people of all nationalities and languages repaired to the Holy City, Jerusalem, to worship the true God. Jerusalem was the one place where the service of the true God was carried on. Matt. 2:1; John 12:20; Acts 8:27. The Saviour, however, told the woman at the well of Sychar that the day was coming when that city would not be the only place where men might worship God. John 4:20-24.

THE CHILDREN OF ISRAEL CROSSING THE JORDAN RIVER INTO THE PROMISED LAND

4. What command was given in regard to the offering of sacrifices at these holy convocations? Num. 28:16-31; 29:1-5.

Many sacrifices must be offered at the time of these holy convocations. On each day during the feasts, in addition to the regular daily sacrifice, there must be made a variety of offerings. The number of sacrifices increased or diminished each day during the holiday season. This was particularly true of the Feast of Tabernacles. (See Num. 29:12-38.)

The Feast of Tabernacles was observed in connection with the dedication of the temple by King Solomon. (See 1 Kings 8:62-66; 2 Chron. 7:8.) At the time of the dedication, the king offered more than 140,000 sacrifices, besides the offerings sacrificed during the following eight days. (See 1 Kings 8:62-65; 2 Chron. 7:4-9.)

"Then king and people offered sacrifices before the Lord. 'So the king and all the people dedicated the house of God.' For seven days the multitudes from every part of the kingdom . . . kept a joyous feast. The week following was spent by the happy throng in observing the Feast of Tabernacles."—*"Prophets and Kings,"* page 45.

5. Although God instituted the sacrificial system, did He always accept these offerings? Isa. 1:11-15.

It is evident that, in giving to the Israelites the system of sacrifices and festivals, the Lord intended to make these gifts acceptable, in view of their purpose and objective. Concerning Abraham's experience in offering up his son, the Spirit of prophecy makes the following observation:

"Abraham learned of God the greatest lesson ever given to mortal. His prayer that he might see Christ before he should die was answered. He saw Christ; he saw all that mortal can see, and live. . . . He was shown that in giving His only-begotten Son to save sinners from eternal ruin, God was making a greater and more wonderful sacrifice than ever man could make.

"Abraham's experience answered the question: 'Wherewith shall I come before the Lord, and bow myself before the high God? shall I come before Him with burnt offerings, with calves of a year old? Will the Lord be pleased with thousands of rams, or with ten thousands of rivers of oil? shall I give my first-born for my transgression, the fruit of my body for the sin of my soul?' In the words of Abraham, 'My son, God will provide Himself a lamb for a burnt offering,' and in God's provision of a sacrifice instead of Isaac, it was declared that no man could make expiation for himself. . . . The Son of God alone can bear the guilt of the world."—*"The Desire of Ages,"* p. 469.

6. Why were these divinely ordained offerings not always pleasing to the Lord? Isa. 66:3, 4; Lam. 2:6.

When sacrifices were offered up to God at a time when all manner of sins and crimes were resting upon the worshiper, these symbols and object lessons were not pleasing to the Lord. They were of no value. God could not accept such worship.

These divinely ordained services had been degraded to such a low level that to the worshiper it made little difference whether he was offering a sacrifice to God or killing a man. God did not want men to shed blood. The Lord expressly commanded: "Thou shalt not kill." When men offered to God sacrifices which were to represent the great sacrifice of Messiah, and at the same time they committed murder and had no compunction of conscience for their evil deeds, how could the Lord accept their gifts?

The "weeping prophet" Jeremiah said: "He hath violently taken away His tabernacle, . . . and hath despised in the indignation of His anger the king and the priest." Lam. 2:6. How could the Lord be pleased with such a degenerate service?

7. Did the worshipers always appreciate the significance of these sacrifices? Isa. 43:22-24.

The Lord planned that when they came to worship Him with the sacrifices, the people should appreciate Heaven's great gift in making such provision for their salvation. He commanded the Israelites to bring to Him sweet spices, fragrant incense, and other gifts of love and appreciation.

God does not need man's gifts; all things belong to the Lord. He desired that the people should call upon Him in a reverential and godly manner, in view of what He had promised to do for His children. What pleasure the Lord took when Noah offered those sacrifices after the patriarch left the ark! While Noah knew it would be some time before the flocks would multiply, he expressed deep gratitude of heart by offering to the Lord what must have meant a sacrifice to himself. Noah appreciated heaven's gifts. He sensed the meaning and the value of sacrifices.

"In the joy of their release, Noah did not forget Him by whose gracious care they had been preserved. His first act after leaving the ark was to build an altar, and offer from every kind of clean beast and fowl a sacrifice, thus manifesting his gratitude to God for deliverance, and his faith in Christ, the great sacrifice. This offering was pleasing to the Lord."—*"Patriarchs and Prophets,"* pp. 105, 106.

8. In what manner did the people pervert the divine plan in the use of these offerings? 1 Sam. 15:8, 9, 13-15, 22, 23.

Under the guise of devotion and loyalty, the people perverted the use of the sacrificial system by various subterfuges and by treacherous conduct. King Saul falsified to the prophet Samuel several times under the pretext that he had reserved some of the finest cattle to offer for sacrifice unto the Lord. The prophet answered the monarch pointedly: "Hath the Lord as great delight in burnt offerings and sacrifices, as in obeying the voice of the Lord? Behold, to obey is better than sacrifice, and to hearken than the fat of rams." 1 Sam. 15:22.

There never would have been need of a Saviour, whom these sacrifices represented, if man had always been obedient. The prophet Isaiah expressed the principle of rectitude in preference to sacrifices when he wrote for God: "I the Lord love judgment, I hate robbery for burnt offering; and I will direct their work in truth." Isa. 61:8.

"When, in direct violation of God's command, Saul proposed to present a sacrifice of that which God had devoted to destruction, open contempt was shown for the divine authority. The service would have been an insult to Heaven."—*Id.,* p. 634.

9. Did the priests always assume a right attitude toward these offerings? 1 Sam. 2:11-17, 27-34; 2 Chron. 36:14.

The priests, the ministers of the Lord, the responsible men chosen to represent God and the meaning of the sacredness of these holy services, did not always assume a right attitude toward the Lord's sacrificial system. The Lord had made ample provision for the needs of the priests and their families. Because the priest was to represent Messiah in His ministry, the people for whom the priest ministered were encouraged to be liberal with these consecrated servants of God. The priests were liberally and generously provided with gifts and offerings. They were given the choice portions of the sacrifices for their use.

The sons of Eli the priest had so grossly and perniciously perverted the purposes of God in the use of the sacrifices that the Lord said: "The sin of the young men was very great: . . . for men abhorred the offering of the Lord." 1 Sam. 2:17.

So awful was the sin of these young men, and such disgrace had they brought upon God's cause by the attitude they assumed toward God's sacred offerings, that through the child Samuel a message came from heaven to the head of the priesthood: "The iniquity of Eli's house shall not be purged with sacrifice nor offering forever." 1 Sam. 3:14.

10. What did the Lord say would eventually become of the feasts and of the sacrifices? Hosea 2:11.

In the days of Isaiah and Jeremiah the prophets, the feasts and the sacrifices had become so degenerated and perverted from their right uses that the Lord cried out against the abuses by these messengers of God. "To what purpose cometh there to Me incense from Sheba, and the sweet cane from a far country?

your burnt offerings are not acceptable, nor your sacrifices sweet unto Me."
Jer. 6:20. "I hate, I despise your feast days, and I will not smell in your solemn
assemblies," cried the Lord through the prophet Amos. Amos 5:21, 22.

Through the prophets the Lord had repeatedly admonished and counseled
the people to reform their ways, and to give their hearts to the Lord that their
worship and their sacrifices might be acceptable. The children of Abraham
finally were told that all their joy in these holy convocations would cease, and
that their feasts would come to an end.

11. What became of the sanctuary and the sacrificial system during
the Babylonian exile? 2 Chron. 36:15-21; Ps. 137:1-4; Dan. 9:16, 17.

During the seventy years of the Babylonian exile, the sanctuary lay desolate,
Jerusalem was in ruins, the priests were either killed or carried away into captivity, and the sacrificial system was temporarily suspended.

How Jeremiah wept for the terrible catastrophe which had overtaken the
worship and service of God! He says: "The Lord hath cast off His altar, He
hath abhorred His sanctuary." "I called for my lovers, but they deceived me: my
priests and mine elders gave up the ghost in the city." "For the sins of her
prophets, and the iniquities of her priests, that have shed the blood of the just in
the midst of her, they have wandered as blind men in the streets." "The anger
of the Lord hath divided them; He will no more regard them: they respected
not the persons of the priests, they favored not the elders." "For these things I
weep; mine eye, mine eye runneth down with water, because the comforter that
should relieve my soul is far from me." Lam. 2:7; 1:19; 4:13, 14, 16; 1:16.

When the people were asked in their exile to recall the songs of Zion, to sing
those joyful melodies they chanted on the feast days, those sweet strains they
used at the time of the offering of the sacrifices, they could not respond. "How
shall we sing the Lord's song in a strange land?" they said. Ps. 137:4.

12. Did the Lord give the people assurance that the sacrificial system
would be restored at the close of the seventy years' exile? Jer. 29:10-
14; Ps. 126:1-4.

Before the Israelites were taken captive by the Babylonians, the Lord assured
them that He would give them another opportunity to serve Him in their own
city. They were promised that they should return to the land of their fathers
at the close of their exile. The godly among the people moaned and sighed during
those seventy years, because they were unable to worship the Lord as they had
been taught. Since they were not in the holy Land of Promise, they were unable
to engage in sacrificial worship. This was a great sorrow to them. But the people
were not left hopeless.

"God left not to hopeless despair the faithful remnant who were still in the
city. Even while Jeremiah was kept under close surveillance by those who
scorned his messages, there came to him fresh revelations concerning Heaven's
willingness to forgive and to save."—*"Prophets and Kings,"* p. 466.

"Humbled in the sight of the nations, those who once had been recognized
as favored of Heaven . . . were to learn in exile the lesson of obedience so necessary
for their future happiness. . . . Those who had been the object of His tender love
were not forever set aside; before all the nations of earth He would demonstrate
His plan to bring victory out of apparent defeat, to save rather than to destroy."—
Id., p. 475.

13. What would be the final results of the sacrificial system and the
sanctuary services if the people failed in carrying out God's will? Jer.
17:21-27.

Many beautiful and outstanding promises were made to the people of God,
if they would only be true and faithful to God and to His message. They were

encouraged to believe that the Holy City would remain forever; that the sacrifices would continue; that the kingdom would go on endlessly; that the Sabbath of the Lord would be the mark of their distinction as the choice of God; that great joy and happiness would be the lot of that people.

If, however, they refused to obey the Lord's commands, if they continued to violate the Sabbath of Jehovah, the city of Jerusalem would be destroyed by a great fire.

Jerusalem was destroyed. The Lord also fulfilled His promise in restoring the people to their own land. They had the privilege of seeing the temple rebuilt, and the sacrifices once more established. The godly of the leaders so recognized the abounding mercy of God in His dealing with the people that Ezra in one of his prayers said: "Should we again break Thy commandments, and join in affinity with the people of these abominations? wouldst not Thou be angry with us till Thou hadst consumed us, so that there should be no remnant nor escaping?" Ezra 9:14.

On their return to the land of their fathers, the sacrificial system had become so despicable in the eyes of priests and people that the Lord was obliged to say to them: "A son honoreth his father, and a servant his master: if then I be a father, where is Mine honor? and if I be a master, where is My fear? saith the Lord of hosts unto you, O priests, that despise My name. And ye say, Wherein have we despised Thy name? Ye offer polluted bread upon Mine altar; and ye say, Wherein have we polluted Thee? In that ye say, The table of the Lord is contemptible? And if ye offer the blind for sacrifice, is it not evil? and if ye offer the lame and sick, is it not evil? offer it now unto thy governor; will he be pleased with thee, or accept thy person? saith the Lord of hosts." Mal. 1:6-8.

The people refused even to close the doors of the temple for the service of God. The whole system had become commercialized. The service of God was profaned and polluted. The sacrificial system, ordained as a sacred and divine institution for the conduct of the true worship of the God of heaven, was despised. The priesthood at the time of Christ's advent on earth had become so vile and degraded that Josephus, the Jewish historian, wrote of the high priesthood as follows:

"Hereupon they sent for one of the pontifical tribes, which is called Eniachim, and cast lots which of it should be the high priest. By fortune the lot so fell as to demonstrate their iniquity after the plainest manner, for it fell upon one whose name was Phannias, the son of Samuel, of the village Aphtha. He was a man not only unworthy of the high priesthood, but that did not well know what the high priesthood was, such a mere rustic was he, yet did they hale this man, without his own consent, out of the country, as if they were acting a play upon the stage, and adorned him with a counterfeit face; they also put upon him the sacred garments, and upon every occasion instructed him what he was to do. This horrid piece of wickedness was sport and pastime with them, but occasioned the other priests . . . to shed tears, and sorely lament the dissolution of such a sacred dignity."—*"The Wars of the Jews,"* book 4, chap. 3, par. 8.

God, seeing what the condition of the people would be following the return from the exile, and foreseeing how they would deport themselves in the ministry of the sacrifice and the temple services, sent a message by the angel Gabriel to the prophet Daniel, telling the time when Messiah should make His advent. Following His earthly ministry, Messiah would be cut off. After Messiah was rejected and cut off, the city and the sanctuary would be destroyed. The sacrifices and the oblations would cease, and never again would the sacrificial system of offerings be revived. During the period of the seventy times seven years (seventy weeks, Dan. 9:24) which were cut off the Jewish people, the transgression would be finished. He would make an end of sins. The Hebrew rendering of the two expressions just mentioned, "to finish the transgression" and "to make an end of sins," is לְכַלֵּא הַפֶּשַׁע וּלַחְתֹּם חַטָּאוֹת וּלְכַפֵּר עָוֹן (*lekalle happesha ulechathem chattawth ulekapper awon*), "to seal up sin offerings, and to forgive sins." When Messiah died on the cross, the sin offerings were finished. The sacrifices were completed and came to an end. By the death of the Son of God, forgiveness of sins, through the great Sacrifice, became an actuality.

"The Holy Spirit through Isaiah, taking up the illustration, prophesied of the Saviour, 'He is brought as a lamb to the slaughter,' 'and the Lord hath laid on Him the iniquity of us all;' but the people of Israel had not understood the lesson. Many of them regarded the sacrificial offerings much as the heathen looked upon their sacrifices,—as gifts by which they themselves might propitiate the Deity. God desired to teach them, that from His own love comes the gift which reconciles them to Himself."—*The Desire of Ages,*" pp. 112, 113.

"Christ was the foundation and life of the temple. Its services were typical of the sacrifice of the Son of God. The priesthood was established to represent the mediatorial character and work of Christ. The entire plan of sacrificial worship was a foreshadowing of the Saviour's death to redeem the world. There would be no efficacy in these offerings when the great event toward which they had pointed for ages was consummated.

"Since the whole ritual economy was symbolical of Christ, it had no value apart from Him. When the Jews sealed their rejection of Christ by delivering Him to death, they rejected all that gave significance to the temple and its services. Its sacredness had departed. It was doomed to destruction. From that day sacrificial offerings and the service connected with them were meaningless. . . . When Christ was crucified, the inner veil of the temple was rent in twain from top to bottom, signifying that the great final sacrifice had been made, and that the system of sacrificial offerings was forever at an end."—*Id.,* p. 165.

"Christ was standing at the point of transition between two economies, and their two great festivals. He, the spotless Lamb of God, was about to present Himself as a sin offering, and He would thus bring to an end the system of types and ceremonies that for four thousand years had pointed to His death."—*Id.,* p. 652.

God's Outstanding Purpose in the Gift of the Scriptures

1. WHAT book of the Bible was the eunuch reading when the evangelist Philip met him by the way? Acts 8:26-28.

In ancient times the Bible was not printed in a book as it is now. The Scriptures formerly were written on parchment by a class of people called scribes. The Hebrew word for scribes is סֹפְרִים (sophrim). While this word sophrim originally meant "books," later it was used also for the person who wrote the books. It is claimed that Ezra was one of the first who belonged to this class. The Scriptures say of Ezra that he was a "scribe, even a scribe of the words of the commandments of the Lord, and of His statutes to Israel." Ezra 7:11.

Each prophet's production was written by itself. Those writings were not carried by the people in bulk. The believers were able to secure the particular writings of a certain prophet. The message of the seer was conveniently obtained, written with a quill pen on parchment. So if a man were financially able, he could employ the scribes to prepare for him the writings of several prophets.

The Ethiopians are mentioned in the Scriptures as manifesting interest in the teaching of God's word. When the queen of Ethiopia heard in her country of the magnificence of the temple of God erected by King Solomon, she journeyed to Jerusalem with a train of servants to make personal investigation. She herself reported her findings in these words: "It was a true report that I heard in mine own land of thy acts and of thy wisdom. Howbeit I believed not the words, until I came, and mine eyes had seen it: and, behold, the half was not told me. . . . Blessed be the Lord thy God, which delighted in thee, to set thee on the throne of Israel: because the Lord loved Israel forever, therefore made He thee king, to do judgment and justice." 1 Kings 10:6-9.

It was an Ethiopian servant who saved the life of Jeremiah the prophet when Zedekiah's princes lowered him into the dungeon and left him to die. "Now when Ebed-melech [the words עֶבֶד מֶלֶךְ (Ebed Melek) are Hebrew, and they mean "servant of the king"] the Ethiopian, one of the eunuchs which was in the king's house, heard that they had put Jeremiah in the dungeon, . . . Ebed-melech went forth out of the king's house, and spake to the king, saying, . . . These men have done evil in all that they have done to Jeremiah the prophet, . . . and he is like to die . . . where he is. . . . Then the king commanded Ebed-melech the Ethiopian, saying, Take from hence thirty men with thee, and take up Jeremiah the prophet out of the dungeon, before he die." Jer. 38:7-10.

Because of his intervention in saving Jeremiah's life, the following message came to the Ethiopian: "Now the word of the Lord came unto Jeremiah, while he was shut up in the court of the prison, saying, Go and speak to Ebed-melech the Ethiopian, saying, Thus saith the Lord of hosts, the God of Israel: Behold, I will bring My words upon this city for evil. . . . But I will deliver thee in that day, saith the Lord: and thou shalt not be given into the hand of the men of whom thou art afraid. . . . And thou shalt not fall by the sword, . . . because thou hast put thy trust in Me, saith the Lord." Jer. 39:15-18.

The Ethiopians had great respect for the words of the prophets, and God honored them for this reverence.

It was necessary for all peoples to go to Jerusalem to worship the true God.

2. What question did Philip ask of the eunuch? Verses 29, 30.

3. How did the eunuch reply to Philip's question? Verse 31.

The leaders of Israel claimed that none were able to understand the Scriptures except those who had been educated in the rabbinical schools. These schools were open to Jewish youth, although those of other nations were permitted to enter such institutions, provided these applicants harmonized with the multitudinous requirements of the rabbinical theologians.

Class distinction developed so rapidly that a vicious antipathy existed between the learned and the illiterate. The uneducated people were called עם הארצים (*am haratsim*), "men of the earth," unlearned, rustics. The rabbis in Christ's day had created such an ill feeling against those who were not educated in the rabbinical schools that the Talmud has recorded strange teachings of the Pharisees against the unlearned. In the Talmudic tract, "Pesachim," we read: "Said Rabbi Eleazar: 'It is permissible to split the nostrils of an illiterate man on the Day of Atonement which occurs on the Sabbath.'"

In a volume entitled, "The Old Paths," we find the following quotation from the Talmud: "Our rabbis have advocated: A man should sell all his possessions, and marry the daughter of an educated person. If he cannot find such a person, let him marry the daughter of one of the great men of the time. . . . If he cannot find such a person, let him marry the daughter of an almoner. If he cannot find such a person, let him marry the daughter of a schoolmaster. But let him not marry the daughter of the unlearned, for they are an abomination, and their wives are vermin; and of their daughters it is said, 'Cursed is he that lieth with a beast'"!

The Scriptures also express the attitude of the Pharisees against those who failed to take a rabbinical theological course. The Saviour was criticized for not attending the popular religious schools. "How knoweth this man letters, having never learned?" John 7:15.

"The question asked during the Saviour's ministry, 'How knoweth this man letters, having never learned?' does not indicate that Jesus was unable to read, but merely that He had not received a rabbinical education."—*The Desire of Ages*," p. 70.

"All wondered at His knowledge of the law and the prophecies; and the question passed from one to another, 'How knoweth this man letters, having never learned?' No one was regarded as qualified to be a religious teacher unless he had studied in the rabbinical schools, and both Jesus and John the Baptist had been represented as ignorant because they had not received this training. Those who heard them were astonished at their knowledge of the Scriptures, 'having never learned.' Of men they had not, truly; but the God of heaven was their teacher."—*Id.*, p. 453.

Again we read: "Have any of the rulers or of the Pharisees believed on Him? But this people who knoweth not the law are cursed." John 7:48, 49.

"Then they reviled him, and said, Thou art His disciple; but we are Moses' disciples. . . . Thou wast altogether born in sins, and dost thou teach us? And they cast him out." John 9:28-34.

This Ethiopian admitted that he could not interpret Scripture. He was not a product of rabbinical learning, but his heart was hungry for the truth. God's Spirit led Philip to instruct him.

4. What portion of Scripture was the Ethiopian treasurer reading? Verses 32, 33; Isa. 53:7, 8.

5. How was the eunuch's interest aroused as he read the sacred scroll? Verse 34.

During the period of the ministry of John the Baptist and of Christ, the writings of the prophet Isaiah had been freely and openly discussed. John told the delegation sent to him by the Sanhedrin that he was fulfilling the "voice" of Isaiah 40:3. John 1:19-23. On a number of occasions the Saviour cited the prophecies of Isaiah, and showed their fulfillment in His mission and teaching. Matt. 8:17; 12:17-19.

At the time of the eunuch's visit to the Holy City, Jerusalem was agitated and stirred by the thousands of Jewish believers who had accepted the Messiah. Without doubt the prophecies of Isaiah were freely discussed. The fifty-third chapter of his prophecy is so outstanding in regard to the treatment and sacrifice of the Saviour, that public sentiment gave heed to those scriptures. This eunuch, an honest man, was looking for light on the passages he was reading, and the Lord sent to him the right man at the right time to give him the correct understanding of the scriptures.

"An angel guided Philip to the one who was seeking for light, and who was ready to receive the gospel; and today angels will guide the footsteps of those workers who will allow the Holy Spirit to sanctify their tongues and refine and ennoble their hearts. The angel sent to Philip could himself have done the work for the Ethiopian, but this is not God's way of working. It is His plan that men are to work for their fellow men."—*"Acts of the Apostles,"* p. 109.

6. What was Philip's response to the Ethiopian's question? Verse 35.

It would appear from Philip's reply to the eunuch that the thirty-fifth verse of this chapter of Acts is one of the key texts of the Bible. The reason for its being a key text is that it unlocks the real purpose of God in the giving of the Holy Scriptures. The Christ of God, the Messiah of heaven, the Holy One of Israel, the Redeemer of mankind, the Deliverer from the woes and sorrows of a lost race,—He is the outstanding message of the whole Bible.

"In every page, whether history, or precept, or prophecy, the Old Testament Scriptures are irradiated with the glory of the Son of God. So far as it was of divine institution, the entire system of Judaism was a compacted prophecy of the gospel. To Christ 'give all the prophets witness.' From the promise given to Adam, down through the patriarchal line and the legal economy, heaven's glorious light made plain the footsteps of the Redeemer. Seers beheld the Star of Bethlehem, the Shiloh to come, as future things swept before them in mysterious procession. In every sacrifice, Christ's death was shown. In every cloud of incense His righteousness ascended. By every jubilee trumpet His name was sounded. In the awful mystery of the holy of holies His glory dwelt."—*"The Desire of Ages,"* pp. 211, 212.

"The miracles of Christ are a proof of His divinity; but a stronger proof that He is the world's Redeemer is found in comparing the prophecies of the Old Testament with the history of the New."—*Id.*, p. 799.

7. When the Saviour met His perplexed disciples on the way to Emmaus, how did He show them that He was the foundation of the Scriptures? Luke 24:27, 44, 45.

The Saviour adopted an unusual method to convince the disciples that He had risen from the dead, and that He was Jesus the Messiah. Those men could easily have been convinced that this was the One who had been with them during the three and a half years, by seeing the wounds made in His hands, the nail prints in His feet, the scar in His side. These outward tokens would have made a deep impression on these men, and they would have been satisfied. This is exactly what doubting Thomas demanded. But it is not possible for the Lord always to be present in person in order to convince each individual that He is the Son of God.

The Lord was thinking of the unborn millions of future generations who must hear the gospel of salvation. They, too, must have indisputable evidence that Jesus lived, died, and rose again from the dead. The people of the future must be convinced, persuaded, and assured that the same Jesus who walked the streets of Galilee, who went about doing good, who wrought mighty miracles for the children of men, is indeed the Messiah of prophecy, the promised Saviour of mankind. The evidence which the disciples on the way to Emmaus would receive must be of such a nature that it would satisfy the millions of tomorrow.

And what better evidence could our Lord give to them that He is the Sent of God, than to point to the writings of the Scriptures? Jesus began at Moses. Why did He begin with Israel's prophet fifteen centuries before?—Because Moses wrote of Him. Had there been inspired writings antedating those of Moses, doubtless the Saviour would have begun with them. Moses was the first person who penned the Sacred Writings, and Moses was quoted to satisfy the disciples that this man was the Messiah of God.

8. What did Jesus tell the Jewish leaders in regard to the relation He bore to the Scriptures? John 5:39.

The Jewish leaders certainly did search the Scriptures. They were diligent students of the Old Testament. According to the Talmudic requirement, a child who was preparing for the rabbinate must begin to study the Scriptures when he was five years old. There were those among the Pharisees who were able to quote the entire Bible. Such an accomplishment was not an unusual experience in Christ's day. There are today, among the devout orthodox Jews, those who are able to quote the entire Old Testament from memory. The writer, when a lad, knew of leaders for whom it was claimed that they could reproduce all the writings of Moses and the prophets, and in addition could recite large portions of rabbinical works, without having recourse to a book. Hours and days they would spend in the study of the Scriptures. This duty was incumbent upon them as leaders of the people, for no rabbi or wise leader in Israel must fail to reply to any question of Scripture asked of him. Yet the real value and purpose of the Scriptures few of them understood. The scholars maintained that the sacred scrolls had more than one meaning. Due to the rabbis' having made contact with Greek philosophy and learning, the leaders introduced a more liberal interpretation of the Scriptures. First it was asserted that the Scriptures could be interpreted in at least four different ways. These ways of interpretation were named: *Peshat*, the simple way; *Remez*, the allegorical or parabolic way; *Derush*, the spiritual way; *Sod*, the secret way. From the first letters of these four words, the acrostic PaRDeS was formed, hence the word "Paradise." Scripture was like a garden: A garden has a variety of flowers and blossoms; the Holy Writings have a variety of interpretations. One, Rabbi Ishmael, introduced the thirteen rules of interpretation, whereas Rabbi Jose, of Galilee, insisted that there were thirty-two rules of interpretation. The Talmud says Scripture may be interpreted in forty-nine different modes. To gain everlasting life, the rabbis taught, one must be acquainted with the words of life as given by Moses. Yet they did not perceive or know that Christ, the Messiah, was the heart of all the prophets. They were ignorant of the real purpose of the Scriptures.

9. If the scribes and Pharisees had really accepted the Old Testament Scriptures, of what would they have been convinced? Verses 45-47.

From their viewpoint, no greater insult could have been heaped upon the Sanhedrin than for the Saviour to accuse them of not believing Moses. Their faith in Moses' writings was boundless. They taught that every word, even every letter, of the writings of Moses, was inspired of God. The rabbis pronounced anathemas and excommunications against those who denied any portion of the writings of Moses. Israel's leaders taught that the traditions and comments on Moses' laws were also inspired.

Nevertheless, those sages knew not the voice nor the spirit of Moses. Had they really believed Moses, they surely would have believed Christ. They did not have the vision of the Saviour.

10. What wise counsel did Paul give to Timothy as to the real value of the Scriptures? 2 Tim. 3:15.

When that proud Pharisee, Saul of Tarsus, caught the vision of the Saviour, he sensed that Christ was found in the writings of Moses. He said: "Having therefore obtained help of God, I continue unto this day, witnessing both to small and great, saying none other things than those which the prophets and Moses did say should come: That Christ should suffer, and that He should be the first that should rise from the dead." Acts 26:22, 23.

"By faith Moses . . . refused to be called the son of Pharaoh's daughter, . . . esteeming the reproach of Christ greater riches than the treasures in Egypt." Heb. 11:24, 26.

"It was Christ who had spoken to Israel through Moses. If they had listened to the divine voice that spoke through their great leader, they would have recognized it in the teachings of Christ. Had they believed Moses, they would have believed Him of whom Moses wrote."—*"The Desire of Ages,"* p. 213.

11. If it were not for God's desire to reveal Christ, would there have been any need of the gift of the Scriptures? John 5:39, 40; 10:10; 5:20-23, 26-29; 10:17, 18.

Old Testament Prophecies and Symbols Illuminated by the New Testament

1. To whom does King David give credit for all he wrote? 2 Sam. 23:1, 2.

Jewish writers claimed there were four degrees of inspiration. The purest inspiration is the decalogue. The next in quality is the Pentateuch, the five books of Moses. The third is the prophets. The fourth degree of inspiration is the writings of the Scriptures, called in Hebrew כתובים (kethubim), "writings." These writings include the following books: Psalms, Proverbs, Job, Song of Solomon, Ruth, Lamentations, Ecclesiastes, Esther, Daniel, Ezra, Nehemiah.

In addition to the four degrees of divine inspiration, the rabbis invented a substitute for inspiration called בת קול (bath qol), "the daughter of a voice."

The fact is that all Scripture is inspired of God. Neither the Old Testament nor the New Testament differentiates in degrees of inspiration. The Spirit of God spoke in and through men. David declares the Spirit of God spoke by him; God's word was in his tongue. The titles to the psalms are part of the psalms, and were written by David himself.

2. What witnesses confirm the foregoing testimony of the psalmist of Israel? Mark 12:35, 36; Acts 1:16; 4:25.

The New Testament writers bear witness that David was inspired of God. Jesus bears testimony that David wrote by the Holy Ghost. The Saviour quotes the very words of Psalms 110:1, and adds: "David therefore himself calleth Him Lord." Mark 12:37. The people in the days of Jesus had unbounded confidence in the writings of David. He was the nation's ideal king and warrior. He was endeared to the people. The Saviour knew that what He said of Israel's psalmist would be accepted by the multitude. Mark gives the people's approval of the Saviour's remarks: "The common people heard Him gladly."

3. What did David prophetically write of Christ's advent? Ps. 40:6-8; 45:6, 7.

Men in Old Testament times wrote under the inspiration of God much that at the time they did not comprehend. The apostle Peter tells us that the prophets themselves inquired and diligently searched their own writings to understand what had been revealed to them. Daniel studied the writings of other prophets, in order to get light on the revelations given to him.

It is true that prophecies given by the writers involved some of their own experiences. Yet the instruction they left on record comprehended more than their own experience.

There are numbers of scriptures which have been difficult for Jewish writers to explain because those writings had no special bearing either on the one who delivered the message or on the people who lived at that time.

Psalms 40:6-8 does not apply to David. This is particularly true of verse 7. In what book can be found the record of David's coming? David was not known until the time the prophet Samuel was told by the Lord to go to Bethlehem and anoint one of Jesse's sons to be successor to King Saul. From then on, and for nearly seventeen years, David fled from Saul to save his life. For a time David was an outcast from the congregation of Israel. Not until King Saul died was much prominence given to David. Then David took the reins of government over the twelve tribes, and Israel developed into a powerful monarchy. In what volume was David's coming foretold?

Numerous stories, legends, deductions, and explanations are suggested by Talmudic teachers of this scripture in the fortieth psalm, but no satisfactory explanation of this verse can be given if it is applied to King David.

While Jewish writers seek to explain Psalms 45:6, 7, by saying these verses apply to King Hezekiah, there is nothing found in history which makes these scriptures fit into Hezekiah's career.

4. What New Testament writer confirms the foregoing prophetic forecasts of our Lord? Heb. 10:5-7; 1:8, 9.

The apostle Paul's application to the Saviour of the two above-mentioned psalms is consistent, fitting. There is no other character in the Bible history in whom they could meet with a fulfillment.

The volume of the Book does make record of Christ, the Son of God. Beginning with Moses, and running through to Malachi, then from Matthew to the Revelation,—in all these books of Holy Writ we find the stately steppings of the divine Lord and Saviour.

5. In the death sentence which was pronounced upon the serpent in the Garden of Eden, was any hope offered to Adam and Eve, and to their descendants? Gen. 3:15; Gal. 3:16, 19; Rom. 16:20.

Before man received the death sentence for his disobedience, God held out to the first pair a comforting hope. Satan had gained control of man when Adam and Eve yielded to the serpent's temptation. 2 Peter 2:19. Yet man's fall was different from that of Satan.

"But even as a sinner, man was in a different position from that of Satan. Lucifer in heaven had sinned in the light of God's glory. To him as to no other created being was given a revelation of God's love. Understanding the character of God, knowing His goodness, Satan chose to follow his own selfish, independent will. This choice was final. There was no more that God could do to save him. But man was deceived; his mind was darkened by Satan's sophistry. The height and depth of the love of God he did not know. For him there was hope in a knowledge of God's love. By beholding His character he might be drawn back to God.

"Through Jesus, God's mercy was manifested to men; but mercy does not set aside justice. The law reveals the attributes of God's character, and not a jot or tittle of it could be changed to meet man in his fallen condition. God did not change His law, but He sacrificed Himself, in Christ, for man's redemption. 'God was in Christ, reconciling the world unto Himself.' "—"The Desire of Ages," pp. 761, 762.

In the promise of the Seed of the woman, man was assured of another probation. The word "it" in Genesis 3:15, is also rendered "He." The Hebrew text is: הוא ישופך ראש (hu yeshupheka rosh), "He will crush thy head." Adam was comforted that "He," the Coming One, would destroy Satan. That Seed of the woman has been the hope of man from the time the promise was given in the garden. In the birth of her first child, Eve thought that the promised Seed who was to crush the serpent's head had come. What a happy hour that would have been to the first pair if that child had been the true Seed! The Seed was promised, but that Seed is Christ. Christ was assured to the race as soon as man needed a Saviour.

6. What veiled prophecy of the Saviour may be seen in Abraham's answer to Isaac's question, "Where is the lamb for a burnt offering?" Gen. 22:7, 8, 13; Heb. 11:17-19; Rom. 4:17-24.

"Abraham had greatly desired to see the promised Saviour. He offered up the most earnest prayer that before his death he might behold the Messiah. And he saw Christ. A supernatural light was given him, and he acknowledged Christ's divine character. He saw His day, and was glad. He was given a view of the divine sacrifice for sin. Of this sacrifice he had an illustration in his own experience.

"The command came to him, 'Take now thy son, thine only son Isaac, whom thou lovest, . . . and offer him . . . for a burnt offering.' Upon the altar of sacrifice he laid the son of promise, the son in whom his hopes were centered. Then as he waited beside the altar, . . . he heard a voice from heaven saying, 'Lay not thine hand upon the lad.' . . . This terrible ordeal was imposed upon Abraham that he might see the day of Christ, and realize the great love of God for the world, so great that to raise it from its degradation, He gave His only-begotten Son to a most shameful death. . . .

"In the words of Abraham, 'My son, God will provide Himself a lamb for a burnt offering,' and in God's provision of a sacrifice instead of Isaac, it was declared that no man could make expiation for himself. . . . Through his own suffering, Abraham was enabled to behold the Saviour's mission of sacrifice." —*"The Desire of Ages,"* pp. 468, 469.

In Genesis 22:8, where, in answer to Isaac's question, Abraham said, "God will provide Himself a lamb," the Hebrew text reads "the lamb," not "a lamb."

7. In whom was fulfilled the prophecy of Jacob, "The scepter shall not depart from Judah until Shiloh come"? Gen. 49:10; Luke 1:31-33; Heb. 7:14.

The majority of the older Jewish commentators acknowledge that Shiloh is Messiah. Among such men are Kimchi, Onkelos, Ben Ganach. Modern commentators are endeavoring to sidetrack the rising generation from that ancient view, for fear some may desire to investigate the meaning of this prophecy of Jacob. Many of the seed of Abraham are today reading and studying Christian literature. The Jewish people are not as estranged from the New Testament as they were formerly. The accepted translation of Genesis 49:10 is being sidestepped, as may be observed by the following:

"It is doubtful if there is a reference to Shiloh in the blessing of Jacob (Gen. 49:10), as the ordinary interpretation assumes: 'as long as [pilgrims] come to Shiloh,' that is, while the sanctuary is established there."—*Jewish Encyclopedia,* Vol. XI, p. 290.

The text of Genesis 49:10 reads: עד כי־יבא שילה (*ad ki-yabo Shiloh*), "till Shiloh comes." There is nothing in the Hebrew text which sanctions the interpretation "as long as [pilgrims] come to Shiloh." The latter portion of this same verse reads: ולו יקהת עמים (*welo yiqhath ammim*), "and to *Him* shall the gathering of the people be." The word *welo,* "and to Him," has reference to a *person.* It is closely related to the word preceding it, "Shiloh." The thought of the text is clear. A *Person* by the name of "Shiloh" will come. When He comes, to Him the people will gather. As has already been stated, many of the ancient writers acknowledged that Shiloh was another name for King Messiah.

To this agrees the angel Gabriel; for when he visited Mary, the angel said to her in regard to the mission of Jesus: "He shall reign over the house of Jacob forever." Luke 1:33.

That divinely enlightened Jew, Saul of Tarsus, also acknowledged Jesus, Messiah, to be the fulfillment of Genesis 49:10. Paul declares: "It is evident that

our Lord sprang out of Judah." Heb. 7:14. From the time of the destruction
of the temple in 70 A.D. till the present hour, no permanent archives have been
preserved of the tribes of Israel, nor of the tribe of Judah. The royal scepter
should be in the hand of Judah till Shiloh came. Nineteen centuries and more
have come and gone. Judah's scepter has passed. For almost twenty centuries,
since the good tidings of Messiah have been heralded to the nations of earth,
wherever men have accepted the good news, they have rallied around the banner
of Immanuel, God with us, Jesus of Nazareth, the Messiah of Israel, the Deliverer
of men. The people have gathered and still are gathering unto Him.

8. Who was in the burning bush when Moses turned aside to see
why the bush was not consumed? Ex. 3:1-6; Acts 7:30-38.

The New Testament illuminates the symbolic teachings of the Old Testament. Referring to the experience of Moses at the burning bush, the apostle
Peter says:

"This is he, that was in the church in the wilderness with the Angel which
spake to him in the Mt. Sina, and with our fathers: who received the lively
oracles to give unto us." Acts 7:38.

The Spirit of prophecy gives added illumination of that experience in the
following language:

"By His humanity, Christ touched humanity; by His divinity, He lays hold
upon the throne of God. As the Son of man, He gave us an example of obedience;
as the Son of God, He gives us power to obey.

"It was Christ who from the bush on Mt. Horeb spoke to Moses saying,
'I AM THAT I AM. . . . Thus shalt thou say unto the children of Israel, I AM
hath sent me unto you.' This was the pledge of Israel's deliverance."—*"The
Desire of Ages,"* p. 24.

"His divinity was veiled with humanity,—the invisible glory in the visible
human form.

"This great purpose had been shadowed forth in types and symbols. The
burning bush, in which Christ appeared to Moses, revealed God. The symbol
chosen for the representation of the Deity was a lowly shrub, that seemingly had
no attraction. This enshrined the Infinite. The all-merciful God shrouded His
glory in a most humble type, that Moses could look upon it and live."—*Id.,* p. 23.

9. Who was foreshadowed in the offering of the paschal lamb? Ex.
12:3, 11; Matt. 26:1, 2; 1 Cor. 5:7; John 19:36; Ex. 12:46.

For fifteen centuries the Jewish race had observed the annual feast of the
Passover. There were periods when it was not observed. This was because
the people had backslidden from God. When prophets or kings introduced
reformations, they invariably commanded the observing of this sacred annual convocation. The Passover was designed to mean much to the people. However,
the significance of this yearly ordinance had been reduced to formal ceremonies.

At the last Passover before the Saviour died, He said to the disciples: "Ye
know that after two days is the feast of the Passover, and the Son of man is
betrayed to be crucified." Matt. 26:2.

The leaders tried to hide the fact that they wished to kill Him at this time.
They feared the crowds who gathered in the Holy City to observe this
yearly feast. Nevertheless they took Him, and through the power of Pontius
Pilate, the Roman governor, who signed the Saviour's death warrant, Jesus was
put to death. In one day twenty-five prophecies of the Old Testament met their
fulfillment in Christ. "For even Christ our passover is sacrificed for us." "These
things were done, that the scripture should be fulfilled, A bone of Him shall not
be broken." John 19:36.

"When the loud cry, 'It is finished,' came from the lips of Christ, the priests
were officiating in the temple. It was the hour of the evening sacrifice. The lamb

representing Christ had been brought to be slain. Clothed in his significant and beautiful dress, the priest stood with lifted knife, as did Abraham when he was about to slay his son. With intense interest the people were looking on.

"But the earth trembles and quakes; for the Lord Himself draws near. With a rending noise the inner veil of the temple is torn from top to bottom by an unseen hand, throwing open to the gaze of the multitude a place once filled with the presence of God. In this place the Shekinah had dwelt. Here God had manifested His glory above the mercy seat. No one but the high priest ever lifted the veil separating this apartment from the rest of the temple. He entered in once a year to make an atonement for the sins of the people. But, lo, this veil is rent in twain. The most holy place of the earthly sanctuary is no longer sacred.

"All is terror and confusion. The priest is about to slay the victim; but the knife drops from his nerveless hand, and the lamb escapes. Type has met antitype in the death of God's Son. The great sacrifice has been made."—*The Desire of Ages,*" pp. 756, 757.

10. Of what special significance was the vision seen by Jacob while on his way to his uncle Laban? Gen. 28:12, 13; John 1:51.

It was Jesus Himself who interpreted the significance of the dream of the patriarch Jacob. The ladder Jacob saw in his dream touched earth and reached to heaven. Angels of God ascended and descended upon that ladder. When Nathanael confessed the divinity of Christ by saying, "Rabbi, Thou art the Son of God; Thou art the King of Israel, Jesus answered and said unto him, . . . Verily, verily, I say unto you, Hereafter ye shall see heaven open, and the angels of God ascending and descending upon the Son of man." John 1:49-51.

Christ is the ladder. As Son of God He grasps the throne of Omnipotence; as Son of man He puts His arms about man and draws him to Himself. In Jesus, God and man meet. Heaven and earth will again be united.

"The ladder represents Jesus, the appointed medium of communication. Had He not with His own merits bridged the gulf that sin had made, the ministering angels could have held no communion with fallen man. Christ connected man in his weakness and helplessness with the source of infinite power. All this was revealed to Jacob in his dream."—*Patriarchs and Prophets,*" p. 184.

11. Who does the apostle Paul say was represented by the rock which Moses smote in the wilderness? Ex. 17:6; Num. 20:7-13; 1 Cor. 10:1-4.

How deeply impressed the Israelites must have been as they watched Moses strike the rock, and saw the clear stream of sparkling waters gush forth from its side! What a sad experience came to Israel's great prophet as a result of his disobedience in smiting the rock the second time, when he had been told to speak to the rock! "And that Rock was Christ." The Saviour was to be smitten but once. After He was smitten, every soul who longed for the waters of salvation needed only to speak, and the water of life was given freely.

Of this experience of Moses the psalmist writes: "It went ill with Moses for their sakes: because they provoked his spirit, so that he spake unadvisedly with his lips." Ps. 106:32, 33. That one mistake shut Moses out of the Promised Land.

"By his rash act, Moses took away the force of the lesson that God purposed to teach. The rock, being a symbol of Christ, had been once smitten, as Christ was to be once offered. The second time, it was needful only to speak to the rock, as we have only to ask for blessings in the name of Jesus. By the second smiting of the rock, the significance of this beautiful figure of Christ was destroyed."—*Patriarchs and Prophets,*" p. 418.

12. What does the Saviour say of the serpent Moses lifted up in the wilderness? Num. 21:4-9; John 3:14; 8:28; 12:32.

JACOB'S LADDER REACHING FROM EARTH TO HEAVEN

13. When and in connection with what event did the star appear which was mentioned by Balaam in his prophecy? Num. 24:17; Matt. 2:1, 2.

14. How many ways of salvation did the Lord tell Israel there are? Jer. 6:16; Isa. 43:11; Acts 4:12.

God has one, and only one, way of salvation. The worthies of all ages, the saints of God during all generations, the loyal defenders of.the faith once delivered to the saints, have been saved by the only means which God has provided. Neither is there salvation in any other. It is only by the sacred name of Jesus, Saviour, Redeemer, Holy One of Israel, that man can come to God and be saved.

15. What outstanding prophecy did Moses leave with Israel, telling of a great Prophet to arise in the future? Deut. 18:15, 18; Acts 3: 22-24; 7:37, 38.

LESSON XVII

Christ the Central Theme of the Prophetic Scriptures

1. WHAT was the burden of Peter's message on the day of Pentecost? Acts 2:14-23, 25-31, 34-36.

Jesus told His disciples that the Spirit of God is the Spirit of truth. The Saviour assured His followers that if He left them, He would send to them this blessed Spirit. This Spirit would be their teacher, and the same Spirit would teach them the truth. John 14:17; 16:7, 13.

When the heavenly enduement came upon the disciples on the day of Pentecost, Simon Peter, with the other apostles, arose before the multitudes and opened to the understanding of the people the prophecies of the Scripture. Although the disciples were accused of being intoxicated, the apostle convinced his audience that it was not wine the Christians were filled with, for it was only the third hour of the day.

The Jewish people divided the twenty-four-hour day into two great divisions, —the day, the light part, and the night, the dark part. The light part was subdivided into four sections; namely, the third hour, the sixth hour, the ninth hour, and the evening. The light part of the day began at six o'clock in the morning. The third hour of the day would be 9 A.M. According to the rabbinical law, the devout worshiper must attend the temple or synagogue service on the Feast of Pentecost. The forenoon devotions of this holy convocation did not terminate till the fifth or sixth hour—at about eleven or twelve in the forenoon. The rabbinical law also demanded that no food or strong drink should be indulged in by the worshiper till the close of the morning service.

The disciples who were filled with the Spirit were talking in other tongues. This in itself was a marvel, since they were uneducated Galileans; but in the various languages they were using, they spoke of "the wonderful works of God." Acts 2:11. Since these men were speaking to the praise of God, how could they be intoxicated, wicked men? But they were good men, and even under rabbinical law they could not have used strong drink until the close of the morning services. It was only the third hour of the day, and the day's worship had not ended. Therefore these men, Peter said, could not be drunken.

Peter then opened the Scriptures to his audience, and assured the multitude that what they saw that day was the fulfillment of prophecy. The apostle quoted from the book of Joel, where the people of God were promised the outpouring of the Holy Spirit. That prophecy in Joel had not met its fulfillment before this time. The people believed that sometime that scripture of the prophet would meet a fulfillment. Peter declared that what they were seeing that morning was the fulfillment of Joel's prophecy.

The apostle continued his discourse by quoting from the Psalms. Peter referred to the sixteenth psalm, and convinced his audience that this particular psalm could not have met its fulfillment in King David; for David's sepulcher was in Jerusalem, not far from the temple. Peter's audience knew the location of the tomb of David. They were able, if they chose, to visit the sepulcher, and they could see for themselves that there had been no resurrection of David's body.

Furthermore, the apostle continued, David, because he was among the dead, had not ascended into the heavens. David himself wrote Psalms 110:1, which Peter was then quoting. Climaxing all that he had already quoted, the apostle said that all those scriptures he referred to met their fulfillment in only one person, and that person is Jesus of Nazareth, who had been raised from the dead, who had ascended into the heavens, and who had sat down at the right hand of God. Christ, Peter told that interested audience, is the one about whom David was prophesying when the king of Israel wrote those holy writings. What the people were witnessing that day was evidence that Jesus of Nazareth is Messiah. Jesus assured the disciples before He left them, that if He went away, He would send them the Holy Spirit. Right before them on that occasion the people had the witness that the words of Jesus were then being fulfilled. Jesus now was exalted at the right hand of God, said the apostle. The house of Israel could be assured that the prophecies he quoted had met their fulfillment in Jesus the Messiah. Therefore, said Peter, this Jesus is the Lord and the Christ.

A mighty conviction gripped that great audience as the Spirit of God impressed the congregation that the Spirit of truth was giving them through Simon Peter the true interpretation of those prophecies.

2. Were the inspired messages given to the prophets always intended for the people living at the time the messages were delivered? 1 Peter 1:9-12.

The apostle Peter, in his epistle, clearly shows that the writings of the prophets were not confined to the time when the messengers delivered their messages to the people. The instruction given the divinely appointed prophets was delivered by them, but it was not necessarily intended for them, or for the people alone who lived in that particular generation. Peter declares that the prophets searched to know the meaning of those prophecies which they received, for their writings testified of the coming of the Christ and the glory which was to follow His advent.

This statement made by the apostle covers a period of almost nineteen centuries. Christ suffered for sins at His first advent; Jesus will come in His glory at His second advent. The messages of both advents were revealed to the prophets, but their fulfillment would be understood by the people who should live at the time of the second advent. Many scriptures of the prophets did not meet their fulfillment in days of yore; they met a partial fulfillment at the Saviour's first advent. Still others are meeting their fulfillment at the present time.

"Even the disciples failed of understanding all that Jesus desired to reveal to them; but from time to time, as they surrendered themselves to the Holy Spirit's power, their minds were illuminated. They realized that the mighty God, clad in the garb of humanity, was among them. Jesus rejoiced that though this knowledge was not possessed by the wise and prudent, it had been revealed to these humble men. Often as He had presented the Old Testament Scriptures, and showed their application to Himself and His work of atonement, they had been awakened by His Spirit, and lifted into a heavenly atmosphere. Of the spiritual truths spoken by the prophets they had a clearer understanding than had the original writers themselves."—*"The Desire of Ages,"* p. 494.

3. Did the disciples always understand the prophecies of the Old Testament? John 2:18-22; Luke 24:4-8.

Many of the Old Testament prophecies were not understood by the disciples when the Saviour was with them. The Lord told His disciples that after He had risen from the dead they would understand the Scriptures. The disciples of Christ were influenced by the rabbis and the religious schools of their day. It is evident by the questions they asked the Saviour that they did not know the meaning of many of the prophecies.

"His disciples asked Him, saying, Why then say the scribes that Elias must first come? And Jesus answered and said unto them, Elias truly shall first come, and restore all things. But I say unto you, That Elias is come already, and they knew him not, but have done unto him whatsoever they listed. Likewise shall also the Son of man suffer of them. Then the disciples understood that He spake unto them of John the Baptist." Matt. 17:10-13.

"The disciples had often been perplexed by the teaching of the priests and Pharisees, but they had brought their perplexities to Jesus. He had set before them the truths of Scripture in contrast with tradition. Thus He had strengthened their confidence in God's word, and in a great measure had set them free from their fear of the rabbis, and their bondage to tradition."—"*The Desire of Ages,*" page 349.

4. Of whom did all the prophets, from the beginning of the world, prophesy? Acts 3:19-21; Luke 1:69, 70; Acts 3:18.

What an unfortunate experience the Jews passed through at the time of the first advent of Christ, because the rabbis had covered up the truth of Scripture with the rubbish of human tradition! Many of the traditions have been handed down from generation to generation through the centuries till the present time. Until this present hour the pious orthodox Jew cannot discern Christ in the Old Testament Scriptures. The apostle Peter declared that God spoke of Christ in all the prophets since the beginning of the world; yet that people to whom were committed the sacred oracles even yet do not see Him in any portion of Moses and the prophets.

The writings of those prophets chosen of God to lead that people for more than fifteen centuries have to a large degree been set aside. The rising generation of Jews hold strange and singular views of the purpose and intent of the Sacred Scriptures inspired by the Spirit of God. Christ in the Old Testament writings is nowhere recognized by the present generation. The "modern view" of the Scriptures is thus set forth:

"Modern Jewish theology of the Reform school, after making full allowance for the human origin of the Holy Scriptures, and recognizing that the matter recorded is sometimes in contradiction to the proved results of modern historical, physical, and psychological research, arrives at the following conclusion:

"While the ancient view of a literal dictation by God must be surrendered, and while the seers and writers of Judea must be regarded as men with human failings, each with his own peculiarity of style and sentiment, the Spirit of God was nevertheless manifested in them. The Holy Scriptures still have the power of inspiration for each devout soul that reads or hears them. They speak to each generation with a divine authority such as no other book or literature possesses. The inspiration of the Bible is different from the inspiration under which the great literary and artistic masterworks of later eras were produced. The religious enthusiasm of the Jewish genius leavens the whole, and the truth uttered therein, whatever be the form it is clothed in, seizes men now as it did when prophet, psalmist, or lawgiver first uttered it, themselves carried away by the power of the Divine Spirit. This view of modern theology, compatible with Biblical science and modern research, which analyzes the thoughts and the forms of Scripture and traces them to their various sources, finds that prophet and sacred writer were under the influence of the Divine Spirit while revealing, by word or pen, new religious ideas. But the human element in them was not extinguished, and consequently, in regard to their statements, their knowledge, and the form of their communication, they could only have acted as children of their age."—*The Jewish Encyclopedia,* Vol. VI, pp. 608, 609.

What a contrast between the foregoing statement and the following testimony of the inspired servant of God: "But those things, which God before had showed by the mouth of all His prophets, that Christ should suffer, He hath so fulfilled." Acts 3:18.

After nineteen centuries we still can hear the lingering echo of those pathetic words which fell from the lips of Him who gave and fulfilled the writings of the prophets. While He wept over His beloved city, He said:

"If thou hadst known, even thou, at least in this thy day, the things which belong unto thy peace!" Luke 19:42.

"Because thou knewest not the time of thy visitation." Luke 19:44.

"How often would I have gathered thy children together, even as a hen gathereth her chickens under her wings, and ye would not!" Matt. 23:37.

5. In quoting from the writings of Moses, whom does the apostle say Moses had in mind when he wrote? Deut. 30:11-14; Rom. 10:6-10; Heb. 11:24-27.

How full of meaning are the Scriptures when they are given in their right setting, under the influence of the Spirit of God. The illustration and comparison made by the apostle Paul of the purpose of God as expressed in Deuteronomy 30:11-14, with its fulfillment in Christ, recorded in Romans 10:6-10, is a forceful application of the fulfilling of prophecy in Christ.

6. Of what did the apostle Paul assure the Corinthian Christians? 1 Cor. 15:3, 4.

7. What did the martyr Stephen tell the Jews the prophets had foretold? Acts 7:38, 52.

8. What effect did the vision which Paul received on the way to Damascus have upon him, and how did he regard the prophecies of the Old Testament? Acts 9:20, 22; 17:1-3.

The apostle Paul was a man of influence and prestige when he was a rabbinical Jew. Many volumes have been written of his wonderful life. His own recital of the experience he had while journeying to Damascus to destroy, if possible, the gospel seed planted by Christ, clearly shows the effect of a perverted interpretation of Scripture upon the mind of a bigoted zealot.

"And having fully decided that the priests and scribes were right, Saul became very bitter in his opposition to the doctrines taught by the disciples of Jesus. His activity in causing holy men and women to be dragged before tribunals, where some were condemned to imprisonment and some even to death, solely because of their faith in Jesus, brought sadness and gloom to the newly organized church, and caused many to seek safety in flight."—"Acts of the Apostles," p. 113.

"His mind was deeply stirred. In his perplexity he appealed to those in whose wisdom and judgment he had full confidence. The arguments of the priests and rulers finally convinced him that Stephen was a blasphemer, that the Christ whom the martyred disciple had preached was an impostor, and that those ministering in holy office must be right."—Ibid.

"A Roman citizen by birth, Saul was nevertheless a Jew by descent, and had been educated in Jerusalem by the most eminent of the rabbis."—Id., p. 112.

"Saul understood the words that were spoken; and to him was clearly revealed the One who spoke—even the Son of God. In the glorious Being who stood before him, he saw the Crucified One. Upon the soul of the stricken Jew the image of the Saviour's countenance was imprinted forever. . . . Into the darkened chambers of his mind there poured a flood of light, revealing the ignorance and error of his former life, and his present need of the enlightenment of the Holy Spirit. . . .

"He saw that his convictions of right and of his own duty had been based largely on his implicit confidence in the priests and rulers. He had believed them when they told him that the story of the resurrection was an artful fabrication of the disciples. . . .

"In that hour of heavenly illumination, Saul's mind acted with remarkable rapidity. The prophetic records of Holy Writ were opened to his understanding. He saw that the rejection of Jesus by the Jews, His crucifixion, resurrection, and ascension, had been foretold by the prophets, and proved Him to be the promised Messiah."—*Id.,* p. 115.

"After his conversion, Saul recognized Jesus as the one who had come into the world for the express purpose of vindicating His Father's law. He was convinced that Jesus was the originator of the entire Jewish system of sacrifices. He saw that at the crucifixion, type had met antitype; that Jesus had fulfilled the Old Testament prophecies concerning the Redeemer of Israel."—*Id.,* p. 120.

To Paul, Christ had become the "all in all." Christ was his life. Everywhere he went he maintained the vision of Christ, and through the Scripture of Moses and the prophets he sought to convince all that Jesus was the great central teaching in those holy records from Genesis to Malachi.

9. What had God promised the prophets in regard to the coming of the Messiah? Rom. 1:1-3.

10. What does Paul's sermon, preached in Antioch in Pisidia, prove in regard to the prophecies of the Old Testament? Acts 13:15-17, 22-27, 32-37.

11. What effect did Apollos' preaching of the Old Testament Scriptures concerning Christ as the Messiah have upon the Jews? Acts 18:28.

12. What did the apostle Paul say to King Agrippa concerning the relationship between the ancient prophecies of the Scriptures and the life of Christ? Acts 26:22, 23.

13. Preaching to the people in the synagogue in His home town, how did Jesus apply the prophecy of Isaiah 61? Isa. 61:1, 2; Luke 4:16-21.

What a different record the people of Nazareth might have left to illumine the pages of history, had they accepted the divine application of Isaiah's prophecy the day that the Lord Jesus brought to them the message from heaven!

The Scriptures in the days of Christ were separated into three great divisions: First was the Pentateuch, the five books of Moses; then came the major and the minor prophets; after that, the Scriptures, the remainder of the canonical books of the Old Testament. The Pentateuch was divided into fifty-two sections. Every Sabbath during each year a section of the Pentateuch was read in the synagogue. Each section was subdivided into seven portions. To seven persons was read a portion during the services on the Sabbath, in the hearing of the congregation.

In addition to this reading of the Pentateuch, a portion of the writings of the prophets was read each Sabbath, at the conclusion of the reading of the weekly section. The person to whom was read the last portion of the section on the Sabbath, was also granted the privilege of choosing a portion of the prophets and reading this prophetic testimony before the service was concluded. Luke 24:44; Acts 13:15; 15:21; 13:27.

Jesus had been absent from His home town for a number of months. He returned on a visit to Nazareth, and on the Sabbath He attended the synagogue in which He had worshiped since His youthful days. The officers of the synagogue conferred the honor upon Jesus on this Sabbath of giving Him the privilege of reading the portion of the prophets, after reading the last section of the day's portion of the Pentateuch. The Saviour chose for His reading this day the first two verses of Isaiah 61. This portion of Isaiah's writings was very precious to the Jewish people. These divine words had for centuries been helpful to them. They often read that portion in the synagogue and in their own homes. This scripture was a comfort to them during the days of the Babylonian exile; it was

ANCIENT MANUSCRIPT SCROLLS ILLUSTRATING THE MANNER IN WHICH THE
SACRED SCRIPTURES WERE PREPARED

a joy to them during the Persian captivity. The writings of Isaiah offered them consolation in the days of Greece. How the Jews were helped as they read that assuring message of freedom and liberty while being oppressed by the iron monarchy of Rome!

The cantor or minister would read the words of the prophets with the rabbinical chant prescribed by the rabbis. A scholar or school teacher would present the message as explained by the sages. When the Saviour read those verses of Isaiah in the synagogue at Nazareth that day, He gave expression to the words in a manner never before listened to by such an audience. His emphasis of the message was different from that of scribe or Pharisee. He made the message personal. He applied the scripture to Himself. He caused the people to understand the reading,—that He was the fulfillment of the message.

Without doubt the audience was thrilled as the Saviour placed that prophetic portion in an entirely new setting. Never man uttered such words as this man spoke. There was a charm, a burning inward appeal, an impression, a conviction, that gripped the people as He read those words from the book of Isaiah. What could Jesus mean by saying, "This day is this scripture fulfilled in your ears"? the wondering congregation asked themselves, and one another. What did Jesus mean when He made a personal application of this oft-repeated portion of the prophets? If that convicted synagogue congregation had responded to the reading of those words by our Lord, when they were thrilled and "wondered at the gracious words which proceeded out of His mouth," what a blessing would have come to them! The Spirit of the Lord surely was upon Him, because the Lord had anointed Him to bring to the world the gospel message of freedom from sin and deliverance from the bondage of Satan. "To Him give all the prophets witness." Acts 10:43.

Christ Described in the Scriptures by Three Outstanding Terms

1. WHAT hymn of praise did the apostle John hear the angels singing around the throne of God? Rev. 5:11, 12.

2. Why did the four living creatures and the four and twenty elders join in singing this grateful song of praise? Rev. 5:8-10.

John the beloved, a prisoner under the condemnation of the Roman government, suffering banishment on the lonely and rocky Isle of Patmos, must have had a keen sense of the bondage of the human race in sin. "We must needs die, and are as water spilt on the ground, which cannot be gathered up again; neither doth God respect any person: yet doth He devise means, that His banished be not expelled from Him." 2 Sam. 14:14.

But when? When will come the glorious consummation? What shall be the sign of His coming? The future is veiled in darkness. We cannot see. The book is written, but on the back side it is sealed with seven seals. We long with great yearning. Our souls cry out, "Come, Lord Jesus; come quickly." But we know not when the time is. And no creature on earth or in heaven can tell us.

3. What man but Christ knows the future? Verses 4, 5.

The book John saw was no ordinary book, but a book of prophecy, a book revealing the future. And when no man could open it, the yearning of John's heart caused him to weep. But when Christ Jesus, "the Lion of the tribe of Juda, the Root of David," the Lamb of God, came forward to open the book, and the saints of God caught a glimpse of the glorious future in store for them, their hearts were filled with joy, and found expression in grateful song.

4. In how much of the Scripture may we find God's revelation of Christ? Luke 24:26, 27, 44, 45; Rev. 22:13.

It is the united testimony of the Holy Scriptures that Christ is revealed through the entire volume of the Sacred Writings. The Saviour Himself bears witness to this fact. Jesus began at Moses, and continued on in the writings of the prophets and the other books of the Old Testament, pointing out to the disciples that those writings spoke of Him. The Saviour Himself says that He is the first and the last.

5. Who does the Bible say created this world? Gen. 1:1; John 1:3-3; Eph. 3:9-11; Col. 1:15-17; Heb. 1:1, 2.

The deity of Christ is clearly set forth from the commencement of the Old Testament. Moses said that in the beginning God created the heavens and the earth. In the first chapter of Genesis the word "God" is found thirty-one times, as many times as there are verses in the chapter. The word "God" is not found in every verse. In some verses it is omitted; in other verses it is found twice.

The word "God" in Genesis 1 is אלהים (Elohim). This word Elohim is the plural form of the word. The singular form is אל (El). Read Genesis 33:20, where the word El is found. Read also the marginal reference of the verse. The plural of the Hebrew noun is formed by adding the Hebrew letter מ (mem). The letter מ (mem) has the sound of the English letter M. (See any Oxford Bible, dividing the 119th psalm in sections, and notice the word heading the section beginning with Psalms 119:97.) That the Hebrew letter *mem* forms the Hebrew plural may be seen by reading Esther 9:26. The word *pur* means "lot." *Purim*, the name given to the feast which commemorates the wonderful deliverance of the Jews from the hands of the wicked Haman, is the plural of the word *pur*.

The word *Elohim* is found in every verse of the first chapter of Genesis where the word "God" occurs, with not a single exception. Not once in the entire first chapter of Genesis is the word *El* found. That the word *Elohim* is a plural form of the word "God," may be seen by reading Psalms 82:6 and comparing this verse with John 10:34. The quotation from the eighty-second psalm is made by our Lord Himself.

If the translators of Genesis had recognized the preexistence of Christ, they would have given the word *Elohim* its proper setting.

This word *Elohim* has been a perplexity to Jewish writers and scholars. In view of the teaching of the "one God" and the "unity of God" idea, it has been difficult for those writers who refuse to believe in the deity of Christ, to present a satisfactory explanation of the word *Elohim*. One of the outstanding Jewish commentators, an authority who for centuries has been regarded as the prime interpreter of Scripture for the Hebrew student, offers the following comment on the first part of Genesis 1:26, ויאמר אלהים נעשה אדם בצלמנו כדמותנו (*yayyomer Elohim naase adam betsalmenu kidemuthenu*), "And God said, Let us make man in our image, after our likeness:" "God said to the angels, Let us make man in our image and in our likeness; that is, with reason and understanding such as we have."

The commentator Rashi, fearing that the foregoing explanation of the verse might not be satisfactory, has elaborated on his comment with the following explanation:

"RASHI'S COMMENT

"From this [that is, "God said to the angels, Let us make man in our image and after our likeness, with understanding and reason such as we have"] we learn concerning the plans of the Holy One, blessed be His name. Because man was made in the image of the angels, and for fear lest the angels should feel provoked concerning this matter, the Lord counseled with these angels, and received their approval in the matter. The Lord said: 'Between the angelic host and Myself there is a similarity in creation; that is to say, the heavenly hosts are created in My image and after My likeness. Now if the earthly creation should not be after My image and My likeness, there would be a jealousy and rivalry in all created works, because the earthly would be jealous of the heavenly.' Therefore He took counsel with the heavenly universe, that is, with the angels, and said, 'Let us make man.' Since, however, they did not assist Him in the creation of the earthly family, and here is an opportunity for the Epicurean [a synonym for the Christian, the follower of Jesus of Nazareth] to contemn the Holy One, blessed be His name, and to say that the angels did assist in the creation of man, for it is written, 'Let *us* make man,' that is to say in the plural form,—it is designed on the part of God to teach us great respect for others, and to inculcate the idea that the greater should counsel with and take advice of the younger.

"If it should have been written in the singular form, 'I will make man in My image and after My likeness,' we would not then have known that He was consulting with the heavenly hosts about the matter, but would have thought that He was speaking to Himself.

"And the alternative we have whereby to answer the Epicurean is written beside this verse, in the next; that is, 'And God created man in His own image, in the image of God created He him; male and female created He them.' It does not say and they created him in their image after their likeness."

Little is written on the plurality of Genesis, chapter one, by Jewish writers before the New Testament times. If the Talmudists had not so bitterly opposed the life and teaching of the Saviour, the later Jewish writers would not have been so confused and perplexed in regard to the deity of the Son of God. Had the Pharisees accepted Jesus of Nazareth as the Messiah, they would have had little difficulty in dealing with those texts which emphasize a plurality in the Godhead.

The New Testament clarifies and simplifies the meaning of Genesis 1. The passages in the New Testament establish the divinity of the Messiah. Those rabbinical commentators would have had little difficulty in harmonizing many of the scriptures which deal with the deity of the Son of God, Messiah, if they had only accepted the inspiration of the New Testament.

The Jewish Encyclopedia makes the following remark on the term "Son of God:"

"In fact, the term 'Son of God' is rarely used in Jewish literature in the sense of 'Messiah.' Though in Sukkah [a Jewish Talmudic work] 52a the words of Psalms 2:7, 8, are put into the mouth of Messiah, Son of David, He Himself is not called 'Son of God.' The more familiar epithet is 'King Messiah,' based partly on this psalm. . . . In the Targum the *Ba-in* [Son of man] of Psalms 80:16 [verse seventeen in our version] is rendered "*Mal-cha M-sha-cha*," "King Messiah," while Psalms 2:7 is paraphrased in a manner that removes the anthropomorphism of the Hebrew: 'Thou art beloved unto Me, like a son unto a father, pure as on the day when I created Thee!'

"The Apocrypha and Pseudepigrapha contain a few passages in which the title 'Son of God' is given to the Messiah."

"The God-childship of man has been especially accentuated in modern Jewish theology, in sharp contradistinction to the Christian God-sonship of Jesus. The application of the term 'Son of God' to the Messiah rests chiefly on Psalms 2:7, and the other Messianic passages quoted above."—Vol. XI, pp. 460, 461.

The portion of the text of Psalms 2:7, which has been paraphrased by the Targum, as mentioned above, is as follows: בְּנִי אַתָּה אֲנִי הַיּוֹם יְלִדְתִּיךְ (*Beni attah ani hayyom yelidtika*). Translators invariably render the text: "Thou art My Son; this day have I begotten Thee."

The Scriptures establish the fact that Christ is divine; He is the Son of God. Not only did Jesus accept the title, Son of God, in its proper sense, a recognition of His deity, but He also received the homage of worship when He was honored by His followers with this term. (See John 1:49; Matt. 14:33.) Jesus on several occasions declared that He is the Son of God. It is written:

"Jesus heard that they had cast him out; and when He had found him, He said unto him, Dost thou believe on the Son of God? He answered and said, Who is He, Lord, that I might believe on Him? And Jesus said unto him, Thou hast both seen Him, and it is He that talketh with thee." John 9:35-37.

"Jesus answered them, Is it not written in your law, I said, Ye are gods? If He called them gods, unto whom the word of God came, and the scripture cannot be broken; say ye of Him, whom the Father hath sanctified, and sent into the world, Thou blasphemest; because I said, I am the Son of God?" John 10:34-36.

A rather interesting terminology has been instituted in modern times in the attempt to overcome the difficulty of the plurality of the term אֱלֹהִים (*Elohim*), the plural form of the word "God," by calling this expression "The Plural of Majesty." The claim is set forth that in ancient times, when a monarch issued a declaration or made a public proclamation, he addressed himself in the "plural" form in preference to the singular form, though the monarch, or his majesty, issued the proclamation singly and alone. As a result of custom and usage, this form of declaration was called "The Plural of Majesty."

Of the time when this novel idea was introduced, neither date nor authority can be found; yet by a large circle of teachers and students it has been accepted as *lux et veritas*, light and truth. However, no such term can be found in the Scriptures nor in the ancient writings of the sages. Moreover, there is no such record to be found in the declarations or in the proclamations issued by kings and rulers in the Sacred Writings. (See Dan. 3:29; 6:25, 26; Ezra 1:1, 2; 6:1, 2, 6-8; 7:11-13; Neh. 2:7, 8.)

6. Do the Scriptures establish that Christ is divine? Deut. 6:4; John 10:30; 11:27; 17:5; 10:17, 18; 5:21-26.

7. What does the apostle say is God's purpose in the gift of Christ? Col. 1:19; 2:9, 10.

In presenting Christ as a gift to the world, God imbued Him with all the fullness of heaven. There was no limit to the plenitude of power existing in the Saviour. For one to receive help from our Lord, it is necessary for the individual not only to make request, but also to believe that Jesus has the ability to grant the petition. (See Matt. 9:28.)

To have faith in the power of the Christ and to make contact with Him, were the qualifications necessary to receive the divine blessing and benefit. Mark 5:25-34.

God anointed Jesus with the Holy Ghost and with power, and He went about doing good. Acts 10:38. Our Lord was not a specialist nor a professionalist. The blind, the lame, the halt, the maimed, received their heart longings, as they made contact with the Saviour.

8. How much wisdom and knowledge are inherent in Jesus? Col. 2:2, 3; 1:9; Eph. 1:8; 1 Cor. 1:24, 30.

Jesus is God's treasure house of wisdom and knowledge. He is the wisdom of God. Jesus is the source of wisdom. Knowledge and wisdom are not existent apart from Him. Scholasticism and intellectualism should not be confounded with divine wisdom. The world seeks human learning. Men who disclaim faith in the divinity of Christ accept the wisdom which "descendeth not from above." The divine storehouse of pure and holy knowledge and wisdom is Jesus, Son of the living God.

9. While God the Father is owner of heaven and earth, to how many of these possessions is Christ heir? Gen. 14:19, 22; Heb. 1:2; Mark 12:6, 7.

God has only one heir. Jesus is that heir. The Saviour admits that He only is the heir to all of God's wealth. To be without Christ is to be separated from life and all its attendant blessings. For "he that believeth on the Son hath everlasting life: and he that believeth not the Son shall not see life." John 3:36.

Jesus said that He and His Father are one. This oneness of Christ with the Father explains that particular scripture which has been so confusing to the Jewish people during many centuries. The creed of Judaism is Deuteronomy 6:4. The first prayer the child is taught in its early years, and the last prayer of the dying aged, is, "Hear, O Israel: The Lord our God is one Lord."

This expression is called the שְׁמַע (shema). This word shema is the first Hebrew word of Deuteronomy 6:4, and it means "hear." No Jew, whether orthodox or reform, who still has lingering in his heart a spark of Judaism, will deny his faith in the shema. Much is written in Talmudic literature on this shema. Without doubt the emphasis placed on the shema is to deny the existence of an equality of the Son of God with the Father. A few excerpts from the Jewish Encyclopedia, written by authoritative Jewish writers, may be of interest on this point:

"The Hellenistic modifications of the Biblical God-concept were further developed in the propositions of the heretical sects, . . . and of the Judaeo-Christians and Christians. To controvert their departures from the fundamental positions of Judaism, the Palestinian synagogue . . . laid all the greater stress on the unity of God, and took all the greater precaution to purge the concept from any and all human and terrestrial similarities. The *shema* (Deut. 6:4 et seq.) was invested with the importance of a confession of faith. Recited twice daily, . . . the concluding word *ehad* [one] was given especial prominence, emphatic and prolonged enunciation being recommended. . . . Audible enunciation was required for the whole sentence. . . .

"Upon Israel especially devolved the duty of proclaiming God's unity. . . . The repetition of 'YHWH' [Jehovah] in the verse is held to indicate that God is one both in the affairs of this world and in those of the world to come. . . . 'The Eternal is Israel's portion,' . . . demonstrates Israel's duty in the *shema* to proclaim God's unity and imperishability. . . . The *ehad* [one] is also taken in the sense of *meyuhad*, i.e., unique, unlike any other being. . . . Two powers, . . . therefore, cannot be assumed. . . . In the historical events, though God's manifestations are varied and differ according to the occasion, one and the same God appears. . . . God has neither father, nor son, nor brother."—Vol. VI, p. 5.

It is unfortunate that Jewish writers do not base their faith more upon the Scriptures themselves, as these writings clarify the meaning of God's word. The word אחד (*echad*), "one," found in Deuteronomy 6:4, which verse is stressed by the children of Abraham in affording them a creed, is not the same word as יחיד (*yachid*), "one." The two Hebrew words *echad* and *yachid* are explained by their context. We find *echad* for the first time in Scripture in Genesis 1:5. ויהי־ערב ויהי־בקר יום אחד (*wayehi ereb wayehi boqer yom echad*), "And there was an evening, and there was a morning, one day."

We next find this word *echad* in Genesis 1:9, 10, which reads: "God said, Let the waters under the heaven be gathered together unto one place, . . . and the gathering together of the waters called He Seas."

The third time we find the word *echad*, "one," it is in the following connection: "Therefore shall a man leave his father and his mother, and shall cleave unto his wife: and they shall be one flesh." Gen. 2:24.

In each of the foregoing scriptures where the word *echad*, "one," is found, its use is associated with more than a single object. The evening and the morning were יום אחד (*yom echad*), "one day." The waters were gathered together מקום אחד (*maqom echad*), "one place;" and the gathering together of the waters was called ימים (*yammim*), "seas." Man and wife shall be לבשר אחד (*lebasar echad*), "one flesh." In none of these places is the Hebrew word *yachid*, "one," used; invariably it is *echad*. The word *echad* indicates "unity," but not merely one individual.

In Genesis 22 God calls upon Abraham to make a sacrifice. The Lord said to the patriarch: "Take now thy son, thine only son Isaac, whom thou lovest." Abraham had more than one son. His elder son by Hagar was called Ishmael. God said to Abraham, קח־נא את־בנך את־יחידך (*qach na eth-binka eth-yechidka*), "Take now thy son, thine *only one* son." The word "one" in this scripture is *yachid*, and not *echad*.

In Zech. 12:10 we read: וספדו עליו כמספד על־היחיד והמר עליו כהמר על־הבכור (*wesaphdu alaw kemisped al-hayyachid, wehamer alaw kehamer al-habbekor*), "And they shall mourn for him, as one mourneth for his *only son*, and shall be in bitterness for him, as one that is in bitterness for his first-born." An only child, a first-born son, is not spoken of among the Jewish people as a בן אחד (*ben echad*), such a child is called בן יחיד (*ben yachid*). There is a difference between an *echad* and a *yachid*. The Scripture, as well as long usage, teaches this. The New Testament has clearly defined the prerogative of the believer in Christ, in the following language: "Wherefore thou art no more a servant, but a son; and if a son, then an heir of God through Christ." Gal. 4:7.

"The Spirit itself beareth witness with our spirit, that we are the children of God: and if children, then heirs; heirs of God, and joint heirs with Christ." Rom. 8:16, 17.

In Christ only do men have heirship with God. Our Lord and Messiah is the *one* and *only* rightful heir to all of God's possessions. Everything in this expansive universe God made *by* and *for* Christ. (See Col. 1:16.) Our Lord Jesus is the divine Son of the living God.

Quoting a portion of Proverbs 8:22-30, wherein the Son of God says He was "brought forth" before the earth was, "when there were no depths," the Spirit of prophecy says:

"Christ, the Word, the only begotten of God, was one with the eternal Father,—one in nature, in character, in purpose,—the only being that could enter into all the counsels and purposes of God. 'His name shall be called Wonderful, Counselor, The mighty God, The everlasting Father, The Prince of Peace.' Isa. 9:6. His 'goings forth have been from of old, from everlasting.' Micah 5:2. And the Son of God declares concerning Himself: 'The Lord possessed Me in the beginning of His way, before His works of old. I was set up from everlasting. . . . When He appointed the foundations of the earth, then I was by Him, as one brought up with Him; and I was daily His delight, rejoicing always before Him.' Prov. 8:22-30."—"*Patriarchs and Prophets*," p. 34.

10. How does Jesus relate Himself to the foregoing statement? John 13:3; 3:35; 16:15; 17:10.

11. How did Jesus express to John His eternal existence? Rev. 1:8, 11; 21:6; 22:13.

12. What twofold relationship does Christ sustain to God and man? 1 Tim. 3:16; Gal. 4:4; Rom. 8:3; Phil. 2:5-8; 1 Tim. 2:5; Heb. 2:14, 16.

The Scriptures teach that Christ is both human and divine. The apostle Paul clearly presents the Biblical view in regard to the humanity of Christ. He says:

"Without controversy great is the mystery of godliness: God was manifest in the flesh, justified in the Spirit, seen of angels, preached unto the Gentiles, believed on in the world, received up into glory." 1 Tim. 3:16.

Both in the Old Testament and in the New Testament the humanity of the Son of God is clearly taught. (See Isa. 9:6.) Jeremiah says that "*The Lord our righteousness*" descends through the seed of David. Without faith it is impossible to please God. (See Heb. 11:6.) Throughout His ministry Jesus was everywhere hailed as the "Son of man."

"Forasmuch then as the children are partakers of flesh and blood, He also Himself likewise took part of the same; that through death He might destroy him that had the power of death, that is, the devil." Heb. 2:14.

As the "Son of man," our blessed Lord overcame Satan. He became the Conqueror, that victory might come to the children of flesh and blood.

13. What name does John say is written on Jesus' thigh and on His vesture? Rev. 19:16; 17:14.

Jesus also is called the "King of kings and Lord of lords." By this title He will be received by His children on His return with power and great glory. The kingdoms of the world then become the kingdom of our Lord and of His Messiah. Jesus is King over all kings; He is Lord over all lords. The armies in heaven, as well as the redeemed of earth, unite their voices in honoring Him as "King of king and Lord of lords," who will reign throughout the ages of eternity.

14. What task has been committed to the church in this generation? Matt. 24:14; Rev. 22:17.

To the people of God in this generation has been committed the task of making known to the world that Christ is the Son of God, that Jesus is the Son of man, and that He is soon to return to this earth in power and great glory, to be welcomed by His people as "King of kings and Lord of lords." The church must be made ready to meet her divine Lord, "the Prince of the kings of the earth," at His glorious second advent.

A world-wide announcement is being heralded of this long-looked-for occasion; all nations of earth must hear the message: "Behold, He cometh with clouds; and every eye shall see Him, and they also which pierced Him: and all kindreds of the earth shall wail because of Him." Rev. 1:7.

While the church in all ages has been blessed with the knowledge that Jesus is divine; while the people of God have always had great reason to be thankful that Jesus is the "Son of man," the church today must be deeply interested that in this age the precious Saviour and glorified Redeemer is to return to earth to take unto Himself His blood-bought people, and by them be received as "King of kings and Lord of lords." This will be the time when He will honor His loyal servants, and bestow upon them the "gift of God," which "is eternal life through Jesus Christ our Lord." Rom. 6:23.

To prepare for this glorious occasion, for the coming of the "King of kings" surrounded by His retinue of angels, who number ten thousand times ten thousand and thousands of thousands, is the chief task of the people of God in this age and generation.

God's Call to the Church to Prepare for Christ's Second Advent

1. WHAT specific calls has God made to His people to prepare to meet the Saviour? Ex. 19:10, 11, 16, 17; Mal. 4:5, 6; Luke 1:17; Amos 4:12.

A number of times in the history of the world God has called upon His people to make preparation to meet Him. The first time the call was made was when God came in person to deliver His law to the Israelites. To have them ready for that outstanding occasion, a command was given to Moses to sanctify the people. The people must be clean in order to meet with a holy God.

The event of the giving of the decalogue on Mt. Sinai was at that time the second greatest in the world's history. In importance it was next to creation. Deut. 33:2; 4:32, 33.

The church was called to meet the Lord at the first advent of the Saviour. All heaven was astir when the word went forth in the heavenly courts: "Lo, I come: in the volume of the book it is written of Me." Ps. 40:7.

For four thousand years the church waited for this most important event. The destiny of the ages depended upon the advent of our Lord to this earth. The time had arrived when He must appear.

"Nearly two thousand years ago, a voice of mysterious import was heard in heaven, from the throne of God, 'Lo, I come.' 'Sacrifice and offering Thou wouldst not, but a body hast Thou prepared Me. . . . Lo, I come (in the volume of the book it is written of Me,) to do Thy will, O God.' In these words is announced the fulfillment of the purpose that had been hidden from eternal ages. Christ was about to visit our world, and to become incarnate. He says, 'A body hast Thou prepared Me.' Had He appeared with the glory that was His with the Father before the world was, we could not have endured the light of His presence."—"The Desire of Ages," p. 23. A great work of preparation was necessary in view of what was about to take place.

The church is now called to prepare to meet her Lord when He returns at His second advent. This coming of the Lord is the greatest scene in human history. No other event can equal in importance the personal appearing of the Son of God. A work of preparation is essential, is vital. When the Lord returns to earth to save His people with an everlasting salvation, those who are alive at His coming must be spotless, faultless, sanctified. For sinful men to stand in the presence of a pure and holy God, it is necessary that a mighty transformation take place in their lives.

2. What preparation is necessary for the people to be ready to meet their God? Ex. 19:10, 14; Isa. 40:3, 4; Matt. 3:7, 8, 11, 12; Luke 3:7, 8, 10, 12, 14; Isa. 62:10, 11.

The standard of righteousness and holiness must be raised in people's lives before they are ready for that solemn and important hour when the Saviour shall return. A great work must be accomplished for them. Of the multitudes who have lived upon this earth, only two individuals have escaped the tomb. Enoch and Elijah are the only ones who left this earth and went to heaven without tasting death. At the return of the Saviour, there will be many thousands of men and women who will be translated from earth to heaven without passing through the tomb. It is vital that an experience be gained by them such as men have not before known. Every stone of stumbling must be removed.

"Said the angel, 'Get ready, get ready, get ready. Ye will have to die a greater death to the world than ye have ever yet died.' I saw that there was a great work to do for them, and but little time in which to do it."—*"Early Writings,"* p. 64.

"Then my eyes were taken from the glory, and I was pointed to the remnant on the earth. The angel said to them, 'Will ye shun the seven last plagues? Will ye go to glory, and enjoy all that God has prepared for those that love Him, and are willing to suffer for His sake? If so, ye must die that ye may live. Get ready, get ready, get ready. Ye must have a greater preparation than ye now have, for the day of the Lord cometh, cruel both with wrath and fierce anger. . . . Sacrifice all to God. Lay all upon His altar. . . . It will take all to enter glory. . . .

"Heaven will be cheap enough, if we obtain it through suffering. We must deny self all along the way, die to self daily, let Jesus alone appear, and keep His glory continually in view."—*Id.,* pp. 66, 67.

"Now is the time to prepare. The seal of God will never be placed upon the forehead of an impure man or woman. It will never be placed upon the forehead of the ambitious, world-loving man or woman. It will never be placed upon the forehead of men or women of false tongues or deceitful hearts. All who receive the seal must be without spot before God—candidates for heaven."—*"Testimonies,"* Vol. V, p. 216.

3. How much of God's word must man believe in order to be saved? 2 Tim. 3:15-17; Luke 6:46; Matt. 4:4.

God's people must be familiar with His word in order that they may know what are His requirements to prepare for the coming of the Lord. God's purpose in giving man the Scriptures was that man may understand what is necessary for his salvation. The Saviour met the devil's temptations with the written word. By this word our Lord overcame all the power of the enemy.

We must ascertain the will of God in order to meet the divine mind. In His word are revealed to us God's wishes for our salvation. How can we be ready for the appearing of our Lord if we do not the things He asks us to do? While man cannot by good works purchase salvation, his character must be changed, that he may be prepared for association with heavenly beings. We are saved by grace, and that not of ourselves; it is a gift of God. To show our appreciation of this gift which God has freely given to us through the Saviour, we should be anxious to search the Sacred Scriptures in order to be wise unto salvation. If we search the word of God, the Holy Spirit will clarify our vision, and we shall receive divine illumination. God will enable us to understand His requirements.

4. In order for God's people to grow spiritually and be ready for the coming of the Lord, how must they relate themselves to God's message of preparation? 2 Peter 2:5; Heb. 11:7; Jonah 3:1-3, 5, 10; Matt. 3:1-3, 9, 10; Luke 1:17.

It is fundamental that man place himself in a receptive attitude. The men God saved in bygone days were those who were on the alert to learn God's will. Their salvation depended upon their accepting the message the Lord had for them during the days in which they lived. Noah, Jonah, and others carried forward the particular work committed to them. By believing and acting on the message delivered to them at the call of God, they were enabled to carry forward the task assigned to their trust. Only in this way, by doing the will of God at the proper time, can men expect to please God and to enjoy His approbation.

5. What special message has God declared will be given preceding the Saviour's coming? Mal. 4:5, 6.

Before the coming of the day of the Lord, God declared He would send the prophet Elijah. This truth the Jewish people feasted on for centuries, prior to the first advent. The leaders of Israel constantly kept before the children of Abraham that the Messiah could not come until Elijah the prophet made his appearance.

A description of Elijah and his work is found in 1 Kings, beginning with chapter 17. Any individual who arose claiming to have a message dealing with the advent of Messiah, was questioned by the leaders of Israel. This was done that the people might not be deceived. The Pharisees and the rulers of Israel did not consider that God, who gave the message, was able also to interpret the message. The Sanhedrin taught that it made no difference who came with a message purporting to be from God; if that person with the message was not the man Elijah, the Tishbite of Gilead, who once lived on earth, and who had been translated to heaven, he could not be the forerunner of the Messiah. This doubtless is why the Sanhedrin sent the delegation to John the Baptist, and inquired of him the questions recorded in John 1:19-22. The question was directed pointedly at John: "Art thou Elias?" He said, "No." The Sanhedrin delegation who waited upon John returned to the council, and told their leaders that this man was not the forerunner of the Messiah. John confessed that he was neither Elijah nor that prophet of Deuteronomy 18:15, 18. The ecclesiastical leaders considered they had fulfilled their mission for the people by the investigation of this "voice in the wilderness." They decided that he could not be the forerunner of the Messiah.

Israel's leaders did not take into consideration what the angel Gabriel told Zacharias, the father of John, that the child would do the work of the prophet Elijah. (See Luke 1:17.) God wanted the leaders of Israel to be so closely in touch with Heaven, that He could point out to them, at the proper time, that the fulfillment of the prophecy in regard to the coming of Elijah the prophet would be met in the work of John, rather than in the man Elijah. It was the *spirit* and the *power* of Elijah that was manifested in John the Baptist, when the time arrived for Messiah's first advent.

To this present hour the Jews say Messiah could not have come, because Elijah the prophet has not appeared. During the Passover supper, as the family, seated about the table, recite the experiences through which their forefathers passed at the time of their deliverance from Egypt, the individual sitting nearest the entrance opens the door, and the family unite in saying: ברוך הבא (*Baruk habe*), "Thou blessed one, come in." They believe that at some time during the Passover, Elijah will appear, and will tell the inmates that he has arrived and will be followed shortly by the Messiah.

The leaders of Israel did not receive the message of the angel Gabriel. They refused to believe the inspired interpretation of Malachi 4:5, 6. The Pharisees insisted that the prophecy of Malachi in regard to Messiah's forerunner could not meet a fulfillment until the man Elijah returned to earth. That people were not prepared for the coming of the Lord. They missed the way, and what a sad, irreparable loss it was, and still is, to them! John was sent from God with a special message from heaven; for it is written: "There was a man sent from God, whose name was John." John 1:6.

"What is our work?—The same as that given to John the Baptist."—"*Testimonies*," Vol. VIII, p. 9.

"In this age, just prior to the second coming of Christ in the clouds of heaven, such a work as that of John is to be done. God calls for men who will prepare a people to stand in the great day of the Lord."—*Id.*, p. 332.

6. What special message was sent to prepare the people for the first advent of the Saviour? Mark 1:1-3.

"Amid discord and strife, a voice was heard from the wilderness, a voice startling and stern, yet full of hope: 'Repent ye; for the kingdom of heaven is at hand.' With a new, strange power it moved the people. Prophets had foretold the coming of Christ as an event far in the future; but here was an announcement that it was at hand. John's singular appearance carried the minds of his hearers back to the ancient seers. In his manner and dress he resembled the prophet Elijah. With the spirit and power of Elijah he denounced the national corruption, and rebuked the prevailing sins. His words were plain, pointed, and convincing. . . . The whole nation was stirred. Multitudes flocked to the wilderness.

"John proclaimed the coming of the Messiah, and called the people to repentance. As a symbol of cleansing from sin, he baptized them in the waters of the Jordan. Thus by a significant object lesson he declared that those who claimed to be the chosen people of God were defiled by sin, and that without purification of heart and life they could have no part in the Messiah's kingdom."—"The Desire of Ages," p. 104.

A special message indeed was John's. The call to repentance to all classes who came within the sound of his voice was the demand of the hour. Jews, soldiers, scribes, Pharisees, taxgatherers, fisherfolk,—all were given the same warning: "Repent, repent, repent, and get ready for the coming of Messiah." This was the Elijah message in the days of the first advent of our Lord. This was the special warning to prepare the people to meet their Lord.

7. What two books of the Bible have a special message of preparation for the second advent of Christ? Dan. 2:44, 45; 7:9, 10, 13, 14, 26, 27; Rev. 1:1, 3, 7; 6:14-17; 11:15.

The books of Daniel and the Revelation deal particularly with counsel, admonition, and instruction concerning the second coming of the Messiah. From the second chapter of the book of Daniel until the close of that book, the prophecy deals with the setting up of the everlasting kingdom of God, the coming of the Son of man, the judgment, and the resurrection of the dead. The entire book is replete with announcements of the kingdom of God.

In the book of Revelation the angel tells the apostle John, at the outset, that the man who reads, who hears, and who obeys the words of the prophecy of this book, is blessed. The outstanding message which the Lord brought to this aged seer on the barren rock of Patmos, was the message of the coming again of the Saviour. The trend of almost every chapter of Revelation is the coming of the King of kings and Lord of lords and the end of all things. These two books of the Old and New Testaments have been bequeathed as a legacy to the church of Christ, to impart to the people of God clear light in regard to the work which must be accomplished in the world and in the lives of all peoples before the coming of the Lord.

8. Are the messages in the books of Daniel and the Revelation vital, and must we study them in order to be ready for the advent? Matt. 24: 15; Rev. 22:6, 7, 11-13.

9. What event immediately occurs when the messages given in these books are proclaimed? Rev. 14:6-12, 14-16.

The prophecy of Revelation is clear in its messages, which are designed to prepare a people for the return of the Lord. When these messages recorded in Revelation 14 have been fully given, the next scene the prophet beholds is the coming of the Son of man sitting on a cloud, with a sharp sickle in His hand. He comes to reap the harvest of the earth. Rev. 14:14-17. The Saviour testifies that the harvest is the end of the world. Matt. 13:39. The messages of these books are vital. They should be read and studied prayerfully, and the counsels contained therein should be obeyed.

10. Where does the voice of God come from when the pronouncement is made that the last message is finished? Rev. 16:17.

11. Where did Mary find the Saviour after she had lost Him for three days? Luke 2:45, 46.

When our Lord completed His work on earth, He said: "I have finished the work which Thou gavest Me to do." John 17:4. When Jesus paid the penalty for sin, and made possible man's reconciliation with his Maker, His dying words were, "It is finished." John 19:30. When human probation is ended, when men have had their day of opportunity and mercy, when men have passed the dead line, there comes a voice from heaven, from the temple, saying, "It is done." Rev. 16:17. Great and grave interests center in the temple in heaven. Our Lord, man's High Priest, intercedes in behalf of poor fallen sinners in His holy temple in heaven. Our holy Messiah pleads the cause of sinful man in the presence of the heavenly Father, in the most holy place of the sanctuary. Each individual has a case pending in the sanctuary in heaven.

12. Where did John say he saw Jesus after His ascension? Rev. 1:12-18.

13. Where should the church of Christ especially study the movements of our Lord, in making preparation for His second advent? Rev. 11:19.

The church of Christ should carefully follow her Lord in the heavenly sanctuary, where He ministers at the right hand of God. The books of Daniel and Revelation are particularly vital for those who are setting their house in order, who are getting ready for the return of their Lord.

"Daniel and Revelation must be studied, as well as the other prophecies of the Old and New Testaments. Let there be light, yes, light in your dwellings. For this we need to pray. . . .

"There is need of a much closer study of the word of God; especially should Daniel and the Revelation have attention as never before in the history of our work. . . . Read the book of Daniel. . . .

"The light that Daniel received from God was given especially for these last days. The visions he saw . . . are now in process of fulfillment, and all the events foretold will soon come to pass. . . . 'Revelation' means that something of importance is revealed. The truths of this book are addressed to those living in these last days. We are standing with the veil removed in the holy place of sacred things."—*"Testimonies to Ministers,"* pp. 112, 113.

"When the books of Daniel and Revelation are better understood, believers will have an entirely different religious experience. They will be given such glimpses of the open gates of heaven that heart and mind will be impressed with the character that all must develop in order to realize the blessedness which is to be the reward of the pure in heart."—*Id.,* p. 114.

"If our people were half awake, if they realized the nearness of the events portrayed in the Revelation, a reformation would be wrought in our churches, and many more would believe the message."—*Id.,* p. 118.

LESSON XX

The Angel Gabriel Visits the Prophet Daniel

1. WHAT appeared to the prophet Daniel in the third year of Belshazzar's reign? Dan. 8:1, 2.

The prophet Daniel acknowledged that the vision given to him in this chapter was not the first he had received. He said that a previous vision had appeared unto him. The record of this other vision we find in chapter seven of the book of Daniel.

2. In that vision what was revealed to the prophet? Verses 3-14.

Five outstanding, distinctive presentations were brought by the angel Gabriel to the attention of Daniel in this vision. These were, first, the ram with two horns; second, the he-goat with a notable horn; third, four horns; fourth, a little horn; fifth, the long prophetic period brought to view in the fourteenth verse of this chapter, namely, "Unto two thousand and three hundred days; then shall the sanctuary be cleansed."

3. Did Daniel understand what had been shown to him in vision? Verse 15.

It is evident from the fifteenth verse of this chapter that after the prophet had seen the vision, it was not clear to him. He says he sought for the meaning of the vision. If Daniel had understood the vision when the angel presented it to him, there would have been no need of his saying he "sought for the meaning."

4. Who was commanded to clarify to the prophet this vision? Verse 16.

The angel Gabriel was commanded to clarify the vision.

5. Who is this angel Gabriel? Luke 1:19; Dan. 10:21.

We have been definitely informed who the angel Gabriel is. In Luke 1:19 we read, "The angel answering said unto him, I am Gabriel, that stand in the presence of God." There is only one angel Gabriel. To this heavenly messenger was committed the trust of making the prophet Daniel understand what had been revealed to him. None other had the commission to fulfill this obligation. No part of this interpretation was entrusted to any other than the angel who stands in the presence of God.

For a right understanding of the vision given to Daniel, found in chapter 8 of his book, we have but one court of appeal. We cannot resort to ancient human folios; we must not appeal to secular records for authority. Historical data may be of value in confirming the interpretation given by the angel Gabriel. The true interpretation of the vision which was shown to Daniel is in the hands of the angel Gabriel. We shall expect this holy messenger to fulfill his commission.

6. As the angel approached the prophet, what assurance was given to Daniel? When was the vision to meet its fulfillment? Dan. 8:17-19.

The angel approached the prophet with calmness and assurance. Gabriel said

124

to Daniel, "Understand, O son of man: for at the time of the end shall be the vision." This vision which was given to Daniel was not to have an immediate fulfillment. This fact was made known to the seer at the beginning of the angel's interpretation. The heavenly visitor told the prophet that he would make known to him "what shall be in the last end of the indignation." The prophet was assured that the angel would fulfill his mission.

7. Whom does Gabriel say the ram represented? Verse 20.

8. What explanation does the angel give of the he-goat? Verse 21.

9. What does he say of the four horns? Verse 22.

Although Gabriel's explanation of the symbols is brief, the interpretation given to the prophet is clear and pointed. The ram is Media and Persia; the rough goat is Grecia; the notable horn between his eyes is the first king. Alexander the great was the first king of Grecia. This fact is universally recognized. The first king being broken,—for Alexander died while he was still a young man,—his kingdom was divided among his four leading generals. So the angel says that four kings shall arise following the death of the first king. And this prophecy was fulfilled. None of the four kings who succeeded Alexander were equal in power to the kingdom built up during the reign of Alexander.

10. What explanation does the angel give concerning the little horn? Verses 23-25.

11. Who is the Prince of princes? Rev. 1:5.

Gabriel points out definitely the little horn. After describing the ability of this little horn to practice and to prosper, the angel specifies in unmistakable language, in the latter part of the twenty-fifth verse, who he is. "He shall also stand up against the Prince of princes." Who is the Prince of princes? The answer to this question is found in Revelation 1:5: "And from Jesus Christ, who is the faithful witness, and the first begotten of the dead, and the Prince of the kings of the earth." "The kingdoms of this world are become the kingdoms of our Lord, and of His Christ." Rev. 11:15. The Lord Jesus is the Prince of princes.

12. What power stood up against Jesus Christ? Ps. 2:1, 2; Acts 4:25-27.

The power which *stood up* against the Lord Jesus is thus described by the apostle Peter: "Why did the heathen rage, and the people imagine vain things? The *kings of the earth stood up,* and the rulers were gathered together against the Lord, and against His Christ. For of a truth against Thy holy child Jesus, . . . both Herod, and Pontius Pilate, with the Gentiles, . . . were gathered together." Acts 4:25-27.

Herod and Pontius Pilate are pointed out, in addition to the Gentiles and the people of Israel, as standing up against the Lord and against the Christ.

13. How did this power stand up against the Saviour? Matt. 2:1-3; 16-18; Luke 3:1; John 19:13-16.

Herod and Pontius Pilate stood up against the Christ; for when the Saviour was a child, Herod issued a decree that all the children in the coasts of Bethlehem under two years of age should be put to death. And all the infants were killed. Matt. 2:16-18. Herod was king of Judea at the time of the birth of Christ. Matt. 2:1, 2. Herod was not an independent ruler, for at the time of the birth of the Saviour the world was under the rule of the Caesars. Luke 2:1. Rome at this time was a universal empire. Jesus escaped the wrath of Herod, for Joseph and Mary were warned by the angel to escape into Egypt. Matt. 2:13-15. Herod ruled under Roman domination.

Pontius Pilate was governor of Judea at the time when John the Baptist and the Saviour carried on their work in Judea; for it is written: "Now in the fifteenth year of the reign of Tiberius Caesar, Pontius Pilate being governor of Judea." Luke 3:1.

Pontius Pilate delivered the Saviour to the Jews, and passed the sentence that our Lord should be put to death. It is written: "Pilate saith unto them, Shall I crucify your King? The chief priests answered, We have no king but Caesar. Then delivered he Him therefore unto them to be crucified. And they took Jesus, and led Him away." John 19:15, 16.

Pilate was governor of Judea in the days of Tiberius Caesar. Both Herod and Pilate ruled Judea by Roman authority. These two men, the apostle Peter said, stood up against the Lord and against His Christ. The predictions of the angel Gabriel plainly reveal that the little horn represented Rome.

14. What did the angel say in regard to the vision of the 2300 days? Dan. 8:26.

Gabriel, having concluded the interpretation of the little horn, said to the prophet: "The vision of the evening and the morning which was told is true: wherefore shut thou up the vision; for it shall be for many days." The vision of the evening and the morning is that of the 2300 days. The Hebrew text for the 2300 days is: עַר עֶרֶב בֹּקֶר אַלְפַּיִם וּשְׁלֹשׁ מֵאוֹת (Ad ereb boqer alpayim ushlosh meoth), "Unto evening morning, two thousand three hundred." In Scripture we first meet with the words "evening and morning," in Genesis 1:5, which in Hebrew reads: וַיְהִי־עֶרֶב וַיְהִי־בֹקֶר יוֹם אֶחָד (Wayehi ereb wayehi boqer yom echad), "And there was evening, and there was morning, one day."

The angel said to the prophet that what had been shown him in regard to the evening and the morning—the two thousand three hundred days—was true, but the heavenly messenger added: "Wherefore shut thou up the vision."

Gabriel had been commanded to interpret to Daniel the vision. The angel already had explained four parts of the vision when he interpreted the little horn. But Gabriel did not attempt to explain the 2300 days just then. He only said to Daniel: The vision of the 2300 days is true, but shut it up.

15. Why did not the angel Gabriel explain to Daniel the meaning of the 2300 days? Verse 27.

The record says that Daniel fainted and was sick certain days. Gabriel had revealed to Daniel the course that would be pursued against the Saviour and God's people by the little horn, Rome. Knowledge that "a king of fierce countenance" would "destroy the mighty and the holy people" was more than the prophet could bear. He could no longer endure what he saw. Hence the angel was unable at that time to proceed with the explanation of the time portion of the prophecy.

Gabriel had been commanded to make known to Daniel the meaning of the vision, and the angel deemed it necessary to give the prophet some assurance in regard to that portion of the vision which he had not explained. Hence he told Daniel to close up the vision. The meaning of the 2300 days was left unexplained at this time by the angel Gabriel.

Daniel Studies the Scriptures to Understand the 2300 Days

1. WHAT effect did the vision have upon Daniel? Dan. 8:27.

When the prophet recovered from his sickness, he recalled that the latter part of the vision, the period of the 2300 days, had not been explained to him. He was greatly troubled because of this, for he was anxious to ascertain the meaning of this unexplained portion of the prophecy.

Daniel was familiar with the prophecies of Isaiah and Jeremiah. From the writings of the apostle Peter it is evident that the prophets studied the writings of other prophets. The seers recognized that the messages given to them from heaven were not always to be immediately understood. 1 Peter 1:10-12; Acts 2:29-31.

Daniel pored over the writings of Jeremiah and Isaiah. The prophet, then at Babylon, was in the land of Israel at the time Jeremiah delivered his warning messages to the kings of Judah. Daniel knew by observation and experience the disastrous results which had come to the people of Judah because of the Israelites' failure to heed the counsels of the prophets.

2. What two outstanding points in the vision of Daniel 8 were left unexplained by the angel Gabriel at his first visit? Dan. 8:14.

The two important points connected with the unexplained portion of the vision were the time (the 2300 days), and the event (the cleansing of the sanctuary). While the prophet Daniel attended to the affairs of state, for he held an important official position in the empire, he was unable to be at ease as long as he did not understand the portion of the vision unexplained by the angel Gabriel.

3. In order to ascertain if possible the meaning of this unexplained part of the vision, what course did Daniel pursue? Dan. 9:2.

Daniel devoted time and study to the writings of the prophets, in order to gain an understanding of the 2300 days and the cleansing of the sanctuary. In the course of his Scriptural investigation, the aged seer was impressed with two passages of Scripture which to him seemed to have some relation to the vision. Daniel felt he was traveling in the path of light.

4. As the prophet studied the sacred rolls, what discovery did he make? Jer. 25:8-13; 29:10-14.

When the prophet read the two predictions of Jeremiah, that at the close of the seventy years of Babylonian captivity, God would punish Babylon, and would again visit His people, and cause them to return to their own land, he must have been thrilled. Daniel understood that the seventy years of exile were almost completed. The reign of Babylon was ended, and the kingdom had passed into other hands. Dan. 5:30, 31.

When Cyrus, the commanding general of the Medo-Persian forces, entered the palace of Belshazzar the night the Babylonian king was slain, Daniel was again elevated to the premiership of Babylon. (See Dan. 5:13-16, 29; 6:1-3.) It is reasonable to believe that when these two men met in the palace hall, the aged prophet called the attention of Cyrus to the prophecies which Isaiah had written foretelling the career of this young man, Cyrus. (See Isa. 44:27, 28; 45:1, 2.) Particularly is this so in view of the statement by Cyrus in his proclamation in behalf of the Jews, made in the first year of his reign: "The Lord God of heaven hath given me all the kingdoms of the earth; and He hath charged me to build Him a house at Jerusalem, which is in Judah." (See Ezra 1:2, 3; 2 Chron. 36:22, 23.)

When he learned that the God of heaven had mentioned him by name more than 150 years before the event which had taken place that day, Cyrus must have related the experience he had with the aged prophet to his uncle Darius. Without doubt Darius was convinced that there was no man more competent to be prime minister over the realm of Medo-Persia than this man of God. So Daniel was made chief ruler of the empire of Medo-Persia. (See Dan. 6:1-3.)

Daniel had entered Babylon as a captive at the beginning of the seventy-year exile. He was in the court of Babylon when the threescore and ten years of exile were ended. The capture of Babylon by its conquering foes, the Medes and Persians, was to the Jews a signal that their captivity was about to end.

The Lord had declared to Jeremiah that at the close of the seventy years He would visit His people, and would perform His good word to them, in causing them "to return to this place," meaning Jerusalem. Jer. 29:10. But Jerusalem at this time, at the close of the seventy years of exile, still lay in ruins. The temple was in a state of desolation. The condition of the temple and the city was the same as it had been when Nebuchadnezzar destroyed them by fire seven decades before.

The center of the temple worship was the sanctuary service. This sanctuary ministry had not been conducted for many years. 2 Chron. 36:20, 21. The holy places had been defiled by the heathen. Lam. 1:10. The worship of the God of Israel had ceased. For threescore and ten years Israel had not observed the feasts of the Lord in the land of their captivity, nor had there been any sacrifices offered during these years of desolation. Lam. 2:6, 7. The songs of Zion were not sung during these sad and mourning decades. Ps. 137:1-4. But God had promised that at the end of the seventy years He would visit His people, and He would cause them to return to the land of their fathers. The prophet must have concluded from his study of the writings of Jeremiah that the time, the set time, had come to rebuild the sanctuary.

5. On finding these scriptures, what course did Daniel follow? Dan. 9:2-4.

As the prophet read these scriptures in Jeremiah, he decided that he would follow the counsel of God. Knowing that light came to those who sought the Lord and who studied God's word, the prophet determined to follow to the letter the instruction given through the weeping prophet. It is written: "Then shall ye call upon Me, and ye shall go and pray unto Me, and I will hearken unto you. And ye shall seek Me, and find Me, when ye shall search for Me with all your heart." Jer. 29:12, 13.

Daniel therefore sought the Lord by prayer and supplications, with fasting and sackcloth and ashes. In ancient times, when God's children sought Him with all the heart, they would lay aside their ordinary clothing, and cover themselves with sackcloth and ashes. (See Esther 4:1.) This outward act was a sign that the people were in trouble, and were in earnest in seeking God to bring deliverance to them. Daniel believed the promise of God. While there is no record that the prophet Daniel had companions with him at this time, to unite their prayers with his in seeking the Lord, the aged seer determined that he would cast himself at the foot of the throne of grace, and would earnestly call upon God to fulfill His promise, which He had made through Jeremiah, to restore the people to the Holy City.

6. What seemed to be the burden of Daniel's most earnest petition? Verses 16-19.

From a study of the prayer of Daniel, found in the ninth chapter of his book, it is evident that the prophet carried upon his soul the burden for the restoration of the sanctuary with its services. We read: "O Lord, according to all Thy righteousness, I beseech Thee, let Thine anger and Thy fury be turned away from Thy city Jerusalem, Thy holy mountain: because for our sins, and for the inquities of our fathers, Jerusalem and Thy people are become a reproach to all that are about us. Now therefore, O our God, hear the prayer of Thy servant, and his supplications, and cause Thy face to shine upon Thy sanctuary that is desolate, for the Lord's sake." Dan. 9:16, 17.

The prophet pleads that the time has come when God should show favor to His people, and should fulfill the promise made to Jeremiah.

In Second Chronicles we read of the condition of the sanctuary at this time: "To fulfill the word of the Lord by the mouth of Jeremiah, until the land had enjoyed her sabbaths: for as long as she lay desolate she kept sabbath, to fulfill threescore and ten years." 2 Chron. 36:21.

7. While Daniel was engaged in this earnest prayer, who visited him? Verses 20, 21.

In response to the prophet's earnest petition in behalf of the restoration of the sanctuary, now that the seventy years of Jerusalem's desolation were nearly fulfilled, the angel Gabriel visited him. In the midst of Daniel's confession and supplication, he says that the angel "Gabriel, whom I had seen in the vision at the beginning, . . . touched me." Dan. 9:21. This angel was the one who brought to the prophet the vision recorded in chapter 8 of this same book. Daniel recognized this heavenly being as the one who had previously visited him.

8. What was the first pronouncement the angel made to Daniel, as he called the prophet by name? Verse 22.

The first words Gabriel spoke to Daniel were: "I am now come forth to give thee skill and understanding." In what did the prophet need skill and understanding? Daniel understood the explanation of the symbols the angel had given to him in the vision of chapter 8, but the 2300 days and the cleansing of the sanctuary part of the vision had not been explained. It is true the prophet was seeking the Lord for light and knowledge on the unexplained portion of the vision. With the best evidence Daniel had from the Scriptures, he was appealing to God to make clear the part of the vision which had not been explained to him by the heavenly messenger. In order to understand this unexplained portion of the vision of chapter 8, the angel knew that the prophet needed skill and understanding from him who stands in the presence of God. The same divine skill and understanding which were given to Daniel in the explanation of the four symbols, revealed to him and recorded in chapter 8, were essential to the prophet, in order that he might gain a correct understanding of that part of the vision which had not yet been explained.

It is evident that the "skill and understanding" now brought by the angel Gabriel to the prophet, is in fulfillment of the angel's commission to "make this man to understand the vision." Dan. 8:16. The ninth chapter of Daniel is a continuation of the eighth chapter. No new vision is brought to the seer by this visit of the angel. Gabriel has come to complete what he left unfulfilled at his previous visit, because Daniel "fainted, and was sick certain days." Dan. 8:27.

9. What encouraging commendation did the angel bring to Daniel? Verse 23.

A beautiful commendation is brought to the aged seer by his heavenly visitor. It must have been pleasing to heaven to witness the prophet's attitude at the time Gabriel was sent to communicate further light to him. At this time Daniel was probably about ninety years old. He entered Babylon at the beginning of the exile. At that time he was old enough to take a three years' course in the university of Babylon. Dan. 1:5. Daniel could not have been less than eighteen or twenty years of age. Adding to these years the period of the exile, we conclude Daniel would be about ninety years old.

Daniel was president of the mighty universal empire of Medo-Persia. He was chief of the 120 princes and of the three presidents appointed by King Darius. But he was subject to the critical eyes of those underchiefs. No doubt these officers watched Daniel in order to discover some error in his administration. His responsibilities were many and they were taxing. (See Dan. 6:3, 4.) Yet a great burden weighed heavily upon Daniel's mind and heart, namely, a desire to understand the rest of the vision. To gain an understanding of the unexplained portion of the vision, this aged man of God prayed night and day. He set aside his robes of state; he clothed himself with sackcloth and ashes; he confessed his sins and the sins of his people, in order that the Lord might have mercy upon him, upon Israel, and upon the Holy City, and restore the sanctuary.

The work and service of God were uppermost in the mind of Daniel. His thoughts were centered upon the work of God in preference to the affairs of state. Daniel felt that more was at stake in Jerusalem than in the 120 provinces over which he was chief administrator. There was a crisis in God's cause, and this man of God felt that nothing was too costly for him to pay, in order to receive a correct understanding of the time and the event connected with that portion of the vision, the 2300 days and the cleansing of the sanctuary, which had not yet been made clear to him. He was willing to forsake all, if Heaven would only hear his appeal in behalf of God's precious cause.

How Heaven must have delighted in the earnestness and sincerity of this aged servant of God. To Daniel was brought the encouraging message by the heavenly minister, "Thou art greatly beloved." God greatly loved this man because his soul was burdened to understand the meaning of the prophetic days and the cleansing of the sanctuary.

We live in the day when this vision is receiving its complete fulfillment. What an incentive to the people of God at this time to study and seek to understand this portion of the vision, in view of the beautiful commendation brought to the seer of Babylon, and in view of the solemn event to take place at the close of the prophetic period.

10. What command was given to the prophet by the angel? Verses 22, 23.

That the mission of Gabriel to Daniel at this particular time was to make clear the unexplained portion of the vision of Daniel 8 is evident from the statement made by the heavenly messenger. Gabriel said: "I am now come forth to give thee skill and understanding; . . . therefore understand the matter, and consider the vision." No vision was given to Daniel at this time, nor had the twenty-three hundred days and the cleansing of the sanctuary yet been explained. Gabriel had come to give to the prophet the explanation of the part of the vision of Daniel 8 which had not been interpreted at Gabriel's previous visit.

The Seventy Weeks Explained to Daniel by the Angel Gabriel

1. How does the angel introduce the explanation of the time vision? Dan. 9:24.

The angel begins the explanation of the 2300 days by saying: "Seventy weeks are determined upon thy people and upon thy holy city, to finish the transgression, and to make an end of sins, and to make reconciliation for iniquity, and to bring in everlasting righteousness, and to seal up the vision and prophecy, and to anoint the most holy." Dan. 9:24.

Ten points are made by the heavenly messenger in causing the prophet to understand the vision, as follows: (1) Seventy weeks (2) are determined (3) upon thy people (4) and upon thy holy city, (5) to finish the transgression, (6) to make an end of sins, (7) to make reconciliation for iniquity, (8) to bring in everlasting righteousness, (9) to seal up, or certify, the vision and prophecy, (10) and to anoint the most holy.

2. What is the significance of the term, "seventy weeks are determined"? Dan. 9:24.

The Hebrew for "seventy weeks" is שבעים שבעים (shabuim shibim). The word shibim is "seventy," but the word shabuim is understood by Hebrew scholars to mean "a period of seven years." All devout orthodox commentators translate this word shabuim,—shmitoth (שמיטות). A שמיטה (shmitah) is "a period of seven years." While the English translations of the Hebrew Old Testament by Jewish scholars render the words shabuim shibim as "seventy weeks," it is clear that these weeks are prophetic rather than weeks of seven literal days. (See Num. 14:34; Eze. 4:6.)

Rabbi Isaac Leeser, who translated the Old Testament into English, is in accord with this prophetic interpretation of shabuim shibim. He says: "Ancient Jewish writers thought that the second temple stood four hundred and twenty years, which, with the seventy years of the Babylonian captivity, make four hundred and ninety years."—*Note 47, Leeser's comments on his Old Testament translation.* The comment of this famous rabbi on these two Hebrew words is agreed to by Hebrew scholars. These words of Leeser indicate that Jewish writers believe the year-day method to be the correct way to reckon the seventy weeks, but they failed to take note of the angel's words that the period "to Messiah the Prince" is to be reckoned "from the going forth of the commandment to restore and to build Jerusalem." Dan. 9:25. The commandment to restore and to build Jerusalem went forth in 457 B.C., and at that time began the seventy weeks.

By a study of the Authorized Version of the Scriptures, King James translation, we arrive at the same result, namely, that the seventy weeks of Daniel 9:24 represent four hundred and ninety years. We have learned that the vision of Daniel 8, given to the prophet, consists of a number of symbols. These symbols are clarified by the angel, by specific application. (Compare Dan. 8:3, 4, with verse 20; verses 5-7 with verse 21; verse 8 with verse 22; and verses 9-11 with verses 23-25.) Since the first four parts of the vision are symbolic, the fifth point in the vision must also be symbolic. The Bible explains the meaning of symbolic time. (See Num. 14:34; Eze. 4:6.) A symbolic day stands for a literal year. These symbolic seventy weeks, being four hundred and ninety days (seven days to a week), are four hundred and ninety literal years.

That the prophet Daniel so understood these words, *shabuim shibim,* "seventy weeks," is evident from the following: Daniel and Ezekiel were contemporary. While Daniel prophesied in the land of Babylon, Ezekiel prophesied for the people of Israel. Eze. 2:3, 4; 3:1, 4, 5, 17. These two prophets doubtless were acquainted with each other. Eze. 14:14, 19, 20; 28:3. Daniel's wisdom had received wide recognition in the days of Ezekiel.

Before Daniel was given the vision recorded in chapter 8 of his book, Ezekiel had a vision of a long period of time. Eze. 4:4-6. The prophet Ezekiel says in the explanation of the time vision given to him, that the three hundred and ninety days in which he was commanded to lie on his side, represented three hundred and ninety years. These days are year-days. The last clause of the fourth verse plainly so states: "I have appointed thee each day for a year." When the angel Gabriel told Daniel that *shabuim shibim,* "seventy weeks," were determined upon his people, the seer of Babylon recognized by the expression that these days were prophetic or symbolic. Each day stood for a year.

The Hebrew word for "are determined" in this twenty-fourth verse of Daniel 9, is נֶחְתַּךְ (*nechtak*). *Nechtak* means "to cut quickly," "to decree." The outstanding Jewish commentator, Rashi, acknowledged as the ablest and most scholarly of Jewish commentators, offers the following comment on the Hebrew word *nechtak:* "These years are decreed ones, in the sense of being cut off."

To clarify still further the force of this word *nechtak,* Rashi introduces as a parallel word to *nechtak* the Hebrew word כרת (*karath*), which means "to cut," "to cut round." *Karath* is an expressive term in the Hebrew Scriptures, meaning "to cut," "to cut off." (See Lev. 23:29, last clause.) The Hebrew word for "was cut off" is נכרת (*nikrath*), from the same word *karath.*

When Gabriel told Daniel, "seventy weeks are determined," as rendered in our version, the prophet understood that the Hebrew words *shabuim shibim nechtak* meant "seventy times seven years were cut off." Two points were at once established in the mind of the prophet. One was that the 2300 days were symbolic or prophetic; the other was that the seventy times seven were cut off from the 2300.

There are two methods of cutting off time. One is by division, the other by subtraction. Subtracting seventy times seven, or 490, from the 2300, leaves a remainder of 1810.

3. To what portion of the time vision does the angel devote his explanation? Dan. 9:24.

It must be remembered that when Gabriel made this second visit to Daniel, in order for the prophet to "understand the matter," to "consider the vision," the heavenly messenger came to explain to him the 2300 days. We find, however, that when the angel said to Daniel, "Seventy weeks are determined upon thy people and upon thy holy city," he was dealing with the seventy times seven which he commanded Daniel to cut off, but he was not dealing with the rest of the 2300 days. The ten points referred to in verse twenty-four dealt exclusively with events to take place during the seventy times seven, or the 490 years.

The rest of the 2300 symbolic days, or literal years, were not considered at this visit of the heavenly messenger. Gabriel confined himself to making clear to the prophet what was to come to pass during the first 490 years of the 2300.

4. How does the angel divide the period of seventy weeks? Dan. 9:25-27.

The attention of Daniel is now called to the division of the seventy times seven. Gabriel divides this cut-off portion into three parts:

1. Seven and threescore and two (sixty-nine) reaches to Messiah the Prince.
2. Following the last threescore and two (sixty-two) of the sixty-nine times seven, Messiah is cut off.
3. Messiah confirms the covenant for one week, at the close of the fulfillment of the sixty-nine; and in the midst of this seventieth week, the one week mentioned in verse 27, the sacrifices and offerings cease.

The heavenly messenger offers a clear and definite analysis of the seventy-times-seven period.

5. What relation exists between the beginning of the 2300-day period and the seventy weeks? Dan. 9:25.

The vital point in connection with this time prophecy is to have a particular starting point from which to count these years. The prophecy would be of little value if the time to begin reckoning the periods were not given prominence by the angel. But Gabriel, who was commissioned to "make this man to understand the vision," does not leave the prophet in uncertainty. He clearly defines when to begin the reckoning. The angel says, "Know therefore and understand." The language is simple and definite. A close relationship exists between the seventy times seven and the 2300; for the 490 are cut off from the 2300. The time to begin counting the two periods, the 490 and the 2300, must be the same. The shorter is cut off from the longer one. Both of these periods begin at the same time.

6. When does the first division of the seventy weeks end? Verse 25.

In marking the beginning of the reckoning of the two periods already mentioned, the angel specifies that the first sixty-nine of the seventy weeks reaches to Messiah the Prince. There are now three periods to consider in dating the beginning of the reckoning of this long-time prophecy; the 2300, the 490, and the sixty-nine times seven to Messiah.

But Gabriel tells Daniel where to begin counting the time: "Know therefore and understand, that from the going forth of the commandment to restore and to build Jerusalem." Verse 25. Somewhere in the Scriptures we must find a commandment "to restore and to build Jerusalem." When this commandment is discovered, we must in that connection be told the particular date to begin to reckon the three periods mentioned. Sixty-nine times seven, or 483 years, from the going forth of that commandment, must reach to Messiah the Prince.

There are six books in the Old Testament which were written after the book of Daniel. These books are Ezra, Nehemiah, Esther, Haggai, Zechariah, and Malachi. In one or more of these six books we must find a decree "to restore and to build Jerusalem." In the book of Ezra we find such a decree, but the decree is thrice repeated. It is written:

"They builded, and finished it, according to the commandment of the God of Israel, and according to the commandment of Cyrus, and Darius, and Artaxerxes king of Persia." Ezra 6:14.

Why do we have three decrees recorded, rather than one? It was customary in ancient times to have two or three witnesses to establish or to certify testimony. One witness was not sufficient. (See Num. 35:30; Deut. 17:6; 19:15.) This law was carried over into the New Testament, and was in vogue in the days of the early Christian church. (See Matt. 18; 16; John 8:17; 2 Cor. 13:1.) Furthermore, God at times repeated a testimony in order that the people might be assured of its accomplishment. (See Gen. 41:32.)

The decree issued by Cyrus is recorded in 2 Chronicles 36:22, 23; Ezra 1:1-4. This decree was given in the year 536 B.C. The command issued by Darius is found in Ezra 6:1-12. This one was proclaimed in 519 B.C. The third decree was issued by Artaxerxes in 457 B.C. Ezra 7:11-13. With which of these three decrees must we start? Between the time of the decree issued by Cyrus and the one given by Artaxerxes there is a difference of seventy-nine years. The commission from heaven was: "Gabriel, make this man to understand the vision." Dan. 8:16. The angel must explain when to begin the reckoning. Much depends upon the accuracy of the starting point. There must be sixty-nine times seven years to Messiah the Prince! The hope of man and the hope of the world depend upon the accuracy of this prediction, for Messiah is the Saviour of the world.

In telling Daniel to "know therefore and understand" when to begin the reckoning of the periods, the angel said that the "commandment" was the one "to restore and to build Jerusalem." The Hebrew expression for "to restore and to build" is להשיב ולבנות (lehashib welibnoth), "fully to restore and to build again." The command fully to restore to Israel in the Holy Land what she had before the captivity, is the starting point from which to begin the reckoning.

Did Cyrus's decree offer such results? According to the prophecy of Isaiah, the Lord did not expect this much of the decree of Cyrus. Isa. 44:28. What God planned through the proclamation of Cyrus was to inaugurate the *foundation work* of restoration. This decree of Cyrus does not completely fulfill the word of the angel.

By reading the commandment issued by Darius, we find that following the decree given by Cyrus, the work of rebuilding Jerusalem was interfered with by the enemies of the Jews. Complaints were made to the Persian king that the Jews were undertaking to rebuild the city of Jerusalem with the purpose of secession. Investigation was made by Darius. The king discovered that Cyrus had issued a decree granting the Jews the privilege of rebuilding their city. Darius proclaimed his command to confirm that of Cyrus. Ezra 6:1-8.

By reading the decree recorded in Ezra 7:11-26, we find that every requirement to grant completely to the Jews the ability to restore their city and their worship as they enjoyed those privileges before the captivity, is comprehended in the law made by Artaxerxes. Full amnesty and complete authority to worship the God of heaven in the offering of the sacrifices are assured and emphasized in the decree of Artaxerxes. This therefore is the decree from which to begin reckoning the time of the prophecy.

We must in this connection, however, find when to begin the reckoning specified by the angel Gabriel. The commandment was issued by Artaxerxes in the *seventh year* of his reign. Ezra 7:7, 8. Not only by the records of secular history, but also by unerring eclipses, it is established that the seventh year of Artaxerxes was 457 B.C.

From that valuable volume, "Certainties of the Advent Movement," by W. A. Spicer, we quote the following:

"One witness to the date 457 B.C. as the seventh year of Artaxerxes, is the famous Canon, or list of kings, compiled by Ptolemy. Claudius Ptolemy, mathematician, astronomer, geographer, and chronologist, dwelt in Alexandria, Egypt. He died about the year 151 A.D. In that ancient seat of learning, with its library collections, Ptolemy compiled his list of kings of the ancient world, with the years of their reigns."—Page 134.

"Along with his list of kings, Ptolemy compiled also a record of ancient astronomical observations, called in later times the 'Almagest' (an Arabic word meaning 'greatest composition'). This 'contains most of what is known of the astronomical observations and theories of the ancients.'—*Webster's Dictionary, under 'Almagest.'* When Ptolemy records the fact that in such and such a year of a king's reign an eclipse of the sun or moon occurred, the modern astronomer and mathematician can verify the chronological record."

"RELIABILITY OF THE RECORD

"The learned Dr. William Hales, chronologist and historian, said of Ptolemy's Canon:

" 'From its great use as an astronomical era, confirmed by unerring characters of eclipses, this Canon justly obtained the highest authority among historians also. It has most deservedly been esteemed an invaluable treasure, . . . and of the greatest use in chronology, without which, as Marsham observes, there could scarcely be any transition from sacred to profane history.'—'Chronology,' Vol. I, p. 166."—Pages 135, 136.

"Of the certainty that Ptolemy's Canon has come down to us correctly copied, Hales says:

" 'To the authenticity of these copies of Ptolemy's Canon, the strongest testimony is given by their exact agreement throughout, with above twenty dates and computations of eclipses in Ptolemy's "Almagest." '—'Chronology,' Vol. I, page 166.

"In a preface to a book on ancient chronology and its astronomical confirmations, James B. Lindsay, an English writer, says:

" 'The Syntaxis of Ptolemy contains an account of many historic events, and blended with them is a multitude of astronomic observations. The astronomic and historic cannot be separated, and they must both stand or fall together. The astronomic can be rigidly verified, and the truth of the historic is a legitimate deduction.'—'The Chro-Astrolabe,' preface, p. vi (London, 1858).

"Again this writer—who has not at all in mind any relation of these facts to Scripture prophecy—goes on to say of Ptolemy's work:

" 'His account of ancient eclipses, and of their connection with historic facts, is more precious than gold.'—Id., p. 86.

"For lack of such perfection of instruments as modern invention has provided, the records of the ancient observations may show some slight variations as now worked out mathematically. But these slight variations, Lindsay exclaims (p. 86), only add confirmation of the authenticity of the record:

" 'The motions and phases of the luminaries are visible every day, and with these alone we have been able to authenticate the whole of the "Almagest." Even the errors of Ptolemy augment, if possible, the evidence for the authenticity of the Syntaxis, and, he cries out in conclusion, 'a foundation is laid for chronology sure as the stars.' "—Id., pp. 146, 147.

The reader will be greatly benefited by reading pages 134-154 of the volume, "Certainties of the Advent Movement," for further and complete evidence that the seventh year of the reign of Artaxerxes is 457 B.C.

God who created the world gave to the world His word. The same authority is the source of both the word and the works. When the Saviour foretold, for the benefit of the church, when the last generation was due, He said to the disciples: "In those days, after that tribulation, the sun shall be darkened." Mark 13:24. The days here mentioned are the 1260 days of papal supremacy. (See Rev. 11:3; 12:6.) The days of papal supremacy began in 538 A.D., and terminated in 1798 A.D. But the papal persecution ended in the year 1775, when Maria Theresa, empress of Austria, issued her decree of toleration. Between the years 1775, the end of the persecution, and 1798, the end of the days, the Saviour said, the sun would be darkened. Most wonderfully was that prediction fulfilled in the "dark day" of May 19, 1780. This unusual phenomenon has not been and cannot be explained on any scientific grounds.

We are told in Scripture that one reason the Lord created the heavenly bodies was "for signs, and for seasons, and for days, and years." Gen. 1:14. God has the right to make use of His works in order to confirm His divine word.

The time to begin the reckoning of the prophetic period is with the decree of Artaxerxes issued in 457 B.C. This date is unalterably and irrevocably fixed. It cannot be gainsaid. The date is determined by the works of God.

The angel Gabriel said that the first sixty-nine times seven of this prophecy extended to Messiah the Prince. That is to say, there must be 483 years, beginning with 457 B.C., to Messiah the Prince. Who is Messiah the Prince?

In the Gospel of John 1:41 we read: "He first findeth his own brother Simon, and saith unto him, We have found the Messias, which is, being interpreted, the Christ." Messiah is derived from a Hebrew word, and Christ comes from a Greek word. But Messiah in the Hebrew means "anointed." (See Ps. 2:1, 2;

compare with Acts 4:25, 26.) *Christos* in the Greek also means "anointed." So the apostle says that "Christ" is the Greek meaning of the Hebrew "Messiah," and both these words mean "anointed." But who is the anointed one, the Messiah?

When Jesus talked with the woman at the well of Sychar, the Samaritan woman said to the Saviour: "I know that Messias cometh, which is called Christ. . . . Jesus saith unto her, I that speak unto thee am He." John 4:25, 26. The Lord acknowledged and admitted that He was the Messiah.

But what made Jesus the Messiah? The meaning of the term "Messiah" is "anointed." With what was Jesus anointed?

"God anointed Jesus of Nazareth with the Holy Ghost and with power." Acts 10:38. If we can learn from the Scripture when Jesus was "anointed with the Holy Ghost and with power," we shall know of a certainty when He became the Messiah.

John the Baptist was born six months before Jesus was born. (See Luke 1:5, 11-13, 26, 27, 36.) It was customary in Bible times for a teacher to begin his work at the age of thirty. (See Num. 4:3, 35, 39; Luke 3:23.) John the Baptist began his work six months before the Saviour began His ministry. We are told just when John the Baptist began his work. This is pointed out in Scripture very definitely. Luke 3:2, 3. The baptism of Christ took place in 27 A.D. (See Luke 3:21, 22, date in margin.) In what part of the year 27 A.D. was the Saviour baptized? The angel Gabriel declared that there must be 483 years, from the going forth of the commandment to restore and build Jerusalem to Messiah the Prince. We have found that the decree of Artaxerxes became effective in the *seventh* year of his reign, which was the year 457 B.C. In what month of the year did the decree become effective? In what month of the year 27 A.D. was Jesus baptized? By His baptism He became the Messiah.

Our calendar, the Gregorian, was not in existence in the year 457 B.C., when the decree went into effect. We must therefore find a Biblical calendar which was in existence in 457 B.C. Such a calendar we have discoverd in the Scriptures. (See Lesson 10 of this series, under question 14.)

The first month of the Bible year (Ex. 12:1, 2) is the one in which the Passover occurs. Verses 6, 11. We are to learn from Scripture in what Bible month our Lord was anointed. When we have learned this fact, we shall be assured of the month in the year 27 A.D. when Jesus became the Messiah. We shall also discover the month when the decree of Artaxerxes became effective.

7. What does the angel say should be done to the Messiah? Verse 26.

The angel Gabriel declared that after 483 years should "Messiah be cut off." Jesus was cut off from the land of the living, as is pointed out by the prophet Isaiah in these words:

"He was oppressed, and He was afflicted, yet He opened not His mouth: He is brought as a lamb to the slaughter, and as a sheep before her shearers is dumb, so He openeth not His mouth. He was taken from prison and from judgment: and who shall declare His generation? for He was *cut off* out of the land of the living: for the transgression of my people was He stricken." Isa. 53:7, 8. Following His Messiahship in the year 27 A.D., He was "cut off."

8. What special work was Messiah to do, as pointed out by the angel? Verse 27.

The angel also points out the work Messiah would perform after His anointing, and the length of time He would minister before He was cut off. Gabriel said:

"He shall confirm the covenant with many for one week: and in the midst of the week He shall cause the sacrifice and the oblation to cease."

This symbolic week represents seven literal years. Messiah was to confirm the covenant with many for seven literal years, three and one-half years by His own ministry, and three and one-half years by the preaching of the apostles to

MESSIAH

69 PROPHETIC
WEEKS TIME
CLOCK

THE
TIME IS
FUL
-FILLED

"JESUS CAME INTO GALILEE
PREACHING THE GOSPEL OF THE
KINGDOM OF GOD AND SAYING
THE TIME IS FULFILLED."
Mark 1:14-15

the people of Israel. This is the last week of the seventy. The Scripture teaches that following the "anointing of Jesus as Messiah" He must personally labor among men for three and one-half years. He was to cause the sacrifice to cease in the middle of this last symbolic week. The Hebrew word for "midst" in this twenty-seventh verse is *chat-tsi,* understood by all Jews to mean "the half," "the middle." So Messiah must minister following His anointing three and one-half years. We learn from Scripture that Jesus died at the Passover. Matt. 26:1, 2; 1 Cor. 5:7. We observed under question 6 in this study, that the Passover occurs in the first Bible month. Jesus died in the middle of the first Bible month. The angel declared that Messiah would minister for three and a half years. He died in the first Bible month, following the three and one-half years of His ministry. Jesus therefore was anointed as Messiah in the seventh Bible month of the year 27 A.D.

The month in which the Passover occurs is the month we call April. Since April harmonizes with the first Bible month, the seventh Bible month is October. Therefore Jesus became the Messiah in the month of October, 27 A.D. The sixty-nine times seven to Messiah the Prince terminated in the seventh Bible month, October, 27 A.D. The decree of Artaxerxes therefore became effective in the seventh Bible month, in October, 457 B.C.; for the angel said there must be 483 years to the Messiah the Prince. Jesus therefore became the Messiah in October, 27 A.D.

What unusual incident occurred in 31 A.D. when Messiah died at this particular Passover? "Jesus, when He had cried again with a loud voice, yielded up the ghost. And, behold, the veil of the temple was rent in twain from the top to the bottom." Matt. 27:50, 51.

What was the meaning of this remarkable occurrence? This veil of the temple was hung by the command of God. This veil separated between the holy and the most holy place of the sanctuary. Ex. 26:31-34; 2 Chron. 3:14. No person but the priest was permitted to look into the most holy place of the sanctuary, and the priest was permitted to enter this most holy apartment on the Day of Atonement only. Even for the high priest to enter this sacred precinct on any day but the Day of Atonement meant instant death. Lev. 16:2.

At the death of Messiah the veil of the temple was rent in twain from the top to the bottom. No visible hand would dare to touch this veil, on pain of instant death. The God of heaven destroyed this hanging, that all might know that sacrifices and offerings had ceased. The sacrificial system was ended. Messiah was the fulfillment of the types and offerings. Messiah's death "caused the sacrifice and the oblation to cease." Just three and one-half years from His anointing as Messiah, Jesus ministered among the people. At His death the system of sacrifices and ceremonies came to an end.

Jesus died at the Passover of 31 A.D., "in the midst" of this seventieth symbolic week. This part of the angel's prophecy was fulfilled. Three and one-half years remained to complete this seventieth week. Three and one-half years added to the spring of 31 A.D., when our Lord died on Calvary, reach to the seventh Bible month, or October of 34 A.D. The seventy prophetic weeks, or 490 literal years, which Gabriel said were cut off from the 2300 years, came to an end at that date.

We found under question 2 of this study that there remained 1810 years after the "cutting off" of the seventy times seven. Adding 1810 to the month of October, 34 A.D., the ending of the 490 years, we arrive at the seventh Bible month, October, 1844, when the 2300 prophetic days, or literal years, ended. Then, said the angel, the sanctuary shall be cleansed. Dan. 8:14. This ending of the 2300 days in October, 1844, has been the position held by the fathers of this message, since the beginning of this great world movement. We observe that, after the preaching of the third angel's message for more than ninety years, the foundations of this movement are as certain as they were when the servants of God, under the guidance of the Holy Spirit, laid them. Truly, "the foundation of God standeth sure." 2 Tim. 2:19.

9. When Messiah was cut off, what was to become of the sanctuary? Verse 27.

10. After the sacrifice and oblations should cease, what was to become of the Holy City? Verses 26, 27.

After Messiah was "cut off," after "in the midst of the week" He had caused "the sacrifice and the oblation to cease," "the people of the prince" were to come and "destroy the city and the sanctuary." Dan. 9:26, 27. In 70 A.D., the city of Jerusalem was destroyed by Titus the commanding general of the Roman armies, and the sanctuary was burned to the ground. From that day to this the Jewish people have never offered sacrifices. We see how literally and completely this prophecy has been fulfilled.

11. Did the angel give the prophet any further explanation of the 2300 days, beyond the interpretation of the seventy weeks? Verses 26, 27.

After the explanation to Daniel of the seventy weeks, the angel Gabriel gave the prophet no further information at this time. However, the aged seer was not content with the partial explanation of the 2300 days given to him by the heavenly messenger. Again he prays, and fasts, and seeks God most earnestly that the remainder of the 2300 days may be made understandable to him.

12. With what particular people does the seventy weeks deal? Verses 24-27.

LESSON XXIII

The Seventy-Week Prophecy Fulfilled, and the Rest of the 2300 Days Explained

1. How many of the ten points mapped out by the angel Gabriel to Daniel met their fulfillment?

Of the ten points given to Daniel when Gabriel came to explain the seventy weeks, we have already fully considered the first two, namely, the seventy weeks and their being cut off. Let us now study the eight points to follow.

Third, "upon thy people." Who were Daniel's people? They were the Jewish people, at that time the people of God.

When the Saviour ordained the twelve apostles to preach the gospel, He commanded them not to go into the cities of the Samaritans, nor to the Gentiles; but to go rather to the lost sheep of the house of Israel. Matt. 10:5, 6. The apostle Paul tells us that "Jesus Christ was a minister of the circumcision for the truth of God, to confirm the promises made unto the fathers." Rom. 15:8.

Although the Saviour was no respecter of persons, and although during His ministry He supplied the needs of all classes of people, yet He told the woman of Canaan, who asked for help for her daughter, "I am not sent but unto the lost sheep of the house of Israel." Matt. 15:24. His ministry was devoted to Daniel's people, for the seventy weeks were "cut off" upon that people.

Before the Saviour left His disciples to return to heaven, He gave them their commission as follows: "Ye shall be witnesses unto Me both in Jerusalem, and in all Judea, and in Samaria, and unto the uttermost part of the earth." Acts 1:8. They were to confine their work at first to the Jewish people. This they did. For three and a half years after the Saviour's ascension, not a sermon was preached outside of Judean territory. While the disciples were fulfilling Christ's command to preach in Jerusalem and in Judea, they were also fulfilling the prophecy of the angel Gabriel, when he said that the seventieth week was to be confined to the Jewish people. The first half of that prophetic week the Saviour Himself used in His ministry; the last half of the week the disciples spent in and about Judea.

Of events at the close of the seventy times seven years, when persecution raged against the church in Judea, we find this account:

"Saul was consenting unto his [Stephen's] death. And at that time there was a great persecution against the church which was at Jerusalem; and they were all scattered abroad throughout the regions of Judea and Samaria, except the apostles. . . . Then Philip went down to the city of Samaria, and preached Christ unto them." Acts 8:1-5.

At the close of the seventieth week, in 34 A.D., the gospel was carried to Samaria, and from there on to the uttermost parts of the earth.

Fourth, "And upon thy holy city." How earnestly the Saviour, while on earth, appealed to the Jews to do the will of God, in order that Jerusalem might remain! By parable and by direct instruction He admonished and counseled them to obey God, that Jerusalem might continue to be "the city of the great King." Matt. 5:35.

The Saviour finally told the disciples that because the Israelites knew not the time of their visitation, there should "not be left here one stone upon another," that should "not be thrown down." Matt. 24:2.

140

With falling tears, the Lord wept over the "Holy City" and over the "temple," which would eventually be destroyed. Jesus said:

"The days shall come upon thee, that thine enemies shall cast a trench about thee, and compass thee round, and keep thee in on every side, and shall lay thee even with the ground, and thy children within thee." Luke 19:43, 44.

"When ye shall see Jerusalem compassed with armies, then know that the desolation thereof is nigh. Then let them which are in Judea flee to the mountains. . . . For these be the days of vengeance, that all things which are written may be fulfilled. . . . And they shall fall by the edge of the sword, and shall be led away captive into all nations: and Jerusalem shall be trodden down of the Gentiles, until the times of the Gentiles be fulfilled." Luke 21:20-24.

After the Saviour made the declaration: "O Jerusalem, Jerusalem, thou that killest the prophets, and stonest them which are sent unto thee, how often would I have gathered thy children together, even as a hen gathereth her chickens under her wings, and ye would not!" He "went out, and departed from the temple." Matt. 23:37; 24:1. After the departure of the Saviour's presence that day from the temple, the glory of God never again entered the temple. Just forty years later, the city and the temple were laid in ruins.

Fifth, "To finish the transgression." The Hebrew expression for "to finish the transgression," is לכלא הפשע (lekalle happesha), "to fill up the transgression," "to make full the transgression." Something was to occur during the four hundred and ninety years which would fill up "the transgression."

When the Jewish people rejected the Saviour, and had determined to take His life, He said to them: "Ye build the tombs of the prophets, and garnish the sepulchers of the righteous, and say, If we had been in the days of our fathers, we would not have been partakers with them in the blood of the prophets. . . . Fill ye up then the measure of your fathers, . . . that upon you may come all the righteous blood shed upon the earth." Matt. 23:29-35.

In rejecting and crucifying the Son of God, their King and their Messiah, the Jews filled up the cup of their transgression.

Sixth, "And to make an end of sins." The word חטאות (chattawth), translated "sins," means also "sin offerings." Sin offerings came to an end when our Lord died on Calvary's cross. This point has already been considered.

Seventh, "And to make reconciliation for iniquity." By man's sin, death passed upon all men, but Christ's great sacrifice was ample to cover all iniquity. Our Lord yielded up His life as a sacrifice for man. 1 Cor. 15:3. As the blood of lambs and goats was offered in the earthly sanctuary for the forgiveness of sin, so the great sacrifice of the Lamb of God upon Calvary's cross made full coverage (Hebrew, כפר, kaphar) for sin, that all who "come unto God by Him" may have pardon and salvation.

Eighth, "And to bring in everlasting righteousness." Everlasting righteousness was brought to man by the Saviour's coming to earth in person, and living the righteous life demanded by the law of God. The apostle thus speaks of Christ: "Of Him are ye in Christ Jesus, who of God is made unto us wisdom, and righteousness, and sanctification, and redemption." 1 Cor. 1:30.

Ninth, "And to seal up the vision and prophecy." The thought in the text is: During the seventy times seven years, events will occur which will seal up, make sure, certify, the prophecy and the vision. The prophecy of the seventy weeks and the 2300 days was sealed up and certified when the Saviour died at the ninth hour, "between the two evenings," the true Paschal Lamb. Ex. 12:6, margin; Matt. 26:1, 2; 27:46, 50; 1 Cor. 5:7. At His death the veil of the temple was rent in twain, indicating that sacrifices and offerings were of no more value.

Tenth, "And to anoint the most holy." The Hebrew words, קרש הקדשים (qodesh haq-qodashim), "the most holy," are applied to things, and not to persons. This term here refers to the heavenly sanctuary, as we shall observe in a future study. Not one feature failed of this remarkable prophecy, included in the ten points uttered by the angel Gabriel, all of which were to be fulfilled during the seventy times seven years. Heaven and earth may pass away, but not a jot or a tittle of the word of God can fall to the ground unfulfilled. Matt. 5:17, 18.

2. What course did the prophet Daniel pursue when the angel did not completely explain to him the 2300 days? Dan. 10:2, 3, 12.

3. How long a time did the prophet spend in seeking the special blessing of the Lord? Verses 2, 3.

The prophet Daniel fasted "three full weeks," with prayer and supplication, during which time He sought God earnestly, in order that added light and information might be given to him in regard to the remainder of the 2300 days. He was visited once more by the heavenly messenger, who told the prophet that his prayer was heard in heaven when he began to seek the Lord at the beginning of his fast. Gabriel came to fulfill the prophet's desire. (See Dan. 10:1-12, 14.)

4. What twofold testimony did the angel bring to Daniel? Verses 11, 19.

5. When did the angel say the 2300 days would terminate? Dan. 10:14; 12:4, 9, 13.

Gabriel impressed upon the mind of the prophet that the rest of the 2300 days would be fulfilled after "many days." When they come to pass, he said, the last days will have been reached. However, the heavenly messenger explained to Daniel that the 2300 days concerned the people of God.

6. What assurance was given to the prophet in regard to what the angel was about to tell him? Dan. 10:21.

The angel assured Daniel that what he was about to tell him was the truth. He was to explain what had already been revealed to the prophet. Gabriel, in visiting Daniel at this time, had not yet shown him, as far as any record indicates, anything in addition to what was revealed to him in chapters 8 and 9. The angel was now to complete his commission: "Make this man to understand the vision." Dan. 8:16.

7. What does Gabriel say will take place during the remainder of the 2300 days?

Ans.—The events described in Daniel 11 and 12.

8. What assurance was given the prophet that God's people would be enlightened at the close of the 2300 days? Dan. 12:8-10.

After Gabriel had enlightened Daniel as to what would occur during the rest of the 2300 days, he told the prophet that the book should be "closed up and sealed" until "the time of the end." When the hour arrived for the unsealing of the book, he said, "Many shall run to and fro, and knowledge shall be increased." Dan. 12:4. Certain events were to take place at the unsealing of the book which were not clear to the prophet. So Daniel said: "I heard, but I understood not: then said I, O my Lord, what shall be the end of these things?" Verse 12. The angel again kindly advised the prophet that the words were sealed up till the time of the end. When that hour should arrive, he said, "the wise shall understand."

9. What encouraging word was given to Daniel to assure him of his standing at the close of the 2300 days? Dan. 12:13.

These words of the heavenly messenger were comforting to the prophet. They were an assurance that at the end of the 2300 days, when certain events were to befall God's people, Daniel would stand in his lot. It must be remembered that it was on the Day of Atonement that the lot was cast.

DIAGRAM OF SEVENTY WEEKS AND 2300 DAYS

"Unto two thousand and three hundred days; then shall the sanctuary be cleansed." Dan. 8:14. These are symbolic or prophetic days. A symbolic day equals a year. Num. 14:34; Eze. 4:6. Twenty-three hundred prophetic days equal twenty-three hundred literal years.

70 weeks=70 × 7 days=490 days

490 years are cut off from 2300 years

1810 years

The cut-off years are divided as follows:

7 wks. and 62 wks. are 69 wks. (7 × 69=483) 69 wks. are 483 days or yrs. to Messiah the Prince

1 wk, or 7 days, equals 7 yrs. to confirm the covenant

RECKON BEGINNING OF THE 2300 DAYS

490 days. 483 days from seventh year of Artaxerxes. Ezra 7:7, 8.
Seventh year of reign of Artaxerxes, 457 B.C. 483 years from 457 B.C. to Messiah the Prince.
Jesus became Messiah in 27 A.D. at His baptism, when He was anointed with the Holy Ghost.
Three and one-half years after His baptism, Messiah was cut off, that is, He died at the Passover, 31 A.D.
Passover occurs in the first Bible month, harmonizing with April of our calendar.
483 years from the seventh year of Artaxerxes to Messiah ended in seventh Bible month, October, 27 A.D.

2300 SYMBOLIC OR PROPHETIC DAYS

October, 457 B.C.

October, 27 A.D.

October, 34 A.D.

October, 1844 A.D.

490 yrs. 69 times 7 is 483 years to 27 A.D.

1 wk. is 7 yrs.

Messiah's baptism

Confirm covenant

Add 1810 to Oct., 34 A.D., or end of 490 yrs.

10. What did the angel say would take place at the close of the 2300 days? Dan. 8:14.

The word "cleansed," found in Daniel 8:14, is a translation of the Hebrew word נצדק (*nitsdaq*). This Hebrew word has its origin in the root צדק (*tsadaq*), which has several meanings, and being used in different texts, is variously translated as "right," "righteous," "just," "justified," "purged," "purified," "cleansed." The Analytical Hebrew and Chaldee Lexicon, published by Bagster, gives the definition of this word, as it is used here in Daniel 8:14, as "purified." Bagster says (page 940): "Niph. Da. 8:14, to be purified, so the Sept. and Vulg."

It will be recognized that "purification," "cleansing," and "purging" may have approximately the same meaning. The Septuagint, or Greek version of the Bible, translates the Hebrew word *tsadaq* as *"katharizo,"* from which comes our English word "cathartic," and which is a synonym for "purge."

This Greek word *katharizo* appears throughout Leviticus 16 wherever the English word is "cleanse." For instance, in Leviticus 16:30 we read, "On that day shall the priest make an atonement for you, to cleanse [*katharisai*] you, that ye may be clean [*katharistheseslhe*] from all your sins before the Lord."

This sixteenth chapter of Leviticus is dealing with the Day of Atonement in the times of ancient Israel. If the high priest among the Jews in olden time cleansed or purged (*katharizo*) the people from all their sins, it is plain that when the angel told Daniel, "Unto two thousand and three hundred days; then shall the sanctuary be cleansed [*katharisthesetai*]," he meant that at the end of the 2300 days, in 1844, the heavenly sanctuary would begin to be purged of sin. Another example of the use of *katharizo* is Leviticus 16:19.

In Hebrews 9:23 we find the apostle Paul using *katharizo* in the sense of "purified." In our English Bibles this text reads: "It was therefore necessary that the patterns of things in the heavens should be *purified* with these; but the heavenly things themselves with better sacrifices than these."

The Hebrew word translated "cleansed" in Daniel 8:14, is in other scripture texts sometimes translated "justified." For instance, Isaiah 53:11 reads in the King James Version: "He shall see of the travail of His soul, and shall be satisfied: by His knowledge shall My righteous Servant *justify* many; for He shall bear their iniquities."

Here we have the great High Priest in heaven *justifying* many, while in the typical service the high priest was to *katharisai* the people from all their sins. One is the type, the other the antitype. The significance of the priestly service is the same in both cases. The cleansing of the sanctuary, or justifying of the sanctuary, is a work of purifying or purging from sin.

In this text, Isaiah 53:11, there can be no mistaking the meaning of the word "justify." In the justification of "many" there is comprehended the forgiveness of sin and the cleansing from sin. This is made clear in 1 John 1:9, where we read: "If we confess our sins, He is faithful and just to forgive us our sins, and to cleanse [*katharisēi*] us from all unrighteousness."

Just as in the type the sins of the people were covered by the blood, and then carried out of the sanctuary, and thereby separated from it, making it clean from sin's pollution, so in the antitype the sanctuary in heaven is being justified, or in other words, cleansed, purged.

This work of cleansing, or blotting out of sins, takes place in the antitypical day of atonement. Peter said, as recorded in Acts 3:19, that it would be "when the times of refreshing shall come from the presence of the Lord; and He shall send Jesus Christ," that sins would be blotted out. This is in harmony with the text we are considering, namely, Daniel 8:14, that "unto two thousand and three hundred days; then shall the sanctuary be cleansed."

That clearer light was to shine upon the sanctuary question in this judgment hour than had been seen during the ages past, is apparent from the first angel's

message of Revelation 14:6, 7, which begins, "Fear God, and give glory to Him; for the hour of His judgment is come." Here is an angel flying in midheaven, and speaking with a loud voice to every nation, kindred, tongue, and people, saying, "The hour of His [God's] judgment is come."

In 1844 the hour arrived when the ministry of Christ in the heavenly sanctuary must be understood in its clear light and in its proper setting. Jesus had fulfilled His priestly service in the first apartment of the heavenly sanctuary, and His intercession now must give way to the closing efforts for the salvation of the human race in the second apartment of the heavenly sanctuary in the antitypical day of atonement. This final chapter of the Saviour's ministry began at the end of the 2300 days. The advent movement which began in 1844 reached its climax when the believers in the return of their Lord expected to see Him whom they loved, on October 22 of that memorable year. These earnest, God-fearing, sincere, waiting saints made no provision for any time in this world following the day they expected to be translated from earth to heaven. They looked for no future on this mundane sphere subsequent to that day.

After their keen and bitter disappointment in not seeing their Lord, all of which had been forecast in the Scripture (see Revelation 10), confusion entered the ranks of the advent band. A ray of heavenly light here and there pierced the gloom which shrouded these waiting ones. Not till the gift of prophecy was restored to God's people by a call from the Lord to Miss Ellen G. Harmon (Mrs. James White), upon whom was bestowed the special heavenly endowment of visions and dreams, did the loyal and faithful remnant have clear divine guidance.

Elder James White declares that from the latter part of the year 1844, when Ellen Harmon was given her first vision, to the year 1868, a period of twenty-four years, she received between one hundred and two hundred visions. Not very long after her early visitations from the angel, she received heavenly explanation of the work of our great High Priest in heaven. (See "Early Writings," p. 32.) The streams of holy light were pouring forth from the heavenly sanctuary to the people of God.

Of a vision which came to her on Sabbath, March 24, 1849, in regard to the ministry of Christ in the heavenly sanctuary, Mrs. White says:

"Then I was shown that the commandments of God, and the testimony of Jesus Christ relating to the shut door, could not be separated, and that the time for the commandments of God to shine out with all their importance, and for God's people to be tried on the Sabbath truth, was when the door was opened in the most holy place in the heavenly sanctuary, where the ark is, in which are contained the ten commandments. This door was not opened until the mediation of Jesus was finished in the holy place of the sanctuary in 1844. Then Jesus rose up and shut the door of the holy place, and opened the door into the most holy, and passed within the second veil, where He now stands by the ark, and where the faith of Israel now reaches.

"I saw that Jesus had shut the door of the holy place, and no man can open it: and that He had opened the door into the most holy, and no man can shut it (Rev. 3:7, 8)."—"Early Writings," p. 42.

In a supplementary note found on page 86 of "Early Writings," we find the following statement made by Mrs. White in regard to the foregoing paragraph:

"The view of the 'Open and the Shut Door,' on pages 42-45, was given in 1849. The application of Revelation 3:7, 8, to the heavenly sanctuary and Christ's ministry was entirely new to me. I had never heard the idea advanced by any one. Now as the subject of the sanctuary is being clearly understood, the application is seen in its force and beauty."

Christ once more gave to the church a revealed knowledge of the sanctuary. This divine illumination came at the close of the 2300 days. Now the sanctuary question is understood in all its bearings, being made clear to the remnant church of Christ. We now understand what is comprehended in the heavenly ministry of our Lord, what is involved in the antitypical work of our High Priest in the cleansing of the sanctuary, and what has taken place in heaven for mankind since Jesus passed from the holy place in the heavenly sanctuary into the most holy place.

In view of the foregoing statements, what significance must be attached to the following counsel from the Spirit of prophecy:

"Many of our people do not realize how firmly the foundation of our faith has been laid. My husband, Elder Joseph Bates, Father Pierce, Elder Edson, and others, . . . were among those who, after the passing of the time in 1844, searched for the truth as for hidden treasure. I met with them, and we studied and prayed earnestly. Often we remained together until late at night, and sometimes through the entire night, praying for light and studying the word. . . .

"When they came to the point in their study where they said, 'We can do nothing more,' the Spirit of the Lord would come upon me, I would be taken off in vision, and a clear explanation of the passages we had been studying would be given me, with instruction as to how we were to labor and teach effectively. Thus light was given that helped us to understand the scriptures in regard to Christ, His mission, and His priesthood. A line of truth extending from that time to the time when we shall enter the city of God, was made plain to me, and I gave to others the instruction that the Lord had given me."—*"Special Testimonies,"* Series B, No. 2, pp. 56, 57.

How God Through the Ages Gave Light on the Sanctuary

1. How was the light on the sanctuary truth originally given? Ex. 25:1, 2, 8, 9, 40; 26:30; 27:8; Num. 8:4.

The light on the sanctuary came to Israel originally through the revelations which God gave to Moses. It was at the direct command of the Lord to Israel, through Moses, that the sanctuary was erected. To Moses were shown the articles of furniture which were to be made for the sacred service, and each particular part was given to him by revelation from God.

2. Where is the true sanctuary, the pattern of which was revealed to Moses? Heb. 8:1, 2, 5; 9:24; Rev. 1:12, 13; 8:3; 11:19.

We read in the book of Exodus that what was being shown to Moses while he was with God in the mount, was a pattern by which he was to make the sanctuary and its instruments; and Paul, in Hebrews 8:5, says the earthly priesthood was an example or "shadow of heavenly things." The Scriptures clearly point out real and actual furnishings in the sanctuary in heaven, the object lesson of which was shown to Moses.

It seems difficult for some to grasp the reality of the objects in the heavenly sanctuary and the ministry of the priesthood carried on there. Due largely to the lack of training and religious instruction in regard to heaven and heavenly things, many believers find it difficult at first to accept the teaching of Scripture that there is a sanctuary in heaven. But the Bible is clear, definite, and specific. The language cannot be misunderstood. The prophet to whom was given a vision and revelation of heavenly things, plainly states that he saw articles of furniture in the heavenly sanctuary, the heavenly temple.

3. Was there any priestly ministry carried on in the heavenly sanctuary during the existence and operation of the earthly sanctuary? Heb. 9:8-10, 23-26; 10:19-21; 8:3, 4.

There was no ministry conducted in the heavenly sanctuary during the time the typical earthly sanctuary was in operation. This the scripture makes clear. After the apostle Paul describes the ministry of the two apartments in the earthly sanctuary, he distinctly says:

"The Holy Ghost this signifying, that the way into the holiest of all was not yet made manifest, while as the first tabernacle was yet standing: which was a figure for the time then present, in which were offered both gifts and sacrifices, . . . until the time of reformation." Heb. 9:9, 10.

4. Where was Moses when he received the information concerning the sanctuary and its ministry? Ex. 24:1, 2, 18; 25:9, 10, 23, 31; 26: 1-7, 31, 34, 35; 28:1, 2; 29:1, 46; 30:1-9; Lev. 8:1-5.

Moses was called of God to come up into the mount. Repeatedly did the Lord instruct Moses to see, to watch, to observe, what was being revealed to him. Day and night, forty days at a time, Moses was with the Lord in the mount, observing what he was being shown. We are told that he neither ate nor drank all through those days and weeks. From the time that Moses left the people until he returned again to the camp, where the Israelites were carrying on their idolatrous worship of the golden calf, the prophet of Israel received by divine revelation the plan of the sanctuary, its furnishings, its ministry. Nothing went into the sanctuary, nor into its services, except what was revealed to Moses.

5. How does David say he was enabled to formulate the plans for the erection of the temple which was built by Solomon? 2 Sam. 23: 1, 2; 1 Chron. 28:2, 3, 6, 9-13, 19.

We have no mention of a temple in the Scriptures until we reach the days of David. During the first three thousand years of human history, no such term as "temple" is found in the Sacred Record. When Joshua with the Israelites possessed the land of Canaan, the tabernacle was located in Shiloh. (See Joshua 18:1; 19:51.) For several centuries the worship of God was conducted in the tabernacle in Shiloh. It was in Shiloh that Samuel ministered in the tabernacle at the time when God called the lad, and bestowed upon him the gift of prophecy. (See 1 Sam. 3:1, 19-21.)

In the days of Samuel, at the time when Eli's sons carried the ark of God into the camp of Israel, the sacred chest was captured by the Philistines. 1 Sam. 4:4. Shiloh was finally destroyed. (See Ps. 78:60; Jer. 7:12, 14; 26:6, 9.)

The ark of God was located for some time in Kirjath-jearim, after the Philistines had returned it to the camp of Israel. 1 Sam. 6:21. It remained in this place for about twenty years. 1 Sam. 7:2. Israel had gone into idolatry. 1 Sam. 7:3, 4. The prophet Samuel sought to bring about a reformation among that people, and he introduced the schools of the prophets. 1 Sam. 7:15-17. No mention is made of the sanctuary services at Shiloh during the reign of Saul, but when David was made king of Israel, he had a burden to establish a permanent place for the ark and the worship of God.

Sometime during the reign of David, to Israel's king was revealed the temple of the Lord. David desired to build a dwelling place for God. With this purpose, God was well pleased. (See 2 Sam. 7:1-11.) During his reign, he gathered vast treasures of gold, silver, brass, iron, and other materials to put into this building for God. 1 Chron. 22:14.

The treasures which the king of Israel gathered for the temple of the Lord were abundant. David says that he had "prepared for the house of the Lord a hundred thousand talents of gold, and a thousand thousand talents of silver; and of brass and iron without weight." Verse 14.

According to our monetary value, a talent of gold is $29,085. That means that Israel's king accumulated in gold alone $2,908,500,000. A talent of silver is valued at $1,940. He gathered in silver $1,940,000,000. The gold and silver together amounted to $4,848,500,000. This amount does not include the brass, iron, and other precious and valuable materials.

In addition to these vast sums, King David said he gave "three thousand talents of gold, of the gold of Ophir, and seven thousand talents of refined silver, to overlay the walls of the houses withal." 1 Chron. 29:4. These three thousand talents of most precious gold, valued at the regular price of the metal, equal $87,255,000. The added seven thousand talents of refined silver would increase the amount another $13,580,000. The total, therefore, of the gold and the silver which David contributed toward the building of that wonderful temple amounted to the staggering sum of $4,949,335,000.

It is not surprising, therefore, in view of the preparation which Israel's king made for the sacred house of God, that he said: "Solomon my son is young and tender, and the house that is to be builded for the Lord must be *exceeding magnifical*, of fame and of glory throughout all countries." 1 Chron. 22:5; 29:1.

Because David was a man of war, God did not permit him to erect this magnificent structure. 1 Chron. 22:7, 8. However, David drew the plans for this temple, for the Scripture says: "Then David gave to Solomon his son the pattern of . . . all that he had by the Spirit." "All this, said David, the Lord made me understand in writing by His hand upon me, even all the works of this pattern." 1 Chron. 28:11-13, 19.

David certifies that the pattern for the temple which was to be erected by his son Solomon was given to him by inspiration. David does not take the credit of personally designing the plans for the temple. He declares that the Spirit of the Lord made him understand how to draft the plans for this sacred edifice.

6. How was the reorganization of the services of the sanctuary effected in the days of David? 1 Chron. 24:1-5, 29, 31; 25:1-7.

Prior to and during the reign of David, the original significance of the sanctuary and its ministry must have been lost. This is evident in view of the experience through which David passed at the time when Uzzah had charge of the ark of the Lord and was so suddenly smitten. (See 2 Sam. 6:6, 7.) David's purpose was to worship the true God, but when this unexpected death of Uzzah occurred, David for a time would have nothing to do with the ark.

Three months later word came to the king that Obededom, in whose care the ark of God was placed after Uzzah's demise, was abundantly blessed of God. David then decided to discover the real cause of the mysterious death of Uzzah. The king made investigation of the Scriptures, and learned that the ark of the Lord must be carried on the shoulders of the Levites rather than placed on a wagon, as the Philistines had done.

During his reign, David also reorganized the work of the sanctuary and the priesthood. This reorganization was carried on under the instruction of the Spirit of God. 1 Chron. 23:25-27; 2 Sam. 23:1, 2.

7. How does the prophet Ezekiel say he received instruction in regard to the measurement of that temple which was never erected? Eze. 40:1-4; 44:4, 5.

Ezekiel describes the year, the month, and the day when the Lord gave him a vision of the temple which was to be erected for the children of Israel, but which never was constructed. The angel said to the prophet:

"Son of man, behold with thine eyes, and hear with thine ears, and set thine heart upon that I shall show thee; for to the intent that I might show them unto thee art thou brought hither: declare all that thou seest to the house of Israel." Eze. 40:4.

Language could not be plainer than that in the foregoing testimony, in which we are told that Ezekiel received the instruction for this temple and its ministry by revelation, not by any research he had made.

8. When the Jewish people lost the significance of the ministry of the sanctuary services, how did the Lord instruct the people as to its meaning? Matt. 23:16, 21; Gal. 1:11, 12, 20; 1 Cor. 14:37; Heb. 2:3, 4; 3:1-5; 8:1, 2.

There came a time in the history of the Israelites when they lost the meaning and significance of the services of the temple. This is evident from the way the Saviour reproved them for placing so much value on the material things of the temple, and regarding so lightly the sacred place and its worship. Jesus, to whom the services of the temple pointed forward, was of no value to that people. The worship in and of the temple consisted of form, ceremony, commercial enterprise, and man-made regulations. The priesthood had become degraded, the ministry powerless, the sacred services demoralized. The time had now come when the earthly priesthood had reached its limit of usefulness.

Intercession for lost man was as necessary as ever. Man needed a Saviour. The human race still was without God and without hope in the world. But the sanctuary ministry and priesthood was to be transferred from earth to heaven, when the everlasting priesthood was to be inaugurated.

The fulfillment of those sacrifices had appeared in the person of the Lord Jesus, Messiah, Saviour. Ps. 40:6-8; Heb. 10:5-9. He was to give His life as man's substitute. With His death these ceremonies and sacrifices would terminate. They would hereafter be meaningless. They would have no more point. The sacrificial system would have no further value, since Jesus is the *Great Offering for lost humanity.*

Because the sacrificial system was now without value, there would be no further need of an organized human priesthood, as had existed from the days of Moses. There would therefore be no further need of an earthly temple, nor of sacrifices and offerings. The entire system of the temple service would be set aside. The Lord predicted that the temple would be destroyed, and every ceremony connected with it as a sacred institution would be forever canceled. Luke 19:41-44; 21:20-24; Matt. 23:37, 38; 24:1, 2.

In order to make plain and intelligible to the Jewish people the whole economy of the sanctuary and the temple ministry, and through them to the church during future centuries until the return of the Lord at His second advent, God raised up a chosen vessel through whom He communicated by revelation the whole gospel scheme embodied in the types and symbols which had been committed to the literal seed of Abraham during fifteen centuries. A learned and scholarly Jew, born and reared among his own nation, trained in the midst of outstanding ecclesiastical leaders, with a background rich in the history of the chosen people, Saul of Tarsus was the choice of God, to set forth the real significance of the types and symbols which originated with the Lord, and which had served their purpose during the centuries of Israel's worship. Acts 9:15; 22:14; 26:16.

The Lord knew the man He needed for such a task, and He chose the one who would serve Him well. Be it remembered that nowhere in the New Testament do we find the heavenly priesthood of the Saviour enlarged upon until we reach the book of Hebrews. This book was God's final appeal to that people whom He had used for a millennium and a half to carry forward His work in the earth. The Lord gave Israel as a race a final opportunity rightly to understand His purposes for them during the centuries. In the book of Hebrews, the apostle Paul by the Holy Spirit revealed to that people, and through them to the world, the temporary and figurative mission of the sanctuary and the temple ministry.

It is true that Peter, Stephen, and other men of God declared that Jesus ascended to heaven, and sat down at the right hand of God, as Saviour, Prince, Mediator. Acts 2:25, 33-35; 7:56. But not until we reach the book of Hebrews do we find mention of the heavenly high priesthood of our Lord. Peter, toward the close of his life, made mention of the priesthood of God's people. 1 Peter 2:9. The Saviour revealed to the apostle John on the Isle of Patmos His priestly ministry in both the holy and the most holy place in heaven. Rev. 1:12; 5:10; 8:3; 11:19. The apostle Paul, however, gives the first declaration of Christ's heavenly priesthood in the book of Hebrews.

9. Is the guidance of the Holy Spirit necessary to an understanding of the Scriptures? Gen. 41:8, 16; Dan. 2:36-38; 4:17, 24, 25, 28; John 1:41, 42; 1 Cor. 9:8-10; 14:6, 26.

It is true that the Saviour promised His followers the Holy Spirit. This blessed gift was to counsel, guide, and lead God's people into all truth. John 14:17, 26. This the Spirit has done. Through the ages the Lord has had His men who have brought to the church precious light and heavenly instruction by the aid of the Holy Spirit. Yet it seems clear from the word of God that in order to bring to men a true and a full understanding of the pure and undiluted truth of God, it has been necessary for Heaven to choose "holy men of God" who "were moved by the Holy Ghost." 2 Peter 1:21. When men and women were under the direct influence of the Holy Spirit, they were preserved from delivering error to the people. Only by the Holy Spirit is one able to differentiate clearly between truth and error.

We are admonished in the Scriptures to study to show ourselves approved unto God, workmen who need not be ashamed, rightly dividing the word of truth. But this division of the word of God must be in accord with what has been given by inspiration. It was in this way that the message for this generation was assured and confirmed to the people of God. In the early days of this message, earnest and God-fearing men gathered to study the word of God. But there were some who cherished error. At such times the Holy Ghost would come upon the servant of the Lord, who was taken off in vision, and the angel of God gave a clear understanding of the Scriptures.

10. How was the full light from the Scriptures on the third angel's message made clear to the people of God in these last days?

Just one illustration will suffice to show how the full light of present truth came to this people:

"Our first general meeting in western New York . . . was held in Volney. . . . About thirty-five were present. . . . But of this number there were hardly two agreed. Some were holding serious errors, and each strenuously urged his own views, declaring that they were according to the Scriptures.

"One brother held that the one thousand years of the twentieth chapter of Revelation were in the past, and that the one hundred and forty-four thousand mentioned in the seventh and fourteenth chapters of Revelation were those raised at Christ's resurrection. . . .

"These strange differences of opinion rolled a heavy weight upon me. I saw that many errors were being presented as truth. It seemed to me that God was dishonored. Great grief pressed upon my spirits, and I fainted under the burden. . . . Brethren Bates, Chamberlain, Gurney, Edson, and my husband prayed for me. The Lord heard the prayers of His servants, and I revived.

"The light of heaven then rested upon me, and I was soon lost to earthly things. My accompanying angel presented before me some of the errors of those present, and also the truth in contrast with their errors. These discordant views, which they claimed were in harmony with the Scriptures, were only according to their opinion of Bible teaching; and I was bidden to tell them they should yield their errors, and unite upon the truths of the third angel's message.

"Our meeting closed triumphantly. Truth gained the victory. Our brethren renounced their errors, and united upon the third angel's message, and God greatly blessed them and added many to their numbers."—*"Life Sketches,"* *edition 1915,* pp. 110, 111. (See also "Gospel Workers," edition 1915, pp. 302, 307, 308.)

Christ the Fulfillment of the Law and of the Types

1. WHAT does the apostle Paul mean by the statement, "Christ is the end of the law"? Rom. 10:1-4; 1 Tim. 1:5; James 5:11.

The popular interpretation of Romans 10:4 is that when Christ came into the world, the law came to an end. It is asserted that all the law which was given to Israel through Moses and the prophets had forever ceased. Mankind was not now obligated to obey the teaching of God's law, for its necessity had come to an end.

But such an understanding of this text is far from the truth, when it is compared with other scriptures of the Bible, particularly in the light of the attitude of our Lord Himself in His exposition of the law in the sermon on the mount. The Saviour taught, as noted in the book of Luke, that "it is easier for heaven and earth to pass, than one tittle of the law to fail." Luke 16:17. "Whosoever therefore, shall break one of these least commandments, and shall teach men so, he shall be called the least in the kingdom of heaven: but whosoever shall do and teach them, the same shall be called great in the kingdom of heaven." Matt. 5:19.

The rabbis divided the ten commandments into two divisions. These divisions were called, מצות גדלות (*mitsvoth gedoloth*), greater commandments; and *mitsvoth qetannoth*, the lesser commandments. The first four commands of the decalogue were designated, *mitsvoth gedoloth*, the greater or larger commandments; the last six were entitled, מצות קטנות (*mitsvoth qetannoth*), lesser or little commandments.

The rabbis had so high a regard for the first four commandments that they said they were very high, that they were outstanding in their requirements. Tracts, pamphlets, and books have been written, setting forth their heights and their greatness. The scribes taught that not a letter of the law could be set aside. To deny even a word of the exalted or greater commandments meant anathema, condemnation. The individual who took such a position was called "the denier of the law."

The rabbis did not place so great an estimate on the last six of the commandments. Those they called *mitsvoth qetannoth*, the lesser commandments. Nevertheless, the scribes taught the people that these commandments must be obeyed, these teachings must be accepted as the words of the living God. The rabbinical leaders exalted in their teachings all the laws which were given to Israel through Moses. For Jesus to have advocated that the law of God, the ten commandments, or the laws given to Israel through Moses and the prophets, had come to an end, or were to be set aside by His advent, or were to be nullified, or were even to be minimized, would have placed Him in an awkward position. Such an attitude on His part would have indicated that He was opposed to the teaching of the Old Testament. But the Lord said that Moses *wrote* of Him. John 5:45-47. Moses "endured, as seeing Him." (See Heb. 11:23-27.)

Moses prophesied of the Saviour. The writings of the wilderness leader pointed to the Messiah. Even the Samaritans recognized that the Pentateuch (the five books of Moses) foretold the coming of Messiah. The woman at the well of Sychar said to our Lord: "I know that Messias cometh, which is called Christ: when He is come, He will tell us all things." John 4:25.

The Samaritans had unbounded faith in the writings of the five books of Moses. To this day the few remaining Samaritans, who still have a synagogue in Sebastian, old Samaria, have a copy of the writings of Moses which they have preserved for nearly three thousand years. Our Lord knew and understood the view of the Jews and the Samaritans in regard to the ten commandments and to the laws of Moses. For Him who is the fulfillment of all these writings to have claimed that by His advent those holy, righteous teachings were no longer obligatory, would have placed Him where the people could not have accepted Him as Messiah, the Sent of God.

Jesus said to the people: "Search the Scriptures; for in them ye think ye have eternal life: and they are they which testify of Me. And ye will not come to Me, that ye might have life." John 5:39, 40.

If the early disciples and apostles had taught contrary to Jesus' instruction, they would have been accused of working against the Saviour and against His mission. But the Saviour said to His apostles, just before He ascended to His Father, "Go ye therefore, and teach all nations, . . . teaching them to observe all things whatsoever *I have commanded you.*" Matt. 28:19, 20. The apostles did not contradict what our Lord commanded them. These chosen apostles followed the instruction our Lord left with them.

The object, the meaning, the purpose of the writings of Moses and the prophets, is *Christ.* He is the fulfillment of the law. Jesus Himself calls attention to this attitude of the writings of Moses and the prophets, as may be seen by the following: "These are the words which I spake unto you, while I was yet with you, that all things must be fulfilled, which were written in the law of Moses, and in the prophets, and in the Psalms, concerning Me." Luke 24:44.

Christ is the end, the intent of the law. This is what the apostle means by that expression, "Christ is the end of the law for righteousness to every one that believeth." Rom. 10:4. In verses 6-11 the apostle gives an illustration of what he means by his statement found in verse 4 of this tenth chapter of Romans, when he applies Deuteronomy 30:12, 13, to the Saviour. Jesus is the fulfillment of the types, the sacrifices, the ceremonies, of the law of Moses.

2. When John the Baptist refused to baptize the Saviour, what explanation did Jesus give to John to show that he should baptize Him? Matt. 3:15.

The Saviour explained to John the Baptist that it was necessary for Him to fulfill all the requirements of the law, in order to assure man that His mission was in harmony with the instruction given in Moses and the prophets. Baptism signifies death, burial, and resurrection—death to the world, burial to all things earthly. Paul declares that the Israelites were "all baptized unto Moses in the cloud and in the sea." 1 Cor. 10:2. That people, as they passed through the sea, virtually said good-by to all that they had left behind them. They were about to enter the land of Canaan, a land of milk and honey, of corn and wine. They were to enjoy a new home, a new experience. This baptism was necessary; by passing through the sea they expressed an outward faith that they believed they were to enter into a new life, a new experience.

Jesus, when He came to John to be baptized, said: "Suffer it to be so now: for thus it becometh us to fulfill all righteousness." Matt. 3:15. Our Lord was about to enter into a new experience in His own life. Never before had He battled singlehanded with the enemy of God and man; now, in His own person, He was to enter such a contest. He was dead to this world. He came to rescue man from the depths of sin into which he had fallen. He must give this outward expression of cleansing, in order that He might fulfill all things written. He was to die for man; He must be buried for man; He must rise again from the dead for man. He must partake of every ordinance of the law, for He is the model, the example, of all righteousness.

The apostle Paul expresses in few words the marvelous attitude of Christ in relation to His mission among men, even though He was the divine Son of God. The apostle says: "Without controversy great is the mystery of godliness; God was manifest in the flesh, justified in the Spirit, seen of angels, preached unto the Gentiles, believed on in the world, received up into glory." 1 Tim. 3:16.

3. In the sermon on the mount, what position did Jesus take in regard to the permanency of the law? Matt. 5:17, 18.

Because the teaching of the Saviour was so different from that of the rabbis of His day, the leaders of Israel sought to accuse Him of being a "denier of the law." Jesus therefore placed Himself on record as to His regard for the writings of Moses and the prophets. The Saviour said: "Think not that I am come to destroy the law, or the prophets: I am not come to destroy, but to fulfill. For verily I say unto you, Till heaven and earth pass, one jot or one tittle shall in no wise pass from the law, till all be fulfilled." Matt. 5:17, 18.

In the days of King David the Hebrew alphabet contained twenty-two letters. The same number of letters constitute the Hebrew alphabet to this day. There were, therefore, the same number of letters in the alphabet in the days of the Master. The tenth letter of this alphabet is *yodh, yod, jot.* ("Jot" is the English for the Greek *iota,* which is translated from the Hebrew *yod.)* This letter is about as large as a comma in English punctuation. It is the smallest letter of the Hebrew alphabet.

In the days of the Saviour, the Scriptures were not printed in a book, as the Holy Scriptures are now; the Sacred Writings were written by the scribes, and were usually written with a quill. These writers were able penmen. Frequently they exhibited this ability by making flourishes on certain letters. These flourishes were very tiny, and they were called crowns or tittles. At times the tittle was put on the *jot,* this smallest letter of the alphabet.

So the Saviour virtually said: The smallest letter of the alphabet, even the little dot on the smallest letter of the law, shall not pass away till all things be fulfilled. The Master emphasized in His teaching that He not only believed and accepted the writings of Moses, He also believed that the least point of the smallest letter of the law could not be done away. His position in regard to the law of Moses and the writings of Moses was more pronounced than that of the Pharisees. How can it be said by a disciple of our Lord that He or His apostles taught that at His advent the law came to an end, or was abolished?

4. Does the apostle Paul state *where* the righteousness of the law is fulfilled? Rom. 8:4.

The apostle declares that the righteousness of the law is fulfilled *"in us."* The law was fulfilled by Christ. He fulfilled every requirement of the Scriptures.

By the life He lived, Jesus demonstrated that God's law must be kept. He demonstrated the importance of obeying the law of God. By so doing He met every requirement of the law. He fulfilled the law. No one accepted His challenge: "Which of you convinceth Me of sin?" John 8:46. He alone is the spotless one. Jesus fulfilled all righteousness. It is written:

"All Thy commandments are righteousness." Ps. 119:172.

"Thy righteousness is an everlasting righteousness." Verse 142.

"This is His name whereby He shall be called, THE LORD OUR RIGHTEOUSNESS." Jer. 23:6.

"Of Him are ye in Christ Jesus, who of God is made unto us wisdom, and righteousness." 1 Cor. 1:30.

"Wherefore when He cometh into the world, He saith, . . . Lo, I come to do Thy will, O God." Heb. 10:5, 9.

He	Daleth	Gimel	Beth	Aleph
ה	ד	ג	ב	א

Yodh	Teth	Cheth	Za-yin	Waw
י	ט	ח	ז	ו

Samkh	Nun	Mem	Labedh	Kaph
ס	נ	מ	ל	כ

Resh	Qoph	Tsadhe	Pe	A-yin
ר	ק	צ	פ	ע

			Taw	Shin
			ת	ש

Finals

ץ ף ן ם ך

Hebrew Alphabet

(Read from right to left.)

155

"I delight to do Thy will, O My God: yea, Thy law is within My heart."
Ps. 40:8.
The issue of His life was to live the law of God in His flesh. He fulfilled
every part of it. When a man accepts the Saviour and gives his life to Christ,
the principles of the law of God are implanted in that man's heart, for Christ
abides in him. The prophet therefore could say of those who are obedient to
Christ and who live in harmony with the teaching of the law of God:
"Hearken unto Me, ye that know righteousness, the people in whose heart
is My law; fear ye not the reproach of men, neither be ye afraid of their revil-
ings." Isa. 51:7. From the sixth verse of this chapter it is apparent that the
prophet is speaking of the people of God who live at the time when our Lord
is to return. Christ is the fulfillment of all righteousness, and in the lives of all
who receive Christ into their hearts, and are obedient to His will, the righteous
law is fulfilled.

5. What application does the angel Gabriel make of certain Old
Testament scriptures? Isa. 7:14; 9:6; Matt. 1:23; Luke 2:11-14.

Certain Old Testament scriptures have neither meaning nor significance if
they do not meet their fulfillment in the Saviour. The expression "a virgin,"
found in Isaiah 7:14, is translated from the Hebrew word ha-almah, "the virgin."
This same word, הָעַלְמָה (ha-almah), is used in Genesis 24:43. Jewish writers
claim that the word עַלְמָה (almah), means a young married woman, but no
Jewish scholar will agree to such an interpretation of the word almah in Genesis
24:43. No child of Abraham will admit that Rebekah was a young married
woman before she was betrothed to Isaac. The Lord revealed to Isaiah that He
had some particular person in mind when He said that a virgin should give birth
to the Child whose name was interpreted, "God with us."
Because of this prophecy, the angel Gabriel said to Mary: "Hail, thou that
art highly favored, the Lord is with thee! blessed art thou among women."
Luke 1:28.

6. How did the Saviour fulfill certain Old Testament scriptures
when healing the sick? Matt. 8:16, 17; Isa. 53:4, 5.

7. When Jesus, permitting the disciples to pluck the ears of corn
on the Sabbath, was accused by the Pharisees of Sabbathbreaking, in
what manner did He defend their course? Matt. 12:1-8; Deut. 23:25.

8. What relationship does Jesus say exists between His acts while
on earth and the teaching of the law? Matt. 26:54; 27:9, 35; Mark
15:28; John 13:18; 17:12; 19:24.

The Jews have for centuries found great difficulty in disposing of the fifty-
third chapter of the book of Isaiah. Their writers undertake to explain that since
the Jewish people have for centuries been a suffering people, this chapter finds
its fulfillment in the sufferings of the children of Abraham. But their perplexity
is increased when they attempt to harmonize this idea of the suffering of the Jews
as the fulfillment of the fifty-third chapter of this prophecy with verses 4-6.
The rabbis maintain that it is the griefs of Israel which have been borne,
theirs are the sorrows which have been carried, they have been wounded and
bruised. They admit they are the sheep who have gone astray; they acknowledge
that they have turned every man to his own way. But the prophet says, "The
Lord hath laid on Him the iniquity of us all." Who is the "Him," if the Jews are
the sheep who have gone astray?
The scripture is harmonious, consistent, when it is understood that Messiah
is the One upon whom the sins of all peoples have been laid. Jesus bears the
sins of Jews and Gentiles. The Lord declares that the fifty-third chapter of
Isaiah meets its fulfillment in Him, and in His healing of the sick.

9. Because the leaders of Israel did not accept Christ as Messiah, what did He say of their attitude toward the law? John 7:19-23.

The Pharisees were confused and angered when the Saviour told them that they did not keep the law. They made such a high profession in their regard for the sacredness of the law of Moses, that when Jesus pointed out to them their inconsistency in circumcising a man on the Sabbath that the law of Moses should not be broken, yet condemning Him for healing a man on the Sabbath, they accused Him of being possessed of a demon.

What angered the Pharisees in regard to the healing of the man on the Sabbath, was that the Saviour told the man to take up his bed and walk. (See John 5:8, 10.) But the circumcision of a child on the Sabbath, makes necessary the carrying of the child from the mother's bed to the appointed place where this rite is to be performed. If the circumcision is to take place in the synagogue, then the child is carried from its mother to the synagogue. Seldom was the infant operated on in the same room with his mother. Even then the child must be taken from its bed and passed to the one who performed the operation. The law of Moses must be obeyed. The child must be circumcised on the eighth day. The leaders of Israel so stressed the importance of circumcision that they affirmed that one reason why the Lord made the world was in order that He might create a man, and the man be circumcised. This rite of circumcision, in the estimate of the Pharisees, was greater than the work of creation.

Furthermore, the rabbis taught that Abraham is stationed at the entrance to Gehenna. When the death angel brings a man who should be cast into Gehenna, they say, Abraham inquires of this angel whether the man has been circumcised. Should the angel reply in the affirmative, Abraham forbids the angel to cast the man into Gehenna.

But in order to circumcise a child on the Sabbath day, they had to acknowledge that they were violating the law of Moses. According to their tradition, no burden can be carried on the Sabbath. But they were obliged to carry a burden on the Sabbath in their endeavor to carry out the rite of circumcision. Thus they condemned themselves in their anger against Christ, when He told the man to carry his bed after He had healed him on the Sabbath.

10. What surprising statement did Jesus make in one of His parables? Luke 16:31.

It must have been a shock to the Pharisees when the Saviour told them that they would not believe though a man were raised from the dead, if they did not believe that the writings of Moses and the prophets were fulfilled in Him. John 8:24. Yet our Lord proved His statement before He completed His work among them. He raised Jairus' daughter from the dead; He raised the only son of the widow of Nain from the dead; and in the presence of a large gathering of people he raised Lazarus from the grave, after decomposition had already begun.

Following this miracle of raising Lazarus from the tomb, the Pharisees took counsel to put Lazarus to death, because through him many of the people believed on Christ. John 12:9-11. It still remains true, that if one does not believe that the writings of Moses and the prophets meet their fulfillment in the Saviour, he will not be convinced though the dead are raised.

11. Were the disciples of Christ able to understand clearly the Scriptures in regard to the life and work of the Saviour while He was on earth? Luke 24:26, 27, 44, 45.

The disciples had been so influenced by rabbinical teaching that it was difficult for them to accept the application of Scripture as interpreted by our Lord while He was with them. (See John 2:18-22; Luke 24:6-8; Matt. 17:9-12.)

Jesus promised the disciples that after He ascended to heaven, He would send them the Holy Spirit. This Spirit would teach them, and would enlighten their minds in regard to the meaning of the Scriptures. This promise was fulfilled soon after Christ's ascension. Acts 1 :16-20; 2 :25-36.

12. Why, according to the apostle Paul, did, the Lord commit the ministry of the sanctuary to the Jewish people? Heb. 9 :9, 10, 24, 25; Deut. 29 :14, 15; Rom. 15 :4; 1 Cor. 10 :11.

To the children of Abraham were committed the oracles of God. Rom. 3 :1, 2. They were a people to whose ancestors God had made definite promises. Rom. 15 :8. These promises and oracles were to meet their fulfillment when Messiah came as a literal descendant of Abraham. The Saviour Himself told the woman at the well of Sychar that "salvation is of the Jews." John 4 :22. The apostle Paul declares that the promises, the worship of God, and the entire service of God were all entrusted to that people. Rom. 9 :1-5. By the training the Lord planned to give them through the centuries, they were to be fitted to demonstrate to the world the real purpose of those shadows and figures in the life and death of Christ, and in the heavenly ministry He would conduct for a lost world.

13. Since God has compared the work of Christ with that of Moses, is the typical sanctuary service essential to a true understanding of the antitypical work in the heavenly sanctuary fulfilled by Christ, our great heavenly High Priest? Heb. 3 :1-5; John 3 :14; Rev. 15 :2, 3; Heb. 9 :6-10, 23, 24.

Repeatedly do we learn from the New Testament that the Lord joined the work of Moses with that of Christ. The apostle tells us that Moses is used as an illustration of those things which were to take place in later times. What God hath joined together, no man can put asunder. The services of the sanctuary which God gave to Israel through Moses will enable the child of God to have a clear conception of the finishing of the ministry of Christ in heaven for the human race.

Our Lord did not overthrow or destroy any of the truth which God gave to Israel through the centuries. It was not the mission of the Saviour to introduce a new religion by His advent. He came to His own, even though they did not receive Him. John 1 :11. His coming was to confirm to the people the promises God made to their ancestors. Jesus had no Gentiles in the circle of His disciples. In His first gospel commission to His followers, He commanded them to go to the lost sheep of the house of Israel. Matt. 10 :1-6. Even after His resurrection and ascension, the apostles were commanded to begin at Jerusalem, then to work in Judea, and later in Samaria; after that they were to go to the uttermost parts of the earth. Acts 1 :8.

Christ came to affirm the truths that people had had in their possession for hundreds of years. His life and teaching were in confirmation of what had been given to them during fifteen centuries. There is no teaching in the New Testament contrary to the truths in the Old Testament. Prophecies and symbols met their fulfillment in Him. The types were met by antitype, in the person of our Lord. Certain of the symbolic teachings ceased by limitation, because Jesus fulfilled them. When Christ's work on earth was completed, He ascended to heaven to carry on His intercession for man at the throne of His Father, in fulfillment of the promises and prophecies given to the children of Israel through prophet and priest.

Christ the Spotless Lamb of God

1. WHAT was Christ's purpose in coming to this world as a man? Luke 19:10; John 10:10; Rom. 4:25; 1 Cor. 1:30; Heb. 2:9; 2 Tim. 1:10.

2. What reply did Jesus give to His mother, when she found Him in the temple discussing with the doctors of the law? Luke 2:49.

3. Was the Saviour always conscious of His mission? John 4: 34; 6:38.

Our Lord had a definite purpose in coming to this world. He was here to attend to the task committed to Him by His Father. This mission was uppermost in His mind from childhood. He never lost sight of the work He came to accomplish.

4. What are two outstanding reasons for Christ's taking upon Himself man's nature? John 1:4; 10:10; 1 Cor. 15:3.

The mission of Jesus to restore man to His Creator may be considered under two heads: First, He came to live for man. He must live the life which God intended man should live. Second, He must pay the penalty for sin. 1 Cor. 15:3. He must die for man.

5. Before completing His ministry as Messiah, what public challenge did Jesus issue? John 8:46.

The law of God demanded a perfect life. Ps. 19:7. Adam forfeited his life, because he disobeyed God's law. Rom. 5:19. The second Adam, Christ, came to accomplish what the first man failed to do. A perfect God gave a perfect law; this perfect law must be kept by a perfect man. Matt. 5:48. The Lord from heaven, who dwelt among sinful men in a sinful world, challenged the world to prove that He had one fault in His character. Neither by thought, nor by word, nor by act did the Saviour as a man deviate from the path of righteousness. He said He always did those things which pleased His Father. John 8:29.

Neither Satan nor men accepted the challenge. Neither friend nor foe confronted Him with a single error or wrong He had done. He lived and dwelt among men, from His childhood to manhood. He toiled as man must toil; He was subject to home influences. He lived in communities under the most peculiar circumstances; yet He never once made a mistake. Not a single fault was found in Him. But Jesus of Nazareth is the only one who ever lived a perfect life since man was placed upon the earth. He is the *one perfect man, the Sinless One.*

6. How did John the Baptist introduce the Saviour to the public? John 1:29, 36.

When John the Baptist introduced the Saviour to the world, He invited the people to "behold the Lamb of God." On at least two occasions the Saviour was mentioned by John in this way. Seven hundred years before His first advent, the prophet Isaiah wrote of Messiah as the lamb led to the slaughter. It is written: "He is brought as a lamb to the slaughter, and as a sheep before her shearers is dumb, so He openeth not His mouth." Isa. 53:7.

7. What outstanding statement did Jesus make in the prayer He offered to His Father, following the last Passover with the disciples? John 17:4.

The Saviour repeatedly told His disciples that He came to do the will of God who sent Him, and to finish His work. John 4:34. This special work committed to the Saviour was to live and to die for man. Jesus called upon mankind to point out a single defect in His life. No one could do this. The Saviour, therefore, in the prayer He offered to His Father, after He partook of the last Passover supper with His disciples, said: "I have finished the work which Thou gavest Me to do."

He had accomplished acceptably this feature of His mission. He had lived in perfect harmony with the precepts and principles of His Father's law. Not a single just charge was preferred against His spotless life. He is the *Lamb of God, without spot and without blemish.* Having lived a pure and holy life, He earned the right to become man's *substitute.* He is the *Lamb* who could be offered as the sacrifice for man's sins.

In the earthly sanctuary the sinner must bring a spotless offering to make atonement for his sins. Lev. 4:3, 23, 28. Our Lord's life was without blemish. He was worthy to be offered for the sins of the people, as man's *substitute.* Rev. 5:1-7.

8. After the close of this prayer, where did Jesus go? John 18:1, 26; Matt. 26:36, 37.

9. What typical feature of the offering for sin was Christ fulfilling while in the Garden of Gethsemane? Isa. 53:5, 6; Matt. 26:38-44; Luke 22:39-44.

The next act of the sinner, after he brought the offering without blemish to the sanctuary, was to place his hands on the head of this substitute, and confess his sins. In this way the sinner transferred his guilt to the blameless offering. Our Lord Jesus, after He had finished the work God gave Him to do, by living the stainless and perfect life, went into the Garden of Gethsemane. While in the garden, He prayed His Father that, if possible, the cup He was to drink might pass from Him. Repeatedly, however, He said, "Not as I will, but as Thou wilt." Matt. 26:39. What was this cup which Christ drank in the garden? The prophet Isaiah declared of Messiah: "All we like sheep have gone astray; we have turned every one to his own way; and the Lord hath laid on Him the iniquity of us all." Isa. 53:6.

Jesus entered Gethsemane to bear the guilt of a sinful world. He entered the garden voluntarily, and upon Him were confessed the sins of the world. Upon Christ were laid the sins which man should bear. Christ was transferring the sins of the sinner unto Himself. He "made Him to be sin for us, who knew no sin." 2 Cor. 5:21. He must drink the cup. He trod the wine press alone; there was none to assist or sympathize with Him. The disciples were asleep while Jesus was agonizing and pleading with God to enable Him to bear the guilt of a sinful world. Our Lord found none to help Him. There was none to uphold Him. He bore the weight and the woe of the sins of a guilty world. The Lord laid upon Him the iniquity of us all. Isa. 63:3-5.

10. What followed immediately after the Saviour had ended His prayer in Gethsemane? John 18:1-7, 28, 29, 31; 19:13-18, 30.

After the sinner confessed his sin upon the head of the sacrifice, with his own hand he took a knife and killed the offering. Lev. 4:4, 15, 24, 29. From Gethsemane the "Lamb of God" went directly to Calvary, and here the Spotless One was taken by cruel hands and put to death. The Sanhedrin, the Roman officials, the officers, and the people,—all had a share in taking His life. He died for all, for Jew and for Gentile. He sacrificed His life for monarch as well as for peasant. The apostle Peter said: "Of a truth against Thy holy child Jesus, whom Thou hast anointed, both Herod, and Pontius Pilate, with the Gentiles, and the people of Israel, were gathered together, for to do whatsoever Thy hand and Thy counsel determined before to be done." Acts 4:27, 28.

11. Just before the Saviour died, what request did He make of His Father? Luke 23:34.

Just before the Saviour died, He prayed for those who took His life. Jesus did not have to die. His life was not taken against His will. He *gave* Himself for our sins, a willing sacrifice and a sweet savor. He died for His love of a lost world. He permitted man to offer Him up in his stead. Our Lord says: "Therefore doth My Father love Me, because I lay down My life, that I might take it again. No man taketh it from Me, but I lay it down of Myself." John 10:17, 18.

The Saviour had no malice in His heart against His murderers. Had they known what they were doing, they never would have killed the Prince of life. Acts 3:14, 15, 17; 1 Cor. 2:8. The sacrifice of the "Lamb of God" for the sins of the world was a freewill offering. Christ *gave* Himself for our sins, that He might redeem us from this evil world, and from the evil of our own hearts. Gal. 1:4.

The last words of Jesus on the cross were, "It is finished." He had finished the work He came to do, by dying as well as by living for man. John 19:30.

12. How does the apostle Peter describe the Saviour after He ascended to heaven? 1 Peter 1:18, 19.

John the Baptist introduced the Saviour as the "Lamb of God," and Peter speaks of Him as the "lamb without blemish and without spot." This latter statement was true at the beginning of the Saviour's ministry, and it was true in a larger sense after Jesus had gained repeated victories over sin and Satan. At the time of His baptism, Jesus had not yet been tempted in the wilderness. But when He expired on the cross, He had gained the victory over the evil one in every struggle. He was indeed the spotless Lamb of God.

After His baptism, Jesus began His ministry. For forty days He was in the wilderness, tempted of Satan. Matt. 4:1-11. During the three years following, our Lord passed through severe conflicts with the enemy. Again and again Satan came to the Saviour to tempt and try Him, peradventure He might cause the Saviour to yield to his temptations. The conflicts through which our Lord passed with Satan were fierce, trying. The devil hoped that he might conquer the Saviour, and by some means seduce Him into sin.

The struggle in Gethsemane was excruciating. The thought of the Father's presence being withdrawn from Him while He was drinking the cup of suffering, almost crushed the Saviour. Amid the fierce conflicts and struggles with Satan, Jesus submitted Himself to the Father. He had absolute confidence in the Father's guidance. "Though He were a Son, yet learned He obedience by the things which He suffered." Heb. 5:8. Through suffering He was made perfect. All this the Saviour did for us. But, thank God, He never sinned. He came off more than conqueror over the powers of darkness. "When a strong man armed keepeth his palace, his goods are in peace: but when a stronger than he shall come upon him, and overcome him, he taketh from him all his armor wherein he trusted, and divideth his spoils." Luke 11:21, 22.

Christ overcame Satan and all the hosts of evil for our sake. He is the "Lamb without blemish and without spot."

Christ's Death, Burial, Resurrection, and Ascension

1. Was Christ compelled to die? John 10:17, 18.
2. How did Christ die? Matt. 27:45-50; Ps. 69:20.

Death is caused by sin. But the apostle Peter says: "Even hereunto were ye called: because Christ also suffered for us, leaving us an example, that ye should follow His steps: who did no sin, neither was guile found in His mouth." 1 Peter 2:21, 22.

Persons put to death by crucifixion usually hung on the cross from twenty-four to forty-eight hours, and even longer. The Saviour hung on the tree from six to nine hours, then He died. When Joseph of Arimathea asked Pilate to permit him to take down the body of the Saviour, because it was the afternoon of the preparation day, "Pilate marveled if He were already dead: and calling unto him the centurion, he asked him whether He had been any while dead. And when he knew it of the centurion, he gave the body to Joseph." Mark 15:44, 45.

The Sanhedrin did not permit bodies of Jews to hang on the cross during the Sabbath day. They, therefore, went to Pilate and requested him to break the legs of the prisoners. The soldiers broke the legs of the thieves, but when they came to the body of the Saviour, they found He was already dead. It was unheard of, for a person to die so quickly by crucifixion.

However, one of the soldiers pierced the side of the Saviour with a spear, and from His side there came forth blood and water. John 19:34. The cause of the Saviour's death is recorded in the following prophecy: "Reproach hath *broken My heart;* and I am full of heaviness: and I looked for some to take pity, but there was none; and for comforters, but I found none."

Yes, the Son of God died of a broken heart. Sin killed Him. "He was cut off out of the land of the living: for the transgression of my people was He stricken. . . . When thou shalt make His soul an offering for sin, He shall see His seed, He shall prolong His days. . . . For He shall bear their iniquities." Isa. 53:8-11.

Sin has made the human heart adamant. Man's heart has become like stone. "Yea, they made their hearts as an adamant stone, lest they should hear the law." Zech. 7:12.

But the Lord promised that under the new covenant He would give to man a new heart. It is written: "A new heart also will I give you, and a new spirit will I put within you: and I will take away the stony heart out of your flesh, and I will give you a heart of flesh." Eze. 36:26.

As the Saviour died of a broken heart, He made it possible that through His death, man might receive another, a different heart. For it is written: "Thou desirest not sacrifice; else would I give it: Thou delightest not in burnt offering. The sacrifices of God are a broken spirit: a broken and a contrite heart, O God, Thou wilt not despise." Ps. 51:16, 17.

3. Why, according to the apostle Peter, could the grave not retain Christ? Acts 2:24.

Peter declares that it was not possible for the grave to hold the Saviour. When Adam sinned, he not only lost his life, he also lost his home; "for of whom a man is overcome, of the same is he brought in bondage." 2 Peter 2:19.

God did not give this world to man as an absolute gift; He gave him this earth as a gift in trust. Man is a steward. 1 Cor. 4:1, 2; 1 Peter 4:10. When Satan seduced our first parents into sin, the earth passed out of the hands of man, and was taken possession of by the enemy. Of Jesus we read: "The devil, taking Him up into a high mountain, showed unto Him all the kingdoms of the world in a moment of time. And the devil said unto Him, All this power will I give Thee, . . . for that is delivered unto me; and to whomsoever I will I give it." Luke 4:5, 6.

In the great plan of salvation, not only must man be bought back, but the earth also must be redeemed. The redemption of the land always accompanied the redemption of its people. Such was an ancient law in Israel. (See Ruth 3:11-13; 4:3-10.)

Man could be redeemed only by blood. "The life of the flesh is in the blood: and I have given it to you upon the altar to make an atonement for your souls: for it is the blood that maketh an atonement for the soul." Lev. 17:11. "Almost all things are by the law purged with blood; and without shedding of blood is no remission." Heb. 9:22.

The blood of Christ purchased man's life. Acts 20:28. We have redemption through the precious blood of the Son of God. Eph. 1:7. The apostle tells us that redemption includes the "purchased possession." (See Eph. 1:11-14.) In ancient Israel the way the land must be cleansed of human blood was by the blood of the man who shed it. Num. 35:33. Christ's agony in Gethsemane and upon Calvary's cross is an assurance that this earth will be cleansed, and will become man's eternal possession, through the precious Saviour. 2 Peter 3:10-13. It is written: "Thou, O Tower of the flock, the stronghold of the daughter of Zion, unto Thee shall it come, even the first dominion; the kingdom shall come to the daughter of Jerusalem." Micah 4:8.

When the earth temporarily passed into the hands of Satan, the devil turned this world into a prison house. Isa. 14:12-14, 17; 24:22. From Adam to the present time, the multitudes who have come into the world have gone down into the tomb, Satan's prison. Of the millions and the billions who have been born into this world, only two have escaped this prison. These two are Enoch and Elijah. Enoch escaped the dark tomb because God took him to heaven, and Elijah was escorted to heaven by thousands of angels. (See Gen. 5:24; Heb. 11:5; 2 Kings 2:11; Ps. 68:17; 2 Kings 6:17.) Since the first man went into the grave, no one who entered the prison house, except Jesus, has been able to unlock the prison doors and to let its captives go free. Excepting Him, all who entered there had sinned, and had come short of the glory of God. Rom. 3:23. There had been no liberator.

Christ died for man. But Jesus did not die for His own sins; He died for the sins of others. But the Saviour also entered the tomb. Matt. 27:60. Satan was able to lock the doors of the tomb upon all others who had gone down into the pit, for they all had transgressed. None were able to unlock that door, and Satan held the key to it. Our Lord entered the grave voluntarily. He was not compelled to enter there because of any wrong He had done. And Satan could not lock the door of the prison house upon Him. Jesus was raised from the dead; He conquered the devil. The Son of God came forth from the grave a victor over death and the tomb. He burst its bars; He unlocked the door. The apostle Peter could well say that it was impossible for the grave to hold the Son of God.

4. Did Jesus come forth from the grave alone? Matt. 27:52, 53; Rev. 1:17, 18.

When Jesus burst the bars of Satan's prison and came forth from the grave, He did not rise alone. At His resurrection "the earth did quake, and the rocks rent; and the graves were opened; and many bodies of the saints which slept arose, and came out of the graves after His resurrection, and went into the Holy City, and appeared unto many." Matt. 27:51-53.

The Saviour demonstrated that He is the resurrection and the life. John 11:25. In conquering the grave, our Lord wrested the keys to it from the hand of Satan. Jesus could encourage the apostle John on the Isle of Patmos with the assurance that death would hold no more terrors for those who died in Christ. Jesus is alive forevermore. He now holds the keys of death and the grave.

Those who came forth from the grave at His resurrection are an illustration of what will happen to all who have died in Christ, when the Lord shall descend from heaven with a shout, with the voice of the Archangel. For at that time all the dead in Christ shall be made alive. 1 Thess. 4:16; John 5:25, 28, 29.

5. What special message did the Saviour give to His disciples just before His ascension to heaven? Luke 24:49; Acts 1:4.

The Saviour admonished His disciples not to enter upon their work immediately at His ascension. He told them to wait at Jerusalem. There was a work of preparation the disciples must experience before they could begin the task committed to their trust, the task of giving the gospel to the world.

There was also a service in which Jesus must engage, when He reached heaven, ere He entered upon His priestly work of intercession. The disciples were not qualified for their work, and our High Priest was not yet prepared to enter upon His heavenly ministry. Jesus first must be consecrated to His priestly ministry in the sanctuary above. Heb. 7:28. He instructed the apostles to tarry in Jerusalem until they received the equipment which would qualify them for their Heaven-sent task, and until His dedication as High Priest had taken place.

Immediately upon His ascension, the disciples gathered together in an upper chamber in Jerusalem, and entered upon the work of heart preparation. They spent days and nights in prayer and supplication, seeking the Lord for the heart cleansing they must have to qualify them for their Heaven-appointed task. Acts 1:13, 14; Luke 24:52.

6. What did Jesus say to His disciples shortly before His death? John 16:7.

Jesus told the disciples that it was expedient for them that He go away. He did not say that it was expedient for Him that He go away, but it was expedient for them. The Holy Spirit would not come to them as long as Christ remained in the world. To accomplish successfully the work He had committed to them, they must have this blessed Spirit. It was therefore essential for Him to leave them, and to return to the Father's house, whence He might send them that blessed gift.

This world was not the Saviour's home. He came to our earth to accomplish a specific work. This He had done. Why, therefore, should He remain here longer in person? Moreover, if the Saviour should still abide in this world, those who needed His help would have to make a pilgrimage to Him, wherever He was located. From far and wide the needy and helpless would be obliged to journey, in order that they might receive the assistance and peace which only the Saviour could give. All such conditions would be unnecessary if He went away and sent the Holy Spirit, His personal representative.

Our heavenly Father permitted men to pass through certain difficult and trying experiences, because of Satan's cruel charges against God and man. The Lord acknowledged that the trials through which Job passed were unnecessary.

But Satan's accusations against God and man were most vindictive. The devil claimed that not even Job loved God unselfishly. God permitted Satan to try Job to the uttermost, that Satan and heavenly intelligences might know there were those who loved God sincerely and unselfishly. Job 1:6-12; 2:3-6; James 5:11.

Jesus was tempted in all points like as man is tempted. Heb. 4:15. He knows from personal experience what man is obliged to suffer at the hands of our common enemy. Our Saviour understands well the unjust and unfounded accusations of Satan against man. Jesus is acquainted with the various schemes and devices of Satan. Our Lord met them all. Heb. 2:14.

Now, at the right hand of God, in the presence of the Father, we have a Saviour who is both God and man. He is able to defend the character of His heavenly Father, and He knows how to intercede mercifully and sympathetically with His Father for man. It was indeed expedient for us that our Lord went away.

7. Where did Jesus say He was going? John 14:1-3; 16:28; 13:3.

Jesus was returning to His home, to the presence of God. He had been absent from His glorious heavenly abode for more than thirty years. He had denied Himself the comforts and delights of heaven. He was the Majesty of the universe. He was the One adored by angel, by seraph, by cherub, by all the heavenly hosts.

Our Lord now was returning to share the throne with His Father. This was His right by inheritance. He had inherited a name more excellent than all the heavenly beings. Heb. 1:4. But He now was returning to the Father's throne in a different relationship to heaven and earth than He had sustained prior to His advent. He was now to become man's Intercessor, man's High Priest. He was to share the Father's throne, and to act as a Mediator on that throne in behalf of those who should place their trust in Him. He was to make His appeal to the Father when Satan made his false charges against poor, weak men.

Jesus also was going to heaven to prepare a place for every one who would overcome sin through the grace of Christ. This world in its present condition, ruined by sin, is no fit place for saints to inhabit forever. Our Lord was going away to prepare a place for the redeemed, an abode fit for God's children. The Saviour promised His disciples that He would not forget them after He departed from them. He assured them that He would make every preparation for their future home with Him. Meanwhile the disciples were to make the proper preparation to fit them to dwell in those mansions He had gone to prepare.

8. Could Satan interfere with the return of Jesus? John 12:31; Rev. 12:10; John 16:33.

Satan could not now interfere with the movements of the Saviour. Having completely conquered Satan in life and in death, Jesus was prepared to leave this earth in absolute control of earth and heaven.

When the Father sent Michael to raise Moses from the dead, Satan interfered with Him. The Archangel did not argue with the enemy; the Son of God said: "The Lord rebuke thee," and He went to heaven with the body of Moses. Jude 9. At the time when our Lord raised Moses and was challenged by the devil, Christ had not yet lived in the flesh as a man. Jesus had not at that time personally met the temptations of Satan and overcome them.

During His earthly ministry, our Lord had been subjected to the fierce assaults of Satan. Jesus had battled with the devil on every point where man had fallen, and He had overcome Satan. In heaven the word had gone forth: "Now is come salvation, and strength, and the kingdom of our God, and the power of His Christ: for the accuser of our brethren is cast down." Rev. 12:10.

9. What became of those who were raised from the grave at the time of Christ's resurrection? Eph. 4:8.

When the Saviour ascended, He took with Him those whom He had brought forth from the grave (Hosea 13:14), and carried them as trophies to heaven. All heaven was assured that in Christ there is sufficient grace and power to defeat the enemy in any part of God's universe. It is written: "Having made peace through the blood of His cross, by Him to reconcile all things unto Himself; by Him, I say, whether they be things in earth, or things in heaven." Col. 1:20. The promised Seed had now come and given His life a ransom for sin. Those redeemed who accompanied our Lord to heaven at His ascension were witnesses to the mighty power of the victorious Christ.

10. How was Christ welcomed by the heavenly hosts at the time of His ascension? Ps. 24:7-10.

What a glorious and triumphant procession was the journey of our Lord to the heavenly mansions, accompanied by the trophies of His resurrection power over the grave! What a welcome was in store for the victorious Son of God and Son of man as He approached the pearly portals to the eternal city! All heaven was waiting for the majestic Commander. They longed for His return to His seat on the Father's throne.

"Lift up your heads, O ye gates; and be ye lift up, ye everlasting doors; and the King of glory shall come in" (Ps. 24:7), was the triumphant song of praise from the myriads of heavenly beings as they joyfully welcomed their adored Commander. With Him He brought the trophies of victory over sin, death, and the grave. How those redeemed from Satan's prison must have thrilled as they accompanied their Lord and Saviour to His heavenly abode!

The scene is to be repeated, we are assured, when our Lord returns for all those who have slept in the silent tomb since sin entered the world. "I will come again," was our Saviour's assurance to His disciples. John 14:1-3. At that time all the dead in Christ shall rise. 1 Thess. 4:16, 17. At that hour a glorious reception in the air will be enjoyed by those who have been held captive in the devil's prison house. Death, the last enemy, shall be destroyed. 1 Cor. 15:26.

The Anointing of the Heavenly Sanctuary

1. FOLLOWING His ascension to heaven, what position was Christ to occupy? Ps. 110:1; Heb. 1:3; 10:12, 13; Acts 2:33.

Repeatedly the Scriptures declare that Christ is to sit at the right hand of God. The Saviour's position in heaven is described by various terms in the Scriptures. David prophesied that He would sit at the right hand of God. The Saviour refers to this Davidic prediction. Mark 12:36. Peter describes our Lord as sitting at the right hand of God. 1 Peter 3:22. He also refers to Christ's exaltation with God's right hand. Acts 5:31. Stephen declares he saw the Saviour standing at the right hand of God. Acts 7:56. Paul writes that Jesus is at the right hand of God, making intercession for us. Rom. 8:34.

In his letters to the Ephesians and to the Hebrews, the apostle says that God set the Saviour at His right hand, and that Jesus sat down on the right hand of the Majesty on high. Eph. 1:20; Heb. 1:3. These expressions mean the same thing. They teach that at our Lord's ascension He took His authoritative position at the right hand of God. Finite man cannot comprehend heavenly dimensions, except as God may reveal them. But the Lord has not revealed to man either the dimensions of the heavenly sanctuary, or of heaven itself. It is true that the Scriptures have given us a glimpse of heaven, but man is unable to determine either size or dimensions of the heavenly abode.

From earliest history it has been the time-honored Scriptural custom to recognize that the "right hand" is a symbol of supreme right, authority, preeminence, and prestige. When Joseph brought his two sons to Jacob for the patriarch's blessing, the aged man placed his right hand on the head of the younger, instead of on the head of Manasseh, the elder. This displeased Joseph, and he told his father of the supposed mistake. Jacob answered: "I know it, my son, I know it: he also shall become a people, and he also shall be great: but truly his younger brother shall be greater than he." Gen. 48:13-19.

It is said that from the right hand of God there went a fiery law. Deut. 33:2. At the right hand of God "there are pleasures forevermore." Ps. 16:11. The mother of James and John asked the Saviour that her two boys might be placed at His right hand and at His left hand in the kingdom. Matt. 20:21-23. It is said that in the judgment the Lord will place all nations on His right hand or on His left. Matt. 25:33, 34. The right hand always has the supremacy.

When King Solomon received his mother, after he had seated himself upon his throne, he tendered her a seat at his right hand. 1 Kings 2:19.

2. In what capacity would Christ minister at the right hand of God? Zech. 6:12, 13; Ps. 110:4; Heb. 8:1.

3. Where would Jesus conduct this priesthood? Zech. 6:13; Rev. 3:21; Heb. 3:1; 4:14-16; 1 Cor. 15:24-28.

While the position of our Lord has been at the right hand of God since the days of eternity, never had He occupied this position as a High Priest until after His ascension following the resurrection. Micah 5:2. Had our Lord remained on earth, He never could have been a priest. Heb. 8:4. The earthly priesthood was given to the tribe of Levi, to Aaron and to his sons. Num. 18:1, 2. The kingdom was a gift to the tribe of Judah. The ruling tribe was foretold by Jacob. Gen. 49:10. Later it was confirmed by the Lord to David. 2 Sam. 7:16.

No person of the tribe of Judah was permitted to engage in any service of the earthly priesthood. King Uzziah attempted to offer incense in the temple, and he was smitten with leprosy. 2 Chron. 26:1, 16-21. No person of the tribe of Levi ever sat on the throne of Judah. The two kinds of services, the kingdom and the priesthood, were gifts to two different tribes. In Christ, however, we find both of these ministries united. He is both King and Priest. He could not have occupied these positions on earth. We already have learned that He could not be a priest while on earth, and His own people refused to accept Him as King. John 1:11; Luke 19:14; John 18:36, 37; 19:15. Jesus Himself said, "My kingdom is not of this world." John 18:36. "When the Son of man shall come in His glory, . . . then shall He sit upon the throne of His glory." Matt. 25:31. Christ now has only a spiritual kingdom upon the earth—a kingdom of grace in the hearts of men. Christ's work now is a work of ministry in man's behalf as High Priest in the heavenly sanctuary. Yet the angel Gabriel said that the Lord God would give unto Him the throne of His father David. Luke 1:31-33. He descended from the ruling tribe, as may be seen by reading Hebrews 7:14.

The psalmist declares that God had sworn, and would not repent, that some person should be a priest "after the order of Melchizedek." Ps. 110:4. This priesthood was not given to King David, and no person on earth ever had received a gift of priesthood aside from that given to Aaron's descendants. The Jewish people are perplexed as to the meaning of this scripture. However, in the prophecy of Zechariah we observe that the prophet declares that a man whose name is the "Branch" would build the temple of the Lord. This Branch would be a priest in that temple, and He would sit upon the throne as priest in that temple.

Who is the Branch? The writers of Israel have acknowledged and recognized that the Branch of Isaiah 11:1 refers to King Messiah. There is general uniformity among those ancient scholars as to who was meant by the Branch. The Talmudical scholars admit that this Branch must come from the lineage of David. Yet the Scriptures declare that no earthly priesthood can descend from Judah's descendants. Furthermore, the temple mentioned in Zechariah 6 cannot be an earthly temple; for the only earthly temple erected by God's people was the magnificent structure built by Solomon, repaired and rebuilt after the restoration of the Jews from Babylonian captivity, and further beautified prior to the advent of our Lord. Zech. 4:7; John 2:20. The temple spoken of in Zechariah is built by the man whose name is the Branch. Since the Branch is Messiah, this temple spoken of by the prophet Zechariah must be of Messianic origin. Messiah must be a priest in this temple which He builds. Neither the temple nor the priesthood prophesied by David and by Zechariah are of earthly origin.

This priestly ministry, conducted by Messiah in His temple, takes place in heaven. Upon the throne of God the Saviour carries forward this priestly ministry. We have a High Priest who is set down on the right hand of the throne of the Majesty in the heavens. He is a minister of the sanctuary and the true tabernacle, which the Lord pitched, and not man. Heb. 8:1, 2.

In describing the throne of God, John the revelator declares: "I heard the voice of many angels round about the throne and the beasts and the elders: and the number of them was ten thousand times ten thousand, and thousands of thousands." Rev. 5:11. The dimensions of the temple where such multitudes minister about the throne of the Infinite, must be immense. Yet we remember that "we have a great High Priest, that is passed into the heavens, Jesus the Son of God." The ministry is an actual service, conducted by our heavenly High Priest, Jesus our intercessor.

4. Before the priesthood in the earthly sanctuary was inaugurated, what special service was conducted? Ex. 30:25-30; 40:9-15; Lev. 8: 12, 13; 21:10; Num. 7:1.

Prior to the ministry of the priesthood in the Levitical sanctuary, the Lord commanded that there should be a dedication, an inauguration, a consecration service. The sanctuary and its furnishings must be dedicated to the service of God, and the priests must be consecrated to their sacred and solemn ministry.

5. What was one of the ten things the angel Gabriel told Daniel must take place during the seventy times seven years? Dan. 9:24.

The angel Gabriel told the prophet Daniel that one of the ten things to take place during the four hundred and ninety years' prophecy was the anointing of the most holy. The Hebrew words translated "most holy" in Daniel 9:24 are *kodesh ka-doshim,* "holy of holies." This term is invariably applied to things, and not to persons. Never in the Scripture do we find the words *kodesh ka-doshim* applied to individuals. They are recognized as applying to the "holy of holies" of the sanctuary.

We have already learned that the four hundred and ninety years of the prophecy of Daniel 9 began in the seventh Bible month of the year 457 B.C., our month October; these years ended in the month of October 34 A.D. The only time the "holy of holies" of the earthly sanctuary was anointed was when it was dedicated. (See Ex. 30:25-28; Lev. 8:10; Num. 7:1.) No sanctuary was erected on earth between 457 B.C. and 34 A.D. at the command of God. This anointing of "the most holy" mentioned by the angel Gabriel could not apply to a sanctuary on earth.

Our Saviour ascended to heaven after His resurrection, between the Passover and Pentecost, in 31 A.D.

6. Was it not necessary, therefore, for Christ to be anointed and consecrated before He began His work in heaven as High Priest? Heb. 1:8, 9; Ps. 45:6, 7; Heb. 7:28.

Before our Lord could enter upon His work as High Priest in heaven, the heavenly sanctuary must be anointed. The angel Gabriel foretold the anointing of the heavenly sanctuary. (See preceding note.)

Concerning the inauguration of Christ's ministry in the heavenly sanctuary, we present the following from "Acts of the Apostles:"

"Christ's ascension to heaven was the signal that His followers were to receive the promised blessing. For this they were to wait before they entered upon their work. When Christ passed within the heavenly gates, He was enthroned amidst the adoration of the angels. As soon as this ceremony was completed, the Holy Spirit descended upon the disciples in rich currents, and Christ was indeed glorified, even with the glory which He had with the Father from all eternity. The Pentecostal outpouring was Heaven's communication that the Redeemer's inauguration was accomplished. According to His promise He had sent the Holy Spirit from heaven to His followers, as a token that He had, as *priest* and *king,* received all authority in heaven and on earth, and was the *Anointed One* over His people."—Pages 38, 39.

LESSON XXIX

Christ Enters Upon His Work as High Priest

1. FOLLOWING the dedication of the earthly sanctuary and the consecration of the priests, where did the priests begin their work of ministry? Ex. 29:38-44.

The priests began their work in the holy place or first apartment of the earthly sanctuary, following the dedicatory exercises. (See also Leviticus 9; Num. 28:1-15.)

At the command of God the tabernacle was divided into two apartments. One apartment was called the holy place, the other was called the most holy. Ex. 26:31-33. The apostle Paul speaks of these two apartments of the sanctuary in a clear, concise way, for he knew that the Jewish people recognized these two apartments of the earthly or Levitical sanctuary. Heb. 9:2, 3.

2. Shortly after His ascension, where was Christ seen by Stephen? Acts 7:55, 56.

To the deacon Stephen there came a vision from God while he was passing through his bitter experience with the Sanhedrin. For this servant of God the heavens opened, and he declared that he saw our Lord standing at the right hand of God.

3. Who visited the apostle John while he was on the Isle of Patmos? Rev. 1:9-11, 17, 18.

Our Lord appeared in vision to the apostle John on the Isle of Patmos, when the latter was an old man. John the beloved had been a devoted servant of Christ, and the Saviour honored him for his faithfulness, while he was banished upon the rock-ribbed, lonely isle for the word of God and for the testimony of Jesus Christ. Rev. 1:9. To John was given the command to write in a book what should be revealed to him. What he saw was to be sent to the people of God.

The revelation given the apostle at this time was so glorious that John said he felt as if he were going to die. The Saviour comforted the aged apostle by telling him that *He* had been dead, but that He had risen again from the dead, and He was to live hereafter forever. Furthermore, He had the keys, and was able to unlock the tomb.

4. Where did John say Jesus was when he saw Him at this time? Rev. 1:12, 13.

John gives us definite information as to where he saw the Saviour at the time the Lord appeared to him in vision on this barren Isle of Patmos. John says: "I turned to see the voice that spake with me. And being turned, I saw seven golden candlesticks; and in the midst of the seven candlesticks one like unto the Son of man, clothed with a garment down to the foot, and girt about the paps with a golden girdle."

A similar description of the Saviour is found in Revelation 14:14. There it is written: "I looked, and behold a white cloud, and upon the cloud one sat like unto the Son of man, having on His head a golden crown, and in His hand a sharp sickle."

There was no mistaking that face. John knew Him. ' The beloved disciple had been with the Saviour for three and one-half years ,on earth. John saw Jesus in the midst of the seven golden candlesticks.

But where was the seven-branched golden candlestick located in the earthly sanctuary? The Scripture says: "Thou shalt set the table without the veil, and the candlestick over against the table on the side of the tabernacle toward the south." Ex. 26:35; 25:31-39; 40:24. This golden candlestick was in the holy place, in the first apartment of the earthly sanctuary.

5. What ministry in heaven did the aged apostle say he saw going on? Rev. 8:2-4.

The apostle beheld the angels standing at the altar. In the hands of one of them was a golden censer, and to him was given much incense, which was offered up with the prayers of the saints. The smoke from the incense ascended up to God, and the prayers of God's people with this incense were accepted before Him. The offering of the incense was a daily service in the first apartment of the sanctuary while the people were praying. (See Luke 1:8-10.)

6. Where in the earthly sanctuary were the altar and the golden candlesticks? Ex. 30:1-6; 40:26, 27; 26:35.

7. Of what was the earthly sanctuary a shadow and figure? Heb. 9:8-10, 24; 8:5.

The Scriptures clearly teach that the earthly sanctuary is a shadow or figure of the heavenly sanctuary. Neither the Saviour nor His apostles destroyed any portion of the Scriptures which the Lord gave to His people anciently. Had either the Saviour or His disciples advocated such a program, the people would have had reason to say that the religion of Jesus and His followers was not in harmony with the teachings of the Old Testament. The Saviour taught that if the people refused to heed the writings of Moses and the prophets, they would not be persuaded though one rose from the dead. Peter declared that Jesus was the prophet like unto Moses. Luke 16:31; Acts 3:22.

At the council held at Jerusalem, the apostles agreed that the Jews were in possession of the writings of Moses, which they read in the synagogue every Sabbath day. Paul avers that the rulers and people who read the prophets every Sabbath fulfilled those writings in putting our Lord to death. The reason the leaders rejected the Saviour was that they did *not understand* those writings. Acts 15:21; 13:27.

Paul never discouraged the reading of, or believing in, the Old Testament. The difficulty with the Jews was that they had a veil on their faces; that is, their minds were blinded when they read the writings of the Old Testament. Had they accepted Christ, their understanding would have been enlightened, for those prophetic Scriptures find their fulfillment in Christ. 2 Cor. 3:13-15.

The revelations given to the prophets in Old Testament times were a forecast of what would be accomplished in reality when Messiah came. The same spirit which gave those revelations to the seers also expounded the interpretations of the same. Dan. 2:19, 36, 45. The Lord never left man to give a human interpretation of the types and symbols. The Holy Spirit made application of the types. John 3:14. For this reason, the apostle says, the earthly sanctuary was the figure or shadow of the heavenly.

8. Do the Scriptures teach that there are holy places in heaven, where God dwells? Ps. 68:35; Heb. 6:19, 20; 9:3-7, 24, 25.

The Scriptures say there are holy places in heaven where God dwells. The

Lord so simplified His instruction as to make it possible for His people to understand the actual work which our High Priest would carry on while in heaven, by giving them an object lesson in the mission of the earthly sanctuary and its ministry. The Bible declares that in connection with the Levitical sanctuary, there were two holy places—the holy and the most holy place. Even so of the heavenly sanctuary the Scriptures declare: "O God, Thou art terrible out of Thy holy places." Ps. 68:35.

9. How long did the priests continue their uninterrupted ministry in the holy place of the sanctuary? Num. 28:3; Ex. 29:38, 39, 42; Heb. 9:6.

The priests in the Levitical sanctuary continued their ministry in the holy place day by day throughout the entire year, with the exception of one day. It must not be understood that the priests remained in the sanctuary every minute during the entire twenty-four hours of each day, of each week, of each month, throughout the entire year, ministering in the holy place by day and by night.

They did carry on the work in the first apartment throughout all the months of the year. Num. 28:14. They did not enter the most holy place at any time during the year while they were daily carrying forward the work of ministry in the first apartment.

10. Where did the high priest complete his annual round of ministry in the earthly sanctuary? Heb. 9:7, 25; Lev. 16:2.

The high priest concluded the year's ministry in the most holy place, the second apartment of the sanctuary. For the high priest to enter the inner apartment at any time during the year, with the exception of the one day, in order to complete the annual round of ministry, would have meant certain death to him. Aaron and his sons were commanded not to minister at any time in the most sacred place, where was the ark of God, except at the time appointed.

In ancient times God, by inflicting sudden death, impressed the people with the importance of obedience to His commands. Aaron's sons died immediately when they offered strange fire before the Lord, instead of offering the fire which God had provided for this purpose. Ananias and Sapphira met instant death when they falsified to the Holy Ghost. Lev. 10:1, 2; Acts 5:1-10. While all cases of disobedience did not meet with the same immediate retribution, God has declared that disobedience to His commands will meet its rightful penalty. Eccl. 8:11, 12.

11. How long must the Saviour have remained in the holy place of the heavenly sanctuary?

From what has been said in the preceding notes, it is evident that Jesus, our great High Priest, must remain in the holy place of the heavenly sanctuary until the time comes for Him to complete His ministry in the most holy place in the heavenly temple. The typical service was not completed in the first apartment of the earthly sanctuary; it was on the Day of Atonement that this work in the Levitical sanctuary was finished for that year. The apostle Paul says: "Nor yet that He should offer Himself often, as the high priest entereth into the holy place every year with blood of others." Heb. 9:25. (Read also Heb. 10:1, 3.) This repetition of the Day of Atonement was an annual affair. This one day which was set apart for the completing of the sanctuary ministry was to impress the Israelites that the work of intercession would sometime come to a final end. For fifteen centuries this typical yearly ministry of the sanctuary was annually repeated.

So likewise must the Saviour conduct His work for sinful man in the holy place in the heavenly temple, until the time came when, in God's plan, our heavenly High Priest should enter the most holy place in the heavenly sanctuary to complete the work of the gospel for sinners.

12. Does John the beloved mention the most holy place of the heavenly sanctuary? Rev. 11:19; 15:5.

The apostle declares that the temple of God was opened in heaven, and in that temple he saw the ark of the testament. In the earthly sanctuary the ark was in the most holy place. Ex. 26:34; 25:21; 40:20, 21. This ark was a shadow of the one in heaven.

The most holy place is again described by the apostle. The next time he speaks of the most holy place he describes it as the temple of the tabernacle of the testimony in heaven. The inner apartment is so designated because the most holy place contained the two tables of testimony. (See Ex. 32:15; 34:29.) On the two tables of stone were written the ten commandments. In the heavenly ark are the two original tables of God's law, the ten commandments, written by the finger of God. Ex. 32:16.

13. What were some of the outstanding features of the ministry on the Day of Atonement? Lev. 16:30, 33.

On the typical Day of Atonement, the tenth day of the seventh Bible month, when the high priest ministered the last rites in the most holy place in the Levitical sanctuary, he performed a thorough cleansing of the sanctuary, and a complete cleansing of the sins of all the people of Israel. This day was a cleaning-up time.

14. At what time did the angel Gabriel say the sanctuary would be cleansed? Dan. 8:14.

The angel Gabriel told the prophet Daniel that at the end of the twenty-three hundred days the sanctuary would be cleansed. This long period of time ended in the seventh Bible month of the year 1844. It was in the seventh Bible month of the year 1844, our month October, that Jesus, our great High Priest, completed His ministry in the holy place in the heavenly sanctuary.

15. When, therefore, must the great antitypical day of atonement have begun, during which our High Priest will complete His ministry as man's intercessor? 1 Cor. 15:24-28.

The great antitypical day of atonement must have begun at the close of the twenty-three-hundred-year period. At this time our Lord entered upon His final work of cleansing the sanctuary and its worshipers. Rev. 11:1. It was announced upon the day of Pentecost that Jesus had entered the holy place of the heavenly sanctuary and that He had begun His work of intercession for sinners. Peter, filled with the Holy Spirit, declared to the assembled multitude that this work of intercession had been entered upon in heaven, that Christ was now seated at the right hand of God. Acts 2:14-36.

For ten days prior to this Pentecostal experience the disciples had been gathered together, preparing for this great work. Acts 1:12-26, 1-3. Would we not expect that when the time arrived for our heavenly Intercessor to enter upon His last effort to save men, God would make this fact known? Can we imagine that the God of heaven, who in all ages of the past has declared His secrets unto His servants the prophets, would permit one of the greatest events in human history to take place, the finishing of the work of salvation for men in the earth, and not give His children warning of it? Would the Lord enter the most holy place in the heavenly temple, when eternal weal or eternal woe for the world is involved, inaugurate the great antitypical day of atonement, and send no message to earth's inhabitants concerning His movements? Amos 3:7.

LESSON XXX

The Great Advent Movement
of the Years 1834-44

1. WAS Christ's work as priest to continue endlessly? Rev. 8:5; 22:11, 12; 15:8.

Christ's ministry as High Priest was not to be perpetual throughout eternity. God has assured us that sin and death will be destroyed. Nahum 1:9. If the priesthood and intercession of the Saviour were to continue endlessly, it would indicate that sin must have perpetual existence. Sin is an intruder; it has no right to an existence. In "Early Writings," pages 279-281, is found the following:

"I saw angels hurrying to and fro in heaven. An angel with a writer's ink-horn by his side returned from the earth, and reported to Jesus that his work was done, and the saints were numbered and sealed. Then I saw Jesus, who had been ministering before the ark containing the ten commandments, throw down the censer. He raised His hands, and with a loud voice said, 'It is done.' And all the angelic host laid off their crowns as Jesus made the solemn declaration, 'He that is unjust, let him be unjust still; and he which is filthy, let him be filthy still; and he that is righteous, let him be righteous still; and he that is holy, let him be holy still.'

"Every case had been decided for life or death. While Jesus had been ministering in the sanctuary, the judgment had been going on for the righteous dead, and then for the righteous living. Christ had received His kingdom, having made the atonement for His people and blotted out their sins. The subjects of the kingdom were made up. The marriage of the Lamb was consummated. And the kingdom, and the greatness of the kingdom under the whole heaven, was given to Jesus and the heirs of salvation, and Jesus was to reign as King of kings and Lord of lords. . . .

"Then I saw Jesus lay off His priestly attire, and clothe Himself with His most kingly robes. Upon His head were many crowns, a crown within a crown."

As man's High Priest, the Saviour will intercede for sinners as long as God sees the necessity for such intercession. Christ reigns as a priest-king on His Father's throne as long as man needs an advocate. Zech. 6:12, 13.

2. Was there to be a succession of high priests in Christ's ministry? Heb. 10:1-14; 7:24.

In the Levitical priesthood there was a succession of priests and high priests. This succession was necessary because of man's limitation. Under that system of priesthood men died. The Levites, the assistants to the priesthood, ministered about the sanctuary from the age of thirty until fifty. Num. 4:3, 35; 8:19. The eldest son of the high priest usually succeeded his father. Ex. 29:29, 30; Num. 20:23-28.

But there was to be no succession of high priests in the priesthood of Christ. After He had offered Himself as the great sacrifice for man, He ascended to heaven and became man's intercessor. This high priesthood of our Lord was not to be succeeded by another. Jesus was to minister for man at the right hand of God as long as man needed an intercessor. Rev. 3:21.

174

3. What was to take place in the heavenly temple when the intercession of Christ for man was finished? Rev. 16:17; 21:6.

When the Saviour completed His work on earth as man's example, living that sinless life which the law of God demanded, He said, in His prayer recorded in John 17, "I have finished the work which Thou gavest Me to do." Verse 4. When the Saviour uttered His last words as He was dying on the cross, He said, "It is finished." John 19:30. By His death the Saviour made possible man's reconciliation with God. Rom. 5:10; 2 Cor. 5:18. When He shall have completed His intercession for the last sinner who can be saved, the word will go forth in the heavenly temple, "It is done."

The plan of God to save lost man will then be finished. There will be no further intercession for a lost race. The final call will have been made, the last prayer for the sinner will have been offered, the last appeal for a lost soul will have been given. No further probation will be extended.

4. When did the high priest complete the annual round of ministry in the earthly sanctuary? Heb. 9:6, 7, 25; 10:1, 2.

The high priest finished the round of ministry in the earthly sanctuary on the tenth day of the seventh Bible month. This tenth day of the seventh Bible month is known among the Jewish people to this day as יום כפור (*Yom Kippur*), the Day of Atonement. Lev. 23:26, 27; Num. 29:7.

While the high priest conducted the ministry in the holiest place of the sanctuary on this most sacred of all days, the people were commanded to afflict their souls. Lev. 16:29-31; 23:27-29, 32; Num. 29:7. All lightness, trifling, every form of joviality which might be indulged in at other times of the year, were set aside during this sacred and solemn period. The Day of Atonement was a life-and-death issue to the people of Israel.

5. How did the Lord instruct the Israelites anciently to introduce the Day of Atonement? Lev. 23:23-25.

The Israelites were prepared for the Day of Atonement by the blowing of trumpets ten days prior to this occasion. In the days of Moses the people were commanded to make "two trumpets of silver, . . . that thou mayest use them for the calling of the assembly." Num. 10:1-8.

One purpose of these trumpets was that "in the day of your gladness, and in your *solemn days,* and in the beginnings of your months, ye shall blow with the trumpets over your burnt offerings, and over the sacrifices of your peace offerings; that they may be to you for a memorial before your God: I am the Lord your God." Verse 10. By the blowing of the trumpets the people were solemnly and seriously impressed, in view of what was to follow. The Israelites understood that from the first day of the seventh month until the tenth day of this same month they were to seek the Lord for what was to take place on the Day of Atonement. To that people the blowing of the trumpets was a loud call to repentance. This seventh month was the closing month of the sanctuary service ministry; all sin must be searched out and put away. During the ten days prior to *Yom Kippur,* earnest and prayerful seasons were observed by the children of Abraham.

The people were taught that on the day of the blowing of trumpets, three sets of books were opened,—the book of life to examine the good deeds, the book of death to examine evil deeds, and an intermediary book to examine into the accounts of those whose cases were to be decided at the Day of Atonement. Not to be prepared for the day of judgment would be tragic. No greater calamity could overtake one than to come up to the Day of Atonement unprepared for an investigation of the records. The Lord offered Israel ten days prior to the Day of Atonement in which to make ready for the investigation to take place on *Yom Kippur.*

6. Could it be possible that the Lord would suddenly introduce the great antitypical day of atonement without giving the world warning of the same? Amos 3:7.

Nowhere in the annals of sacred history do we find that the Lord came to His people, at a time of crisis, without first giving them ample warning of what was to take place. The world was warned of the deluge; Sodom was notified of its impending destruction; Pharaoh was warned prior to Israel's release from Egypt; the prophets warned the ten tribes before they were led into captivity. Judah was repeatedly entreated to turn from their evil ways in order to escape the Babylonian exile. The Jews were notified of the first advent of the Messiah, and they were commanded to prepare for His coming. (See Gen. 6:3, 12, 13, 17, 18; 18:17-32; 19:12-14; Ex. 5:1-4; 2 Kings 17:6-18; Jer. 25:2-14; Luke 1:17.)

It is unthinkable that God would permit the antitypical day of atonement, the day of investigative judgment, to come upon the church and upon the world, without notifying the inhabitants of earth of this unusual and outstanding event.

7. What message did God send to the church and to the world to prepare for the great antitypical day of atonement? Acts 17:31; 1 Peter 4:17; Rev. 14:6, 7.

The Scriptures declare that the day of judgment will come, and that when that day of judgment comes, it will begin with the church. 1 Peter 4:17. Therefore God sent a judgment-hour message to every nation, kindred, tongue, and people. This judgment-hour message was carried to the world by the church, and it was the gospel message for that time.

For at least ten years prior to the opening of the antitypical day of atonement, God's professed people sounded to all parts of the earth the judgment message as it is declared in the Scriptures. From the book, "Rise and Progress of Seventh-day Adventists," by J. N. Loughborough, we quote the following:

"The evidences that these symbols, found in Revelation 10 and 14, represent the advent proclamation, are set forth in a volume entitled, 'Thoughts on Daniel and the Revelation.' . . .

"The reader will observe in the above texts that the 'time' for the concluding work of the gospel, and the announcement, 'The hour of His judgment is come,' are to be made known by 'sea' and 'land' 'to every nation, and kindred, and tongue, and people.' To show that such was the extent of the advent movement from the years 1831 to 1844, we notice again the words of Mourant Brock:

"'It is not merely in Great Britain that the expectation of the near return of the Redeemer is entertained and the voice of warning raised, but also in America, India, and on the Continent of Europe. In America, about three hundred ministers of the word are thus preaching "this gospel of the kingdom;" while in this country, about seven hundred of the Church of England are raising the same cry.' "—Page 27.

"Elder Joseph Marsh, in his advent paper entitled the *Voice of Truth,* January, 1845, said:

"'The everlasting gospel, as described in Revelation 14:6, 7, has been preached to every nation, kindred, tongue, and people, saying with a loud voice, "Fear God, and give glory to Him; for the hour of His judgment is come, and worship Him that made heaven, and earth, and the sea, and the fountains of waters." No case can be more clearly substantiated with facts than that this message has been borne to every nation and tongue under heaven, within a few past years, in the preaching of the coming of Christ in 1843, or near at hand. Through the medium of lectures and publications, the sound has gone into all the earth, and the word unto the ends of the world.' "—Page 28.

8. What has been God's plan through the ages in conducting His work? 1 Kings 8:56; Eccl. 3:1, 17; Rom. 13:11; 1 Thess. 5:1, 4.

When the time arrives for the Lord to do a certain work, God's providences are set in motion to carry out His plan. The work of the Lord is conducted with precision. The Lord never delays. His work is carried forward on time. The sun, moon, and stars rise and set precisely on schedule time. Not one of the heavenly bodies is ever late. God's word cannot return to Him void. There is no such word as failure with the Lord. No man or combination of men can hinder the fulfillment of the purpose of God.

9. What were two outstanding scriptures used in connection with the great advent movement of 1834-44? Dan. 8:14; Rev. 14:6, 7.

When the hour arrived for the preaching of the judgment-hour message to the church and to the world, at the appointed time the Lord raised up men in all sections of the earth to declare this message. We have no record that men in various portions of the world delivered to its inhabitants simultaneously a message that the great judgment hour of God had come, until the great advent movement of 1834-44.

And in a most singular manner the two outstanding features of the message proclaimed by those godly men in connection with the advent movement during the middle of the nineteenth century, were, "Then shall the sanctuary be cleansed," and, "The hour of His judgment is come." The gospel of our Lord, God's power to save men, had never been proclaimed *in this form* at any previous time in the world's history. While the Lord Jesus was held up before men as the only means of salvation, the cry was everywhere raised, "The hour of God's judgment is come," the sanctuary will be cleansed. "Fear God, and give glory to Him," was sounded nigh and far off. Wherever the message was proclaimed, hundreds, yes, thousands, embraced the teaching.

10. What was the view of the believers in regard to the cleansing of the sanctuary at the close of the 2300 days? 2 Peter 3:10-12.

In connection with the declarations found in Daniel 8:14 and Revelation 14:6, 7, those messengers and believers preached that the Lord would return at His second advent with power and great glory. In all places where the message was proclaimed, the advent believers taught that the cleansing of the sanctuary meant the destruction of the earth at His second coming. The earth then would be burned with fire, and the new heavens and the new earth would be ushered in. This burning of the earth by fire was understood to be the cleansing of the sanctuary.

Nowhere in the Scripture is the earth said to be the sanctuary. There is not to be found, between Genesis and Revelation, a single text which says that the earth is the sanctuary. The word "sanctuary" means a "holy place." Ever since sin entered this world, this earth has been anything but a holy place. Of particular places God has declared that His presence made them holy; but the earth as a planet is nowhere regarded in the Scripture as a sanctuary. Strong was the faith of those devout advocates of the judgment-hour message that the Lord would come at the end of the twenty-three hundred days, which terminated in the seventh Bible month, the month of October, 1844.

11. Does the Scripture teach that the Lord will come and destroy the earth at the close of the 2300 days? Dan. 8:14; Rev. 14:6, 7.

12. What caused the people to be so greatly disappointed when the Lord did not come at the end of the 2300 days? Rev. 10:10.

The symbolic prophecy of the great advent movement had forecast that while the message of the second coming of Christ, which is so clearly taught in the word of God, would be sweet to those who proclaimed it, after they had delivered the message, their disappointment at not seeing their Lord would be bitter. And what a bitter disappointment it must have been to those saints of God who faced a scoffing and frowning world, after they had given their time, money, and energy in the service of their Lord's cause! Everywhere the believers declared their Lord would come at the end of the 2300 prophetic days. That time would be their hour of glory, of deliverance and joy. How they anticipated the arrival of that supreme moment when the Son of God would appear with all His holy angels for their salvation, for the destruction of the wicked, for the destruction of this evil world! But alas! The 2300 years ended, and the Saviour did not appear as those devoted believers expected. Bitter indeed was their disappointment. One writer says of that experience:

"The tenth day of the seventh month, Jewish time (Oct. 22, 1844), at last came. It found thousands upon thousands who were looking to that point for the consummation of their hopes. They had made provisions for nothing earthly beyond that date. They had not even cherished the thought, 'If it doesn't come,' but had planned their worldly affairs as they would if they had expected that day to end the period of their natural lives. They had warned and exhorted the wicked to flee from the wrath to come, and many of these *feared* that the message might prove true. They had counseled and prayed with their relatives, and had bidden good-by to such as had not given their hearts to God. In short, they had bidden adieu to all earthly things with all the solemnity of one who regards himself as about to appear face to face with the Judge of all the earth. Thus, in almost breathless anxiety, they assembled at their places of worship, expecting, momentarily, to hear 'the voice of the Archangel and the trump of God,' and to see the heavens ablaze with the glory of their coming King.

"The hours passed slowly by, and when at last the sun sank below the western horizon, the Jewish tenth day of the seventh month was ended. The shades of night once more spread their gloomy pall over the world; but with that darkness came a pang of sadness to the hearts of the advent believers, such in kind as can only find a parallel in the sorrow of the disciples of our Lord, as they solemnly wended their way to their homes on the night following the crucifixion and burial of Him whom, but a little while before, they had triumphantly escorted into Jerusalem as their King."—*"Rise and Progress of Seventh-day Adventists,"* by J. N. Loughborough, pp. 74, 75.

13. What gave the disappointed ones in those days precious comfort? Hab. 2:1-3.

14. Was the Lord responsible for the disappointment of these disciples? Luke 24:17-21; 9:43, 44.

While the disappointment which came to those believers who expected the Lord to come at the close of the 2300 prophetic days, was bitter, the Lord was not responsible for their sorrow, neither were the Scriptures to blame for their mistake. The message of the judgment they proclaimed was correct; for this message was in perfect accord with the Sacred Writings. The proclamation of the 2300 days to end in the seventh Bible month in 1844, October 22, was in harmony with the Bible; for that prophetic period did terminate on that date. From that time to this, the dates of the beginning and ending of that long Bible prophetic period have been regarded as absolutely reliable, in complete harmony with the word of God.

But the idea that the cleansing of the sanctuary at the close of the 2300 days was the purifying of the earth by fire, and therefore that the Lord would come when that long time period ended, on October 22, 1844,—this view was not in agreement with the Scriptures. The mistake of the believers of that day was in supposing that the sanctuary was the earth. The believers in the advent message in 1844 did not at that time understand the subject of the sanctuary as it is taught in the word of God. Their burden was to make known the judgment-hour message, and the cleansing of the sanctuary, which was to take place at the close of the 2300 days. God impressed those people to announce this judgment-hour message, for the church and the world must prepare for the antitypical day of atonement.

Had they studied the advent message more closely, they might have discovered their mistake earlier. But the Lord comforted their hearts, and assured them that in spite of their mistake, He had not failed them. Their message was given at the proper time. They announced the correct time when the sanctuary should be cleansed. They voiced heaven's message of the judgment to come. Their faith in God and in His word was severely tested, but many of the earnest and sincere believers held fast their confidence.

When the disciples of Christ proclaimed: "Blessed be the King that cometh in the name of the Lord: peace in heaven, and glory in the highest" (Luke 19:38), they were fulfilling the prophecy foretold by the prophet Zechariah more than five centuries before. The Saviour Himself said to those Pharisees who demanded that the people be restrained from making such a disturbance: "I tell you that, if these should hold their peace, the stones would immediately cry out." Luke 19:39, 40.

Yet a little later, when the disciples thought that Jesus was to be crowned as Israel's King, but instead He was crucified and buried, they were bitterly disappointed. Hear the pathetic statement of those disappointed ones in their conversation with the Master, when Jesus overtook them on their way to Emmaus: "We trusted that it had been He which should have redeemed Israel." Luke 24:21.

Why should they have entertained such an idea? Jesus was not responsible for the belief to which they clung. Nor were the Scriptures accountable for their adhering to such an idea. The Saviour had admonished them months before: "Let these sayings sink down into your ears: for the Son of man shall be delivered into the hands of men. But they understood not this saying, and it was hid from them." Luke 9:44.

Why was this important statement of the Saviour's hid from them? Why did they not understand it? The Scripture tells us: "Then there arose a reasoning among them, which of them should be the greatest." Verse 46. Their minds were centered upon another theme. They were thinking who of them would have the largest responsibility in that kingdom which they expected Jesus would set up. They did not let those sayings of the Saviour sink down into their ears. Eventually they were disappointed.

The Adventists in 1844 had so set their affections upon seeing the Lord return that their minds were not open to all the sayings of the Scripture. At the end of the 2300 days the sanctuary must be cleansed, the judgment must begin. These ardent believers expected that at the close of the prophetic time the Saviour would come and destroy the earth. The event they expected to take place at the seventh Bible month was not in accord with the teaching of Scripture. The expectation of the disciples that Jesus would set up His kingdom, instead of dying, was not in harmony with what the Lord had told them. The disciples of Christ proclaimed Christ as the coming King in fulfillment of prophecy; the advent believers proclaimed the message of the judgment and the cleansing of the sanctuary in perfect fulfillment of what Daniel the prophet had foretold would come to pass in the middle of the nineteenth century.

Christ Entered the Most Holy Place in the Heavenly Sanctuary in 1844

1. WHAT prediction did the angel Gabriel make in regard to Christ's mission upon earth? Dan. 9:25-27; Gal. 4:4; Mark 1:14, 15; Rom. 5:6, margin; Acts 2:23; 3:18; 4:28; Luke 1:67-70.

Although the first gospel sermon was preached in the Garden of Eden in the presence of Satan, although prophets, kings, and righteous men longed to be alive when the promised Messiah should appear, the Lord prophesied that when the Redeemer did come to earth, He would come in the fullness of time. Five centuries prior to the advent of the Saviour, the angel Gabriel declared the month and the year when Israel's Deliverer should appear in person, and when that hour arrived, all the angels of heaven united in proclaiming the good news of the Saviour's birth. Luke 2:8-14.

Jesus became the Messiah when He was anointed with the Holy Ghost and with power. Luke 3:21, 22. The announcement that the time of His Messiahship had arrived, was proclaimed. His death took place on time. Jesus foreannounced His betrayal, His crucifixion, His death, and His resurrection. Matt. 16:22, 23. One reason why He foretold these events was that the disciples might be assured that all the Scriptures clustering about the first advent of Messiah and His mission met their fulfillment in Him. John 16:4. Every feature of His ministry, from His birth to His death, was forecast, and a perfect fulfillment of those predictions was realized.

2. Which two books of the Bible particularize the second coming of Christ, and contain messages preparatory for that event? Dan. 2:44; 7:9, 10, 13, 14; 12:1, 2; Rev. 1:7; 6:14-17; 11:19; 22:12, 20.

The two outstanding books of the Bible which deal largely with the second coming of our Lord and the necessary preparation for it, are Daniel and the Revelation. The former is in the Old Testament and the latter is in the New Testament. In the closing portion of Daniel's writings, the setting up of the everlasting kingdom at the return of the Saviour is mentioned again and again. The pages of the closing book of the New Testament, from its first chapter to the end of the last chapter, are replete with instruction in regard to the second coming of the Lord.

3. Were all the prophecies of Daniel to meet their fulfillment at the same time? Dan. 12:4, 9.

While Daniel was informed by the angel Gabriel that the words given to him would not meet with an immediate fulfillment, the heavenly messenger assured the seer that when the hour arrived for the messages contained in his sealed book to be made public, God would cause "the wise" to understand. For this reason the prophet was advised by the angel to rest calmly and contentedly. God has a care over His work and over His word.

4. What class of people only would understand the true meaning of the events described in the book of Daniel? Dan. 12:10, 13.

"The wise shall understand," said the angel Gabriel. Men receive heavenly wisdom when they need it. James 1:5. God furnishes His servants who long to know His will with divine skill and wisdom for the particular time and purpose. Those who were anxious to understand the messages contained in the books of Daniel and Revelation when the hour arrived for that instruction to meet its fulfillment, were assured of wisdom and knowledge from God. For the angel said: "Blessed is he that readeth, and they that hear the words of this prophecy, and keep those things which are written therein: for the time is at hand." Rev. 1:3.

In the days of the first advent, the Saviour said to His disciples: "Blessed are your eyes, for they see: and your ears, for they hear." Matt. 13:16.

To the scribes and Pharisees of that day, our Lord remarked: "By hearing ye shall hear, and shall not understand; and seeing ye shall see, and shall not perceive." Matt. 13:14.

God is no respecter of persons. He is willing and anxious that all shall see and shall hear. While a certain class are anxious to know His will and to perform it, others there are who profess to know His will, but they prefer not to do it. The latter may have excellent physical sight, but they do not have proper spiritual vision.

5. What is represented by the angel clothed with a cloud, and having in his hand a little book open? Rev. 10:1, 2.

An excellent exposition of Revelation 10:1, 2, is given by the author of that valuable book, "Thoughts on Daniel and the Revelation," Elder Uriah Smith. He says:

"'He had in his hand a little book *open.*' There is a necessary inference to be drawn from this language, which is, that this book was at some time closed up. . . . .

"Since this book was closed up only *till* the time of the end, it follows that *at* the time of the end the book would be opened; and as this closing was mentioned in prophecy, it would be but reasonable to expect that in the predictions of events to take place at the time of the end, the *opening* of this book would also be mentioned. There is no book spoken of as closed up and sealed except the book of Daniel's prophecy; and there is no account of the opening of that book, unless it be here in the tenth of Revelation. We see, furthermore, that in both places the contents ascribed to the book are the same. The book which Daniel had directions to close up and seal had reference to time: 'How long shall it be to the end of these wonders?' And when the angel of this chapter comes down with the little book open, on which he bases his proclamation, he gives a message in relation to time: 'Time shall be no longer.' Nothing more could be required to show that both expressions refer to one book, and to prove that the little book which the angel had in his hand open, was the book of the prophecy of Daniel."—*Edition 1897*, pp. 488, 489.

Elder J. N. Loughborough also gives a clear exposition of this same scripture:

"The work of preaching the gospel has been committed to man, and the Lord has promised His blessing on that instrumentality till the 'end of the world.' So the angel bearing this message must be a symbol of a message concerning *time* which is to be preached to earth's inhabitants. The message is proclaimed from a book that is 'open,' clearly implying that it had once been *closed.* These messengers are esteemed of God; for the 'bow,' a token of God's covenant, is over them, and they stand clothed with the light of God's glory, and declare the message on the authority of the Creator of all things. That which is here declared is a *time* message, once 'sealed,' but now proclaimed from an 'open' book."

6. What is the extent of the message to be given by this angel with the little open book? Rev. 10:2, 5.

This message of the angel with the little book open must be world wide, for it is to go on both sea and land. This earth consists of water and dry land. Says the Scripture: "God said, Let the waters under the heaven be gathered together unto one place, and let the dry land appear: and it was so." Gen. 1:9.

Since the angel with this message sets his "right foot upon the sea, and his left foot upon the earth" (Rev. 10:2), his message must go where there is earth and sea. The message of Revelation 10 is a complement to the message of Revelation 14:6, 7. They harmonize; they are in accord.

7. **What outstanding declaration is made by this angel in giving his world-wide message?** Rev. 10:6.

This world-wide message deals with time. But the message declares that time shall be "no longer." The Scriptures deal with both prophetic time and ordinary or probationary time. Which kind of time does this message indicate? That it cannot be probationary time is evident from the fact that the following verse declares that the seventh angel is to sound, and in the days of the sounding of this seventh angel the mystery of God is to be finished. Probationary time is to continue for the giving of the gospel message, following the one announced by the angel whose feet cover sea and land. Hence the kind of time mentioned by the angel must be prophetic time. It is evident that in the little book "open" in the hand of the angel is a message containing prophetic time. This angel declares that the prophetic time mentioned in that book is ended.

8. **What particular book of Scripture did the angel Gabriel say should be sealed and later be unsealed?** Dan. 12:4, 8, 9.

9. **What time is meant by the statement made by this angel with the little book open?** Rev. 10:6-8.

10. **What was the nature of this world-wide message, and what was its aftereffect?** Rev. 10:9, 10.

We find other scriptures where the prophet is commanded to take a book and to eat it. (See Jer. 15:16; Eze. 3:1-3.) The eating of the book indicates that the messenger is to give the message contained in the book. The message of a soon-coming Saviour was indeed a sweet message, but the misapplication of the event, proclaimed by those who gave the world-wide message to take place at the end of the prophetic time, the 2300 days, resulted indeed in a bitter experience.

11. **Following this bitter disappointment, what command did the angel give to the prophet John?** Rev. 10:11.

The announcement was made by the angel that at the close of the message given by those believers in 1844, another message must follow. And the message which should follow must be given as extensively as that given by the angel with one foot on the land and the other foot on the sea. That is to say, another message must be given following the bitter disappointment.

It is clear from this tenth chapter of Revelation that God foresaw the disappointment of those who gave His message to every nation, kindred, tongue, and people. It was to those disappointed ones that the words came, "Thou must prophesy again before many peoples," etc. Rev. 10:11. The message that "there should be time no longer" (verse 6) must be given, even though the messengers should meet with a bitter experience after they had eaten the little book, which at the first was so sweet to them.

How literally was this prophecy fulfilled by those who preached the advent message which culminated in the year 1844! Elder Uriah Smith says:

"A mistake had been made which apparently involved the integrity of the little book they had been eating. What had been so like honey to their taste, suddenly became like wormwood and gall. But those who had patience to endure, so to speak, the digesting process, soon learned that the mistake was only in the event, not in the time, and that what the angel had given them was not unto death, but to their nourishment and support."—*Thoughts on Daniel and the Revelation,"* ed. 1897, p. 496.

12. **Immediately following this command of the angel, what does the prophet say was given to him?** Rev. 11:1.

The attention of the prophet is now called to the temple of God in heaven and to its worshipers. John is told to measure those who worship in the temple. God does have a rule of worship for His followers. (See Gal. 6:16.) The Scriptures tell us that God's rule of right is His commandments. Eccl. 12:13, 14. Associated with the keeping of the commandments of God is the faith of Jesus. Rev. 14:12. In order for God's people to be prepared to meet their Saviour at His second coming, they must measure their lives by God's rule.

At the time when the message of the 2300 days was given and the people expected their Lord to return, God's church was not spiritually prepared to meet the Lord. The church as a whole was breaking one of God's commands, the fourth, by observing the first day of the week instead of the seventh day. The church also was teaching things not in harmony with the true faith of Jesus. The church of Christ must receive another message which would reveal to them what is necessary for them to be prepared for the coming of the Lord. Luke 3:4, 10-14.

Until the close of the seventh Bible month, October, 1844, our heavenly High Priest had been ministering in the holy place, in the first apartment of the heavenly temple. The attention of the church and the world was directed, through the message of the prophet John, to the measurement of the worshipers of the true God. The people of God were to be measured according to Heaven's rule of true worship. All those who had their sins blotted out at the close of the typical Day of Atonement, fully harmonized with all of God's requirements. The people were led to investigate their conduct while the high priest interceded for them in the most holy place of the sanctuary. So in this antitypical day of atonement the church of Christ must be investigated, to determine whether their lives have been in harmony with God's commandments and with the faith of Jesus, before they are translated from this world into the kingdom of God.

13. What did John say he saw in heaven? Rev. 11:19.

John declares that he saw the temple of God opened in heaven. He had seen the heavenly temple open at other times during the vision given to him and recorded in the Revelation. Rev. 1:12; 8:3. But he points out that at this time he saw that part of the temple open in which is the ark.

We know from the Scriptures that no person anciently was permitted to look into the most holy place of the sanctuary, where the ark was placed, except the high priest, and that only on the Day of Atonement. It is evident that the Saviour, in permitting the apostle to see the temple where the ark of God is, had entered the most holy place of the heavenly sanctuary. The disappointment among those who accepted the message of the 2300 days and the cleansing of the sanctuary, was widespread. They had planned and hoped that they would see their Lord at the close of the tenth day of the seventh month, Jewish time (October 22, 1844). They had not expected to live on this earth another day following this one. They had no further message to give. To them their mission was completed.

They did not at that time sense that they were to follow their High Priest into the most holy place in the heavenly temple, where had begun the antitypical day of atonement, His work of investigating those who should be ready to meet Him in peace at His coming. The antitypical day of atonement must begin with the church of God. 1 Peter 4:17.

During the centuries and millenniums of the past, God's people have lived and died. They are at rest, waiting for the great resurrection day. Dan. 12:13. Before they are raised from the dead, it must be determined by the records that they are worthy of that resurrection. Luke 14:14; 20:36. The heavenly Intercessor must be their Advocate before the Father and before the heavenly hosts. Dan. 7:9, 10.

Our heavenly High Priest entered the most holy place of the heavenly temple in 1844, to perform the final work of intercession, prior to the completion of the plan of human redemption. Christ entered into the holy of holies in the heavenly temple at the termination of the 2300 days.

Christ's Ministry in the Most Holy Place in the Heavenly Temple

1. WHILE the prophet Daniel was still in vision, what question did a "certain saint" ask, and of whom? Dan. 8:13.

By reading verse 13 of Daniel 8, it is evident there were three individuals present at the time Daniel received his vision. One was the angel Gabriel, the second was Daniel, and the third was a "certain saint" who asked a question. The original text for the words of our translation, "Then I heard one saint speaking, and another saint said unto that certain saint which spake," is ואשמעה אחד־קדוש מדבר ויאמר אחד קדוש לפלמוני המדבר (*Wa-eshmaah echad-qadosh medabber wayyomer echad qadosh lappalmoni hamdabber*). Rendering the Hebrew text literally, we have the following: "I heard one holy one who was the speaker; and a holy one said to פלמוני (*Palmoni*) who was the speaker." From the foregoing we learn that the speaker of the vision is one whose name is *Palmoni*. *Palmoni* is a contracted Hebrew word, derived from two words, פלא (*Pele*) and מנא (*mcna*). *Pele* means "wonderful." (See Isa. 9:6, where the word *pele* is translated "wonderful.") *Mena* means "numberer." (See Dan. 5:25, 26, where the words "mene, mene," are translated "numbered.") *Palmoni* means "wonderful numberer." (See Dan. 8:13, margin.) This "wonderful numberer" is none other than our Lord Himself.

2. To whom did the prophet say was given the answer to this question? Dan. 8:14.

Our Lord, Gabriel, and Daniel are the three persons taking part in the vision. (Compare Dan. 10:21.) Gabriel (see Luke 1:19) asks *Palmoni* a question: "How long . . . the vision?" There are a number of supplied words in verse 13. These supplied words do not belong to the text. Instead of *Palmoni* directing His answer to the angel, the prophet said, "He turned unto me," and said: "Unto two thousand and three hundred days; then shall the sanctuary be cleansed." Verse 14. Our Lord spoke directly to the prophet. Gabriel evidently raised the question for Daniel's benefit.

3. Following the disappointment in the advent message in 1844, to what place was the attention of the believers directed? Rev. 11:19; Heb. 8:1.

When the 2300 days terminated, the believers who had so earnestly proclaimed the advent message could not understand why the Lord had not come as they expected. We have already learned that knowledge of the sanctuary ministry came to the people of God through the gift of prophecy. (See Lesson 24.) Within a few weeks following the disappointment in October, 1844, there was restored to the church the gift of prophecy. Light had shone from the heavenly sanctuary upon certain of the disappointed ones who were earnestly praying for divine knowledge as to what was to take place at the close of the 2300 days, but with the restoration of the gift of prophecy the light from the sanctuary became brighter, and shone more clearly upon those who were so solicitous to know the will of God. The seekers after truth now turned their attention to the most holy place of the heavenly sanctuary, where they found their Lord had entered to complete the priestly ministry for His people. They found Him whom for a time they had lost. (See Luke 2:45, 46.) He was in His holy temple, ministering before the ark of God. By faith they recognized that the original deĉalogue, the ten commandments, was in the heavenly ark. The purpose which God explained to Moses in having an ark made in the earthly sanctuary, was that there might be a place for the law of God, the divine and immutable law, the basis of divine authority. Ex. 25:16.

4. What two outstanding characteristics mark the remnant church of Christ? Rev. 12:17; 19:10.

The Lord has marked His remnant church. He has stamped upon it such indubitable recognition that none of His children can mistake it. God saw the necessity of placing upon His true people these two outstanding signs, for the Scriptures declare that in the last days Satan will work with all power, signs, and lying wonders, so that if it were possible he would deceive the very elect. Matt. 24:24; 2 Thess. 2:9, 10; Rev. 12:12. That His chosen ones might be saved from the snares and deceptive power of the evil one, God has pointed out such distinct characteristics of His own true remnant church that the sincere, honest believers need not be misled. 2 Cor. 2:11; Eph. 4:14.

A firm belief in the commandments of God and the testimony of Jesus Christ are two outstanding characteristics of the remnant, the true church of Christ. That church which bears these marks is the church which will wait for the glorious appearing of the Lord. 1 Cor. 1:4-8; 1 Thess. 4:16, 17.

Within two months after the disappointment in October, 1844, the gift of prophecy was restored, and accepted by those believers who by faith had followed our great High Priest into the most holy place of the heavenly sanctuary, to conduct His final intercession for sinners. (See 1 Sam. 3:19-21.) In various parts of the field where the advent message had been proclaimed, there arose men and women who abandoned the observance of the first day of the week as a religious day of rest, and observed the seventh day of the week as the Sabbath of the Lord.

When the believers who followed their Lord into the most holy place in the heavenly sanctuary after the seventh month (October, 1844), saw in the heavenly temple the ark of God, they recognized that there was written on the stone tablets contained therein the command, "The seventh day is the Sabbath of the Lord thy God." This commandment had not been changed by divine authority. This law could not be changed. Ps. 89:34. The purpose of the Creator in originally giving the seventh day for the Sabbath was to memorialize the Creator's works. In order that man might always acknowledge that this world was created in six days, God made the seventh day His Sabbath, *His* day of rest. There would have been no Sabbath had there been no creation. The seventh-day Sabbath cannot be dissociated from creation. They stand together. The world-wide message declares: "Worship Him that made heaven, and earth, and the sea, and the fountains of waters." Rev. 14:7.

To worship Him who made all things is to honor the day He made to memorialize creation. God used only six days in which to create. Whatever was essential for man's welfare upon this earth, God made in those six days. There would have been only a six-day week, if God, through our Lord Jesus, had not established a memorial of His creation. The one and only reason the seventh day was made was so that as long as the earth existed God's creatures might recognize and understand that He made this world and all in it in six days.

With the observance of the seventh day of the week as the Sabbath of the Lord was joined the gift of prophecy. Those who accepted and obeyed God's commandments, recognized the necessity of accepting the gift of prophecy. 2 Chron. 20:20.

When the people of God through the ages kept the commandments of God, they had entrusted to them the gift of prophecy. 2 Kings 17:13. The two always have been associated, and the Lord promised they would again be joined in the last days. The true remnant church would be recognized by those two significant divine marks. We have the remnant church located by the holy Scriptures.

5. What class of worshipers is described by the prophet Ezekiel, as perverting the true services of the sanctuary? Eze. 8:15, 16.

When the Lord commanded Moses to arrange the furnishings of the sanctuary, He gave particular directions as to their location. (See Ex. 26:30-35.) The people of God were to enter the sanctuary at the east, and they were to face

Diagram Illustrating the Sanctuary of Israel, and Showing the Arrangement of the Furniture

the west in their worship, where was the most holy place, with the ark, and the law of God. This mode of worship was reversed when Israel turned away from God. That people often apostatized from the worship of the true God, and indulged in sun worship. (See Judges 2:11-13; 10:6; 2 Kings 23:3, 11.) So long as they worshiped with their faces toward the west, they honored the Creator of the heavens and the earth, and they also observed God's holy Sabbath, His memorial of creation.

Frequent mention is made in the Scriptures of the Israelites' turning their backs upon God. It is written: "Saying to a stock, Thou art my father; and to a stone, Thou hast brought me forth: for they have turned their back unto Me, and not their face." "And they have turned unto Me the back, and not the face." Jer. 2:27; 32:33.

By turning their backs toward the sanctuary and their faces toward the east, they adopted heathen worship, the worship of the sun. Ezekiel says: "Their backs" were "toward the temple of the Lord, and their faces toward the east; and they worshiped the *sun* toward the east."

Sun worship always involved Sunday worship, for the *Dies Solis,* the day of the sun, has been recognized among heathen worshipers from time immemorial, as the day set apart for the worship of this false deity. When Israel followed idolatry, they abandoned the Sabbath of the Lord, the seventh day. God warned that people not to forsake the Sabbath. He promised them that if they would observe His holy day, Jerusalem should stand forever. If they refused to sacredly observe His rest day, they would be punished, and their land would become desolate. Jer. 17:19-27. In their departure from God's Sabbath, they made no difference between the sacred and the secular. Eze. 22:26. They were finally sent into Babylonian exile for seventy years, in order that the land might enjoy the Sabbath. (See 2 Chron. 36:14-21.)

6. What glorious light came to God's waiting people as they turned their faces toward the most holy place of the heavenly sanctuary? Rev. 11:19.

When the believers, following the disappointment, saw that the seventh day is the Lord's holy day, they were convicted of its importance, and began to observe it as the true rest day. They turned their faces toward the sanctuary of

Israel, Worshiping the Sun, With Their Backs to the Law of God, Enshrined in His Temple

the Lord, where the great High Priest ministered in their behalf. The light on the Sabbath shone brightly, and they were impressed that they must obey all of God's commandments.

This glorious light of God's true Sabbath led them to follow the Lord in keeping the fourth commandment, which had been set aside for centuries. In giving themselves fully to the Saviour, in turning their faces toward the temple of the Lord, they turned their backs on Sunday worship. In keeping the seventh-day Sabbath they acknowledged their obligation to sacredly observe this day because of Christ's ministry in the most holy place of the heavenly sanctuary. This is what made those believers Seventh-day Adventists. It is true that the law of God always taught that the seventh-day is the Sabbath of the Lord thy God. There are others, aside from the Jews and the Seventh-day Adventists, who observe the seventh day as the sacred day of worship. These Sabbathkeeping worshipers do not accept the teachings of the sanctuary in connection with the last-day message going to all nations, kindreds, tongues, and peoples. They do not observe God's holy day from the same viewpoint as do those who follow their High Priest into the most holy place of the heavenly sanctuary. Seventh-day Adventists keep the Sabbath because they have repudiated every form of error, including the day devoted to the worship of the sun. Seventh-day Adventists recognize the necessity of obeying their Lord in all things. They recognize the necessity of repentance from *every* sin, and humble obedience to *every* command of God, that all their sins may be blotted out while the High Priest is completing His work of intercession for them in the heavenly sanctuary. Acts 3:19.

7. When the believers, following the disappointment in 1844, recognized the importance of observing the Sabbath of Jehovah, and accepted the Spirit of prophecy, what was inaugurated? Rev. 14:12; 1 Cor. 1:3-6; Rev. 12:17.

It was after the disappointment of 1844 that the remnant church was organized. Following the announcement of the threefold message going into all the world, is the declaration: "Here is the patience of the saints: here are they that keep the commandments of God, and the faith of Jesus." Rev. 14:12.

The next scene the prophet beheld was the coming of the Son of man with a sharp sickle in His hand to reap the harvest of the earth. The harvest is the end of the world. Matt. 13:39. The remnant church was separated from the world when the people of God by faith followed the Saviour into the most holy place of the heavenly sanctuary, when they began the observance of God's holy Sabbath day, when they became a part of the message which is to go to every nation, kindred, tongue, and people, and when they accepted the gift of prophecy as of God's own appointment, which is to confirm the church waiting for the coming of the Lord.

8. Upon what special phase of His ministry had the Saviour now entered? Heb. 9:7; Rom. 9:28; Rev. 7:3; 14:9-12.

Our Lord could not have entered upon the work of the great antitypical day of atonement until the announcement of the judgment-hour message had been given. His ministry in the most holy place did not begin until 1844. Then the final phase of the threefold message was launched. When our Lord passed into the holiest of the heavenly sanctuary, in 1844, He entered upon His final intercession for a lost world. We are living in the great antitypical day of atonement, and mercy is now offered to all nations, kindreds, tongues, and peoples. Mercy is making her final appeal.

LESSON XXXIII

A Special Message to a Particular People

1. To how many peoples must be given the message to prepare for the return of the Lord? Rev. 14:6-11; Matt. 24:14; 28:18-20.

The gospel message commanded by the Saviour to His disciples was to be preached to all the world. Acts 1:8. In the days of the apostles the good tidings of salvation were carried to the ends of the earth. Rom. 10:18; Col. 1:27. The Master said that the gospel of the kingdom should be preached in all the world for a witness unto all nations, and then should the end come. But He also told His disciples that persecution would come to the church during the 1260 years. Matt. 24:21, 22; Rev. 12:6; 13:5; Dan. 7:25. If God had not stayed the hand of persecution, there would no flesh have been saved. But for the elect's sake, those days were shortened. And the gospel message recorded in Revelation 14:6-12, particularizes by describing in detail the extent of its mission,—to every nation, kindred, tongue, and people.

The world never has been so fully discovered as in this generation. During the past centuries cities, countries, and continents have been discovered. Today there are no new continents or countries to discover. The airplane has found the North Pole, the South Pole, and all places on the earth between the poles. The frozen and torrid sections are known today, and no part of this mundane sphere, where human beings are found, is unknown. The highest mountains have been scaled, and the flying machine has brought to light all the ends of the earth.

The message described in Revelation 14:6-9 is sent from heaven, and it is to be carried to every nation, kindred, tongue, and people. No work as extensive as that described in this chapter in Revelation has ever before been conducted for mankind. The Israelites were located in the Near East, and for many centuries they conducted their work in that section of the world. During the Christian Era the good news of salvation was carried into many lands, but there were some sections of the world which had not been reached. This was due in part to the fact that a large portion of the earth was undiscovered. But with the invention of the telegraph, the telephone, radio, television, aviation, and other forms of rapid transmission, the almost insurmountable difficulties in reaching the high points and the extremely difficult portions of earth have all been overcome.

At this writing the message of Revelation 14 has entered more than three hundred countries and islands, and is being preached in more than five hundred and fifty languages and dialects. New languages and tongues are being added at the rate of more than twenty-five a year. This message has believers in every well-known country, and its influence is being exerted to the ends of the world.

Such a work is indeed a miracle of grace when it is remembered that the message of Revelation 14 has been preached for less than a century. This message is indeed a special message, and it is winging its way to all peoples in all continents.

2. What particular name is given to the people who accept this world-wide message? Rev. 14:12; 22:14.

God Himself has designated the name of the people who give and accept this final warning message of Revelation 14. They are called commandment keepers. The body who have obligated themselves to carry it to all the world are called Seventh-day Adventists. And what an appropriate name this is! They are called *Adventists* because they believe in the near coming of the Saviour. They are designated *Seventh-day* Adventists because they observe the seventh-day Sabbath.

What a close relationship exists between God's commandment-keeping people and the name the denomination bears! Wherever they are found, they are known as commandment keepers. They are a called-out people.

The followers of our Lord when He was on earth were first called disciples. Later the twelve were called apostles. By some Christ's followers were named Nazarenes. Still others called them Christians. All these names applied to the same people. Matt. 10:1, 2; Acts 24:5; 11:26.

3. What immediately follows upon the acceptance or the rejection of this message? Rev. 14:14-16.

4. Will there follow other messages after this international message is given? Matt. 13:38, 39.

No other world-wide message will follow that of Revelation 14. The closing message announced in the Old Testament is that of the coming of the Lord, prefaced by the appearance of Elijah the prophet. Mal. 4:5, 6. The angel Gabriel declared that John the Baptist came in the spirit and power of Elijah. Luke 1:17. John did the preparatory work for the Messiah's advent. Matt. 11:10. And there was no other message given among the Jews, until the forerunner of Messiah heralded the news through the Jordan valley to prepare for the Messiah's appearing. Matt. 3:1-5.

There follows no world-wide message in the New Testament after the one announced in Revelation 14. In chapters 15 and 16 we have a record of the seven last plagues to be poured out upon those who reject the message of Revelation 14. In Revelation 18 there is a reinforcement of the message of Revelation 14. Then follows the announcement in chapter 19 to prepare for the marriage supper of the Lamb. This marriage supper will be enjoyed by those who have obtained the victory over the evil powers spoken of in the message of Revelation 14. The binding of Satan, recorded in chapter 20, will take place after human probation closes, and when the Lord comes in glory to take the righteous to heaven and to destroy the wicked.

When death and the grave are destroyed, sin and sinners will be no more. Eternity with its joys is to be enjoyed by those who are conquerors through the sacrifice made by our Lord. (See Revelation 21, 22.) There is no further message recorded in the Scriptures to be given to the world after the one noted in Revelation 14.

5. What effect will the completion of this message have upon the human race? Rev. 16:17; 22:11; Luke 13:24, 25.

When the proclamation of the third angel's message is finished, human probation will cease. All peoples in all lands will have had their day of opportunity. Savages, cannibals, heathen, and civilized people will have been granted the opportunity of hearing and receiving this final message of hope and mercy. By its acceptance or rejection every class and every race will have decided for eternal weal or for everlasting woe.

When the Lord informed Abraham that He was on His way to destroy Sodom, the patriarch interceded for the people in the cities of the plain. In response to Abraham's appeal for mercy for the inhabitants of those cities, the Lord said that if there were ten people in those cities who loved and feared God, the destruction would not take place. When Abraham learned that God would spare Sodom if there were ten righteous persons there, He knew that a loving God would dispense mercy as well as mete out justice. The hour soon arrived when these cities met their fate. There were not five people in that entire section who were righteous. When the Lord closed the door of the ark which Noah and his family built, there were none left outside who would change their course of conduct. As long as God sees a penitent soul, He gladly grants grace and favor.

As long as this message of Revelation 14 is being carried to earth's remotest bounds, the nations, kindreds, and tongues will have the privilege of hearing this final appeal of God's mercy to the sinner.

It is immaterial what the past record of peoples may have been. The blood of the Son of God can cleanse every sinner from the stain of every sin. 1 John 1:7, 9. On the typical Day of Atonement, the man who obeyed God's requirements during that day, while the high priest was engaged in ministry in the most holy place, enjoyed the favor of God. At the close of that day such a person was approved of God. His past record was not held against him. For the Scripture declares: "On that day shall the priest make an atonement for you, to cleanse you, that ye may be clean from all your sins, before the Lord." Lev. 16:30. The Day of Atonement was man's final opportunity.

A thorough and complete cleansing from sin took place on that day. That day was a cleaning-up day. No remembrance of sin was left in the sanctuary when the high priest completed his intercession at the setting of the sun on that day, and carried out the sins at his exit, and placed them on the head of *Azazel*, the scapegoat. The atonement on that day was made for all the sins of all the people, and the atoning work for that year was complete. Lev. 16:33.

This last message of mercy is today being carried to the wildest men the world has known. The Spirit of God speaks to their hearts, and they respond to the call of Heaven. Their sins are forgiven. Isa. 1:18. They accept and receive divine grace. Eph. 2:8. If they continue to adhere to God's commandments and to obey His entire will, they are received and accepted in heaven, and are regarded as though they had never sinned. 2 Cor. 6:16-18. Their sins and their iniquities will be remembered against them no more forever. Jer. 31:34.

The same privileges and blessings are available to all classes. Our High Priest, His heart overflowing with love for all people, offers the abundance of His grace to all races, to all nations. Deut. 33:27. This is the day of man's final opportunity. The sins of those who have confessed and repented of their past wrongs, will all be blotted out of the record books above when the High Priest leaves the throne of mercy in the most holy place of the heavenly sanctuary. Acts 3:19, 20; Jer. 50:20; Heb. 4:14-16.

6. How must this movement start? What will be its result when the work is completed? Mark 4:30-32; Rev. 7:1-3.

In all ages of the world's history the Lord has undertaken His work of recovery and redemption in a simple and an unostentatious manner. 1 Cor. 1:27-29. The foundation work of redemption for lost man and for the recovery of a lost world was started with a Seed. The woman's Seed was to bruise the serpent's head. That seed is Christ. Gen. 3:15; Gal. 3:16; Rom. 16:20. That undertaking will prove successful. Rev. 11:15.

When the Lord was about to deliver Israel from the land of Egypt, He chose two aged men and one woman as the visible agents of that movement. Micah 6:4. Those two men were fourscore and more years old, and the woman was older still. Ex. 7:6, 7; 2:4. The material facilities for conducting that campaign consisted of a rod. Ex. 4:2. Yet the Lord assured Moses that He would perform wonders with that rod. Verse 17. Moses was given a pledge that the people would be delivered by a mighty hand and a stretched-out arm, though the human leadership was weak and helpless. Ex. 6:1; Num. 12:3; Ex. 3:10-17.

The Israelites were delivered; they came forth from the land of their serfdom on time. Ex. 12:40, 41. They sang their song of deliverance. Exodus 15.

The world-wide gospel movement of Revelation 14 started small, like a seed. The original pioneers of the message were few. The material facilities of the undertaking were exceedingly meager. The first biographer of the movement,

Elder James White, gives the following description of the launching of this world-wide message:

"We entered upon our work penniless, with few friends, and broken in health. . . . Without means, with very few who sympathized with us in our views, without a paper, and without books, we entered upon our work. Most of our meetings were held in private houses. Our congregations were small. It was seldom that any came to our meetings excepting Adventists, unless they were attracted by curiosity to hear a woman speak."—*"Life Sketches,"* ed. 1888, p. 127.

At the present time the territory of the whole world is embraced in the organizations of Seventh-day Adventists. The organizations include the General Conference of Seventh-day Adventists, which comprises twelve divisions, embracing seventy union conferences, 148 local conferences, and 237 missions. These various organizations have a constituency of nearly 450,000 members, in 8,139 churches.

To conduct the world-wide work through these organizations there are employed 2,356 ordained ministers, 1,213 licensed ministers, 3,428 missionary licentiates, 3,378 colporteurs, or a total of 12,185 laborers.

To man the institutions connected with this movement there are employed 3,074 teachers in the primary schools, and 2,698 teachers in advanced schools. One thousand ninety employees operate the publishing houses, and 6,138 are employed in sanitariums, medical institutions, and food factories. Both classes of employees, evangelical and institutional, number 25,185.

To carry forward this international message in the year 1935, the believers contributed in tithes $5,743,281. For the conduct of the work in fields outside of the home bases, there was contributed $3,150,404. In addition to these sums there was donated $1,599,448. The average amount given by the membership of the denomination was $24.81 for each person. The combined gifts for the conduct of this world work for the year 1935 amounted to $10,493,134.

God's last message is indeed a growing message. What hath God wrought, may be loudly acclaimed. To Him the praise and the honor are rendered, for He has accomplished this wonderful result. In one single generation this message has embraced the world, and it has brought forth a multitude of believers. This work has indeed become great, going to all parts of the world, and one day it will sing its triumphant song. Rev. 15:2, 3.

7. What four outstanding events will take place during the progress of this message, similar to those which were accomplished during the typical Day of Atonement? Dan. 8:14; Rev. 14:6; 1 Peter 4:17; Acts 3:19; Jer. 50:20; Rev. 7:2-4.

Four outstanding events were accomplished on the typical Day of Atonement by the high priest. These were: The cleansing of the sanctuary, the work of judgment, the blotting out of sin, and the sealing work. (See Lesson 12, question 4.)

Four prominent fundamental beliefs of Seventh-day Adventists are: The cleansing of the sanctuary, the blotting out of sin, the investigative judgment, and the sealing work. Wherever this world-wide message is preached, these four fundamental Scriptural teachings are recognized and accepted by the believers.

With such clear, simple, and fundamental instruction given to the Israelites in the types during the centuries of their existence as the people of God, and with the further divine amplification of those teachings passed on to the church of Christ through the apostles of our Lord, it is singular that there are those who become confused in regard to the fulfillment of the mission of our High Priest, the Lord Jesus, in His intercessory work in the heavenly temple. Deut. 29:14, 15; Rom. 15:4; 1 Cor. 10:11; Heb. 9:1-10, 23, 24.

There are those who say that the seventy weeks of Daniel 9 are weeks of literal days instead of periods of prophetic days. This view of literal days is contrary to the writings of Hebrew scholars. Jewish writers, those of modern times as well as those of ancient days, unite in maintaining that the 2300 days of which the seventy times seven are a part, are symbolic. Each day represents a year. Num. 14:34; Eze. 4:4-6. Though Jewish writers admit they do not have a clear understanding of the significance of those prophetic periods, there is no dissonance among the large number of scholastic writers in regard to the symbolic meaning of those days.

The view held by some that the original record of Daniel 8:14 should be 2200 days is groundless; there is no foundation for such a position. It is altogether untenable. Every Hebrew Bible reads "2300 evenings mornings."

To attempt to link the feast mentioned in John 10:22 with the cleansing of the sanctuary of Daniel 8:14, is decidedly farfetched. In the *Review and Herald,* published at Takoma Park, Washington, D.C., issue of August 31, 1933, appeared the following article, entitled: "The Feast of Dedication. It Was Winter:"

"This feast of the Jews, recorded in the tenth chapter of the Gospel of John, has been celebrated by that people since the middle of the second century before the Christian Era. In late years a strange interpretation of the origin of this festival has been advocated. We therefore present to the readers of the *Review* the facts in regard to this annual holiday observed by the Jewish people for more than twenty centuries.

"In the year 165 B.C. Judas Maccabeus fought against the Greeks, and wrested the Holy City from the hands of their heathen enemies. And three years prior to this time, the Greeks entered the temple at Jerusalem, and placed a heathen idol upon the holy altar and offered sacrifice to it. Great consternation was manifested among the children of Abraham, that a heathen people should enter the holy precincts of their sacred house, and thus defile the temple of God. For three years the abominable idolatrous shrine remained in the house of the Lord, until in the year 165 an army of the Jews was raised by the Maccabees, who drove the ungodly from Jerusalem, and again took possession of the temple with its sacred places.

"The heathen idol was cast out of the temple, the altar was cleansed from its uncleanness, and the sanctuary was again set in order. That the Jewish people might ever after remember this great victory over their enemies, the Maccabees, with the elders of the Jews, decided to rededicate the altar to the service of God and to reconsecrate the temple. A feast of eight days was appointed as a dedication service, similar to the observance of the Feast of Tabernacles, which lasted eight days. During each day and night of these memorial services the lights were burning in the temple, and all the Jewish people greatly rejoiced in their deliverance from the heathen.

"An Annual Feast Instituted

"It was decided by the elders of the Jews that the Jewish people should hereafter observe this feast annually. They were commanded to burn lights in their homes and in their synagogues for eight nights, by the doing of which they would annually call to mind the great deliverance which had come to them over their heathen enemies. The feast was called 'The Feast of Dedication.' In later years other reasons were set forth for the observance of this feast. All later suggestions offered were traditional.

"One tradition says that when the enemies of the Jews were driven from the temple, the lamp ceased to burn; and when the holy places were recaptured, there was no oil in the sacred precincts to feed the lamp. In cleansing the temple the high priest discovered one small sealed flask of oil which had been overlooked by the heathen. The priest lighted the lamp with this small amount of oil, and a messenger was dispatched to secure a fresh supply. This oil which the priest placed in the lamp ordinarily would have been sufficient to burn for about twenty-four hours, whereas it required eight days for the messenger to return with the oil supply. So tradition says that a miracle was wrought, and that the lamp kept burning till the fresh supply of oil reached the temple.

"During the first century of the Christian Era, many added traditions were introduced by the elders. The people were taught that the lighting of the lamps was to commemorate the miracle which was wrought in keeping the lights burning during the eight days when there was only enough oil for one day. The feast then was called 'Chanuka,' the 'Feast of Lights.' The custom was continued, the lights in the homes of the people and in the synagogues being burned during the eight days of the feast.

"Rabbis Shammi and Hillel Discuss This Feast

"In the first century before Christ, there lived two great rabbis, one named Hillel and the other Shammi. It is claimed that the latter was a Greek convert to Judaism. In a discussion between these two rabbis in regard to the observance of the 'Feast of Lights,' Shammi argued that on the first day of the feast the entire eight lights should be lighted, and that on each night following, one light less should be lighted till the eighth night, when one taper only should be lighted. Hillel argued that the reverse should be the custom. He taught that on the first day one taper only should be lighted, and an additional luminary should be burned each night till the eighth night, when all eight lights should burn. Since the days of Hillel, the orthodox Jews have followed the custom advocated by Hillel.

"Four names have been given to this feast,—the 'Feast of Dedication,' the 'Feast of the Maccabees,' 'Chanuka,' and the 'Festival of Lights.' This annual holiday occurs in the ninth Bible month, called *Kisleu*. It begins on the twenty-fifth day of the month, and coincides with our month of December. The Jewish Encyclopedia, Volume VI, article 'Hanukkah,' published by Funk and Wagnalls, New York, gives a full statement of the origin and development of this festival among the Jewish people.

"That tradition for the observance of this annual feast is followed, is evident from the following benedictions pronounced by the Jews during the eight days of this feast, when the lamps are lighted:

" 'Blessed art Thou, O Lord, our God! King of the universe, who hath sanctified us with Thy commandments, and commanded us to light the lamp of dedication.

" 'Blessed art Thou, O Lord, our God! King of the universe, who wrought miracles for our fathers in those days, and in this season.

" 'Blessed art Thou, O Lord, our God! King of the universe, who hath preserved us alive, and brought us to enjoy this season.'—*'Prayers of Israel,'* pp. 196, 197.

" 'These lights we light to praise Thee for the miracles, wonders, salvations, and victories which Thou didst perform for our fathers in those days, and in this season, by the hands of Thy holy priests. Wherefore, by command, these lights are holy all the eight days of the dedication; neither are we permitted to make any other use of them, save to view them, that we may return thanks to Thy name, for Thy miracles, wonderful works, and salvation.'—*Ibid*.

"It is difficult to explain how a person at all familiar with the history of the Jewish people, with their customs and manners, can suggest that the 'Feast of Dedication,' originating in the second century before the Christian Era, had anything in common with a cleansing of the temple at the close of the 2300 days revealed to the prophet Daniel and recorded in the eighth chapter of his book. Those days were prophetic time, and had their fulfillment in harmony with the explanation given to the prophet by the angel, as noted in Daniel 9."

8. Will this work be finished according to God's promise? and to how many peoples in the world will mercy be offered? Rom. 9:28; Isa. 27:12; Eccl. 7:27.

9. Who only will be benefited by Christ's ministry in the most holy place in the heavenly sanctuary? 1 Tim. 5:24; Matt. 25:8-13.

"I saw angels hurrying to and fro in heaven. An angel with a writer's ink-horn by his side returned from the earth, and reported to Jesus that his work was done, and the saints were numbered and sealed. Then I saw Jesus, who had been ministering before the ark containing the ten commandments, throw down the censer. He raised His hands, and with a loud voice said, *'It is done.'* And all the angelic host laid off their crowns as Jesus made the solemn declaration, 'He that is unjust, let him be unjust still; and he which is filthy, let him be filthy still; and he that is righteous, let him be righteous still; and he that is holy, let him be holy still.'

"Every case had been decided for life or death. While Jesus had been ministering in the sanctuary, the judgment had been going on for the righteous dead, and then for the righteous living. Christ had received His kingdom, having made the atonement for His people, and blotted out their sins. The subjects of the kingdom were made up. The marriage of the Lamb was consummated. And the kingdom, and the greatness of the kingdom under the whole heaven, was given to Jesus and the heirs of salvation, and Jesus was to reign as King of kings, and Lord of lords. . . .

"There was then no mediator between guilty man and an offended God. While Jesus had been standing between God and guilty man, a restraint was upon the people; but when He stepped out from between man and the Father, the restraint was removed, and Satan had entire control of the finally impenitent. It was impossible for the plagues to be poured out while Jesus officiated in the sanctuary; but as His work there is finished, and His intercession closes, there is nothing to stay the wrath of God, and it breaks with fury upon the shelterless head of the guilty sinner, who has slighted salvation and hated reproof. In that fearful time, after the close of Jesus' mediation, the saints were living in the sight of a holy God without an intercessor. Every case was decided, every jewel numbered. Jesus tarried a moment in the outer apartment of the heavenly sanctuary, and the sins which had been confessed while He was in the most holy place, were placed upon Satan, the originator of sin, who must suffer their punishment.

"Then I saw Jesus lay off His priestly attire, and clothe Himself with His most kingly robes. Upon His head were many crowns, a crown within a crown. Surrounded by the angelic host, He left heaven. The plagues were falling upon the inhabitants of the earth. Some were denouncing God and cursing Him. Others rushed to the people of God and begged to be taught how they might escape His judgments. But the saints had nothing for them. The last tear for sinners had been shed, the last agonizing prayer offered, the last burden borne, the last warning given. The sweet voice of mercy was no more to invite them. When the saints, and all heaven, were interested for their salvation, they had no interest for themselves. Life and death had been set before them. Many desired life, but made no effort to obtain it. They did not choose life, and now there was no atoning blood to cleanse the guilty, no compassionate Saviour to plead for them and cry, 'Spare, spare the sinner a little longer.' All heaven had united with Jesus, as they heard the fearful words, 'It is done. It is finished.' The plan of salvation had been accomplished, but few had chosen to accept it. And as mercy's sweet voice died away, fear and horror seized the wicked. With terrible distinctness they heard the words, 'Too late! too late!' "—*"Early Writings,"* pp. 279-281.

The Investigative Judgment; The Close of Human Probation

1. WHAT does the Scripture state in regard to the extent of the judgment? Acts 17:31.

It is clear that the entire world will be judged. This idea of the judgment of all peoples, is again expressed with emphasis by the apostle Paul in the following language: "Therefore thou art inexcusable, O man, whosoever thou art that judgest: for wherein thou judgest another, thou condemnest thyself; for thou that judgest doest the same things. . . . And thinkest thou this, O man, that judgest them which do such things, and doest the same, that thou shalt escape the judgment of God?" Rom. 2:1-3. "Now we know that what things soever the law saith, it saith to them who are under the law: that every mouth may be stopped, and all the world may become guilty before God." Rom. 3:19.

There are three kinds of days mentioned in the Bible. The twenty-four-hour day (Gen. 1:5, 8, 13, 18, 19, 23, 31; Lev. 23:32); the prophetic or symbolic day (Eze. 4:4, 5; Dan. 8:14; Rev. 12:6); and the day of judgment. A prophetic day represents one year. Num. 14:34; Eze. 4:6. The day of judgment covers the time from the beginning of the investigative judgment until the work of judging all who are to be judged, shall be ended. 1 Cor. 6:2, 3.

The day Paul speaks of in Acts 17:31 is the day of judgment.

2. Will the cases to be investigated in the judgment be passed upon as a whole? Rom. 14:10-12; 2 Cor. 5:10.

God does not deal with mankind in the judgment as a whole, without reference to individuals. In the beginning, God made one man and one woman. The Lord did not create a nation, or a race, or a world of peoples at one time. While there have been times in the world's history when the Lord has dealt with nations and with races in a national and racial capacity, the fact must not be overlooked that each individual has a personal case to be decided before the throne of God.

The Scriptures plainly teach that in the judgment God will handle each individual case on its own merit. Eccl. 7:27. Because of the statement made in the second commandment of the decalogue, that the Lord will visit the iniquities of the fathers upon the children unto the third and fourth generation, the idea developed among the Hebrew people that the children are responsible for the parents' sins. Another idea which took root was that the father is responsible for a son's sins until the son reaches the age of thirteen. At this age, the son becomes כר־מצוה (bar-mitsvah), "son of the commandment." That is, at the age of thirteen the lad assumes responsibility for his own wrongs.

The Sabbath following the thirteenth birthday, the orthodox lad is obliged to attend the synagogue, and he reads a portion of the Pentateuch set apart for this particular Sabbath day. (See Acts 13:14, 15.) At the close of the reading of the law by this youth, the father steps upon the rostrum, and standing beside the lad, in the presence of the congregation, offers a prayer, the concluding words of which are: כרוך שפוטרני (Baruch Sheputrani). A free translation of these words is: "I am blessed now I have no further responsibility for this lad."

Through the prophets the Lord sought to correct this wrong interpretation of the second commandment by Israel's leaders. This is evident from the following testimony: "What mean ye, that ye use this proverb concerning the land of Israel, saying, The fathers have eaten sour grapes, and the children's teeth are set on edge? As I live, saith the Lord God, ye shall not have occasion any more to use this proverb in Israel. Behold, all souls are Mine; as the soul of the father, so also the soul of the son is Mine: the soul that sinneth, it shall die." Eze. 18:1-4. "In those days they shall say no more, The fathers have eaten a sour grape, and the children's teeth are set on edge. But every one shall die for his own iniquity: every man that eateth the sour grape, his teeth shall be set on edge." Jer. 31:29, 30.

However, this wrong view of that commandment had not been overcome in the days of the Saviour, for the disciples asked our Lord this question in regard to the blind man whom Jesus was about to heal: "Master, who did sin, this man, or his parents, that he was born blind? Jesus answered, Neither hath this man sinned, nor his parents." John 9:2, 3.

3. According to the Scripture, how many classes of people does God recognize? Rom. 2:6-11; Matt. 13:30, 38, 39.

The Bible recognizes but two classes of people in the world, the good and the bad, the righteous and the wicked, the wheat and the tares, saints and sinners. The Talmud introduced a third class, who were said to be neither sinners nor saints. In the rabbinical code a man is a saint if he is pious, or if he is philanthropic. He also may be a saint if he closely follows the rabbinical traditions. A man who is extremely wicked, one who commits certain outrageous evil acts, is a sinner. But the man who is not extremely wicked nor devoutly religious according to the Talmudic understanding, may belong to an intermediate class. This intermediate would be classed as a neutral. Such a person would have to pass through Gehenna before he could be classed as a saint or a sinner. It might require a long process for him eventually to be classed with either the good or the bad. Yet they held it was possible for him to attain to one of the two classes. No such third class is mentioned or recognized in the Scriptures. There are certain religious people at the present time who believe in a third class. Both the good and the bad grow together till the harvest, says our Saviour; and the harvest is the end of the world.

4. Who will be prepared to meet the Lord at His second advent? Isa. 25:9; 2 Thess. 1:7, 10; Heb. 9:28; 1 Thess. 5:23, 24; Jude 24.

Those only will be ready to meet the Saviour at His second advent who have made proper preparation for that event. Our Lord has promised ample grace to overcome every sin and every temptation. 1 Cor. 10:13. The Lord assured Zacharias, the father of John the Bapist, that his son would have a message which would prepare the people for the first advent of Messiah. Luke 1:13-17. The Master acknowledged that John the Baptist did a thorough work in his day. (See Matt. 11:7-14.)

The forerunner of Jesus told the people what they must do in order to be prepared when Messiah came. Luke 3:10-14. Had the multitudes who came to John for counsel followed his advice, they would have been ready to receive Messiah at His advent.

In these days God has sent a message to the children of men to prepare them for the coming of the Lord. The message is able to make every one fit to meet the Master when He returns from heaven. Our Lord has promised to keep His children unto that day. He has assured them that He is able to present them faultless before the presence of His glory with exceeding joy. God expects His people to follow His counsel, if they are to receive the reward awaiting the righteous. Obedience to all of God's commands on the part of God's children is essential to their enjoyment of the blessings of eternal life. Isa. 1:19.

5. What decision must be reached in heaven before the people can be translated at the second advent of Christ? Rev. 22:11.

It is evident that a decision in regard to the character of those who shall be found worthy to enter the kingdom of glory with our Lord at His second advent, must have been reached before the Saviour descends from heaven to gather His saints into His heavenly abode. It is not supposable that God would give to men a title to the mansions above, before it had been determined whether such individuals were worthy of a place in God's kingdom. The Scripture says that before Christ's return to earth, each case has already been decided for eternal weal or eternal woe.

Those whose cases have been passed upon and who have received a favorable decision, will forever be among the saved. The same certainty is fixed for those whose cases have received an adverse decision. These are eternally lost. It is after every case has been decided that the Lord comes and brings His reward with Him.

6. Will both classes of people be judged at the same time? Matt. 10:32, 33; Mark 8:38; 1 John 4:17; Rev. 3:5.

7. Where will this investigative judgment take place? Dan. 7:9, 10; Rev. 20:12.

The Scripture is clear that a faithful record is preserved of every person's thoughts, words, and deeds. Matt. 12:36, 37; 5:37; Col. 4:6; James 5:12; Eccl. 12:14. As soon as one is born into the world, his name is enrolled. Matt. 18:10. When a person is converted and gives his heart to the Lord, his name is entered in another book called the book of life. Phil. 4:3. This book of life is in the possession of our Lord Himself. Rev. 13:8. Our High Priest has charge of this book.

In the days of Israel, when the sanctuary service was introduced, the high priest was commanded to carry the names of the children of Israel "in the breastplate of judgment upon his heart, when he goeth in unto the holy place, for a memorial before the Lord continually." Ex. 28:29.

When the individual's name is recorded in the book of life, it is expected that his conduct from then on will be in accord with his new, converted, and transformed life. The records of his entire career are still preserved in the book where his name was enrolled at his birth.

The time comes when the individual's case is to be investigated. The hour arrives when it is to be decided whether a person, either dead or alive, is found worthy to be accounted among those who are to share the glories of eternity. Luke 20:35, 36; 21:36. The Saviour says that those who confess Him before men, He will confess before the Father and before the heavenly angels. Only those who have given their hearts to the Saviour are enrolled in the Lamb's book of life. Those who have not accepted Christ as their Lord and Saviour do not have their names entered in that special book which our Lord Himself has in charge.

It is therefore evident that those who have professed to love their Lord, those who claim to have given their hearts to the Saviour, and who have believed that their names are entered in the book of life, are considered in the investigative judgment. If a person has not accepted the Saviour, his name has not been written in the book of life of the Lamb. Such a person's case cannot be considered at the time when the investigation is being conducted for those whose names are in the book of life.

The question may be asked, "What does it mean to confess Christ?" The following statement by the Spirit of prophecy is a pointed reply to this question:

"He who would confess Christ, must have Christ abiding in Him. He cannot communicate that which he has not received. The disciples might speak fluently on doctrines, they might repeat the words of Christ Himself; but unless they possessed Christlike meekness and love, they were not confessing Him. A spirit contrary to the spirit of Christ would deny Him, whatever the profession. Men may deny Christ by evilspeaking, by foolish talking, by words that are untruthful or unkind. They may deny Him by shunning life's burdens, by the pursuit of sinful pleasure. They may deny Him by conforming to the world, by uncourteous behavior, by the love of their own opinions, by justifying self, by cherishing doubt, borrowing trouble, and dwelling in darkness. In all these ways they declare that Christ is not in them. And 'whosoever shall deny Me before men,' He says, 'him - will I also deny before My Father which is in heaven.'"—"*The Desire of Ages*," p. 357.

8. Will there be a rule to guide the Judge in each case? Eccl. 12:13, 14; James 1:25; 2:8-12.

It is unfortunate that many religious people have so erroneous a view of the work of the judgment. In the business world, men have certain well-regulated, established principles to guide them in the conduct of their administrative affairs. Yet it is hard for a certain class to believe that the Creator has a well-established rule in His universal affairs.

Repeatedly does the Bible state that God's rule of life is His law. The Scriptures declare that our first father sinned. Isa. 43:27. The first father was Adam. 1 Cor. 15:45, 47. But we are told that sin is the transgression of the law. 1 John 3:4. The law of which sin is the transgression is that law which declares, "Thou shalt not commit adultery," "Thou shalt not kill," "Thou shalt not steal." James 2:11. Adam therefore violated that law. Rom. 7:7. Adam could never have become a sinner if he had violated no law.

Furthermore, the Scripture declares: "He that committeth sin is of the devil; for the devil sinneth from the beginning." 1 John 3:8. Sin originated with Satan. Satan's home originally was in heaven. Isa. 14:12-14; Eze. 28:11-16.

Our Saviour said of Satan: "I beheld Satan as lightning fall from heaven." Luke 10:18. Satan first sinned in heaven. From heaven was this fallen angel cast out because of his sin. God's divine law, therefore, must be in heaven. This fact we have already seen in these studies. Rev. 12:7-9. (See Lesson 32, question 3.)

The Bible iterates and reiterates that God is a King. Jer. 10:7, 10. He has a kingdom, and "His kingdom ruleth over all." Ps. 103:19. Can there be a kingdom without law and without authority? A government that is not ruled by law soon finds itself in confusion. Wherever God's kingdom rules, there must be recognized His law. God is no respecter of persons. Rom. 2:11. He loves all His creatures alike. John 17:23. There are no favorites with Him. Acts 10:34. The origin of sin, the beginning of disturbance and confusion in God's universal kingdom, was caused through Lucifer's desire to be an exception. He became dissatisfied with the position appointed to him by the great King of the universe. Eze. 28:14, 15.

The law of the Lord is perfect. Ps. 19:7. A perfect God gave a perfect law. Deut. 32:4; Matt. 5:48. This perfect royal law is the standard by which God's creatures are to be judged. James 2:8-12.

9. With whom will the judgment begin? Phil. 4:3; Rev. 13:8; 1 Peter 4:17.

The judgment will begin with those whose names have been entered in the book of life. The records of their lives will be compared with God's standard of judgment, the law of God, the ten commandments. According to the Scriptures, those individuals who have lived in harmony with God's will and who have died with a hope in Christ, will first be investigated. (See Heb. 11:4-40.)

The people of God, from Adam's day to the last one who shall enter the tomb, will have their cases examined, and the decision of heaven will be in accordance with that which the records disclose. If they have sown to the Spirit, they will "of the Spirit reap life everlasting." Gal. 6:8; Rom. 2:7.

After the cases of the dead in Christ have been passed upon, then the records of the living will be considered. There will be no exceptions. Rev. 20:12, 13. How important it is that those who now live shall appreciate their privileges in this unusual day and hour!

10. At the time when their cases are investigated, what decision will be made concerning those whose names have been entered in the book of life, but whose sins are not pardoned? Ex. 32:32, 33; Eze. 18:25-30; 33:17-20.

11. What will be the attitude of the heavenly High Priest toward those who have lived in past generations, whose conduct has measured up to the rule of the judgment, and whose sins have been pardoned? Rom. 3:24-26.

God will judge men according to the light they have had, and which they have followed. Ps. 87:6. There will be those in the kingdom of God who have never heard of the crucifixion. Zech. 13:6. There is only one way of salvation. Isa. 43:11; John 14:6; Acts 4:12. Jesus is the light that lighteth every man that cometh into the world. John 1:4; 8:12; 9:4. But many who have believed in Him have not known Him by name. They have not had the advantages of light and truth which others have had in later times.

Our Lord commanded the disciples to preach the gospel and to baptize the believers. This is God's method, in Christ, of saving men. Matt. 28:18-20; Mark 16:15, 16. We have no record that the thief on the cross was baptized, yet our Lord assured that dying thief that he would be with the Saviour in the kingdom. Luke 23:39-43. Our Lord saw the sincerity and honesty of the man's faith. The thief was convinced that Jesus was the Messiah, and he courageously and publicly confessed the Saviour.

The leaders of Israel, however, had had great light. They refused to walk in it. To them the Saviour said: "If I had not done among them the works which none other man did, they had not had sin: but now have they both seen and hated both Me and My Father." John 15:24.

"And Jesus said, For judgment I am come into this world, that they which see not might see; and that they which see might be made blind. And some of the Pharisees which were with Him heard these words, and said unto Him, Are we blind also? Jesus said unto them, If ye were blind, ye should have no sin: but now ye say, We see; therefore your sin remaineth." John 9:39-41.

Because those men refused to practice the light that had come to them, our Lord said to them: "That upon you may come all the righteous blood shed upon the earth, from the blood of righteous Abel unto the blood of Zacharias son of Barachias, whom ye slew between the temple and the altar. Verily I say unto you, All these things shall come upon this generation." Matt. 23:35, 36.

Those men of Israel knew what had overtaken their ancestors who refused to follow the light given to them. The rabbis of Israel, by their attitude toward the Saviour, declared that had they lived in the days of their fathers they would have walked in the same footsteps. Those leaders incurred the guilt of their ancestors. By rejecting the light which had come to them through the Saviour, they decided their destiny.

For those who in all ages have desired to obey, but have unwittingly lived in error, our great High Priest mediates before the Father. The apostle Paul says of the intercession of the Saviour: "Whom God hath set forth to be a propitiation through faith in His blood, to declare His righteousness for the remission of sins that are past, through the forbearance of God; to declare, I say, at this time His righteousness: that He might be just, and the justifier of him which believeth in Jesus."

Christ's righteous life is presented to God in place of the imperfect life of him who followed the Lord to the best of his ability. Only God is able to determine correctly who has fully lived up to all the light. The Judge of all the earth will do right. Gen. 18:25.

This present generation enjoys the light of the ages. To the people of today is presented the accumulated light and truth of the centuries. Every truth of the Scriptures which is essential for men and women, and which will enable them to understand how to prepare for the return of the Lord, is given in its completeness. God's rule of right may be understood today, clearly and definitely. There is no excuse for this generation if they are not able to understand all of God's requirements. Rom. 1:20. The prophet, speaking for God, asks a pertinent question of the church of the twentieth century: "What could have been done more to My vineyard, that I have not done in it?" Isa. 5:4. God has given us His only-begotten Son. In Jesus, God has poured out the wealth of the universe. The riches of His grace are boundless. His supply of mercy is fathomless. All the resources of His throne are pledged for the salvation of those who put their trust in Him.

The Lord has given us the Bible. The book of God is able to make us wise unto salvation through faith in the Lord Jesus. 2 Tim. 3:15-17. To make more clear to the people of today God's plan for the church, the Lord has bestowed the gifts of the Spirit. Nothing necessary for the church, in order that she may be prepared for the return of her Lord, has been omitted or overlooked. All the counsel of God has been declared. Acts 20:27. Our heavenly High Priest will present every man's case to the Father according to righteousness, holiness, and truth.

12. Will the Judge of the judgment also act as a Judge-Advocate? John 5:22; 1 John 2:1; Heb. 7:25; Rom. 8:34.

Our Lord said, "The Father judgeth no man." All judgment is committed unto the Son. The Father is present in the judgment. The Son is Judge on the throne with the Father, and conducts the judgment in the Father's presence.

Christ can act as Judge, for He is both God and man. As God, the Father has appointed Him heir of all things. Heb. 1:2. His judgment is just. He also is Son of man. 1 Cor. 15:47. He lived on earth as man must live, and He lived His life in full accord with His Father's will. John 8:29.

He is man's Advocate. He intercedes in man's behalf. When unjust accusations are presented by Satan to the Father, our High Priest pleads for man before His Father, as may be seen by the following experience:

"He showed me Joshua the high priest standing before the Angel of the Lord, and Satan standing at his right hand to resist him. And the Lord said unto Satan, The Lord rebuke thee, O Satan; even the Lord that hath chosen Jerusalem rebuke thee: is not this a brand plucked out of the fire? Now Joshua was clothed with filthy garments, and stood before the Angel. And He answered and spake unto those that stood before Him, saying, Take away the filthy garments from him. And unto him He said, Behold, I have caused thine iniquity to pass from thee, and I will clothe thee with change of raiment." Zech. 3:1-4. (See also Isa. 61:10.) "I said, Let them set a fair miter upon his head. So they set a fair miter upon his head, and clothed him with garments. And the Angel of the Lord stood by." Zech. 3:5. (See also Isa. 64:6.)

Of the experience recorded in the foregoing scriptures, the Spirit of prophecy makes the following comments:

"In his own strength, man cannot meet the charges of the enemy. In sin-stained garments, confessing his sins, he stands before God. But Jesus, our

Advocate, presents an effectual plea in behalf of all who by repentance and faith have committed the keeping of their souls to Him. He pleads their cause, and by the mighty arguments of Calvary, vanquishes their accuser. His perfect obedience to God's law has given Him all power in heaven and in earth, and He claims from His Father mercy and reconciliation for guilty man. . . .

"Zechariah's vision of Joshua and the Angel applies with peculiar force to the experience of God's people in the closing scenes of the great day of atonement."—*"Prophets and Kings,"* pp. 586, 587.

13. How long will Christ act as Judge and Judge-Advocate? 1 Cor. 15:24, 25.

Christ will act as Judge and Judge-Advocate until the close of human probation. As long as there is an honest soul who longs for deliverance from the power of Satan, and who earnestly desires to give up all for the Saviour, and to prepare himself for the coming of the Lord, so long will Jesus intercede in man's behalf. Jesus will reign till all enemies of God and man are put under His feet.

Cleansing of the Heavenly Sanctuary: The Church of Christ Prepared for Her Lord

1. WHAT was the high priest, in the Levitical sanctuary, commanded to do at the completion of his ministry in the most holy place? Lev. 16:20.

The high priest on the Day of Atonement must not leave the most holy place until his ministry was completed. The Scripture says that when his labors in this sacred apartment were ended, the sanctuary was reconciled. In Leviticus 16:20 the Hebrew word translated "holy place" is קֹדֶשׁ (kodesh). Although the Hebrew word מִקְדָּשׁ (mikdash) is the predominating term used in the Old Testament for "sanctuary," we find the word kodesh is translated "sanctuary" nearly seventy times. The Hebrew expression for the first clause in Leviticus 16:20, "And when he hath made an end of reconciling the holy place," is וְכִלָּה מִכַּפֵּר אֶת־הַקֹּדֶשׁ (Wekillah mikkapper eth-haqqodesh), "And when he hath made an end of atoning for the the sanctuary." The words "reconcile" and "atonement" are translated from the same word, כַּפֵּר (kaphar).

The Scripture suggests that when the high priest had finished his work on the Day of Atonement, the sanctuary had been atoned for; the sanctuary had been reconciled; the sanctuary had been cleansed. This thought is in perfect harmony with the statement found in the thirty-third verse of this same chapter of Leviticus. Nothing further can be done in the ministry of the sanctuary or in ministering for the people when the Day of Atonement is ended. It is then that the priest calls for the live goat, the עֲזָאזֵל (Azazel). Verse twenty offers conclusive evidence that Azazel, the scapegoat, had no share in the ministry of the sanctuary on this most sacred of all days, until the atoning ministry was fully ended.

2. What ceremony did the high priest perform when he left the sanctuary? Lev. 16:21.

3. What was done with Azazel, the scapegoat, when the sins of Israel had been confessed upon him? Verses 21, 22.

On leaving the sanctuary, the priest was to lay his hands upon the live goat, and confess on this goat all the iniquities of the children of Israel. All the transgressions of the people of God were placed on this Azazel. These transgressions which were placed upon the head of Azazel were not the sins or wrongs of the strangers nor of the Gentiles. These transgressions of Israel had already been confessed, forgiven, pardoned.

Be it remembered that in Leviticus 4 we have the record showing how the people of Israel came to the sanctuary with their offerings, and confessed their sins on the head of those sacrifices. These sins were transferred to the sanctuary, either by the blood of the offering, which was slain as the atonement for the guilty individual, or by the priest's eating the flesh of the offering in the holy place. (See Lev. 4:3-6, 13-17; 6:24-26, 30.) When the penitent soul had offered the sacrifice to the Lord as his substitute, he went home forgiven. Lev. 4:26, 31, 35.

The sins and transgressions of Israel had gone before them into the sanctuary prior to the Day of Atonement. When the blood was sprinkled upon the veil in the holy place, there was, in type, the record of man's confession of guilt, and the assurance of pardon. The sins which had been gathering in the holy place during the year, and those which had been confessed and blotted out during this special day, all were brought forth at the close of the Day of Atonement by the high priest, and these pardoned and atoned-for sins were placed upon the head of Azazel, the scapegoat. But when these sins were placed upon Azazel, this goat *was not slain.* He was not offered up as an atonement before the Lord. This goat was *sent out of the camp.* By a fit man was Azazel sent away into the wilderness, where he remained with those pardoned sins of Israel. This goat never returned to the camp. He was banished to a desolate place. He was forever separated from the congregation of Israel. Azazel was not sacrificed for the sins of the people.

4. When Azazel was removed from the camp of Israel, what was the condition of the sanctuary and of the people of Israel? Verses 30, 33.

The condition of the sanctuary and the character of the people are thus described by the Scripture: "He shall make an atonement for the holy sanctuary, and he shall make an atonement for the tabernacle of the congregation, and for the altar, and he shall make an atonement for the priests, and for all the people of the congregation." "On that day shall the priest make an atonement for you, to cleanse you, that ye may be clean from all your sins before the Lord." Lev. 16:33, 30.

Nothing could be clearer than that the sanctuary and all the congregation of the people of Israel, including the priests, were cleansed during the time that the high priest ministered in the most holy place of the sanctuary on the Day of Atonement.

5. What would be the fate of those who did not conform to the commands of God upon the Day of Atonement? Lev. 23:28-30.

For those who did not accept the provision of God's mercy on this "sabbath of sabbaths," on this tenth day of the seventh month, on this Day of Atonement, there was no further probation. Mercy was no longer extended to them. They had had their day of opportunity, and when they failed to improve the final hour of mercy, they were cut off from among their people.

So when the Day of Atonement was finished, the congregation of Israel were cleansed, the sanctuary was cleansed, and the sins were carried away, in type, by Azazel into an uninhabited place in the wilderness. The obedient were sealed; the disobedient were cut off from the congregation of the Lord.

6. When the Saviour shall complete His work in the heavenly sanctuary, what will become of the original Azazel? Isa. 14:5-17, 19, 20; Rev. 20:1, 2.

When our heavenly High Priest completes His work for sinners in the most holy place of the heavenly sanctuary, at the close of the antitypical day of atonement, the record of every individual whose sins have gone before him to judgment will have been investigated, and all sin will have been blotted out. 1 Tim. 5:24. The people of God have accepted the final proffers of mercy; and in every land and among all peoples the obedient have been accepted and have been sealed.

The disobedient and unregenerate have stilled the appeals of mercy. Our Lord will soon leave the most holy place of the heavenly sanctuary, with the sins of those who have confessed and whose sins have been blotted out. These pardoned transgressions of the people of God are now placed upon the head of the original Azazel—Satan, the devil. Ancient peoples have believed that Azazel, the scapegoat, represents the devil. Doctor Gesenius, in his Hebrew Lexicon, on the word "Azazel," says: "The name Azazel is also used by the Arabs for an evil demon."

No longer will there be a record of sin remaining in the books of heaven against those who have accepted the merit of a Saviour's blood. The names of God's loyal, faithful people will be retained in the Lamb's book of life. Dan. 12:1; Luke 10:20; Rev. 21:27. They are God's precious chosen ones. Mal. 3:16, 17. The sanctuary in heaven will have been cleansed. Dan. 8:14. Intercession for man will be at an end. The dead line will have been reached. The church of God will have been sanctified, made clean. 1 Thess. 5:23. Upon Satan, the originator of sin, will be rolled the sins which he caused the children of God to commit while they in their heart loved and followed their Lord.

The unrepentant, with the professed followers of the Master whose record did not stand the heavenly investigation, will be cut off from the congregation of God's people. Then Satan will be bound, and will never again be permitted to tempt the children of the Lord.

"Jesus tarried a moment in the outer apartment of the heavenly sanctuary, and the sins which had been confessed while He was in the most holy place, were placed upon Satan, the originator of sin, who must suffer their punishment."—"Early Writings," pp. 280, 281.

7. To what place will Satan be consigned? Rev. 20:2, 3, 7; Isa. 24:21.

Satan, bearing the sins of the righteous which have been placed upon him, will be a prisoner on this earth as it is returned to its original chaotic state at the coming of the Lord. Jer. 4:23-26. For one thousand years this earth, which has been Satan's prison house for those whom he has taken captive during the reign of sin, will become the devil's jail, from which he has no means of escape.

Bound by a chain of circumstances stronger than links forged by the most powerful brawn of man or of demons, Satan will be cast out into the wilderness of this dark and disarranged earth, which will revert to the condition in which it was at creation, before the Lord made it beautiful and glorious. For a thousand years the originator of sin and sorrow will have the opportunity to meditate upon his work of destruction and desolation. He will have ample time to consider the results of his disobedience to the commands of God. The advantages which he promised men if they would only follow him and disobey their Maker, are nowhere to be seen. The terrors of desolation and death face him in their enormity. Satan will observe the ruin caused by his career, as he considers his lot and the lot of those who enlisted under his banner. An outcast, an exile, abandoned, forsaken by God and by man, Satan for an entire millennium will reap the fruit of his sinful course, and of the "good time" he promised his followers.

8. What has become of the records of those who have lived righteous lives? Jer. 31:33, 34; 50:20.

The righteous will enjoy to the full the promise of the new covenant: "They shall all know Me, from the least of them unto the greatest of them, saith the Lord: for I will forgive their iniquity, and I will remember their sin no more." Jer. 31:34.

"I have blotted out, as a thick cloud, thy transgressions, and, as a cloud, thy sins." Isa. 44:22.

"I, even I, am He that blotteth out thy transgressions for Mine own sake, and will not remember thy sins." Isa. 43:25.

"Thou wilt cast all their sins into the depths of the sea." Micah 7:19.

In that day the sins of Israel cannot be found. Should any want to uncover or remember them, they cannot be found, for they will have been blotted out. The church of our Lord will have been made ready and prepared to meet her Lord.

9. What will be the fate of those who have made a profession of religion, but whose conduct has not been in harmony with the will of God, and who have unconfessed and unforgiven sins upon their life record? Matt. 24:50, 51, margin.

Our Lord Returns for His People; Reunion of God's Family

1. WHEN the Saviour returns to earth, what will be done for those who have died in Christ? 1 Cor. 15:51-54.

The hope of a resurrection from the dead has anchored God's people through the ages. In Isaiah's day the prophet encouraged the people to believe that the time would come when death would be conquered, at the coming of Messiah, who would raise the dead. Isa. 25:8, 9. Our Saviour made clear in His day that there must be a resurrection of the righteous patriarchs, for God had declared that He is the God of Abraham, of Isaac, and of Jacob. Mark 12:26, 27. The Sanhedrin and the scribes knew that those fathers of Israel were still in their graves.

Our Lord gave the people assurance that the righteous would be recompensed at the resurrection of the just. The Jews, to this hour, believe in the resurrection at the coming of Messiah. The two following statements are taught the Jewish lad in his early days:

"He will send the Messiah at the end of the days."

"God will raise the dead according to the multitude of His mercies."

This teaching is impressed upon the young child, that he may always cling to the hope of a resurrection.

The apostle Paul wrote that sublime chapter on the resurrection, in order that God's people might be confirmed in the prophet's teachings, that death is not an eternal sleep. The day will come when the reign of that cruel enemy, death, will be broken. All God's sleeping saints will be raised from the dead at the second coming of Christ.

2. What will become of the righteous living when the saints are raised? 1 Thess. 4:15-17.

When the Lord descends from heaven with a shout, with the voice of the Archangel, and with the trump of God, to raise the dead, the living righteous will also be rewarded. The apostle Paul declares: "These all [the worthies who died in Christ], having obtained a good report through faith, received not the promise: God having provided some *better thing* for us, that they without us should not be made perfect." Heb. 11:39, 40.

The two classes, the living and the dead, mentioned in the above scripture, are the righteous. One class died before they received the promise of the inheritance; but they looked forward to a resurrection from the dead, when the reward of the faithful would be given them.

The other class are assured *something better* even than a resurrection from the dead. This something better is to be alive when the Lord comes, and to go to heaven without tasting death. At that time they expect to be translated by the Saviour without having to pass through the tomb. The reward to both the dead and the living is sure. God's remnant people will be alive when the Saviour returns to earth at His second advent.

Two classes will be redeemed at the second advent of our Lord. Of one class it is written: "I will ransom them from the power of the grave; I will redeem them from death." Hosea 13:14. It is doubtless to this class that Paul refers when he rejoicingly exclaims: "O death, where is thy sting? O grave, where is thy victory?" 1 Cor. 15:55.

Of the other class we read: "These were redeemed from among men, being the first fruits unto God and to the Lamb." Rev. 14:4. Commenting on the first five verses of Revelation 14, the Spirit of prophecy says:

"Upon the crystal sea before the throne, that sea of glass as it were mingled with fire,—so resplendent is it with the glory of God,—are gathered the company that have 'gotten the victory over the beast, and over his image, and over his mark, and over the number of his name.' With the Lamb upon Mount Zion, 'having the harps of God,' they stand, the hundred and forty and four thousand that were redeemed from among men; and there is heard, as the sound of many waters, and as the sound of a great thunder, 'the voice of harpers harping with their harps.' And they sing 'a new song' before the throne, a song which no man can learn save the hundred and forty and four thousand. It is the song of Moses and the Lamb,—a song of deliverance. None but the hundred and forty-four thousand can learn that song; for it is the song of their experience,—an experience such as no other company have ever had. 'These are they which follow the Lamb whithersoever He goeth.' These, having been translated from the earth, from among the living, are counted as 'the first fruits unto God and to the Lamb."— *"The Great Controversy,"* pp. 648, 649.

Both the righteous dead who have been raised and the righteous living are together caught up to meet the Lord in the air. At His second advent our Lord will not touch the earth. Jesus with His trumpet will awaken the sleeping saints, and they, with those who have never died, will at once ascend to meet Him on the cloud. Isa. 26:19.

3. What will the Lord then do for all the righteous? John 14: 1-3; Acts 1:11; Matt. 16:27; 25:31.

Our Saviour assured His disciples that if He went away, He would come again. At His coming He would take His followers with Him to those mansions He went to prepare for them. What an occasion that reception in the air will be! Jesus, surrounded by millions of angels, will have come to fulfill His promise to His children,—to escort His faithful servants to those heavenly homes of which He had told them. They hold a reception in the air, on their journey to heaven.

The unbeliever today has no ground for disputing the reality of the heavenly chariots. Who would have dreamed, a few decades ago, that aviation could have existence, and, if it were realized, that it would assume the proportions it has? Who could have imagined it possible for men to raise a machine from the ground, against the well-established laws of gravity, and by the development of motor power transport human beings with safety, miles high in the air, and traverse seas and oceans? The Oriental "Clippers" travel at a tremendously rapid pace.

Since to frail, puny man has been given the ability to do such seemingly impossible things, can we doubt God's ability to do more? Does not the Creator and Redeemer possess more power than finite man? Hear the voice of God speaking to the children of men concerning His almighty power and ability to poise and uphold all the worlds in their places: "Lift up your eyes on high, and behold who hath created these things, that bringeth out their host by number: He calleth them all by names by the greatness of His might, for that He is strong in power; not one faileth." Isa. 40:26. (See also verses 12-18.)

Jesus with the righteous will make the ascent to His Father's home and to the heavenly throne.

4. What Scriptures will meet their fulfillment as the Saviour approaches the New Jerusalem? Isa. 26:2; Matt. 25:34; Rev. 22:14.

As the happy throng of the redeemed, accompanied by the angels, follow their blessed Master, they approach the glorious golden city of God. The pearly gates swing back on their glittering hinges, even as the arms of a mother open wide to receive her long-looked-for child, and in that day the words of the Scripture are heard: "Open ye the gates, that the righteous 'nation which keepeth the truth may enter in." Isa. 26:2.

5. As the Saviour approaches the throne of God, what promise will He say He has fulfilled? Gen. 43:8, 9; Heb. 7:14; John 20:25-27.

The Scriptures say that our Lord sprang out of Judah. Judah is said to be the lawgiver. Ps. 108:8. Jacob forecast that the scepter should not depart from Judah until Shiloh should come. Gen. 49:10.

It was Judah who made so earnest an appeal to Joseph in behalf of Benjamin. Judah was willing to become a substitute for his brother. Our Lord made an appeal to His Father to allow Him to become man's substitute. He promised the Father He would bring back lost man. (See "Early Writings," p. 126.) The marks on the palms of His hands are eloquent evidence of the infinite price He has paid to bring man back. Isa. 49:15, 16. He fulfilled what He promised His Father. Man is restored; the precious blood of the Son of God was the price of restoration. Acts 20:28.

6. What promise does Jesus ask His Father to fulfill to Him? John 17:24.

7. What presentation will the Father then make to the Saviour? Eph. 5:26, 27; Col. 1:22; 2 Cor. 11:2; Rev. 14:5.

After our Lord gathers His redeemed church around the Father's throne, the blood-bought throng are then presented to our Saviour by the Father. God presents to Jesus His own saved ones. As a parent offers a bride to her husband, so does the heavenly Father present the church as a gift to the Son of God. What an honor it will be to be gathered with those who shall constitute the redeemed host in the presence of God!

8. What privilege will then be afforded the redeemed? Matt. 5:8; Rev. 22:4; 1 Cor. 13:12.

During the ages of the reign of sin, man has not been permitted to see the Father's face. In response to an earnest appeal of Moses to behold the presence of God, the prophet of Israel was told: "Thou canst not see My face: for there shall no man see Me, and live. . . . I will take away Mine hand, and thou shalt see My back parts: but My face shall not be seen." Ex. 33:20, 23.

God talked to Moses face to face and mouth to mouth. Ex. 33:11. He made it possible for Moses to listen to His voice. When our Saviour receives His church as a gift from the Father, it is then that the people of God will be able to look into the beautiful face of God undimmed and unveiled.

9. What great gathering will assemble around God's throne, upon the Saviour's return with the redeemed church? Eph. 3:14, 15; Luke 15:4-6.

God's family consists of those on earth and those upon other planets, as well as those in heaven. Since sin entered God's domains, one member of the family has been lost. When Jesus returns to heaven with the redeemed from this earth, there will be present about God's throne, inhabitants of other planets. The missing member has been found. The family of God around His throne will once more be united. What a universal family reunion that will be! The lost will have been found.

14

10. With the family of God united, what will take place around God's throne? Zeph. 3:17; Rev. 15:2, 3; 5:11-13.

With a united family about God's throne, a song of praise and thanksgiving will be heard from every voice in the universe. The apostle says of this hymn of praise: "Every creature which is in heaven, and on the earth, and under the earth, and such as are in the sea, and all that are in them, heard I saying, Blessing, and honor, and glory, and power, be unto Him that sitteth upon the throne, and unto the Lamb forever and ever." Rev. 5:13.

From every tongue is heard the voice of joy and thanksgiving to the Father and to the Son who manifested such abounding love to those creatures who once were rebellious. There is no silence in heaven. Everything that has breath praises the Lord. Psalms 150.

11. What will become of the wicked dead at the close of the millennium? Rev. 20:7; Matt. 25:46; Rev. 20:4, 12; 1 Cor. 6:2, 3.

At the second coming of Christ all the wicked will be destroyed. 2 Thess. 1:7-10; Rev. 6:14-17; Jer. 4:26. The righteous will all leave the earth, and the wicked will all be slain by the brightness of Christ's glory. When the Saviour with His saints leaves this earth for heaven, there will be no living human beings left on the earth. There can be no funerals, for there will be none to gather the dead or to bury them. Jer. 4:25; 25:31-33. The earth will be in its former void and chaotic condition. Jer. 4:24-27.

For one thousand years the earth will lie bare and barren. It will remain in this state during ten centuries.

Christ, in conjunction with the righteous saints, will pass judgment upon the wicked during the thousand years. At the close of the millennium, our Lord will again return to earth, and then all the wicked will be raised. The Saviour said that "all that are in the graves shall hear His voice, and shall come forth; they that have done good, unto the resurrection of life; and they that have done evil, unto the resurrection of damnation." John 5:28, 29. Paul declares that there is to be "a resurrection of the dead, both of the just and unjust." Acts 24:15. The apostle makes clear that the resurrection of the just will take place first. 1 Thess. 4:16. It is at the resurrection of the just that the righteous will receive their reward. Luke 14:14. The apostle John tells us the two resurrections will be one thousand years apart. The wicked will come forth from their graves at the end of the thousand years to hear the sentence of eternal death passed upon them.

12. What will eventually become of Satan and his evil angels? Rev. 20:10; Heb. 2:14; Mal. 4:1, 3.

With all the wicked again raised to life, Satan will gather the evil hosts for a final stand against the Lord and against His people. Then fire will come down from God out of heaven, and destroy the devil and all his evil hosts. They will be burned up, root and branch.

13. What disposition will God make of all His foes, and of death itself? Isa. 33:14; Rev. 21:4; 1 Cor. 15:26; Rev. 1:18; 20:14.

With the destruction of Satan, death and the grave will also be destroyed. Every influence which the originator of sin has exerted is to be brought low. There will be a clean universe. Not a weed will be seen; not a thorn will be left. All the foes of God are to become ashes. "One reminder alone remains: our Redeemer will ever bear the marks of His crucifixion. Upon His wounded head, upon His side, His hands and feet, are the only traces of the cruel work that sin has wrought. Says the prophet, beholding Christ in His glory: 'He had bright beams coming out of His side: and there was the hiding of His power.' Hab. 3:4, margin."—"The Great Controversy," p. 674.

14. Upon what supreme experience will the people of God then enter? Isa. 65:17; 66:22; Rev. 21:1, 2; Isa. 65:22; Nahum 1:9.

Eternity, with all its significance, is the lot of the redeemed. There will never again be sorrow, sighing, or death. Separation and suffering will not enter the domains of God. The redeemed will have learned the awful lesson of disobedience. The unfallen worlds will have observed the experiences through which the redeemed have passed.

The story of redemption will never lose its sweetness for the saved. As eternity rolls on, Jesus will become more and more precious to those who have been given such rich treasures through His saving grace. What a treasure of truth God has entrusted to His church in these last days! Could the people of God catch the vision of the sanctuary truth in its clearness, it would daily be a fresh revelation to them.

What precious instruction has been bequeathed to the remnant church through the Spirit of prophecy, and how this information should be heeded and treasured up! Says the servant of the Lord:

"God's people are now to have their eyes fixed on the heavenly sanctuary, where the final ministration of our great High Priest in the work of the judgment is going forward,—where He is interceding for His people."—*"Life Sketches,"* p. 278, ed. 1915.

A Study of the Atonement

Part 1. The Principle of Substitution Introduced

1. WHAT was man's condition at creation? Eccl. 7:29; Gen. 1:31.

God made man upright. The Hebrew word for "upright" is יָשָׁר (yashar). By all orthodox Jewish commentators the word yashar is translated "rechtfertig." Man was made perfect. Man could not be improved upon. Another Hebrew word closely associated with yashar is שַׂר (sar), which means "prince." The angel changed Jacob's name to "Israel." The term "Israel" is a contracted expression derived from two Hebrew words, Sar El, "prince of or prevailer with God." The Lord created man a noble and princely being.

The following from "Patriarchs and Prophets" is illuminating in regard to the creation of man:

"God created man in His own image. Here is no mystery. There is no ground for supposition that man was evolved . . . from the lower forms of animal or vegetable life. Such teaching lowers the great work of the Creator to the level of man's narrow, earthly conceptions. . . .

"He who set the starry worlds on high, and tinted with delicate skill the flowers of the field, . . . when He came to crown His glorious work, to place one in the midst to stand as ruler of the fair earth, did not fail to create a being worthy of the hand that gave him life. . . .

"He was placed, as God's representative, over the lower orders of being. . . .

"Man was to bear God's image, both in outward resemblance and in character. . . . His nature was in harmony with the will of God. His mind was capable of comprehending divine things. His affections were pure; his appetites and passions were under the control of reason. He was holy and happy in bearing the image of God, and in perfect obedience to His will.

"As man came forth from the hand of his Creator, he was of lofty stature and perfect symmetry. His countenance bore the ruddy tint of health, and glowed with the light of life and joy. Adam's height was much greater than that of men who now inhabit the earth."—Pages 44, 45.

2. How does the psalmist describe God's character? Ps. 92:15.

3. In whose image and likeness was man made? Gen. 1:26, 27.

4. For what purpose was man created? Rev. 4:11; 1 Cor. 6:19, 20.

Man was created for God's pleasure. The Lord made man to live for His glory. Our heavenly Father was under no obligation to create man. God is the possessor of heaven and earth. Gen. 14:19; Job 35:5-8. God is love. 1 John 4:8. Man was created to glorify his Maker, and to share with the Creator the joys and delights of a pure, holy, unselfish love.

5. Is the pleasure of God temporary or permanent? Ps. 16:11; 36:8.

God's works are neither temporary nor limited. Our Creator is the "eternal God" "who only hath immortality." Deut. 33:27; 1 Tim. 6:16. The works of God abide; they last always. Eccl. 1:4. The pleasures which God desired man to enjoy were to be lasting, perpetual, endless.

In creating man, God did not experiment. The Lord was not making a test or trial when His hands brought forth man. The Maker designed that the perfect man He made should always retain the same perfection.

6. How does man compare with the angels? Ps. 8:4, 5.

7. What pronouncement of His work did God make at the close of the sixth day of creation? Gen. 1:31.

Repeatedly we read in Genesis 1 that what God made was good. When we reach the climax of His creation, the making of man, at the conclusion of the sixth day, it is written: "God saw everything that He had made, and, behold, it was *very good*. And the evening and the morning were the sixth day." Gen. 1:31. The Hebrew words, טוֹב מְאֹד (*tob meod*), translated "very good," mean good in the extreme. Man could not have been made better. Nothing could have been added to man when God pronounced him "very good."

8. In the beginning, what gift was bestowed upon man? Ps. 115:16.

9. Was the earth presented to man as an outright gift? 1 Cor. 4: 1, 2; 1 Peter 4:10; Luke 12:42.

At creation, God gave to man all things, with one exception, the tree of knowledge of good and evil. Man was assured that this world with all its contents was a free gift to him. This gift was not an absolute one. The earth was not given to man as an independency, apart from God. Man could not be independent of God. Man always must be dependent on his Creator. This world was presented to man as a "gift in trust." Man was God's steward. All that he enjoyed was to be considered a sacred trust. Man did not create any part of the world. Creation existed prior to man. God did not make man in the morning of the first day. All things were made prior to man. Adam was formed after the world was made. Man has not a thing he can call his own, apart from what was given to him by his Maker.

Man was made a steward over this world, and the Creator would not interfere with man's control of it as long as he conducted its affairs in harmony with the will of the Creator. Man never would have surrendered this earth if he had constantly followed the instruction of his Creator. Adam was given authority over this earth as God's steward.

10. Was evil or sin a part of God's original program? James 1:13.

11. Was death part of the pleasure of God? Eze. 18:32.

Sin, sickness, and death were no part of God's program for man or for this earth. God created man perfect, and at creation the Lord gave him a dietary which would enable him to live forever. There could not have been disease or disturbance in the world if man had continuously followed the instruction of his Maker.

12. What brought about sin and death? James 1:14, 15; Rom. 5:12, 19.

Sin and death, with the brood of evils and sorrows which accompany them, are the result of man's failure to adhere to God's wishes. Man was not compelled to do wrong. The Creator endowed our first parents with faculties able to carry out His wishes. It is true that Adam and Eve were tempted, but it was not necessary for them to yield to the temptation. They could have remained steadfast to Heaven. All the power of God was at their command, to enable them to continue in the path of right. Had they not *yielded* to the suggestions of evil, sin would never have entered this earth. Force was not and could not have been used to compel them to commit sin. Adam and Eve departed from God's program when they failed consistently to heed the instructions which they well understood.

13. Was man advised against disobedience? Gen. 2:16, 17.

14. Did the first parents plunge into sin of their own choice? 2 Cor. 11:3; 1 Tim. 2:13, 14.

Adam was instructed not to disobey His Creator. Heaven took all precautions against the possibility of the first parents' being led into disobedience. The Lord had said to them: "Of the tree of the knowledge of good and evil, thou shalt not eat of it: for in the day that thou eatest thereof thou shalt surely die." Gen. 2:17.

This warning was not to intimidate Adam and Eve. God was advising them to remain loyal and true. Since the Lord placed man where he was, the responsibility for man's protection rested upon the Creator. Heaven assured man that this continued care would never fail, but he must guard strictly the admonition to be obedient. Adam must not depart from the command of God. To give careful and consistent heed to this admonition was to ensure man's success and continuance.

In the statement, "In the day that thou eatest thereof thou shalt surely die," God was explaining to Adam and Eve the consequence should they fail to heed the counsel given them. God is not arbitrary. The Lord loves His creation.

Adam and Eve failed to accept fully God's word. They were seduced into sin. They were deceived by a foe. They were duped and misled; but their disobedience showed their lack of confidence in their Creator. They failed fully to believe the word of God.

15. When man disobeyed his Creator, was he left in despair, or was an opportunity offered him of recovery? Gen. 3:15; Gal. 3:16.

By sinning against the Lord, man subjected himself to the consequences of disobedience. There was no excuse for him. Adam knew what was expected of him; he was told the result of disobedience. There was no justification for Adam's wrong course, though he attempted to cast blame for his sin upon Eve, and eventually upon the Creator. Sin cannot be excused.

By secreting themselves in the garden, Adam and Eve acknowledged their guilt, admitted their sin. They could not face their Creator. Thus they condemned themselves.

Had God manifested no mercy, had His attribute of justice alone been displayed, judgment would have become effective immediately. Death would have gone into effect at once. The sentence would have been equitable. Man brought nothing into the world. He had no basis for an appeal for a stay of execution. Man must die, for God's word is immutable. "The word of the Lord endureth forever." Had the death sentence gone into effect then, eternal despair would have been seen in all nature. But God delights in mercy. "The mercy of the Lord is from everlasting to everlasting." Ps. 103:17; also verses 8-14.

Before pronouncing the death sentence, God offered man a hope. A way of escape for him had been arranged, a door of opportunity for his recovery was opened. The Lord proclaimed: "I will put enmity between thee and the woman, and between thy seed and her seed; it [He] shall bruise thy head, and thou shalt bruise His heel." Gen. 3:15.

The word "it," the Hebrew word, *hoo,* is usually translated "he" in the Scriptures.

God assured Adam that a "He" should crush the head of him who caused man to sin. In the beginning, God introduced the principle of *substitution.* For man a substitute had been found. The substitute would accomplish everything necessary for the complete recovery of man, and of all that Adam lost by his disobedience.

There are a number of concrete object lessons in the Scripture, illustrating this principle of substitution. The Levites were substituted for Israel's first-born. Num. 3:11-13. In making provision for man's recovery, God's original purpose in the creation of man and of the world must be met.

There was one, and only one, being in the universe who could become man's substitute. Sin is an intruder. It has no right to an existence. It cannot continue in God's realm. To recover man, sin must be destroyed. There is only one being, apart from God the Father, who understands fully the seriousness and ultimate results of sin, and who is able to bring about man's recovery. The scripture says of Him: "Then Thou spakest in vision to Thy Holy One, and saidst, I have laid help upon one that is mighty; I have exalted one chosen out of the people." Ps. 89:19.

Of this one, the beloved John writes: "One of the elders saith unto me, Weep not: behold, the *Lion of the tribe of Judah* . . . hath prevailed to open the book, and to loose the seven seals." Rev. 5:5.

Man's substitute must be a prevailer. He must have the ability to prevail over every force of evil. He must be stronger than the strong one who brought about man's downfall and ruin. "When a strong man armed keepeth his palace, his goods are in peace; but when a stronger than he shall come upon him, and overcome him, he taketh from him all his armor wherein he trusteth, and divideth his spoils." Luke 11:21, 22.

This one who could accomplish man's recovery, and who became man's substitute, is Christ, Messiah, the Sent of God.

"The Son of God, heaven's glorious Commander, was touched with pity for the fallen race. His heart was moved with infinite compassion as the woes of a lost world rose up before Him. But divine love had conceived a plan whereby man might be redeemed. The broken law of God demanded the life of the sinner. In all the universe there was but one who could, in behalf of man, satisfy its claims. Since the divine law is as sacred as God Himself, only one equal with God could make atonement for its transgression. None but Christ could redeem fallen man from the curse of the law, and bring him again into harmony with Heaven. Christ would take upon Himself the guilt and shame of sin,—sin so offensive to a holy God that it must separate the Father and His Son. . . .

"Before the Father He pleaded in the sinner's behalf. . . . Long continued was that mysterious communing,—'the counsel of peace' for the fallen sons of men. The plan of salvation had been laid before the creation of the earth; for Christ is 'the Lamb slain from the foundation of the world:' yet it was a struggle, even with the King of the universe, to yield up His Son to die for the guilty race. But 'God so loved the world, that He gave His only-begotten, Son, that whosoever believeth on Him should not perish but have everlasting life.' "—"*Patriarchs and Prophets*," p. 63.

Man had no part in the plan for his recovery. Only God could devise a way whereby man might again be restored to the favor of Heaven. This purpose of God to recover man is forcefully suggested in the following statement: "We must needs die, and are as water spilt on the ground, which cannot be gathered up again; neither doth God respect any person: yet doth He devise means, that His banished be not expelled from Him." 2 Sam. 14:14.

God condescended to join Himself to man, in order to raise man from the depths into which he had fallen. No angel could restore man, for angels are a different order of creation from man. (See question 6, this lesson.) Man's substitute must not only be God; he must also be man.

This joint combination of God and man is beautifully taught by the dream which God gave to the patriarch Jacob at the time he fled from his brother Esau to journey to his uncle Laban. In his dream Jacob saw a ladder extending from earth to heaven. One end of the ladder was in heaven; the other end was fixed upon earth. (See Gen. 28:10-15.)

"Christ took upon Himself humanity, that He might reach humanity. Divinity needed humanity; for it required both the divine and the human to bring salvation to the world."—"*The Desire of Ages*," p. 296.

"And so it is written, The first man Adam was made a living soul; the last Adam was made a quickening spirit. . . . The first man is of the earth, earthy: the second man is the Lord from heaven." 1 Cor. 15:45-47.

The Son of God would become man. God accepted the substitute, and the first part of the atonement was effected.

A Study of the Atonement

Part 2. The Son of God Becomes the Second Adam and Lives the Life of Man

1. WHAT effect did man's sin have upon his relation to his Maker? Isa. 59:1, 2; Ex. 20:20.

Man's disobedience separated him from God. God's attitude toward man was in no wise changed, for God still loved him. Jer. 31:3. God is unchangeable; He does not change. Mal. 3:6; James 1:17. While sin is heinous in the sight of God, the love of the Lord toward the sinner remains the same. The measure of God's love for the sinner is the measure of His hatred of sin.

As a result of man's disobedience, his attitude toward God changed. He was conscious he had disobeyed his Creator. His own conscience condemned him. Man knew he now stood in a relationship to his Maker different from that he enjoyed when he was in harmony with God's will. Had not God intervened, this separation would have been eternal. God cannot countenance sin. James 1:13. Evil has nothing in common with God. Sin is subversive of every right and noble principle. Sin is an unsheathed sword, waiting the opportunity to plunge itself into the heart of its victim. Sin cannot abide with God.

A forceful illustration of this fact is given in the Scripture in connection with the sin of Achan. When the Israelites attempted to capture Ai, following the victory God had given them over Jericho, they were smitten before their enemies. Their leader became disheartened. Joshua clothed himself with sackcloth and ashes, and from morning till evening he humbled himself before God with weeping and mourning. At the time of the evening sacrifice the Lord came to Joshua with the question: "Wherefore liest thou thus upon thy face? Israel hath sinned; . . . therefore the children of Israel could not stand before their enemies, . . . neither will I be with you any more, except ye destroy the accursed from among you." Joshua 7:10-12.

2. Was it not possible for man to return to God? Gen. 2:17.

Man was unable to find his way back to God. Sin is inexcusable. Man could not apologize to God for his wrong course by saying, "Lord, excuse me; I am sorry for what I did." The integrity of God's law and government was involved. If God could excuse sin, it would be an indirect admission of a need for its existence. God's standard of right demands perfect conduct. His law is faultless. All subjects of that law must be in perfect harmony with its precepts. There can be no exceptions.

Satan, the originator of sin, maintained that God's law could not be fully obeyed. For God to excuse man for his sin would be to countenance the devil's unjust accusation against God's rule. The law has its penalty, death; and this penalty must be met. "The wages of sin is death." "The soul that sinneth, it shall die." Rom. 6:23; Eze. 18:4.

The only answer Adam could have received from his Creator, had he asked to be excused, would have been the pronouncing of the death penalty. God must be just. God would not torture man for the sin he had committed. To do that would be to manifest cruelty. The wages, or penalty, for sin is not torture or vindictiveness. To consign man to endless suffering for his disobedience would manifest a spirit of revenge. But God must be obeyed; if man disobeys his

Creator, he must suffer the consequence of his disobedience. This is why the Lord said to man, when passing sentence upon him: "In the sweat of thy face shalt thou eat bread, till thou return unto the ground; for out of it wast thou taken: for dust thou art, and unto dust shalt thou return." Gen. 3:19.

By his course Adam showed himself unworthy to enjoy a continuity of life. He must die. In his own estate, man had no way to break down the wall of separation between himself and his Maker.

3. How only does Jesus say man can approach his Maker? John 14:6; Eph. 2:18; John 10:9.

God *could* provide a way of escape by accepting a substitute for man. The penalty for man's transgression could not be minimized. Sin cannot be lightly regarded. The one accepted as substitute for man must become responsible for man's wrongdoing. He must measure up to the standard of the divine requirements. He must meet every condition which was expected of man. If man was ever again to find his way back to God's throne and to heaven's family, it must be through this substitute. Jesus offered Himself as man's substitute. He was accepted by the Father. The Saviour could truthfully and properly say: "No man cometh unto the Father, but by Me." Man's own efforts could give him no approach to God; for over man hung the sentence of death. Since sin entered the world, every man who has approached the Father and been accepted of God has come by the way of our Lord and Saviour, Jesus.

4. When did Christ offer Himself to atone for sin? 1 Peter 1:20.

The Scriptures clearly teach that Christ was "foreordained before the foundation of the world" to become the sinner's substitute, should the occasion arise that demanded a substitute. To the human mind the secrets and mysteries of God are unknown, except in so far as the Lord sees fit to reveal them. The prophet Isaiah, to whom were given such wonderful revelations from God, raises this question: "Who hath directed the Spirit of the Lord, or being His counselor hath taught Him? With whom took He counsel, and who instructed Him, and taught Him in the path of judgment, and taught Him knowledge, and showed to Him the way of understanding?" Isa. 40:13, 14.

By another man who had an abundance of revelations, is raised this question: "O the depth of the riches both of the wisdom and knowledge of God! how unsearchable are His judgments, and His ways past finding out! For who hath known the mind of the Lord? or who hath been His counselor? or who hath first given to Him, and it shall be recompensed unto him again?" Rom. 11:33-35. Man cannot know the ways or the mind of God, except as they are made known to him. All divine knowledge must be accepted by faith, but it is easy for the child of faith to understand. "Without faith it is impossible to please Him." Heb. 11:6. "Through faith we understand." Verse 3.

Christ is declared to be the "Lamb slain from the foundation of the world." Rev. 13:8. The question of the atonement is most interesting when it is considered in the light of the Scriptures. The word is translated from the Hebrew word, כפר (*kaphar*). (See Ex. 29:36.) The Hebrew word *kaphar* means "to cover." Gesenius, in his Hebrew and English Lexicon, on the word *kaphar*, says: "To cover over, to overlay with anything." "To cover over sins, i.e., to forgive." We first find this word *kaphar* in Genesis 6:14. Again we meet with this same Hebrew word in Genesis 32:20, where it is written: "Jacob is behind us. For he said, I will appease him with the present that goeth before me, and afterward I shall see his face."

Jacob thought that this gift might be a covering for his past wrongs. In this way he might again see his brother's face, and be forgiven.

In 1 Samuel 12:3 we read: "Whose ox have I taken? or whose ass have I taken? or whom have I defrauded? whom have I oppressed? or of whose hand have I received any bribe [*kaphar*], to blind mine eyes therewith?" Samuel asked of whom did he take a *kaphar* (a cover), to cover up wrongs of some person, or to accept a bribe; for a bribe blindeth the eyes.

The word *kaphar* is also used in connection with the covering of the mercy seat. The Scripture says: "The cherubim shall stretch forth their wings on high, covering the mercy seat." Ex. 25:20.

Gesenius comments as follows on the word כפרת (*kapporeth*), from the root *kaphar*, found in Exodus 25:20: "A cover, lid, only of the lid of the ark with cherubim upon it." This word, *kaphar* (cover), is also translated "mercy seat." (See Ex. 25:17; 30:6.) In 1 Chronicles 28:11 it is associated with the word בית (*bayith*), "house;" and *beth hakkapporeth* (from the root, *kaphar*), is translated, "the place of the mercy seat."

In the early days of human history the word *kaphar* was a legal term for propitiation, for the ransoming of a person or object. (See Job 33:24, margin, where the word "atonement" is used; also Job 36:18.)

From this word *kaphar* there developed the idea of ransom, propitiation, atonement. The word *kaphar* came to have many meanings, some of which included at-one-ment, setting at one persons having enmity toward each other, covering up sins and wrongs, wiping out offenses against offended individuals, pardoning wrongs, making settlement by expiation, etc.

When God chose the Israelites as His people, He desired to use them as an object lesson, in order that the nations around them might learn of the purity and holiness of the true God, and also of the sinfulness of disobedience. Through this people the Lord sought to make the nations understand how vile and evil sin is. Ex. 15:26; 20:20; 19:10-13, 21; Lev. 11:44; 19:2; Ex. 19:6; Deut. 4:5-10. Israel was commanded to have nothing in common with the surrounding nations; they were not to follow the customs of the Canaanites; they were to keep themselves clean and pure in the sight of God. Ex. 23:23, 24, 31, 32; Lev. 18:3, 24-30; 20:23; Jer. 10:1-3.

Every act of Israel not in perfect accord with the will of God must be atoned for. (See Lev. 4:2, 3; 5:15-19.) However small the act, even to touching that which was not perfectly clean and wholesome, an atonement must be offered for that offense. Forgiveness was immediately granted to the one who recognized his wrong, and who offered sacrifice for the offense as commanded by the Lord. If the offender repeated the same wrong, it would be necessary for him to repeat the act of sacrifice in order to be clean.

5. In order to restore man to God, what must Christ become? Ps. 40:6-9; Heb. 10:5-10.

6. What kind of life did God demand of man? Matt. 5:48; Col. 4:12.

7. What must be the character of man's substitute? 1 Peter 1:15, 16.

8. What question did Christ ask of His enemies? John 8:46.

That Christ might accomplish all that was necessary for man's complete recovery and restoration, He Himself must become man. He must place Himself in the position where He could reach and raise man. Christ must partake of man's nature; He must subject Himself to man's experiences and environments. The apostle Paul states in few words Christ's program for man's full recovery, in the following scripture: "Let this mind be in you, which was also in Christ Jesus: who, being in the form of God, thought it not robbery to be equal with God: but made Himself of no reputation, and took upon Him the form of a servant, and was made in the likeness of men: and being found in fashion as a man, He humbled Himself, and became obedient unto death, even the death of the cross." Phil. 2:5-8.

Our Lord must reach down to the humblest, the poorest, and the most needy, in order to raise the fallen and to lift up those who are bowed down. Heb. 2:14-18.

9. How did the people commend Christ for His conduct? Matt. 7: 29; Mark 7:37; Luke 23:4; John 19:6.

Christ's manner of conversation was different from that of the ordinary man. Christ spoke words of certainty, of positiveness, of truth. Our Lord never uttered a doubt in regard to any statement He made; He spoke with firmness and with accuracy. He uttered nothing superfluous. Although the people tried to catch Him in His words, they were unsuccessful. Mark 12:13, 17. He realized that He must speak only as would a godly man; therefore He carried with Him certain authority. All men in His day could have used pure language as He did, but religion had become so formal that men had lost a sense of the value of pure speech. The conduct of our Lord was perfect.

10. By what three names was Christ particularly recognized when on earth? John 1:49; Matt. 20:30; 8:20.

Christ was recognized while on earth as Son of God, Son of man, Son of David. Repeatedly men acknowledged Jesus to be the Son of God. He accepted that recognition. He called Himself the Son of God. He accepted worship, and no person but God can be worshiped. Matt. 16:16; John 6:68, 69; 11:27; 9:35-38.

Some twenty or more times in the Gospels it is recorded that Christ is the Son of man. He was generally known and called by this name. Among the children of Abraham it was current that "Son of David" was the title to be given to Messiah. To this day in the synagogue literature the Talmudists use the term, Son of David, as a synonym for Messiah, as may be seen in the following prayer: "Our God and the God of our fathers, . . . remember us, remember our ancestors, and remember Messiah, the Son of David Thy servant."—*"Prayers for the Holy Days."*

For centuries before the advent of the Saviour it was a common belief among the Jewish people that Messiah is Son of God, Son of man, Son of David.

11. Was any sin found in Christ? 1 Peter 2:22; Heb. 4:15; 2 Cor. 5:21.

Every divine requirement was fulfilled in the life and conduct of Jesus of Nazareth. He is the only perfect man. No flaw contaminated His conduct. The divine ideal was realized in Him. He pleased God in every detail of character. God could find no fault in Jesus. By His holy and wholesome life He made possible man's salvation. Jesus is able to save man from sin, because He lived a perfect life. His life is able to cover the imperfections of those who fully and completely surrender themselves to Him. Christ's life does not save man *in* sin; His life saves man *from* sin.

The angel Gabriel said of Christ at His birth: "Thou shalt call His name Jesus: for He shall save His people *from* their sins." Matt. 1:21. Christ's perfect life, His vicarious sacrifice on Calvary, and the divine power of the Holy Spirit are sufficient to enable every one who desires to live the life demanded by God's law, to meet the divine standard of heavenly behavior.

Just prior to the Saviour's death, He said to His Father: "I have finished the work which Thou gavest Me to do." John 17:4. His labor of love for the saving of man was accomplished. By His upright conduct He had made it possible for every man to live again in full harmony with God's will, if the man accepted the life of Jesus. Jesus earned the right to be man's Saviour.

A Study of the Atonement

Part 3. Christ's Death and Resurrection Make Possible Man's Reconciliation to His Maker

1. WHAT is the penalty for sin? Rom. 6:21, 23.

When the death sentence was passed upon Adam by the Creator, the Lord said: "Dust thou art, and unto dust shalt thou return." Gen. 3:19. Man was taken from the dust when he was created, and he was to return to dust. There was no hope of life for man after his death. Man brought nothing into the world; he could take nothing with him out of the world. 1 Tim. 6:7. Man had no future ahead of him, as far as his own ability to provide it was concerned. Death would have been eternal for mankind, if some provision for his future had not been planned by His Maker.

As mentioned in a previous study, a forceful illustration of man's helpless condition, cut off from God and without a way of escape, is found in the following language: "We must needs die, and are as water spilt on the ground, which cannot be gathered up again; neither doth God respect any person: yet doth He devise means, that His banished be not expelled from Him." 2 Sam. 14:14.

Eternal expulsion from the presence of God was the only thing man could hope for, unless God should devise a plan for his deliverance from the grave. There was no light shining beyond the tomb. Man must reap what he had sown, except as God should make provision for his future.

2. How many are included under this death penalty? Job 4:19.

3. Does man have a way whereby he can redeem himself or his fellows from the grave? Ps. 49:7, 8.

4. Had not God provided a substitute, could man have found a way whereby he could be reunited to God? Ps. 146:3, 4.

5. What is God's plan for again joining man to Himself? 1 Tim. 2:5, 6; 2 Cor. 5:21.

Christ's perfect life assures repentant man of salvation. But man has a past which must be atoned for. Man is born in sin. Ps. 51:5. His whole life is sinful, from his birth until the time he surrenders his life to the Lord, when he may receive the new birth through faith in the death and resurrection of the Son of God.

There is a plan whereby man's past sinful record can be forgiven. Sin separated man from his Creator; how can he again come to God? The gulf between him and his God must be bridged. The penalty for his past wrongs must be met. Sin must receive its just penalty. Death, separation from God, is the penalty. If man himself must meet his own penalty, then he is forever shut away from his Maker.

But Christ, man's substitute, died for man. 1 Peter 3:18; Rom. 5:6. Through the eternal years, Christ, the co-Creator, never had been separated from His Father. They together had shared the glories of the eternal days. Micah 5:2; Prov. 8:22-31. Our blessed Saviour, in offering Himself as man's substitute, was willing to leave His home in glory, separate Himself from His Father, and allow Himself to enter the recesses of the grave, in order that man might again be brought into communion with God. 1 Cor. 15:3, 4. In order that man may be at one with his God, man must pay the penalty for his wrong. 1 Cor. 15:21. The man Christ Jesus substituted Himself for mankind, and by His death bridged the gulf which separated the children of Adam from the presence of their heavenly Father.

6. How may man avail himself of this provision of grace? Acts 16:31; 1 John 1:9.

If the Father Himself had not accepted the plan for human salvation, if He had not permitted the Son to forfeit His life, man could never have been saved. The Father shared the suffering in the price which was paid for human redemption. "God so loved the world that He gave His only-begotten Son." John 3:16. The Father and the Son are indeed one in the great purpose of saving lost man. Deut. 6:4; Zech. 6:12, 13; Mark 12:29.

The Father never harbored ill feelings toward man. Man became afraid of his Creator. His own course of conduct kept him in a state of condemnation. Mal. 1:2; Gen. 3:10; Ex. 20:18-21; John 3:17, 18. God desired that man should be free from this condemnation. Rom. 8:1. Jesus was delivered for our offenses. Rom. 4:25. It is the blood of Jesus Christ His Son that cleanseth from all sin. 1 John 1:7.

7. Was Christ forced to die? John 10:17, 18; 5:26.

Christ's death was not a forced one. Even after His murderers had arrested Him in the Garden of Gethsemane, He had power to deliver Himself from them. He said He could ask of His Father legions of angels who would give Him deliverance. Matt. 26:52-54. But the Scripture declared that Christ must die a sacrifice for man. Isa. 53:4-12. He came to this hour for the very purpose of fulfilling the Scripture. Jesus willingly allowed Himself to be taken. He died the cruel death that man again might have life. The forfeiture of His life was vicarious. The sacrifice of Christ for man was a part of the plan of reconciliation, atonement, redemption.

8. Was it possible for the grave to retain Christ? Acts 2:24.

Since Christ did not commit sin, death could not hold Him in the grave. The tomb had held its prisoners for four thousand years. Except Moses and Lazarus, no person ever had entered the grave, and come forth from it again to live. Moses and Lazarus were restored to life at the command of the Son of God. Jude 9; John 11:14, 43. Certain persons had died, and had been revived in answer to the prayers of the prophets of God. 1 Kings 17:17-24; 2 Kings 4:20, 32-37. No person had been able to burst the bars of the tomb and free its prisoners.

The Lord Jesus entered the tomb, but death, which had separated man from God, was unable to hold the Saviour in the grave. No seed of sin was found in Him. Nothing in His conduct gave offense. He never once disobeyed the will of Heaven. He strictly observed every enactment demanded of man. Through suffering, Jesus learned obedience. Heb. 5:8. No displeasure of the Almighty rested upon our Lord, man's substitute. How could the grave hold Him? Since Jesus was perfect and His life pleased God, why should He not have the power to burst the bars of the tomb, and to bring release to those who were in the grave, to those who had performed the will of God? Matt. 27:51-53. Why should He not be permitted to ransom the captives and to restore them to the Father's presence? Hosea 13:14; Eph. 4:8. The keys of death and the grave which for forty centuries had been held by Satan now passed into the hands of Jesus, Substitute, Saviour. Isa. 14:12-17; 24:21, 22; Rev. 1:17, 18. Death now was broken. Man could hereafter, through our blessed Lord, be brought into the Father's presence. Man could now be joined to God's family. The family circle of heaven and earth once more could be made whole. Eph. 3:14, 15.

9. Can there be a future hope for man aside from the resurrection? 1 Cor. 15:17-19.

The family tie of heaven and earth will be joined through the death and resurrection of our blessed Lord. The new birth offers a hope that man shall once more live with his God. Truly the resurrection from the dead is an anchor to the human soul. Heb. 6:19.

10. What assurance does Christ offer to man by His death and resurrection? 1 Cor. 15:22.

11. Can death again take possession of Christ? Rom. 6:9; Heb. 9:26.

12. Will man ever again be separated from God? Rev. 7:15-17.

Not to believe in the glorious resurrection through the blessed Messiah is to debar oneself forever from joining the family of God. We can understand why man has no future, if he does not believe that our blessed Lord and Messiah will raise the dead. What assurance has man of returning to the Father's house and to the Father's heart unless there be a resurrection from the dead? When our Saviour died on Calvary's cross, He said, "It is finished." John 19:30. Christ's death was God's assurance that man should live again. The way had been opened whereby the children of Adam can be restored to the presence of God. The death and resurrection of the Saviour opened a new and living way for man to return to the Father's family. Heb. 10:20.

A Study of the Atonement

Part 4. What Christ's Intercession Means to the Atonement

1. WHAT important principle did Christ state to Nicodemus? John 3:3.

It was a great surprise to Nicodemus, a ruler of the Jews, when the Saviour told him it was necessary for him to have a new birth. Conversion as recognized in the New Testament was not accepted by the Jewish people. It is true that the psalmist understood the need of such an experience. Ps. 51:10-13. The prophets also admonished Israel of the necessity of having a new, clean heart. Eze. 11:19, 20; 36:26. The rabbis, however, impressed the people with the importance of following the teachings of God's word, but only in the letter. Rom. 2:17-20, 28, 29. The Talmudists exalted the letter of the law, but said little in regard to the necessity of obeying God's word in the spirit. 2 Cor. 3:6.

Position and ability carried great weight among the Jewish leaders. Wealth, talent, and genius exerted much influence upon the laity. Religion belonged to Israel. It was theirs exclusively. They were assured by the rabbis, "All Israel have a part in the world to come."—"*Ethics of the Fathers,*" chap I. The Gentiles, they said, were outcast; they were not accepted with God. The other nations were not circumcised. They did not possess any of Abraham's virtue. "We have Abraham to our father," was a slogan. "We be Abraham's seed, and were never in bondage to any man" (Luke 3:8; John 8:32), was a national teaching. The people were weighted down with forms and ceremonies. Without doubt the disciples were startled when the Saviour explained to them the meaning of the barren fig tree.

"Christ's act in cursing the fig tree had astonished the disciples. It seemed to them unlike His ways and works. Often they had heard Him declare that He came not to condemn the world, but that the world through Him might be saved. They remembered His words: 'The Son of man is not come to destroy men's lives, but to save them.' His wonderful works had been done to restore, never to destroy. The disciples had known Him only as the Restorer, the Healer. This act stood alone. What was its purpose? they questioned. . . .

"But it is in mercy and love that He lifts the veil from the future, and reveals to men the results of a course of sin.

"The cursing of the fig tree was an acted parable. That barren tree, flaunting its pretentious foliage in the very face of Christ, was a symbol of the Jewish nation. The Saviour desired to make plain to His disciples the cause and the certainty of Israel's doom. For this purpose He invested the tree with moral qualities, and made it the expositor of divine truth. The Jews stood forth distinct from all other nations, professing allegiance to God. They had been specially favored by Him, and they laid claim to righteousness above every other people. But they were corrupted by the love of the world and the greed of gain. They boasted of their knowledge, but they were ignorant of the requirements of God, and were full of hypocrisy."—"*The Desire of Ages,*" pp. 582, 583.

2. Why is it necessary for man to have a new birth if he would enter the kingdom of God? Eph. 2:1, 5.

The Bible emphasizes the fact that man is dead in trespasses and sin. He is compared to a dead man, as far as his relationship to his God is concerned. Rom. 5:12, 15, 17, 18; 6:2, 6, 7, 11; Col. 2:13. In order for man to have hope of a future, he must have a new birth. Man must enter into a new life as real as was his birth when he first came into the world.

"Being born again, not of corruptible seed, but of incorruptible, by the word of God, which liveth and abideth forever." 1 Peter 1:23. It is impossible for one to have a part in the kingdom of God without a new heart. Sin and righteousness cannot dwell together. Holiness and iniquity have nothing in common. "Shall the throne of iniquity have fellowship with thee?" Ps. 94:20. "Can two walk together, except they be agreed?" Amos 3:3.

3. After one has been born again, what experience is necessary? 1 Peter 2:1; 2 Peter 3:18.

4. To what heights must one attain? Eph. 4:13.

As the natural-born child must partake of food in order to grow and develop, so the child of God, having received the new birth, must partake of spiritual food in order to grow up into Christlikeness. But the natural child first takes its milk, and later takes other kinds of food, in order to develop strength and physique. The Christian, likewise, must not remain in the earlier stages of Christian growth and development. It is expected that a Christian will continue to rise in stature, until he reaches the perfect state of the Christian. Heb. 5:13, 14; 6:1-4; Eph. 4:13.

5. How only can a person reach such an experience? John 15:5; Phil. 4:8; 2 Cor. 12:9.

6. Will such a person be free from Satan's temptations? 1 Cor. 10:13; 1 Peter 5:8; Rev. 12:12, 17.

The only way that a Christian can reach the heights of a perfect man in Christ is by following the means provided for him by our High Priest, Christ Jesus. When a person surrenders his life to the Saviour, he learns that without Christ he can do nothing. Sin slew the natural-born man. Rom. 7:9. Christ came to his rescue, breathed the life of the Spirit into his soul, raised him from the death of sin, and gave him a new birth. Our Lord, through the divine Spirit, breathed into his soul the life-giving power, and it is only by this same divine power that man is able to make progress in the Christian life. 1 Peter 1:3; 2 Peter 1:4.

Satan will bring his forces to bear against that man, and the enemy will do everything in his power to conquer him. Temptations, enticements, and allurements will steadily pursue the child of God. At times, like a roaring lion will the devil seek to devour him. For man's safety and security there has been provided a complete spiritual armor to meet every dart of the enemy. Eph. 6:10-17. No defense has been provided for the Christian's back; it is not expected that a Christian will turn his back to the foe. Man is admonished that Satan will flee from him if he stands his ground. 1 Peter 5:9; James 4:7. As the end draws near, the bitter and relentless foe will work with all power and might, if by any means he can deceive and conquer the followers of Christ. Matt. 24:24; 2 Thess. 2:8-11. But our Intercessor has offered every assurance that He will furnish power and grace to meet every issue. Heb. 4:15, 16.

7. How only is one able to overcome the fierce assaults of Satan? John 16:33; 1 John 4:4; Rev. 3:10; 12:11.

8. If after one is born again he is overcome by Satan, what is such a person to do? 1 John 1:9.

It is possible, however, for a person to be overcome by Satan. While our Mediator has all power in heaven and in earth, and has promised the trusting soul that he may be victorious over every assault of the enemy, man may be overcome by Satan and commit sin. But ample provision has been made by our Lord for the forgiveness of sin. Matt. 28:18-20; Luke 10:19. By repentance and confession, our Intercessor, who stands in the presence of God, appeals to His Father in behalf of the one who has missed his way; for Jesus shed His blood that sin may be pardoned. Forgiveness is granted the penitent; and again man is taken into favor with God, for the blood of Christ has cleansed the soul from every sin. The sinner is accepted, and he is looked upon as if he never had committed an offense against God. 1 John 1:7.

9. Can a person make confession once or twice, and then become immune from sin? Luke 17:4.

If the servant of Christ will constantly keep his mind stayed on God, he has the promise that Heaven will keep him in perfect peace. Isa. 26:3. No forces can conquer a person as long as he has his hand in the hand of his Father. John 10:28, 29. The Lord never wearies of listening to the appeals of the weak and tempted soul. He knows our weaknesses and our perplexities. Ps. 103:8-14. Our Mediator is anxious to do much more for us than we can do for one another; for He is so much mightier than we are. Isa. 55:8, 9. When a person who is born of God meets with a misfortune, his Intercessor at the right hand of God is always prepared to appeal in his behalf, should he miss the way and commit sin. 1 John 3:9; 2:1.

10. How is this forgiveness made possible? Acts 2:32, 33; 3:26; 5:31; 13:38.

Forgiveness for every sin is made possible because Christ on the cross paid with His life the penalty for all sin. He was raised from the dead and has ascended to heaven. Man should reckon himself to be dead to sin. He should so yield his life to the Saviour that he may know the constant keeping power of Christ. Rom. 6:11, 13, 14, 16. Christ did not die in vain. His death and resurrection from the dead opened the way for Him to become man's Intercessor. Rom. 14:9; 2 Cor. 5:15. As often as man approaches the throne of grace, seeking pardon, he is assured that he will in no wise be cast out. John 6:37.

In the days of Israel the sinner often came with his sacrifice to receive forgiveness. (See Lev. 6:1-7; Num. 5:5-8.) It made no difference the number of times sin had been committed, each time a sacrifice must be brought to the sanctuary, and the priest, after the blood had been sprinkled, assured the penitent that his sin was forgiven. Lev. 17:11. Whenever the sinner approached the sanctuary, an atonement was made. The priest did not offer one sacrifice to cover every sin that the individual might commit. Each time an offering was accepted, and the transgressor was pardoned.

It is true that our Saviour was not often to be sacrificed. He made one sacrifice of Himself. His sacrifice was sufficient to cover every sin that might be committed. Heb. 9:25, 26.

But while an atonement was made each time the sinner offered his sacrifice, the atonement in the days of the sanctuary was not fully perfected each time a substitute sacrifice was offered. The atonement was not completed and perfected until the close of the Day of Atonement, when the ministry was conducted in the most holy place. Forgiveness of sin was granted as often as the sinner brought his offering; but the completing of the atonement did not occur until the intercession of the high priest was finished in the inner apartment of the sanctuary at the close of the tenth day of the seventh month.

It must not be understood that the atonement was conducted on the installment plan. The sinner, in bringing his sacrifice, was gladly and freely forgiven. The atonement for that occasion was finished. The man, having confessed his sins, was accepted of God. The blood that was carried into the holy place was ample provision to cleanse the sinner from the sins he had committed at that particular time. But there still was a record preserved of the sins. The time must come when the record of all the sins the individual had committed should be blotted out. But this *blotting out* of sin took place on only one day in the year. This was one purpose of the Day of Atonement; for the Scripture clearly states: "On that day shall the priest make an atonement for you, to cleanse you, that ye may be clean from *all* your sins before the Lord." "And he shall make an atonement for the holy sanctuary, and he shall make an atonement for the tabernacle of the congregation, and for the altar, and he shall make an atonement for the priest, and for all the people of the congregation." Lev. 16:30, 33. The atonement was completed and perfected in the type at the close of the Day of Atonement. The ministry was ended for that year. Intercession had ceased. The congregation and the sanctuary were clean.

11. What relationship does Christ, seated at the right hand of God, sustain to man? 1 John 2:1; Rom. 8:34; Heb. 7:25.

Having obtained complete victory over Satan, both in His life and through His death, our Lord Jesus ascended to heaven to become man's Intercessor, Advocate, Mediator. Of His own free will, our precious Saviour became man's servant. Matt. 20:28; Luke 22:27; John 13:13, 14; Phil. 2:7. He had lived for man, and for man He had died. He was given *for* man, and was *a gift to man.* Isa. 9:6; 2 Cor. 5:14, 15. Our Lord has bound Himself to mankind by a tie which can never be severed. Into heaven He ascended that He might appeal before God in behalf of man. Man is guilty before God. Rom. 3:19. He has no means of his own to reach the ear of God. Micah 6:6, 7. But the blessed Christ had the right to become man's Intercessor. He is God; and being divine, His position is at the right hand of God's throne. He also is man. But He is a perfect man. He has the right, therefore, to entreat the throne of God in behalf of man.

When Satan's accusations are presented to the throne against those who earnestly long to do the will of God, but who have sinned and fallen under the enemy's severe temptations, our Intercessor appeals to God to pardon and spare the sinner, when he makes confession of his wrong and asks for pardon. Zech. 3:1-4. Our Intercessor presents His shed blood for the poor sinner. Heb. 10:19-22. Jesus offers Himself as man's substitute. 2 Cor. 5:21. Pardon is granted the sinner. He is forgiven. Atonement for the sins of the sinner is made. It is made that the forgiven sinner may live a holy life, for Christ said in His prayer in the garden: "I have finished the work which Thou gavest Me to do." John 17:4. The atoning sacrifice was made when Christ died on Calvary's cross, when He uttered those agonizing words: "It is finished." John 19:30. Yet, when a man receives pardon for his sins, the record of those forgiven sins is not immediately blotted out. The time must come, however, when the record shall be completely expunged from the heavenly books. Jer. 50:20; 31:34.

That the records of sin are not blotted out each time the sinner confesses his sins, is evident from the following scripture: "The righteousness of the righteous shall not deliver him in the day of his transgression: as for the wickedness of the wicked, he shall not fall thereby in the day that he turneth from his wickedness; neither shall the righteous be able to live for his righteousness in the day that he sinneth. When I shall say to the righteous, that he shall surely live; if he trust to his own righteousness and commit iniquity, all his righteousnesses shall not be remembered; but for his iniquity that he hath committed, he shall die for it. . . . When the righteous turneth from his righteousness, and committeth iniquity, he shall even die thereby. But if the wicked turn from his wickedness, and do that which is lawful and right, he shall live thereby." Eze. 33:12-19. (See also 18:25-30.)

God declares through the prophet Ezekiel that He will judge every one of the house of Israel. Eze. 18:30. The Lord also says that He will judge the people according to their ways. Eze. 7:3. And God's people will be called to give an account of themselves one by one. Eccl. 7:27; Isa. 27:12; Rom. 14:10-12.

That sin is to be entirely blotted out from God's record is evident from the following: "Repent ye therefore, and be converted, that your sins may be blotted out, when the times of refreshing shall come from the presence of the Lord; and He shall send Jesus Christ, which before was preached unto you: whom the heaven must receive until the times of restitution of all things, which God hath spoken by the mouth of all His holy prophets since the world began." Acts 3:19-21.

All iniquity is marked. Ps. 130:3. There is no substance on earth that can erase it. Jer. 2:22. Through the blood of Christ it is forgiven and pardoned. At the close of Jesus' intercession in heaven, and before the Lord returns to earth, all marks of confessed and forgiven sin will be erased, blotted out of God's books. Ex. 32:32, 33.

12. How long will Christ remain in His position as advocate? Heb. 7:24.

13. What pronouncement is made in heaven when Christ's intercession for man ends? Rev. 16:17; 22:11.

14. Will there be opportunity for repentance and forgiveness after Christ completes His intercession for man? 1 Cor. 15:24-28.

Jesus our High Priest will continue in His intercessory ministry until the last needy, repentant soul craves pardon and mercy. The door of mercy will remain open for that man or woman who longs for deliverance, freedom from sin, complete and full salvation. Only God knows who and where that individual is.

But the hour finally arrives when the atonement is finished and perfected. The last prayer is offered, the last appeal is made, to the last sinner is offered hope. The curtain falls, and the atonement for sin and sinners is completed. The heavenly Intercessor announces before the heavenly universe, "It is done." The fourth, the concluding act in the atonement, intercession for guilty man, has been completed.

"When the third angel's message closes, mercy no longer pleads for the guilty inhabitants of the earth. . . . An angel returning from the earth announces that his work is done; the final test has been brought upon the world. . . . Then Jesus ceases His intercession in the sanctuary above. He lifts His hands, and with a loud voice says: 'It is done;' and all the angelic host lay off their crowns as He makes the solemn announcement: 'He that is unjust, let him be unjust still: and he which is filthy, let him be filthy still: and he that is righteous, let him be righteous still: and he that is holy, let him be holy still.' Every case has been decided for life or death. Christ has made the atonement for His people, and blotted out their sins."—*The Great Controversy*," pp. 613, 614.

"He [Aaron] entered the most holy place on the Day of Atonement, 'not without blood,' as a mediator for all Israel. He came forth from that work to bless the congregation, as Christ will come forth to bless His waiting people when His work of atonement in their behalf shall be ended."—*Patriarchs and Prophets*," p. 426.

Hebrew Expressions With Their Meaning

Adar, twelfth Bible month, ... 59
Ad ereb boker alpayim ushlosh meoth, unto evening and morning, two thousand and three hundred 126
Ad ki yabo Shiloh, till Shiloh come 100
Almah, a virgin, not a young married woman 156
Am haratsim (Biblical form, Am haaratsoth), men of the earth, or lands, illiterate 94
Ammah, cubit 31
Azazel, scapegoat 203

Bar mitsvah, son of the commandment 196
Baruch sheputrani, I am blessed now, I have no further responsibility 196
Baruch haba, Thou blessed one, come in 121
Bath qol, daughter of voice, substitute for gift of prophecy 98
Bayith, house 218
Ben echad, one son 116
Beni attah Ani Hayyom yelidtika, Thou art My Son, this day have I begotten Thee 114
Ben yachid, an only son 116

Chasid, holy 11
Chattath, sin offering 72
Chattawth, sins or sin offerings... 141

Ebed melek, servant of the king.. 93
Echad, one, meaning unity 116
El, singular form of the word "God" 112
Elohim, plural form of the word "God" in Genesis 1.........112, 114
Eth-pene paroketh, face of veil ... 56

Goral echad la-Yehovah, the Lord's lot 63

Haalmah, the virgin 156
Hu yeshupheka rosh, He will crush thy head 99

Kaphar, to cover, to make atonement 141, 217
Kapporeth, a cover 218
Kapharoth, sacrifices (literally, atonements) 55
Karath, to cut, to cut round 131
Ken, foot of laver 33
Kethubim, writings or Scriptures.. 98
Kodesh, holy place, also sanctuary 203
Kohen, priest 77

Lebasar echad, for one flesh 116
Lehashib welibnoth, fully to restore and build again 134
Lekalle happesha, to fill up the transgression 141
Lekalle happesha ulechathem chattawth, wekapper avon, to seal up sin offerings, and to forgive sins 91
Liphene, face or presence 25, 56

Man hu, manna 27
Maqom echad, one place......... 116
Mashach, to anoint 43
Mem, Hebrew letter 25, 112
Mena, numberer 184
Miqdash, sanctuary 11, 203
Miqqets yamin, end of days 76
Mishkan, tabernacle 29
Mishkan ha-eduth, tabernacle of the witness 29
Mitsvoth gedoloth, greater commandments 152
Mitsvoth ketannoth, lesser or little commandments 152
Moshia, Saviour 58

Nasi, prince 77
Nechosheth, brass 32
Nechtak, to cut off, to cut quickly 131
Nichrath, was cut off............. 131
Nitsdak, to be made right, to be righted 144

Ohel, tent 29
Ohel moed, tabernacle or tent of the congregation 29
Oklah, diet 51
Omer, period between Passover and Pentecost 85

Palmoni, Wonderful Numberer... 184
Paroketh, veil 31
Pele, wonderful 184
Pur, lot 25
Purim, feast of Jews 25

Qach-na eth-binka eth-yechidka, "Take now thy son, thine only son" 116
Qodesh, holy (place) 11
Qodesh haqqodashim, holy of holies, refers to things, not persons 141

Rosh hashanah, beginning of year. 61

Sar, prince 212
Shabbath Shabbathon, Sabbath of Sabbaths 67

Shabuim shibim, seventy times the period of seven years. Among Orthodox Jews these terms are spoken of as seventy shmitoth.. 131
Shaken, neighbor 12
Shekinah, God's glory 12
Shema, a Jewish prayer 115
Shmitah, a period of seven years.. 131
Shmitoth, a period of seven years. *Shmitah* is singular; *Shmitoth,* plural 131
Sophrim, scribes 93

Tamid, daily or continual........ 51
Tob meod, very good 213
Tsadak, to be just, to justify, Niph (passive), to be purified 144

Wayehi ereb wayehi boqer yom echad, "And there was evening, and there was morning, one day" 116, 126
Waeshmaah echad qadosh medabber wayyomer echad qadosh lappalmoni hamdabber, "I heard one Holy, one who was the speaker; and a holy one said to (Palmoni) who was the speaker" 184
Wayyashilum, and they solicited.. 84

Wayehi miqqets yamim, and it came to pass at end of days ... 76
Wayyomer Elohim naase Adam betsalmenu kidemuthenu, "And God said, Let us make man in our image, after our likeness"... 113
We-Adar, month Adar repeated.. 59
Wegoral echad la-Azazel, and lot to Azazel 63
Wekillah mikapper eth-haqqodesh, "And when He hath made an end of reconciling the holy place" 203
Welo yiqhath ammim, to Him shall the people gather 100
Wesaphdu alaw kemisped al-hayyachid, wehamer alaw kehamer al-habekor, "And they shall mourn for him, as one mourneth for his only son, and shall be in bitterness for him, as one is in bitterness for his first-born"...... 116

Yachid, one, individuality 116
Yamim, days 116
Yasha, Saviour 58
Yashar, upright 212
Yom haddin, day of judgment 71
Yom Kippur, Day of Atonement.62, 175
Yom le-yom, day unto day 51

Scriptural Index

Genesis

1:	112, 114
1	112
5	76, 196
8	76, 196
9	116, 181
10	116
13	76, 196
14	135
18	196
19	76, 196
23	76, 196
26	113, 212
27	212
29	51
31	76, 196, 212
2:2	76
3	11, 12, 76
16	213
17	213, 214, 216
24	116
3:10	221
15	18, 99, 214
19	217, 220
4:3	18
3-5	76
5:3, 5, 6, 9, 12, 15, 18, 21, 25, 27, 28	75
24	163
6:3, 12, 13	176
14	217
17, 18	176
7:11	58, 75
24	58
8:3, 4	58
20, 21	75
9:4	17
13:14-17	15
14:18	75, 76, 77
19	115, 212
22	115
15:13-16	14
18-21	15
18:17-32	176
25	201
19:12-14	176
22:	116
2	77
7	53, 77, 79, 100
8	53, 100
9, 10	77
13	53, 100
24:43	156
28:10-15	215
12, 13	102
18	41
31:13	41
54	77

32:20	217
33:20	112
41:8, 16	150
32	133
45	76
43:8, 9	209
46:3	15
48:13-19	167
49:10	100, 167, 209

Exodus

2:	76
4	191
16	76
3:1-6	101
6-10	15
7. 8. 12	84
10-17	191
21, 22	24
4:2, 17	191
5:1-4	176
6:1	191
7:6, 7	191
12:1, 2	59, 136
1-6	16
3	79, 101
5	79
6	79, 136, 141
7	17
8-12	16
10	79
11	101, 136
13	17
14-20	16
34, 36	84
40, 41	14, 191
46	101, 191
13:1, 2. 14, 15	34
17, 18	15, 84
14:10, 11	84
15:	191
17	11
26	19, 80, 218
16:1	59
1-3	84
15, 31	27
32-34	25
17:5-7	40
6	102
18:5	84
21	52
25	52
19:1	59, 84
2	84
3-6	12
4-8	18
5	34
6	34, 218

10, 11, 14, 16, 17	119
10-13, 21	218
20:18-20	81
18-21	221
20	81, 216, 218
22:29	34
23:14-19	85
23	16, 218
24	218
27-33	16
31, 32	218
24:1	20, 147
2	147
6-8	13, 19
12, 15	20
12-18	81
18	20, 147
25:1	147
1-7	24
1-9	12, 81
2	147
8	11, 12, 21, 147
9	21, 147
10	147
10-15	25
16	25, 185
17	218
17-21	25
20	218
21	31, 173
22	28
23	147
23-30	28, 31
31	147
31-39	171
31-40	28
40	21, 147
26:1	29
1-7	147
1-29	29
15-29	31
30	21, 29, 147
30-35	186
31	147
31-33	29, 170
31-34	138
33	29
34	147, 173
35	31, 32, 147, 171
27:1-18	32
8	21, 147
20	51
21	47
28:1, 2	35, 147
1-3	82
3	13
4, 6-43	35

231

29 198
41..13, 36, 41, 45, 47
29:1 .... 43, 147
4-9 43
7-9 .... 36, 41
7, 9, 20, 35 45
29 174
30 .... 45, 174
38 .... 51, 172
38-42 50
38-44 170
39 172
42 .... 32, 51, 172
42-44 .... 32, 53
43 .... 32, 46
44 ....29, 32, 41, 47
45 12
46 .... 12, 147
30:1-6 171
1-10 28
6 218
7-9 59
7-10 47
10 60
18-21 33
22-25 35
25-28 169
25-30 .... 41, 168
26-29 44
26-38 36
30 45
31:1-11 23
32:15, 16 173
32, 33 .... 200, 227
33:11, 20, 23 209
13-15 13
16 .... 12, 13
34:1-4 20
22-25 85
28 .... 20, 21, 25
29 173
29-35 21
35:4-9 24
21-29 24
21, 25, 26, 30-35.. 37
36:1-3 .... 23, 25
1-4 37
4-7 25
8 29
20-34 31
38:1-7, 9-20 32
8 33
21 29
39:27-29 35
32 37
33-43 38
40:1, 2, 16, 17, 19, 23, 25, 29 38
6, 8, 22 32
7 33
9 41
9-15 168
13 13
13-15 45

20 173
21 .... 38, 173
24, 26 .... 32, 171
27 .... 38, 171
33, 34, 36-38 39

Leviticus

1: 51
4 72
2: 51
3: 51
2, 8, 13 72
4: 51, 203
2 .... 52, 218
3 .... 52, 160, 218
3-6 203
4 .... 53, 72, 160
5-7 54
6 31
13, 14, 22, 27 52
15 .... 53, 72, 160
16, 17, 25, 30.... 54
20 57
23, 28 .... 52, 160
24, 29 .... 53, 160
26 .... 57, 204
31 .... 57, 204
35 204
5: 51
15-19 218
6: 51
1-7 225
24-26 .... 56, 203
30 .... 56, 203
7: 51
27 17
8: 51
1-5 43
6-9 43
10 ....41, 44, 45, 169
11 .... 41, 44, 45
12 .... 45, 168
13 168
24, 30 45
33 .... 45, 46
34, 35 46
9: 170
1 49
10:1, 2 ...52, 59, 172
17 56
11:44 .... 11, 218
45 11
16: 51
2 ....31, 65, 138, 172
5 63
7, 8 .... 63, 72
9, 10 63
14, 15 64
5-22 35
16 .... 64, 65
17 .... 65, 66
18 69
19 .... 69, 144
20 .... 71, 203

21 ....72, 73, 203
22 203
29..60, 63, 66, 67, 175
30 .....66, 67, 71, 74, 144, 173, 191, 204, 226
31 .... 68, 175
33 .... 63, 66, 69, 74, 173, 191, 204, 226
34 60
17: 51
10 17
11 .... 18, 225
10-14 55
12-14 17
18:1-4 80
3 218
24-30 218
19:2 .... 11, 218
26 17
30 12
20:22 80
23 .... 80, 218
21:10 .... 45, 168
23: 51
4-22 51
23-25 ....51, 61, 175
26 ....59, 62, 175
26-32 51
27..59, 62, 67, 68, 175
27-29 175
28 .... 66, 68, 74
28-30 204
29 ....67, 71, 132
30 .... 67, 71
31 68
32 ...67, 68, 175, 196
33-42 51
24: 51
3, 4 47
25:1-6 61
26:2 12

Numbers

1: 43
3:2, 3 47
5-10 34
5, 6, 9, 10 35
10-38 48
11-13 .... 34, 214
4:3 .... 136, 174
5 ....27, 31, 47
6, 15, 16 47
35 .... 136, 174
39 136
5:5-8 225
7:1 .... 41, 169
9 27
8:4 .... 21, 147
5-22 35
9 35
19 174
9:15-23 39
16 51

10:1-8, 10 175
12 12
33-36 39
12:1, 2, 4, 5 32
3 191
7 39
14:1, 2 16
28-30, 32-35 85
28-35 16
34 ....131, 132
143, 193, 196
15:28 57
16:1-3 52
8-11, 23-25 48
28-33 ....48, 52
36-40 33
17:2-5 49
5 28
7-11 40
8, 10 ....28, 49
18:1 ....35, 47, 167
1-7 82
2 ....35, 167
5, 7-20 47
8, 20........... 45
19:1-10 51
20:7-13 102
23-28 174
21:4-9 102
23:9............... 12
24:17 104
25:1, 2 79
26:1-3, 63-65 85
28:1-4 58
1-6 76
1-15 170
3 172
3-10 50
6 51
9 ....58, 76
10 76
11-15 ....51, 58
14 ....59, 172
16-31 ....51, 87
17-23 58
29:1-5 87
1-11 51
7 ....67, 175
12-38 ....51, 87
35:30 133
33 163

Deuteronomy
1:2 ....15, 84
3 59
19-21 ......15, 84
39 85
3:11 31
4:2 38
5-9 ....12, 82
5-10 218
7 39
32, 33.........20, 119
32-35 82

6:1, 2............. 86
1-3 85
4 ......115, 116, 221
21-23 15
24 80
7:6-8 12
8:4 85
15, 16........27, 85
9:9 21
10:1-5 20
15 12
12:1-11 16
4-14 84
5-12 19
10, 11, 21 86
23 17
16:1-8 16
5-16 86
17:6 133
9-12 45
18:15, 18 ....104, 121
19:15 133
23:25 156
29:5 85
14, 15..84, 85, 158, 192
30:11-14 108
12, 13 153
32:4 199
33:2 ....20, 119, 167
27 ....191, 212

Joshua
7:10-12 216
18:1 148
19:51 148
24:2 77

Judges
2:11-13 186
10:6 186

Ruth
3:11-13 163
4:3-10 163

1 Samuel
2:11-17, 27-34 89
3:1 148
13 18
14 ....18, 89
19-21 ......148, 185
4:4 148
6:19 27
21 148
7:2-4, 15-17 148
10:1 43
12:3 217
14:32, 33 17
15:8, 9, 13-15, 22, 23 89
16:1, 13 43

2 Samuel
6:6, 7 149
7:1-11, 16 148

14:14..12,23,112,215, 220
23:1, 2 ......98, 148, 149

1 Kings
1:39 29
2:19 167
4:7 59
7:26 31
27, 37 33
8:9 27
10 39
56 176
62-65 88
62-66 87
10:6-9 93
11:36 87
12:32 59
17: 121
17-24 221

2 Kings
2:11 163
4:20, 32-37 221
6:17 163
17:6-18 176
13 186
23:3, 11 186

1 Chronicles
22:5, 7, 8, 14 148
23:25-27 149
24:1-5, 29, 31...... 149
25:1-7 149
27:1-15 59
28:2, 3, 6, 9-13 148
11 218
11-13 149
19 ....148, 149
29:1, 4 148

2 Chronicles
2:6 19
3:3 31
14 138
7:4-9 88
8 87
12 19
19:7 12
20:20 185
26:1, 16-21 168
16-21 48
18-20 49
33:9 13
36:14 89
14-21 187
15-21 90
20 128
21 ....128, 129
22, 23 .....128, 133

Ezra
1:1 115
1-4 133
2 ....115, 128

3 128
6:1-8 134
  1-12, 14 133
  1, 2, 6-8 115
7:7, 8 ....134, 143
  11 93
  11-13 ......115, 133
  11-26 134
9:14 91

Nehemiah

2:7, 8 115
6:15 61

Esther

3:7 61
4:1 128
9:1 59
  26 ....25, 113

Job

1:6-12 165
2:3-6 165
4:19 220
33:24 218
35:5-8 212
36:18 218

Psalms

2:1, 2 ....125, 135
  7, 8 114
8:4, 5 213
16:11 ....167, 212
19:2 51
  7 ....159, 199
23:4, 5 40
24:7-10 166
25:15 51
36:8 212
40:6-8 ....98, 150
  6-9 218
  7 119
  8 156
45:6, 7 ...98, 99, 169
49:7 ....23, 220
  8 ....23, 220
51:5 220
  10-13 223
  16, 17 162
68:17 163
  35 ....171, 172
69:20 162
78:18, 19 40
  24, 25 27
  29 85
  60 148
80:1 32
  16 114
82:6 113
87:6 200
89:19 ....11, 215
  34 185
92:15 212
94:20 224

99:1 32
103:8-14 .....214, 225
  17 214
  19 199
105:37 80
  43-45 81
106:15 85
  32, 33 102
108:8 209
110:1 ....98, 167
  4 ....167, 168
115:16 213
119: 112
  97 ....25, 113
  142, 172 154
126:1-4 90
130:3 227
133:1, 2 45
137:1-4 ......90, 128
146:3, 4 220
150: 210

Proverbs

8:22-30 117
  22-31 220

Ecclesiastes

1:4 212
3:1, 17 176
7:27 ......194, 196, 226
  29 212
8:11, 12 172
12:13 ....183, 199
  14 .....183, 198, 199

Isaiah

1:11-15 88
  18 191
  19 ....80, 198
  20 80
5:4 201
7:14 156
9:6 ......117, 156, 226
11:1 168
14:5-17 204
  12-14 ...... 163, 199
  12-17 221
  17 163
  19, 20 204
24:21 ....205, 221
  22 ....163, 221
25:8 207
  9 ....197, 207
26:2, 19 208
  3 225
27:12 ....194, 226
33:14 210
37:15, 16 32
40:3 ....95, 119
  4 119
  12-18. 26 208
  13, 14 217
43:11 ....104, 200

22-24 88
  25 205
44:22 205
  27 128
  28 ....128, 134
45:1, 2 128
49:15, 16 209
51:7 156
53:4-6 156
  4-8 54
  4-12 221
  5 ....156, 160
  6 160
  7 ....94, 136, 159
  8 ....94, 136
  8-11 162
  11 144
55:8, 9 225
58:13 50
59:1, 2 216
61:1, 2 109
  8 89
  10 201
62:10, 11 119
63:3-5 160
  7-11 58
64:6 201
65:17, 22 211
66:3, 4 88
  22 211

Jeremiah

2:22 227
  27 186
4:23-26 205
  24-27 210
6:16 104
  20 90
7:12, 14 148
  21, 22 ......79, 80
  22-24 19
  23-26 80
10:1-3 218
  7, 10 199
15:16 182
17:19-27 187
  21-27 90
23:6 154
25:2-14 176
  8-13 127
  31-33 210
26:6, 9 148
28:1 59
29:10 128
  10-14 ....90, 127
  12 128
  13 ....67, 128
  14 67
31:3 216
  29, 30 197
  34 ....191, 205
32:33 186
38:7-10 93
39:2 59

15-18 93
50:20..191, 192, 205, 226
    31, 34 226

Lamentations

1:10 128
    16, 19 90
2:6 ....88, 128
    7 ....90, 128
3:7 33

Ezekiel

2:3, 4 132
3:1-3 182
    1, 4, 5, 17 132
4:4 196
    4-6 ....132, 193
    5 196
    6...131, 132, 143, 196
7:3 226
8:15, 16 186
11:19, 20 223
14:14, 19, 20 132
18:1-4 197
    4 216
    25-30 ....200, 226
    30 226
    32 213
22:26 187
24:1 59
28:3 132
    11-16 199
33:17-20 200
36:12, 19 226
    26 ....162, 223
40:1-4 149
44:4, 5 149

Daniel

1:5 130
2:19, 36 171
    36-38 150
    44 ....122, 180
    45 ....122, 171
3:29 115
4:16 58
    17, 24, 25, 28 ... 150
5:13-16, 29-31 127
    25, 26 184
6:1-3 ....127, 128
    3, 4 130
    25, 26 115
7:9, 10..122, 180, 183, 198
    13, 14 ......122, 180
    25 189
    26, 27........ 122
8: 129, 130, 132
    1-14 124
    3-11 131
    13 184
    14 ...7, 127, 138, 143,
       144, 173, 177, 184,
       192, 193, 196, 205

15 124
16..124, 129, 134, 142
17-19 124
20-25 ....125, 131
26 126
27 .....126, 127, 129
9:............... 194
    2 127
    2-4 128
    3 67
    16, 17 ....90, 129
    16-19 128
    20, 21 129
    22 ....129, 130
    23 ....129, 130
    24 ..91, 131, 132, 169
    24-27 139
    25 ....131, 133
    25-27 ....132, 180
    26 ....136, 139
    27 .....133, 136, 139
10:1-12, 13, 14, 19 .. 142
    21 .....124, 142, 184
    23 63
11: 142
    13 58
12: 142
    1 ....180, 205
    2, 10 180
    4 ......142, 180, 182
    8 182
    8-10, 12 142
    9 ....180, 182
    13 ......142, 180, 183

Hosea

2:11 89

Amos

3:2 12
    3 224
    7 176
4:12 119
5:21, 22 90

Jonah

3:1-3, 5, 10....... 120

Micah

4:8 163
5:2 .....117, 167, 220
6:4 191
    6, 7......... 226
7:19 205

Nahum

1:9 ....174, 211

Habakkuk

2:1-3 178
3:4 210

Zephaniah

3:17 210

Haggai

1:1 59

Zechariah

3:1-4 ....201, 226
    5 201
4:7 168
6: 168
    12, 13 ..167, 174, 221
7:1 59
    12 162
12:10 116
13:6 200

Malachi

1:2 221
    6-8 91
3:6 216
    16, 17 205
4:1, 3 210
    5, 6.....119, 121, 190

Matthew

1:21 219
    23 156
2:1 ....87, 104, 125
    1-3 125
    2 ....104, 125
    13-18 125
3:1-3, 9, 10 120
    7, 8, 11, 12 ... 119
    15 153
4:1-11 161
    4 120
5:6 21
    8 209
    17, 18 ......142, 154
    19 152
    35 140
    37 198
    48 ......159, 199, 218
7:29 219
8:16 156
    17 .... 95, 156
    20 219
9:28 115
10:1 190
    1-6 158
    2 190
    5, 6 140
    32, 33 198
11:7-14 197
    10 190
12:1-8 156
    5 50
    17-19 95
    36, 37 198
13:14, 16 181
    30 197
    38 ....190, 197
    39..123, 188, 190, 197
14:33 114
15:24 140

16:16 219
22, 23 180
27 208
17:9-12 157
10-13 107
18:10 198
16 133
20:21-23 167
28 226
30 219
21:43, 44 82
23:16, 21........ 149
29-35 141
35, 36 200
37 ......108, 141, 150
38 150
24:1 ....141, 150
2 ....140, 150
14 ....117, 189
15 122
21, 22 189
24 ......185, 224
50, 51 206
25:8-13 194
21 39
31 ....168, 208
33 167
34 ....167, 208
46 210
26:1, 2 101
36-44 160
52 221
54 156
27:9, 35......... 156
45-50 162
46 141
50 ....138, 141
51 138
51-53 ......164, 221
52, 53, 60 163
28:18-20 ...189, 200, 225
19, 20 153

Mark

1:1-3 122
14, 15 180
4:30-32 191
5:25-34 115
7:37 219
8:38 198
12:6, 7 115
13, 17 219
26, 27 207
29 221
35, 37 98
36 ....98, 167
13:24 135
15:28 156
44, 45 162
16:15, 16.......... 200

Luke

1:5, 26, 27, 36 136
8, 9 59

8-10 171
11-13 136
13-17 197
17 ....119, 120, 121, 176, 190
19 ....124, 184
28 156
31-33 ....100, 168
33 100
36 136
67-70 180
69, 70 107
2:1 125
8-14 180
11-14 156
45 ....123, 185
46 ....123, 185
49 159
3:1 125
2, 3, 23 136
4 183
7, 10, 12, 14 119
8 ....119, 223
10-14 ......183, 197
21, 22 ......136, 180
23 136
4:5, 6........ 163
16-21 109
6:46 120
9:43 178
44 ....178, 179
46 179
10:18 199
19 225
20 205
11:21, 22........161, 215
12:42 213
13:24, 25.......... 190
14:14 ....183, 210
15:4-6 209
16:17 152
31 ....157, 171
17:4 225
19:10 159
14 168
38-40 179
41-44 150
42 108
43 141
44 ....108, 141
20:35 198
36 ....183, 198
21:20-24 ... 82, 141, 150
36 198
22:27 226
39-44 160
23:4 219
34 161
39-43 200
24:4-8 106
6-8 157
17-21 178
21 179
26 ....112, 157

27 ....95, 112, 157
44 ....95, 109, 112, 153, 157
45 .....95, 112, 157
49, 52 164

John

1:1-3 112
4, 29, 36 159
11 ....158, 168
19-22 121
19-23 95
41 ....135, 150
42 150
49 .... 114, 219
49-51 102
2:18-22 ......106, 157
20 168
3:3 223
14 ......102, 158, 171
16-18 221
35 117
36 115
4:20-24 87
22 158
25, 26 ....136, 153
34 ....159, 160
5:8, 10 157
20-23 97
21-26 115
22 201
25 164
26 221
26-29 97
28, 29 ......164, 210
39 ....96, 97, 153
40 ....97, 153
45-47 ....96, 152
6:37 225
38 159
68, 69 219
7:15 94
19-23 157
48, 49 94
8:17 133
28 102
29 ....159, 201
32 223
46 .....154, 159, 218
9:2, 3 197
28-34 94
35-37 114
35-38 219
39-41 200
10:9 217
10 ....97, 159
17, 18 ......97, 115, 161, 162, 221
28, 29 225
30 115
34 113
34-36 114
11:14 221
25 164

27 ....115, 219
43 221
12:9-11 157
20 87
31 165
32 102
13:3 117
13, 14 226
18 156
14:1-3 .....165, 166, 208
6 ....200, 217
17 ....105, 150
26 150
15:5 224
24 200
16:4 180
7 ....105, 164
13 105
15 117
28 165
33 ....165, 224
17:4 ....123, 160. 175, 219, 226
5 115
10 117
12 156
23 199
24 209
18:1-7, 26, 28, 29, 31. 160
36, 37 168
19:6 219
13-16 125
13-18 160
15 .... 126, 168
16 126
24 156
30 .... 123, 160, 161, 175, 222, 226
36 101
20:25-27 209

Acts

1:1-3, 12-26 173
4, 13, 14 164
8 ....140, 189, 158
11 208
16 98
16-20 158
2:1 85
11, 14-23, 25-31, 34-36 105
14-36 173
23 180
24 ....162, 221
25, 33-35 150
25-36 158
29-31 127
32 225
33 167
3:14, 15, 17 161
18 ....107, 180
19..144, 187, 191, 192
19-21 ......107, 227
20 191

22 171
22-24 104
26 225
4:12 ....104, 200
25 ....98, 136
25-27 125
26 136
27 161
28 ....161, 180
5:1-10 172
31 ....167, 225
7:30-38 101
37 104
38 ....104, 108
52 108
55 170
56 ...150, 167, 170
8:1-5 140
26-28 93
27 87
32-34 94
35 95
9:15 150
20, 22 108
10:34 ....12, 52, 199
38 ....115, 136
43 111
11:26 190
28-30 24
13:14 196
15 ....109, 196
15-17, 22-27, 32-37 109
27 ....109, 171
38 225
15:20 ....18, 56
21 ....109, 171
28 18
16:31 221
17:1-3 108
31 ....176, 196
18:28 109
20:27 201
28 163
22:14 150
24:15 210
26:16 150
22, 23 ....97, 109

Romans

1:1-3 109
20 201
2:1-3 196
6-11 197
7 200
11 199
17-20, 28, 29..... 223
3:1, 2 158
1-3 82
19 ....196, 226
24-26 200
23 163
4:17-24 100
25 ....159, 221
5:6 ....180, 220

10 175
12 ....213, 224
15, 17, 18 224
19 .... 159, 213
6:2, 6, 7 224
9 222
11 ....224, 225
13, 14, 16 225
21 220
23 ..... 118, 216, 220
7:7 199
9 224
8:1 221
3 117
4 154
16, 17 116
34 ..... 167, 201, 226
9:1-5 158
28 ....188, 194
10:1-4 152
4, 6-11 153
6-10 108
18 189
11:33, 35........... 217
13:11 176
14:9 225
10-12 226
15:4 ...... 27, 158, 192
8 ..... 12, 140, 158
26 24
16:20 ....99, 191
25, 26 23

I Corinthians

1:4-8 185
24 115
27-29 191
30..115, 141, 154, 159
2:8 161
4:1, 2 ....163, 213
5:7 ....17, 101, 141
6:2, 3 ....196, 210
19, 20 212
9:8-10 150
10:1-4 ....57, 102
2 153
11 ......27, 158, 192
13 ....197, 224
18 82
20 79
13:12 209
14:6, 26 150
37 149
40 52
15:3 ...108, 141, 159, 220
4 ....108, 220
17-19, 22 222
21 221
24, 25 202
24-28 ...167, 173, 227
26 ....166, 210
45 199
45-47 215
47 ....199, 201

51-54 207
55 208

2 Corinthians

2:11 185
3:6 223
    13-15 171
4:3, 4 23
5:10 196
    14 226
    15 .... 225, 226
    18 175
    21 ..160, 219, 220, 226
6:16 12
    16-18 191
11:2 209
    3 213
12:9 224
13:1 133

Galatians

1:4 161
    11, 12 ......23, 149
    20 149
3:16 ......99, 191, 214
    19 99
4:4 ....117, 180
    7 116
6:8 200
    16 183

Ephesians

1:7, 11-14 163
    8 115
    20 167
2:1, 5 223
    8 191
    18 217
3:3-8 23
    9-11 112
    14, 15 .....209, 221
4:8 ....166, 221
    13 224
    14 185
    18 23
5:26, 27 209
6:10-17 224

Philippians

2:5-8 ......117, 218
    7 226
4:3 ....198, 199
    8 224

Colossians

1:9, 19........... 115
    15-17 112
    16 117
    20 166
    22 209
    27 189
2:2, 3, 9, 10 115
    13 224

4:6 198
    12 218

1 Thessalonians

4:15-17 207
    16 ......63, 164, 166,
             185, 210
    17 ....166, 185
5:1, 4 176
    23 ....197, 205
    24 197

2 Thessalonians

1:7, 10 197
2:8-11 224
    9, 10 185

1 Timothy

1:5 152
2:5 ....117, 220
    6 220
    13, 14 213
3:16 ....117, 154
5:24 194
6:7 220
    16 212

2 Timothy

1:10 159
2:15 23
    19 138
3:15 97
    15-17 ......120, 201

Hebrews

1:1 112
    2 ....112, 115, 201
    3 167
    4 165
    8, 9 ....99, 169
2:3 149
    9 159
    14 .....117, 165, 210
    14-16 117
    14-18 219
3:1 167
    1-5 ....149, 158
    5 39
4:2 57
    14-16 .....167, 191
    15 ......165, 219, 224
    16 224
5:8 ....161, 221
    13, 14......... 224
6:1-4 224
    19 ....171, 222
    20 171
7:11 82
    14 .....100, 101, 168
    24 ....174, 227
    25 ....201, 226
    28 ....164, 169

8:1 ...147, 149, 167, 168
    2 ......147, 149, 168
    3 147
    4 ....147, 167
    5 ......23, 147, 171
    6, 7 82
    13 82
9:1-10 192
    2 170
    2-4 29
    3 ....25, 170
    3-7 171
    4 25
    6 ....57, 58, 172, 175
    6-10 158
    7 ....58, 60, 65,
             172, 175, 188
    8-10 ......147, 171
    9, 10 .....147, 158
    19-22 13
    22 ....18, 163
    23 ....144, 158, 192
    23-26 147
    24 ..147, 158, 171, 192
    25 .....60, 65, 158,
         171, 172, 175, 225
    26 ....222, 225
    28 197
10:1 ....172, 175
    1-14 174
    2 175
    3 172
    5, 9 154
    5-7 99
    5-9 150
    5-10 218
    12 167
    19-21 147
    19-22 226
    20 222
11:3 217
    4-40 199
    5 163
    6 ....117, 217
    7 120
    17-19 100
    23-27 152
    24, 26 97
    24-27 108
    39, 40......... 207

James

1:13 ....213, 216
    14, 15 213
    17 216
    25 199
2:8-12 199
4:7 224
5:11 ....152, 165
    12 198

1 Peter

1:2 17
    3 224

9-12 106
10-12 127
15, 16 218
18, 19 161
20 217
23 224
2:1 224
9 150
21 162
22 .... 162, 219
3:15 23
18 220
22 167
4:10 ....163, 213
17..176, 183, 192, 199
5:8, 9 224

2 Peter
1:4 224
21 ....23, 151
2:5 120
19 ....99, 163
3:10-12 177
10-13 163
18 224

1 John
1:7 ....191, 221, 225
9 ...144, 191, 221, 224
2:1 ....201, 225, 226
3:4, 8 199
9 225
4:4 224
8 212
17 198

Jude
9 ....63, 165
24 197

Revelation
1:1 122
3 ....122, 181

5 125
7 ....118, 122, 180
8, 11 117
9-11 170
12..147, 150, 170, 183
12-18 123
13 ....35, 147, 170
17 ..... 163, 170, 221
18..163, 170, 210, 221
3:5 198
7, 8 145
10 224
21 ....167, 174
4:11 212
5:1-7 160
4, 8-10, 12 112
5 ....112, 215
10 150
11 ....112, 168
11-13 210
6:14-17 ...122, 180, 210
7:1-3 191
2-4 192
3 188
15-17 222
8:2-4 171
3 ....147, 150 183
5 174
10: 145, 176, 182
1, 2, 5 181
6-11 182
10 ....177, 182
11:1 182
3 135
15 ......122, 125, 191
19 ..... 123, 147, 150,
173, 180, 183, 187
12:6 ....59, 135, 189, 196
7 63
7-9 199
9 58
10 165
11 224
12 ....185, 224
17 ......185, 188, 224

13:5 ....59, 189
8 ......198, 199, 217
14: 176, 189, 190, 191
4 208
5 209
6 .... 145, 176,
177, 182, 192
6-11 189
6-12 ....122, 189
7 ...145, 176, 177, 185
9-12 188
12 ......183, 188, 189
14 170
14-16 ....122, 190
14-17 123
15:2, 3.....158, 192, 210
5 173
8 174
16:17..123, 175, 190, 227
17:14 117
19: 190
10 185
16 ....63, 117
20: 190
1 204
2 ....204, 205
3 205
7 ....205, 210
10, 14 210
12 ......198, 200, 210
13 200
21: 190
1, 2 211
4 210
6 .... 117, 175
27 205
22: 190
4 209
6, 7, 11-13 122
11..174, 190, 198, 227
12 ....174, 180
13 ....112, 117
14 .... 189, 208
17 117
20 180

Spirit of Prophecy Index

Acts of the Apostles

109	95
112	108
113	108
115	109
120	109

Desire of Ages

309, 310	13
31, 32	15
76	16, 80
77	17
82	17
157	19
121	27
284-286	50
28	79
77	80
27	82
29	82
52	83
652	85
785, 786	86
463	86
469	88
112, 113	92
165	92
652	92
70	94
453	94
211, 212	95
799	95
213	97
761, 762	99
468, 469	100
24	101
23	101
756, 757	102
494	106
349	107
23	119
104	122
357	199
296	215

Early Writings

63	7
32	27
16, 17	35
64	120
66, 67	120
32	145
42	145
279-281	195
280	205
281	205

Gospel Workers

302, 303	8
302, 307, 308	151

Great Controversy

648, 649	208

Life Sketches
1915 edition

278	7
110, 111	151
278	211

1888 edition

127	192

Patriarchs and Prophets

25	14
137	14
281, 282	15
232	15
118	15
277	17
279	17
71	18, 76
358	20, 69, 74
592	21
356	21, 64
281	24
344	25
297	27, 37
403	28
343	29
347	29, 31, 32, 33
348	33, 36
274-277	34
350	34, 35, 39, 44, 47
351	35, 44, 48
353	36, 53
349	37, 39
376	38
293	40
303	41
305	41
252	41
282	43
323	47
425	47
426	47
395	48
359	50, 59
527	51
352	53
354	53, 55, 56
355	56, 60, 67, 71, 74
360	59
356	71

68	76
125	77
128	77
245	77
332, 333	77, 80
141	79
154, 155	79
576	79
120-123	79
364	80
309, 310	81
312	81
313	81
314	82
373	82
369	82
539, 540	85, 86
105, 106	89
634	89
184	102
418	102
34	117
63	215
426	227

Prophets and Kings

304	49
45	88
466	90
475	90
586	202
587	202

Testimonies for the Church
Vol. III

389	24

Vol. IV

123	18

Vol. V

216	120

Vol. VIII

9	121
332	121

Vol. IX

264	38

Testimonies to Ministers

112, 113	123
114	123
118	123

Special Testimonies
Series B, No. 2

56, 57	146

240

Bibliography

"Certainties of the Advent Movement," by W. A. Spicer, pp. 134-154.

"Daniel and the Revelation," by Uriah Smith, ed. 1897, pp. 488, 489, 496

Gesenius' Hebrew Lexicon, ed. 1871.

Jewish Encyclopedia, by Funk & Wagnalls, N.Y.:

    Vol. II, pp. 280, 281, 288, 365, 366, 367,

    Vol. VI, pp. 5, 608, 609; also article, entitled, "Hanukah."

    Vol. VIII, ed. 1904, pp. 630-632.

    Vol. XI, pp. 114, 290, 460, 461.

"Jewish Prayer Book," article, "Method of Atonements."

Josephus, "Wars of the Jews," Book 4, chap. 3, par. 8.

Popular and Critical Encyclopedia, Vol. II, p. 479.

"Prayers of Israel," pp. 196, 197.

"Prayers for the Day of Atonement."

"Prayers for the Holy Days."

"Rashi's Comment on Genesis 1:26."

Review and Herald, August 31, 1933.

"Rise and Progress of Seventh-day Adventists," by J. N. Loughborough.

Talmud, Tractate, Mishnah, Rosh Hashonah, Treatise VII, chap. 1.

    Baal Aruch.

    Hilchoth Shabbath.

    Hilchoth Shechita.

    Hilchoth Talmud Torah.

    Hilchoth T-Choo-Vah.

    Hilchoth Youm Touv.

    Orach Chayim.

General Index

AARON, priesthood conferred upon, 47, 48.

Abraham, faith of, in circumcision, 157; God fulfilled promise to, 15; God's promises to, 14; sought to preserve knowledge of God, 79; symbols revealed to, 15; why, offered sacrifice, 14, 77; why God chose, 14.

Advent, cause of disappointment in, movement, 145, 177-179; essential preparation for second, of Christ, 120; no new religion introduced at first, 158; righteous dead to be raised at second, 166.

Adam, did he offer sacrifices? 75.

Alphabet, same today as in King David's day, 153; the Hebrew, 155.

Altar, angels ministered at, in heaven, 171; censers covered the, 32, 49; the golden, 32; of incense, 36; the, of burnt offering, 32.

Ark, Aaron's rod in, 25; borne by priests, 39; description of, 25; John beheld, in heaven, 173; pot of manna in, 25; testimony put in, 25; Uzzah's experience with, 7; why manna was placed in, 23.

Atonement, a thorough work done by high priest on day of, 173; all people could share in efforts on the day of, 66; Christ the promised, 18; day of, 60, 85; day of, a day of sealing, 71; day of, a work of judgment, 71; God's message to prepare for antitypical day of, 176; God's special requirements for day of, 67; goats used on typical day of, 63; Hebrew name of day of, 62; how Israel prepared for day of, 175; how Jewish people now observe day of, 68, 69; how services were conducted on day of, 63; is made for sanctuary at close of day of, 203; people to afflict souls on day of, 175; sealing on day of, 61; services on day of, divided into four parts, 68; sins blotted out on day of, 71; studies on atonement, 6, 212-227; the antitypical day of, began at close of 2300 days, 173; the, must be completed, 57; the blood made the, 18, 25; the sinner's part in, 55; virtue of the Lord's goat on day of, 73; what happens on day of, 144; what this day of, meant to high priest, 69; what this day of, meant to the Israelites, 67; when typical work of, ended, 71; where blood was sprinkled in sanctuary on day of, 64;

why day of, was instituted, 65; work accomplished on day of, 60, 66, 67; would the Lord introduce the great antitypical day of, without warning the world? 175.

Azazel, not needed for reconciliation, 72; sins confessed on head of, 72, 74; twelve reasons why, represents Satan and not Christ, 71-73; was removed to uninhabited place, 204; when, is called for, 71.

BIBLE, the, foretells, 5.

Blood, New Testament forbids eating of, 18, 55; not permitted to eat, 17, 55; of Christ to be applied, 18; Orthodox Jews do not eat, 17, 18; people who ate, were to die, 17; rabbinical laws concerning eating of, 18; sprinkled on horns of altar, 56; the, only can redeem, 63; what was represented by, 65; without shedding of, there is no remission of sin, 18.

CALENDAR, a Biblical, 59; the, followed by the Jews, 59.

Candlestick, the golden, 32.

Cherubim, the, 25; location of, 28; the Lord dwells between, 32.

Christ, a glorious welcome was given, at His ascension, 166; all the dead in, will arise at His second advent, 166; a personal Saviour, 17; blood of, purchased man's life and home, 163; death of, caused by a broken heart, 162; death of, efficacious for all, 161; first advent of, confirmed truth of Bible, 158; God imbued, with the fullness of heaven, 115; great sacrifice of, 19; heirship with, only, 117; how, read the Scriptures, 111; intercedes for man, 123; is God's only heir, 115; is the spotless Lamb, 159, 160; man's only hope, 201; men can overcome through the grace of, 165; message of, to His disciples just before His ascension, 164; mission of, 17; Old Testament writers spoke of, 107; only, knows the future, 112; others came from grave at resurrection of, 164; Peter speaks of, as lamb without blemish, 161; power that stood up against, 125, 126; prayer of, before His death, 161; price of our redemption is paid by, 210; prophecies fulfilled in, 106; return of, for His church, 208; sacrifice of, a freewill offering, 161; saved only through, 104; Scriptures establish that, is divine, 113; Scriptures foretold sufferings of, 107; Scriptures teach that, is also to come as King of kings and Lord of lords, 117, 118; Scriptures teach that, is man as well as divine, 117, 118; sits at right hand of God, 167; the deity of, 112; those raised at the resurrection of, were taken with Him to heaven, 166; two reasons why, took human nature, 159; value of communion with, 21; virtue of the blood of, 17; visits His home town, 109; was not compelled to die, 162; weeps over Jerusalem, 141; what happens in heaven when, completes His ministry as High Priest, 175; what it means to confess, 198, 199; who will be benefited by the ministry of, 194; why, came to this world, 159; why, died, 161; why it was expedient for, to go away, 164; why it was impossible for the grave to hold, 162, 163; wonderful prayer of, 160; work of, compared to that of Moses, 158; world not the home of, 164.

Church, God's description of remnant, 185, 189; organization of the remnant, 192; Satan persecutor of, 58, 59.

Cleansed, meaning of the word, in Daniel 8:14, 144.

Cleansing, a thorough, 65; disciples seek for heart, 164; of the camp of Israel, 71, 74.

Commandments, the greater and the lesser, 152.

Condemnation, man not under, 57.

Consecration, oil for, 35; service of, 43, 45, 46.

Court, dimensions and description of, 32.

Cubit, length of, 31.

DANIEL, angel Gabriel again visits, 129; angel Gabriel visits the prophet, 124; assurance given to the prophet, 124; a twofold testimony given to, 142; book of, 11; book to be closed for a time, 142; book used in giving the message, 180; effect of the vision upon, 127; encouraging message brought to, 129, 130; Gabriel explains to, ten points dealing with seventy weeks, 140; Gabriel tells, most holy must be anointed, 169; Gabriel interprets prophecy to, 125; makes discovery as he studies the prophecies, 127; meets Cyrus in the palace, 128; messages in, are vital, 122, 123; need of understanding book of, 122; prophecy of, unsealed, 5; prophet, familiar with the prophecies, 127; the angel brings to, five out-

standing features, 124; the angel explains vision to, 129, 130; the burden of petition of, 128, 129; the prophet faints, 127; the prophet seeks the Lord, 127, 128; vision not fully explained to, 139; wise to understand messages in, 180, 181, 182.

Day, God's cleaning up, 65.

Days, antitypical day of atonement began at end of the 2300, 173; Daniel seeks to understand prophecy of the 2300, 127; feast of dedication has nothing in common with the 2300, 192-194; Gabriel comes to explain the 2300, 131; Hebrew expression of the 2300, 126; message given at the close of the 2300, 177, 178; prophecy of the 2300, 126; three kinds of, mentioned in the Bible, 96; when the 2300, will end, 142, 144; why Gabriel did not at first explain the, 126.

Death, destruction of, 210; not perpetual, 5.

Deception, what constitutes, 13.

Dedication, the Jewish feast of, and the 2300 days, 192-194.

Disciples, Jesus defends His, 156.

Disobedience, how God regards, 59.

Division, of Israel's camp, 52.

ELI, sons of, carry the ark into the camp, 148; the sin of house of, 18.

Elijah, Jews say Messiah cannot come until, first comes, 121; the work of John the Baptist is message of, 121, 122; work and message of, 121.

Eternity, the people of God to enjoy an, 211.

Evil, disposition of, 6; God not responsible for, 5; will not rise the second time, 5.

Excommunication, rabbinical, 61, 62.

FEASTS, many sacrifices offered at, 87; where, to be kept, 86.

Firstborn, 17, 34; redeeming the, 34.

First fruits, Feast of Weeks, 85; when offered, 16.

GIFTS, God's call for, 24; of Israelites, 51.

Goat, offering of the Lord's, 64.

God, a dwelling place for, 11; a, of order, 38; a, of system, 52; forbearance of, 15; is holy, 11; meaning of the word, in the Hebrew, 112, 113; no respecter of persons, 12, 52; preparation to meet, 119; purposes of, 14; Rashi's comment on the Hebrew word, 113, 116; Sabbath of, 12; the righteous approach the city of, 209.

Gospel, why believe? 20.

HOLY, anointing the most, 141, 169; blood sprinkled in most, place on Day of Atonement, 65; Christ began His work in heaven in the, place, 170; Jesus enters the most, place in heaven, 146; John saw Christ in the, place, 171; meaning of the word, 11; places, 31; priests enter most, for cleansing, 74; priests ministered in the, place every day, except one, 172; Scriptures teach there are, places in heaven, 171, 172; sins carried into the, place, 65; special significance to the, festivals, 85; the apostle saw the most, place in heaven, 173; the priests begin their work in the, place, 170.

Hope, a, God gave to Adam, 99.

INCENSE, meaning of, 36; offering of, 59; use of, 36.

Inspiration, David acknowledges light on erection of temple was given to him by, 149; Jews believed in different degrees of, 98; Old Testament writers were under the, of God, 98.

Institutions, God's are sacred, 12.

Israel, heavy obligations rested upon leaders of, 52; leaders of, 52, 200; rejected her king, 83; special commands given to, on Day of Atonement, 67.

Israelites, a series of feasts given to, 85; camp of, divided, 52; census of, 43; deliverance of, 17; did not die, 17; disregarded divine instructions, 13; Egyptians eager to release, 24; experience in wilderness an emergency, 84; experiences of, for our learning, 40; God gave, favor, 24; God works miracles for the, 85; God's demands of, 18; God's plan for, 15; God's protection over, 84; had divine guidance, 39, 43; how the, came to the sanctuary with their offerings, 203, 204; lessons the, had to learn, 79; meaning of sanctuary service was lost to, 149; meaning of wandering of, 15; Moses encourages the, to enter Promised Land, 84; murmurings of, 37, 84; not one weak person among, 80; offerings of, 51; relation of, to heathen, 13; solicited the Egyptians, 84; sprinkled the blood, 16; sprinkled with blood, 13; statutes given to, 12; suffering of, 14; tempted the Lord, 40; the, in Egypt under the lash, 80; the, lost meaning of sacrifices, 82; the, must afflict their souls, 67; the, promised a return to Palestine, 90; the, refuse to enter the Promised Land, 84; the, watch Moses smite the rock, 102; the, were depositaries of God's law, 77; the, were to have God's abiding presence, 81; the, were to prepare for Day of Atonement, 176; to be a separate people, 12, 13; to be a wonderful people, 13; to the, was given God's law, 81; urged to free themselves from heathen customs, 13; were the, the first people to offer sacrifices? 75; what the, did when they rejected their Lord, 141; when the, could not sing the songs of Zion, 90; why God chose the, 12; why God permitted the, to go to Egypt, 80; why, sent into captivity, 13; why, went into Egypt, 15.

JERUSALEM, agitation in, because of fulfillment of prophecy, 95; destruction of, 91; Jesus wept over, 141; people went to, to worship, 87, 94; restoration to, 91; service in, was desolate, 128.

Judgment, a rule to guide the judge in the, 199; Christ will act as judge and judge advocate in the, 201, 202; Day of Atonement a work of, 68, 71; decisions to be made in, 200; hour message, 145, 188; how God will deal with men in, 196; the Bible's description of, 196; the investigative, message, 196; where the investigative, will take place, 196; with whom will the, begin? 199.

KORAH, rebellion of, 48.

LADDER, of Jacob's dream, 102.
Lamb, passover, 17; was eaten, 17.
Laver, description of, 33.
Law, a fiery, issued from the right hand of God, 167; Adam disobeyed God's, 159; a perfect God gave a perfect, 159; Christ fulfilled the, 153-155; Christ lived the, in His flesh, 156; giving of the, world's second great event, 119; how rabbis violated the, 157; impossible for the disciples to repudiate the, 153; meaning of the expression, "the end of the," 152; righteousness of the, fulfilled, 154; the, demands a perfect life, 159; the, is God's rule in the judgment, 199; when the Jews believe the, was given, 86.

Leaders of Israel men of piety, 52.
Levi, God chose the tribe of, 34.
Levites, inauguration of, 35; no inheritance given to, 45; work of, 35.
Lot, casting the, 63; the Lord's, first offered, 63.

MANNA, nature of the, 27; the meaning of the word, 27; the miracle of the, 27; where the pot of, now is, 27.

Meat, meaning of the word, 51.

Melchizedek, Christ is a priest after the order of, 168; first mention of, 76.

Mercy seat, description of, 25; location of, 28.

Message, God carries forward His, on time, 176, 177; God's last, of mercy to the world, 190, 191, 194, 195; God's special, 189; God's special, given in Revelation 14, 189; how God carries forward His, 191, 192; the last day, 6.

Messiah, Abraham's answer a veiled prophecy of, 100; angel foretold the coming of, 91; coming of, 122, 135; death of, 138; divinity of, established, 114; feasts point to, 86; God's promise of, 109; how Jesus convinced the disciples that He is the true, 96; how John the Baptist introduced the, 159, 161; is God's only way of salvation, 104; Jesus tells the Samaritan woman that He is the, 153; means anointed, 43; older Jewish commentators acknowledge that Shiloh is, 100; Paul finally believed that Jesus is the, 108, 109; priests to represent the, 89; prophecies fulfilled in, 95; prophecies of Isaiah regarding the, 95; public challenge issued by, 159; Samaritans had faith in, 153; Scriptures fulfilled in, 156; the fulfillment of the sacrifices in, 150; to be cut off, 136, 139; vindicates His disciples, 50; work, must do at His coming, 136, 138.

Moses, builds according to pattern, 21; came down from Sinai with the law, 20; experience, had with God, 21; foretold the coming of Messiah, 104, 108; faithfulness of, 39; God depended on, 39; God has interview with, 20, 21, 47; God met, at the bush, 84; had associates to build the sanctuary, 23; Israelites refuse to follow, into the Promised Land, 84; Jews in possession of writings of, 171; Jewish leaders, knew not the voice or the spirit of, 97; learned obedience, 38; light given to, on the sanctuary, 147; meeting rebellion, 48; people watch, smite the rock, 102; Pharisees claimed to believe, 157; prophesied of the Saviour, 152; revelations given to, 21; rod of, 40; the face of, shone, 21; work of Christ compared to that of, 158.

NEIGHBOR, meaning of word, among the Jews, 12.

Noah, God accepted sacrifices of, 89.

OBEDIENCE, the Lord requires, 80.

Offering, blood of, taken into the holy place, 55; Christ the spotless, 160; Day of Atonement sin, 65; spotless, bore the guilt of the sinner, 53; the sinner slew the, 160.

Offerings, five general classes of, 51; sin, 52; sin, ended, 141; sinners benefit by the, 53; various kinds of, 58; were without blemish, 52; where the, were presented, 53.

Oil, Moses uses the anointing, 45; pouring the, on the priests, 45; the holy, for consecration, 41, 42.

Organization, God recognizes, 52.

PASSOVER, a memorial, 17; how often, to be observed, 16; Messiah died at the, 138; observed for fifteen centuries, 101; observance of, 16, 79, 80, 85; the month in which, occurs, 135, 138.

Pentecost, outpouring of the Holy Spirit on day of, 86; the feast of, 85.

Pharisees, claims of the, 13; disciples perplexed by teaching of, 107; Jesus told the, that they did not keep the law, 157; perverted the types, 13; righteousness of, 13.

Priest, attitude of our heavenly High, toward those who have lived in days past, 200; Christ's ministry as High, cannot continue endlessly, 174; Jesus our great High, 168; mediation of our great High, 200; no succession to Christ's ministry as High, 174; our High, remained in the holy place until antitypical day of atonement, 172; the earthly high, remained in the most holy place till his work was completed, 172, 203.

Priesthood, a succession of, in Levitical ministry, 174; Christ's, in heaven, 168; Christ must be prepared for His heavenly, 164; demoralization of, 91; where we have the first mention made of Christ's heavenly, 150; why no further need of an earthly, 150.

Priests, ample provision was made for the needs of, 89; consecration of, 36, 41, 45; dress of, 35; flesh eaten in the holy place by, 56; garments for, 35, 44; inauguration of, 45, 160; make the atonement, 57; meaning of the garments of, 35; ministry began following their consecration, 50; ministry of the, in the sanctuary, 47, 65; ministry on the Sabbath, 50, 76; only, could minister in sanctuary, 48; origin of the, 76; preparing the, for consecration, 43, 44; robes of, 35; setting apart of, 13; the, did not always rightly represent the sacrificial system, 89; were leaders of the people, 52; work of, on Day of Atonement was comprehensive, 66.

Prophecies, disciples did not at first understand the, 106; Jews are disturbed over the, of Isaiah 53, 156; made sure, 141.

Prophecy, counsel from the Spirit of, 146; gift of, connected with the keeping of the commandments, 185; light came to the church through the Spirit of, 145, 146, 151; restoration to the church of the gift of, 145.

RECONCILED, how men became, 57.

Reconciliation, 141.

Redemption, Israel's deliverance is an object lesson of, 17; what was involved in the plan of, 163.

Remission, no, without shedding of blood, 56.

Repentance, ten days of, 61.

Revelation, book of, important messages in, 180, 181; we should understand, 122.

Revelation, gospel given by, 23; light came to David by, 148.
understand the book of, 122.

Reward, 5.

Righteous, to inhabit the earth, 5.

Righteousness, bringing in everlasting, 141; Christ is our, 154.

Rod, Aaron's, 28, 40.

SABBATH, a holy institution, 11; existed before sin, 11; God only can make a, 12; God sends His people light on, 187; proper observance of, 50, 91; the, was made for man, 12; why God gave the, 12.

Sacred, God's work is, 28.

Sacrifice, Christ offered the great, 160; spirit of, 37; the Israelites had the spirit of, 51.

Sacrifices, all, cease at the death of Messiah, 139, 150; ceased to be offered, 83, 90; God required many, 51; Israel did not always appreciate the system of, 88, 89; Jewish people now have no, 68; meaning of daily, 51; misunderstood, 19; Noah offered, 75, 89; not confined to the wilderness, 84; offering of, 50, 60; pointed to Christ, 18; purpose of, 17; rabbis obscured the meaning of, 19; system of, 18; system of, was perverted, 89; temporarily ceased, 90; the system of, was understood by Cain and Abel, 18; to Israel only was entrusted the system of, 82; to whom did the heathen offer? 79; were a revelation, 21; what eventually was to become of the system of? 90; when did the

system of, begin? 75, 76; when the system of, ended, 82; why the Lord did not always accept the, 88; why the Lord would not accept King Saul's, 89.

Salvation, God introduced the plan of, 23; how much is involved in the plan of, 163; the plan of, 18.

Sanctify, meaning of the word, 12.

Sanctuary, annual service in the, 58; anointing the, 44, 46; atonement for the, 69; attention of God's people called to the heavenly, 183; blood taken into, 56; built according to the pattern, 21; Christ enters most holy place of the heavenly, 180; church should follow her Lord in the heavenly, 123; cleansing of, 69; cleansing of the heavenly, 203; commercialization of, 91; confessed sin only, taken into, 56; continual service in, 58; David reorganizes the work in, 149; dedication services of, 35, 36, 41, 43, 160; earthly, a shadow of the heavenly, 171; erected, 38; erected by the order of God, 25; explained, 6; fascinating study of, 6; first mention of Christ's priesthood in the heavenly, in book of Hebrews, 150; furnishings of, 25, 147; furniture in, 28; God dwelt in, 12; God raised up Paul to make clear the meaning of, 150; God's glory covered the, 39; God's people turn their faces toward the heavenly, 186; heavenly, anointed, 167, 169; how light on the, originally was given, 147; how the Israelites built the, 24; Israelites lost the meaning of, 149; lay desolate during the Babylonian exile, 90; length of time to build the, 37; light on the, given to the prophet Ezekiel, 149; light on the, promised, 144-146; man unaided cannot grasp meaning of, 21; meaning of, to the Israelites, 20; ministry in, 5; ministry in, following the consecration, 49; ministry of heavenly, must be understood, 145; ministry ordained by the Lord, 50; no labor performed in, when it was dedicated, 46; no ministry in heavenly, while earthly was in operation, 147; number of times the word is mentioned in the Scriptures, 11; offerings for, 25; only priests could minister in, 48; origin and definition of, 11; originated with God, 21; other terms associated with the word, 11; priestly ministry completed in the, on Day of Atonement, 176; purpose of, 5, 19; revealed to Moses, 11; services of, were most sacred, 65; sinner must bring a spotless offering to the, 160; tabernacle of, 29; the cleansing of, 144; the Lord met the priests at the door of, 32; the real, in heaven, 147; the, service was the center of worship, 128; the, was rebuilt, 91; to diffuse light, 5; to whom God entrusted the, 12; two apartments to the, 172; types in, 5; when was Moses called to receive light on? 81, 82; where first mentioned, 6, 11; why the, was committed to the Jews, 158; why, was given, 11, 12.

Satan, bound for a thousand years on this earth, 205; charges of, are cruel, 164, 165; Christ overcomes, 161; evil inventions of, in Egypt, 80; final destruction of, 210; is an innovator, 5; Jesus completely conquered, 165; opposition of, to the work of God, 73; purpose of, is to counterfeit, 77; should be responsible for sins he caused the righteous to commit, 73; the Saviour subjected to fierce assaults of, 165; the sins of the righteous confessed upon Azazel, who is, 205; the world turned into a prison by, 163.

Saviour, meaning of the word, 58; our, is both God and man, 165.

Scapegoat, meaning of the, 63.

Scribes, Ezra said to belong to the, 93; meaning of the word, 93; wrote the Scriptures, 154.

Scriptures, all the, inspired, 98; certain class only supposed to understand the, 94; neither Christ nor apostles destroyed any part of the, 171; Christ revealed in the, 112; Christ the central theme of the, 105; disciples assured they would understand the, 106; disciples did not always understand the, 157; few leaders in Israel understood the, 96; given by revelation, 23; God's people must be familiar with, 120; how the, were written in the days of Christ, 154; Jesus fulfills the, when healing the sick, 156; Jesus tells the people to search the, 153; Jesus the outstanding purpose of the, 95; Jewish leaders professed to have faith in, 96; Jewish writers find certain, difficult to understand, 98, 99; key text of the, 95; meaning of the name of Ebed Melech spoken of in the, 93; modern view of the, 107; our great need of the, 97; rabbis introduce various interpretations of, 96; rabbis misapply the, 156; the angel's application of Old Testament, 156; the angel gives clear light on, 151; the apostle Peter opens the, to the people, 105; the, are translated, 5; the Ethiopian acknowledged he could not understand the, 94; the Ethiopians mentioned in,

93; the, foretold the sufferings of Christ, 107; the, recognize two classes of people, 197; the sacred, 5; the Saviour opened to His disciples the, 95; the Spirit necessary to a proper understanding of, 150, 151; teaching of, in regard to the Pharisees, 94; to study the, 23; the, were divided into three parts, 109; the, were not anciently printed in a book, 93, 154; why God gave the, 93.

Shekinah, meaning of the, 12; place of the, 28; where the, dwelt, 32.

Showbread, meaning of the, 12.

Sin, a remedy for, 20; deliverance from, 17; final disposition of, 6; is blinding, 23; no part of God's program, 5; not to be perpetual, 5; shall forever cease, 5; to be destroyed, 5.

Spices, for dedication, 35.

Spirit, Christ promised the gift of the, 105; guidance of the, necessary to understand the Scriptures, 150.

Sprinkled, Christ's blood, 17; the blood, 17.

Substitute, Jesus is our, 160; the sinner placed his hands on the head of, 160; the sinner's, 53; the sinner's guilt transferred to a, 53.

Substitution, God introduces the principle of, 18, 34; orthodox Jews recognize the principle of, 55; was known among the ancient Israelites, 53.

Symbols, gospel in, 19; meaning of, perverted, 17, 34; no human interpretation of, 171; Old Testament, 98, 101; pointed to the Saviour, 82.

TABERNACLE, built after pattern, 29; construction of, 29; dimensions of, 31; God gave Moses plan of, 29; how divided, 29; location of furnishings in, 31, 32; meaning of ministration of, 20; the, divided into two parts, 170; various names of, 29.

Tabernacles, feast of, 86; many sacrifices offered at feast of, 87, 88.

Talmud, numerous legends told in, 99; teachings in, 62, 94.

Temple, great wealth expended on, 148; John saw heavenly, opened, 183; the first time we meet with the word in the Scriptures, 148; why David was not permitted to erect the, 148.

Time, Biblical reckoning of, 58.

Tithing, 24.

Traditions, Jews made many, 61.

Tribes, no permanent record preserved of the twelve, 101.

Trumpets, blowing of, 60, 171; feast of blowing of, 61; secular service laid aside at the blowing of, 61; to observe feast of, 85.

Types, became valueless, 19; Christ fulfillment of, 152; come to an end, 83; gospel in, 23, 43; purposes of, 5, 15; the sacrifices were, 19, 92; the Saviour manifested in the, 82; to express faith in Christ, 18.

VEIL, 31; a preserver of records, 56; a typical record book, 56; blood sprinkled on, 56, 65; Jews had a, over their face, 171; the, rent in twain, 138; when blood was not sprinkled on, 56.
Virgin, meaning of the word, in the Hebrew, 156.

WEEKS, angel divides the seventy, 132, 133; angel Gabriel explains the seventy, 131, 132; certainty of the beginning of the reckoning of the seventy, 134, 135; diagram of seventy, 143; first division of seventy, end, 133, 134; meaning of the term seventy, 131, 132; relation between the seventy, and the 2300 days, 133; the angel enlightens Daniel on the seventy, 140; the seventy, 91; the seventy, deal with Daniel's people, 139.
Wicked, destruction of, 210.
Wilderness, Israelites remain in the, till they die, 85; the wandering in, no part of God's program, 85.
Worshipers, Ezekiel describes sun, 186; sun, turn their backs on the sanctuary, 186.

YEAR, Jewish new, 61.
Yom Kippur, name of Day of Atonement, 175.

We'd love to have you download our catalog of
titles we publish at:

www.TEACHServices.com

or write or email us your thoughts,
reactions, or criticism about this
or any other book we publish at:

TEACH Services, Inc.
254 Donovan Road
Brushton, NY 12916

info@TEACHServices.com

or you may call us at:

518/358-3494

Produced in partnership with
LNFBooks.com

CPSIA information can be obtained
at www.ICGtesting.com
Printed in the USA
LVHW052155160422
716065LV00003B/50